AMERICAN AMNESIA

HOW THE WAR ON GOVERNMENT LED US TO
FORGET WHAT MADE AMERICA PROSPER

JACOB S. HACKER *and*
PAUL PIERSON

SIMON & SCHUSTER PAPERBACKS

New York   London   Toronto   Sydney   New Delhi

PRAISE FOR *AMERICAN AMNESIA*

"*American Amnesia* provides chapter and verse on why the public has good reason to be angry."

—*The New York Times*

"In this lively, engaging, and persuasive book, Hacker and Pierson explain how much of our health and prosperity rests on what governments have done. *American Amnesia* will help slow the intellectual pendulum that is currently swinging toward ananarchic libertarianism that threatens more than a century of American progress."

—Angus Deaton, winner of the
Nobel Memorial Prize for Economics in 2015

"This is a fascinating and much-needed book. America once invented universal public education and sharply progressive taxation of income and inherited wealth, and has shown to the world that strong government and efficient markets are complementary—not substitutes. But since 1980 a new wave of anti-government ideology has prospered, and is about to make America more unequal and plutocratic than Europe on the eve of World War I. If you want to understand why this great amnesia occurred, and how it can be reversed, read this book!"

—Thomas Piketty, author of *Capital in the Twenty-First Century*

"If you are curious about why our infrastructure, our roads and bridges and water systems, is falling apart—then read *American Amnesia*. Curious about why the US spends almost 18 percent of our GDP on medical care, but has health outcomes that are at levels of many developing countries—then read *American Amnesia*."

—*Inside Higher Ed*

"Progress and prosperity in the United States, they demonstrate, have rested in no small measure on a constructive relationship between an effective public authority and dynamic private markets. We are now paying a terrible price for 'forgetting this essential truth.'"

—*The Philadelphia Inquirer*

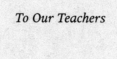

To Our Teachers

CONTENTS

INTRODUCTION

· ★ ★ ★ ·

Prosperity Lost

55 signers
of Dec. of Ind?

T HIS BOOK is about an uncomfortable truth: It takes government—
a lot of government—for advanced societies to flourish.

This truth is uncomfortable because Americans cherish freedom. Government is effective in part because it limits freedom—because,
in the language of political philosophy, it exercises legitimate coercion.
Government can tell people they must send their children to school
rather than the fields, that they can't dump toxins into the water or air,
and that they must contribute to meet expenses that benefit the entire
community. To be sure, government also secures our freedom. Without
its ability to compel behavior, it would not just be powerless to protect
our liberties; it would cease to be a vehicle for achieving many of our
most important shared ends. But there's no getting around it: Government works because it can force people to do things.

The authors of the US Constitution were keenly aware of this fact.
Eleven years after the Declaration of Independence—with its ringing
declaration of "certain unalienable rights" and its clear-eyed recognition
that "to secure these rights, governments are instituted among men"—
fifty-five American notables gathered in Philadelphia because they had
become convinced that the absence of effective public authority was
a mortal threat to the fledgling nation.[1] Perhaps the most influential
of them all, James Madison, put the point bluntly in arguing against
those at the Virginia ratifying convention who worried that the Constitution would create too strong a national government: "There never

was a Government without force. What is the meaning of government? An institution to make people do their duty. A Government leaving it to a man to do his duty, or not, as he pleases, would be a new species of Government, or rather no Government at all."[2] In calling on Americans to discard the loose Articles of Confederation that had brought so much instability and vulnerability, the Virginian known as the "Father of the Constitution" declared, "A sanction is essential to the idea of law, as co-ercion is to that of Government. The [current] system being destitute of both, wants the great vital principles of a Political Constitution."[3]

But Americans have never been good at acknowledging government's necessary role in supporting both freedom and prosperity.[4] And we have become much less so over the last generation. We live in an era of pro-found skepticism about government. Contemporary political discourse portrays liberty and coercion as locked in ceaseless conflict. We are told that government is about "redistribution" and the private sector about "production," as if government only reshuffles the economic deck rather than holding many of the highest cards. We are told "free enterprise" and "big government" are engaged in a fierce zero-sum battle (one side's gain is the other's loss), when, in fact, the modern partnership between markets and government may well be humanity's most impressive positive-sum bargain (making both sides better off). We are told that the United States got rich in spite of government, when the truth is closer to the opposite: The United States got rich because it got government more or less right.

We suffer, in short, from a kind of mass historical forgetting, a dis-tinctively "American Amnesia." At a time when we face serious chal-lenges that can be addressed only through a stronger, more effective government—a strained middle class, a weakened system for generating life-improving innovation, a dangerously warming planet—we ignore what both our history and basic economic theory suggest: We need a *constructive and mutually beneficial tension* between markets and govern-ment rather than the jealous rivalry that so many misperceive—and, in that misperception, help foster. Above all, we need a government strong and capable enough to rise above narrow private interests and carry out long-term courses of action on behalf of broader concerns. At the Constitutional Convention in 1787, one of the delegates noted: "It has never been a complaint of [the Confederate Congress] that they governed overmuch. The complaint has been that they governed too little."[5] Today there are complaints only about our leaders governing "overmuch." But the truth is that although areas of government overreach certainly do exist, we have "too little" effective government, not too much.

We recognize that these words are likely to provoke doubt, if not disbelief. We ask only that these reactions be suspended long enough to consider the evidence. Fortunately, it is close at hand: in our nation's history and in the history of every nation that has transited from poverty, sickness, and mass illiteracy to wealth, health, and enlightenment. Still, the forgotten roots of our prosperity are well buried. We have to dig deeply into the debris left behind by nearly a half century of ideological warfare to unearth the economic model that—in remarkably short order, beginning little more than a hundred years ago—made us the richest nation the world has ever seen.

Why Markets Need Government

Like other advanced democratic nations, the United States has what economic analysts call a "mixed economy." In this public-private arrangement, markets play the dominant role in producing and allocating goods and innovating to meet consumer demand. Apple brings us iPhones, and it earns sizable profits by doing so. Visionaries such as Steve Jobs see untapped opportunities to make money by satisfying human wants, and then draw on the knowledge and technology around them to produce goods and services for which people are willing to pay. Markets are the most powerful institutions yet developed to encourage and coordinate decentralized action in response to individual desires.

Alongside companies like Apple, however, government plays a dominant or vital role in the many places where markets fall short. Look inside that iPhone, and you'll find that nearly all its major components (GPS, lithium-ion batteries, cellular technology, touch-screen and LCD displays, internet connectivity) rest on research that was publicly funded—and, in some cases, carried out directly by government agencies.[6] Jobs and his creative team transformed all this into something unique, and uniquely valuable. But they couldn't have done it without the US government's huge investments in technical knowledge—knowledge that all companies can use and thus none has strong incentives to produce. That knowledge is embodied not just in science and technology but also in a skilled workforce that government fosters directly and indirectly: through K–12 schools, support for higher education, and the provision of social supports that encourage beneficial risk taking. And even if government had played no role in seeding or enabling Apple's products, it would be responsible for much of the economic and physical infrastructure—from national monetary policy to local roads—on which the California tech giant relies.

Of course, affluent democracies differ in the exact form that this public-private mix takes, and not all mixes are equally effective. Public policies don't always foster prosperity. Those within government can hurt rather than harness the market, directing special favors to narrow interest groups or constraining economic dynamism in ways that stifle growth. No less important (though much more neglected), they can fail to respond to problems in the market that could and should be addressed by effective public action, hindering growth through omission rather than commission. For all this, however, no country has risen to richness without complementing private markets with an extensive array of core functions that rest on public authority—without, that is, a mixed economy.

That markets fall short under certain conditions has been known for at least two centuries. The eighteenth-century Scottish economist Adam Smith wrote enthusiastically about the "invisible hand" of market allocation. Yet he also identified many cases where rational actors pursuing their own self-interest produced bad outcomes: underinvestment in education, financial instability, insufficient infrastructure, unchecked monopolies.[7] Economists have been building on these insights ever since to explain when and why markets stumble and how the *visible* hand of government can make the invisible hand more effective.

The visible hand is needed, for example, to

- provide key collective goods that markets won't (education, infrastructure, courts, basic scientific research);
- reduce negative spillover costs that parties to market exchanges don't bear fully, such as pollution;
- encourage positive spillover *benefits* that such parties don't take fully into account, such as valuable shared knowledge;
- regulate the market to protect consumers and investors—both from corporate predation (collusion, fraud, harm) and from indi-

viduals' own myopic behavior (smoking, failing to save, under-
estimating economic risks);
- provide or require certain insurance protections, notably, against
the costs of health care and inadequate retirement income; and
- soften the business cycle and reduce the risk of financial crises.

The political economist Charles Lindblom once described markets
as being like fingers: nimble and dexterous. Governments, with their
capacity to exercise authority, are like thumbs: powerful but lacking
subtlety and flexibility.[8] The invisible hand is all fingers. The visible
hand is all thumbs. Of course, one wouldn't want to be all thumbs. But
one wouldn't want to be all fingers, either. Thumbs provide countervailing power, constraint, and adjustment to get the best out of those nimble
fingers.

To achieve this potential requires not just an appropriate division of
labor but also a healthy balance of power. Markets give rise to highly
resourceful economic actors who want government to favor them. Absent measures to blunt or offset their political edge, their demands will
drown out the voice of broader groups: consumers, workers, concerned
citizens. Today the message most commentators take from Adam Smith
is that government should get out of the way. But that was not Smith's
message. He was enthusiastic about government regulation so long as it
wasn't simply a ruse to advantage one set of commercial interests over
another. When "regulation . . . is in favor of the workmen," he wrote in
The Wealth of Nations, "it is always just and equitable." He was equally
enthusiastic about the taxes needed to fund effective governance. "Every
tax," he wrote, "is to the person who pays it a badge, not of slavery but
of liberty."[9] Contemporary libertarians who invoke Smith before decrying labor laws or comparing taxation to theft seem to have skipped these
passages.

Far from a tribune of unregulated markets, Smith was a celebrant of
effective governance. His biggest concern about the state wasn't that it
would be overbearing but that it would be overly beholden to narrow
private interests. His greatest ire was reserved not for public officials
but for powerful merchants who combined to rig public policies and
repress private wages. These "tribes of monopoly" he compared with an
"overgrown standing army" that had "become formidable to the government, and upon many occasions intimidate the legislature." Too often,

Smith maintained, concentrated economic power skewed the crafting of government policy. "Whenever the legislature attempts to regulate the differences between masters and their workmen," he complained, "its counsellors are always the masters. . . . They are silent with regard to the pernicious effects of their own gains. They complain only of those of other people."[10]

In the more than two centuries since Smith wrote, the world's advanced economies have grown vastly more complex and interdependent, creating many new sources of market failure. Moreover, the extraordinary scale of modern capitalism has repeatedly fostered the sharp concentrations of economic power that so worried Smith. What Smith saw in the protodemocracies of his day—concentrated interests converting power into profits—has become only more sophisticated and common in the advanced democracies of our day. Smith's intellectual heirs even have a term for such politically generated rewards. They call them "rents," and efforts to secure them "rent seeking."

Contemporary economists sometimes write of rent seeking as if it's only a problem when government is active. Conservative commentators often argue as if all it takes to "reduce the scope of rent extraction" (in the words of one *Wall Street Journal* columnist) is "shrinking the ambitions and power of government."[11] But as Smith clearly recognized, the intermingling of markets and politics is inevitable: A private sector completely free of government influence is just as mythical (and undesirable) as a government completely free of private-sector influence. And a government that doesn't act in the face of distorted markets is imposing costs just as real as those imposed when a government acts in favor of narrow claimants. Crippling active government to reduce rent seeking is a cure far worse than the disease.

The mixed economy, in short, tackles a double bind. The private markets that foster prosperity so powerfully nonetheless fail routinely, sometimes spectacularly so. At the same time, the government policies that are needed to respond to these failures are perpetually under siege from the very market players who help fuel growth. That is the double bind: Democracy and the market—thumbs and fingers—have to work together, but they also need to be partly independent from each other, or the thumb will cease to provide effective counterpressure to the fingers. Smith recognized this dilemma, but it was never resolved adequately during his lifetime, in part because neither markets nor democracies had achieved the scale and sophistication necessary to make broad prosperity possible. When that changed, the world did, too.

The (Forgotten) Triumph of the Mixed Economy

The mixed economy is a social institution, a human solution to human problems. Private capitalism and public coercion each predated modern prosperity. Governments were involved in the market long before the mixed economy. What made the difference was the marriage of large-scale profit-seeking activity, active democratic governance, and a deepened understanding of how markets work (and where they work poorly). As in any marriage, the exact terms of the relationship changed over time. In an evolving world, social institutions need to adapt if they are to continue to serve their basic functions. Money, for example, is still doing what it has always done: provide a common metric, store value, facilitate exchange. But it's now paper or plastic rather than metal, and more likely to pass from computer to computer than hand to hand. Similarly, the mixed economy is defined not by the specific forms it has taken but by the specific functions it has served: to overcome failures of the market and to translate economic growth into broad advances in human well-being—from better health and education to greater knowledge and opportunity.

The combination of energetic markets and effective governance, deft fingers and strong thumbs, has delivered truly miraculous breakthroughs. Indeed, the mixed economy may well be the greatest invention in history. It is also a strikingly recent invention. Plot the growth of Western economies on an axis marking the passage of time, and the line would be mostly flat for thousands of years.[12] Even the emergence of capitalism, momentous as it was, was not synonymous with the birth of mass prosperity. Trapped in a Malthusian race between population and sustenance, societies remained on the brink of destitution until well into the nineteenth century. (Thomas Malthus, born when Adam Smith was completing *The Wealth of Nations*, was an English cleric who predicted that population growth would continually outstrip the food supply.) Life expectancy rose only modestly between the Neolithic era of 8500 to 3500 BC and the Victorian era of 1850 to 1900.[13] An American born in the late nineteenth century had an average life expectancy of around forty-five years, with a large share never making it past their first birthdays.[14]

Then something remarkable happened. In countries on the frontier of economic development, human health began to improve rapidly, education levels shot up, and standards of living began to grow and grow. Within a century, life expectancies had increased by two-thirds, average years of schooling had gone from single to double digits, and the productivity of workers and the pay they took home had doubled and doubled and then doubled again. With the United States leading the way, the rich world crossed a Great Divide—a divide separating centuries of slow growth, poor health, and anemic technical progress from one of hitherto undreamed-of material comfort and seemingly limitless economic potential. For the first time, rich countries experienced economic development that was both broad and deep, reaching all major segments of society and producing not just greater material comfort but also fundamental transformations in the health and life horizons of those it touched. As the French economist Thomas Piketty points out in his magisterial study of inequality, "It was not until the twentieth century that economic growth became a tangible, unmistakable reality for everyone."[15]

The mixed economy was at the heart of this success—in the United States no less than in other Western nations. Capitalism played an essential role. But capitalism was not the new entrant on the economic stage. Effective governance was. Public health measures made cities engines of innovation rather than incubators of illness.[16] The meteoric expansion of public education increased not only individual opportunity but also the economic potential of entire societies. Investments in science, higher education, and defense spearheaded breakthroughs in medicine, transportation, infrastructure, and technology. Overarching rules and institutions tamed and transformed unstable financial markets and turned boom-bust cycles into more manageable ups and downs. Protections against excessive insecurity and abject destitution encouraged the forward-looking investments and social integration that sustained growth required. At every level of society, the gains in health, education, income, and capacity were breathtaking. The mixed economy was a spectacularly positive-sum bargain: It redistributed power and resources, but as its impacts broadened and diffused, virtually everyone was made massively better off.

It's an impressive record. If advanced democratic capitalism won the twentieth century, the mixed economy deserves to stand atop the podium. If foundations are giving out X Prizes for technological innovation, ribbons should be pinned onto the modern machinery of economic statecraft. In a sense, they are: Nearly every one of the gee-whiz innovations that we shower with prizes and profits—indeed, virtually the entire range of computing technologies that so define our present era—owe their origins to the "military-industrial-academic complex" (Senator William Fulbright's reworking of President Dwight Eisenhower's famous phrase) that America's political and economic leaders built in the twentieth century.[17]

There's just one problem: We're trashing the mixed economy.

The Man Who "Ruined the Twentieth Century"

With increasing vigor and volume, some of the most powerful actors in American politics are sabotaging government's essential role in the economy. The assailants include antigovernment politicians and conservative media celebrities, ultrawealthy activists and influential corporate leaders, idea warriors bankrolled by the rich and the right and business associations dominated by the extreme and the acquisitive. Some mount the vanguards. Others cheer on the assault. And still others—the silent majority of the American political class—remain quiet amid the carnage, indifferent to or untroubled by the titanic stakes.

The most active combatants are not simply taking issue with recent departures from their preferred policies. They are taking issue with the entire edifice of modern public authority. They don't think things went wrong in the 1970s. They think things went wrong in the 1930s. Actually, many of them think things went wrong even earlier than that. They conjure up a mythical vision of the Constitution's authors as free-market fundamentalists and of the country's early economic rise as a triumph of laissez-faire. They downplay the depredations of the industrial economy that first prompted social reform and celebrate as geniuses and giants the men whom previous generations called "robber barons."[18] When they tell their stories of declension, they pin the blame on a Democratic president who sought to harness government to address emerging economic and social challenges. But that president is not always FDR. To a surprisingly large number of their intellectual leaders, it is Woodrow Wilson, the southern-born governor of New Jersey who in 1912 became president of the United States.

Wilson has recently attracted criticism from the left, mainly because of the intensely racist views he brought to the White House. Yet since the late 2000s, it has been the right—especially the vocal and vehement "Tea Party" wing that emerged in 2009 to become a major activist force within the Republican Party—that has cast its critical gaze on Wilson. Or, to be more accurate, directed at Wilson a "virulent, obsessive hatred" (in the words of the historian David Greenberg) that borders on hysteria.[19] The *National Review* columnist Jonah Goldberg dubs Wilson "the 20th Century's first fascist dictator."[20] The conservative talk-show host Glenn Beck manages to go one better. According to a recent article in *American History* magazine, "Wilson is No. 1 on his 'Top Ten Bastards of All Time' lists—ahead of not only both Theodore and Franklin Roosevelt, but also Pontius Pilate, Hitler, and Pol Pot."[21] "This is the architect that destroyed our faith," Beck said in 2010. "He destroyed our Constitution, and he destroyed our founders, okay?" Even the establishment conservative George Will has gotten into the hate fest. At a banquet held at the libertarian Cato Institute the same year, he declared that Wilson had "ruined the 20th century."

"Ruined the twentieth century"? That's a big accusation. What did he do to deserve it? Though the bill of particulars varies from critic to critic, the right's objections have nothing to do with Wilson's reactionary views on race. Instead, the charges seem to boil down to one great crime: Wilson directed his domestic policy agenda toward building the mixed economy. With the United States becoming for the first time a truly national industrial economy, with huge financial and manufacturing "trusts" wielding enormous power over markets and public officials alike, the nation's twenty-eighth president argued that a capable federal government was necessary to address the festering problems of his time.[22]

Even worse, apparently, Wilson delivered. Working with a supportive Congress, he created the Federal Reserve System, which rescued the United States from almost a century of recurrent bank panics caused by the proliferation of private bank–issued scrip, a hodgepodge of state currencies, and the lack of any agency charged with regulating banking or credit.[23] He backed the nation's first graduated federal income tax, which allowed the United States to move away from its excessive dependence on tariffs while ensuring that the growing ranks of the superrich helped finance basic government operations.[24] He championed the Clayton Antitrust Act of 1914 to try to break up the uncompetitive monopolies fueling many of those great fortunes. His administration established the Federal Trade Commission (FTC)—"the world's first independent 'competition' agency," in the words of two of its former leaders—whose appointed commissioners oversaw antitrust actions without fear of congressional or presidential removal.[25]

More heretical still, Wilson claimed that common understandings of what the Constitution dictated were misaligned with the nation's expanding industrial society. "The Constitution was not meant to hold the government back to the time of horses and wagons," Wilson complained as a Princeton University professor of government in 1908. (We are professionally obligated to note that Wilson was the first and last political scientist to occupy the Oval Office.)[26] To catch up, Wilson supported a stronger executive branch with greater power to regulate the national economy. He saw the strengthening of central authority as the natural evolution of American government in response to the profound transformations taking place around it.

Ultimately, Wilson's insistence that government and the economy should grow and adapt together is what most enrages today's conservatives. To the outraged George Will, "The very virtue of a constitution is that it's not changeable. It exists to prevent change, to embed certain rights so that they cannot easily be taken away. . . . Gridlock is not an American problem, it is an American achievement!"[27] Will wants us to look to another Princetonian for the true nature of American government: James Madison. "When James Madison and fifty-four other geniuses went to Philadelphia in the sweltering summer of 1787, they did not go there to design an efficient government. That idea would have horrified them. They wanted a safe government, to which end they filled it with blocking mechanisms: three branches of government, two branches of the legislative branch, veto, veto override, supermajorities, and judicial review."[28]

What the "geniuses [who] went to Philadelphia" wanted remains the subject of endless debate—a debate fueled by the real differences among them and the very real ambiguities of the compromises they forged. But James Madison did not go to Philadelphia seeking gridlock. Quite the opposite: The Virginian who played such a critical role in the nation's founding led the charge for a powerful national government. He pushed for a new constitution specifically because its predecessor, the Articles of Confederation, adopted in 1777, had been a catastrophe—a decentralized arrangement too weak to hold the country together or confront pressing problems that needed collective solutions. Madison arrived at the convention with one firm conviction: Government needed the authority to govern.[29]

In the deliberations that followed, Madison stayed true to that cause. He argued tirelessly for the power of the federal government to be understood broadly and for it to be decisively superior to the states. He even supported an absolute federal veto over all state laws, likening it to "gravity" in the Newtonian framework of the new federal government.[30] Most of the concessions to state governments in the final document were ones that Madison had opposed. He was a practical politician, and he ultimately defended these compromises in the public arena—the famed *Federalist Papers* Madison penned with his colleagues Alexander Hamilton and John Jay are an advertisement, not a blueprint—but he did so because he saw them as necessary, not because he saw them as ideal.[31] Throughout, Madison kept his eyes on the prize: enactment of the more vital and resilient government he regarded as a national imperative.

As for minority vetoes, Madison fought a losing battle to eliminate some (most crucially the disproportionate power of small states in the Senate). He accepted others as necessary safeguards. But in "The Federalist No. 58," he made clear why supermajority requirements should be avoided whenever practicable: "In all cases where justice or the general good might require new laws to be passed, or active measures to be pursued, the fundamental principle of free government would be reversed. It would be no longer the majority that would rule: The power would be transferred to the minority."[32]

So much for the virtues of gridlock.

Like the demonization of Woodrow Wilson, the morphing of Madison into some sort of protolibertarian is a manifestation of American Amnesia. The position embraced by George Will and other self-proclaimed "constitutional conservatives" isn't the position of James Madison. It's the position of those who opposed creating the Constitution in the first place. Transport today's Tea Party movement, with its hostility to the national government and celebration of states' rights, back to 1787, and it wouldn't be leading the Federalist campaign for the constitution. It would be leading the anti-Federalist charge against it.

But there is something even more confusing in Will's attack. What's this about Wilson *ruining* the twentieth century? All centuries have their ups and downs, but the twentieth, despite some terrible downs, was an extraordinary one for the United States and the larger community of emerging affluent democracies. The century that Will thinks Wilson ruined brought greater increases in human prosperity—measured not just by income but also by life expectancy and education and much else—than the entirety of prior human history.

So Will's Cato Institute speech delivers a powerful message. Only it's not a message about Madison or Wilson. It's a message about American Amnesia and the damage it inflicts on our democracy and our democratic society.

Falling from Grace

At least since Alexis de Tocqueville visited the United States in the early nineteenth century, American democracy has been seen as a beacon of popular rule and material opportunity. Yet that beacon is dimming. Beset by polarization and intransigence, flooded with the lobbying dollars of narrow interests and the campaign dollars of a tiny slice of the nation's wealthiest citizens, our political institutions look increasingly incapable of handling even routine matters, much less our biggest challenges. Public trust in government is at record lows; Congress is so unpopular that Americans say they prefer head lice and root canals to their elected legislature. The twin pillars of a successful mixed economy—well-functioning private markets and an effective democratic government—are crumbling.

Saying that the United States is coming up short is never easy or popular. Tocqueville himself worried that the deep patriotism of Americans sometimes prevented a "reflective" assessment of their nation's strengths and weaknesses. "A foreigner would indeed consent to praise much in their country," Tocqueville complained, "but he would want to be permitted to blame something, and this he is absolutely refused."[33]

Almost two centuries later, Tocqueville's words still ring true. To question any aspect of American greatness, according to many commentators, is to deny "American exceptionalism": the notion that the United States is not just singular but singularly awesome. In recent years, the two-word phrase has become a rhetorical battering ram, used more and more to quell a long-overdue conversation about America's faltering performance. (Between 1980 and 2008, according to Google's catalog of English-language books, the number of references to "American exceptionalism" increased almost eightfold.)[34] But celebrating America's enormous achievements does not require ignoring the many ways in which we are coming up short. We should cheer the great American experiment—the "shining city upon a hill" (Reagan), "the New World in all tongues, to all peoples" (FDR).[35] But we should also embrace the reflective patriotism that Tocqueville advocated, a patriotism that acknowledges the challenges we face—and recognizes that many of them cannot be addressed without effective governance.

For those challenges are mounting. Over the last decade or so, a growing body of evidence has shown that the United States is indeed exceptional, just not always in a good way. In a range of areas—human health, high-quality education, economic opportunity, broad-based income gains—we are losing the significant lead over other democracies that our successful mixed economy produced.[36] In some areas, such as health and education, we are moving from the top part of the international rankings to the bottom.[37] In others, we are failing to address emerging challenges, such as global warming and rising obesity.

Worse, even our relatively poor performance often *understates* how far we have fallen. In some cases, the best aspects of our performance reflect the lingering impact of past investments no longer being made—in basic scientific research, for example, or modern infrastructure. In others, measures of "average" performance provide a false reassurance because they reflect extremely strong outcomes among older Americans, based on the efforts of a generation or two ago. When we focus on the young, however, we see a bleaker picture of a nation failing to ensure what was once assumed: that each generation would do better than the last.[38]

What makes these trends especially troubling is that they constitute such a stark departure from the successful mixed economic model that marked America's long and extraordinary ascent. From the end of the nineteenth century, the United States led a revolutionary transformation experienced by a small club of rich nations. We were the first middle-class nation, the runaway leader in high school and then college graduation rates, the unrivaled champion in medical innovation and basic scientific research. Our infrastructure was world class and included some of the greatest engineering achievements in human history. Our economy was a model of productivity-driven growth. Our conservation and environmental programs set the standard for other rich nations. Our public health efforts, from sanitation, to smoking control, to auto safety, inspired those seeking to improve health worldwide. Now, on the most critical measures of social success, we are sliding slowly from the front to the back of the pack. What happened?

The Great Forgetting

The signs read Republicans for Romney. A prominent Republican businessman and former governor is seeking to unseat a Democrat in the White House. The candidate typifies business thinking—perhaps a bit more moderate than the norm but well within the mainstream of corporate opinion. And he is a man who says he can get things done, given his practical experience governing a highly unionized "blue" state with a progovernment electorate.

But this is not the Romney you know—not Mitt, the unsuccessful candidate in 2012, but his father, George, the unsuccessful candidate in 1968.[39] They shared a name; they shared a business background; they even shared a stint in a statehouse (Michigan in George's case; Massachusetts in Mitt's). Yet in all the ways that mattered for how they led companies and citizens, they occupied radically different economic and political worlds.[40] The transit between these worlds traces the erosion of the mixed economy and, with it, the foundations of our shared prosperity. Between Romney and Romney, American Amnesia took hold.

George Romney's private-sector experience typified the business world of his time. His executive career took place within a single company, American Motors Corporation, where his success rested on the dogged (and prescient) pursuit of more fuel-efficient cars.[41] Rooted in a particular locale, the industrial Midwest, AMC was built on a philosophy of civic engagement. Romney dismissed the "rugged individualism" touted by conservatives as "nothing but a political banner to cover up greed."[42] Nor was this dismissal just cheap talk: He once returned a substantial bonus that he regarded as excessive.[43] Prosperity was not an individual product, in Romney's view; it was generated through bargaining and compromises among stakeholders (managers, workers, public officials, and the local community) as well as through individual initiative.

When George Romney turned to politics, he carried this understanding with him. Romney exemplified the moderate perspective characteristic of many high-profile Republicans of his day. He stressed the importance of private initiative and decentralized governance, and worried about the power of unions. Yet he also believed that government had a vital role to play in securing prosperity for all. He once famously called UAW head Walter Reuther "the most dangerous man in Detroit," but then, characteristically, developed a good working relationship with him.[44] Elected governor in 1962 after working to update Michigan's constitution, he broke with conservatives in his own party and worked across party lines to raise the minimum wage, enact an income tax, double state education expenditures during his first five years in office, and introduce more generous programs for the poor and unemployed.[45] He signed into law a bill giving teachers collective bargaining rights.[46] At a time when conservatives were turning to the antigovernment individualism of Barry Goldwater, Romney called on the GOP to make the insurance of equal opportunity a top priority. As Richard Nixon's secretary of the US Department of Housing and Urban Development from 1969 to 1973, he courageously tried to tackle the de facto racial segregation that plagued America's urban centers.[47]

George Romney sought a party that reached toward the broad middle. His allies were figures such as New York governor Nelson Rockefeller, who argued for an effective partnership between government and the private sector. In contrast to Goldwater's famous dictum that "extremism in defense of liberty is no vice," Romney maintained that "dogmatic ideological parties tend to splinter the political and social fabric of a nation, lead to governmental crises and deadlocks, and stymie the compromises so often necessary to preserve freedom and achieve progress."[48]

Fast-forward a generation. Like his father, Mitt Romney reflects key economic and political features of his time. Along with other firms in the burgeoning world of "private equity," Bain Capital—the business Romney cofounded and led—helped pioneer a new corporate model in which individual companies were not socially embedded communities of stakeholders but commodities ripe for financial restructuring.[49] Partly by exploiting legal opportunities tied to the tax code, Bain could extract enormous resources, even if the "reengineered" companies failed to thrive. Corporate rearrangers are the masters of this new economic universe. According to Mitt Romney and all other contemporary GOP candidates, they are the vital entrepreneurs ("the job creators") who should be unhindered—and virtually untaxed—by governments.[50]

The corporate world of Mitt Romney's day is far more globalized than that of George Romney's. But even more fundamentally, it is far more financialized.[51] Compared with George Romney during his career at American Motors, CEOs today are far less closely bound to a particular community or even a particular company.[52] Their rewards come increasingly from the short-term movement of share prices, which dominate the huge pay packages they demand.[53] And the financial rewards at the top, both on Wall Street and in executive suites, generate enormous fortunes. Just as in Woodrow Wilson's day, these concentrated resources threaten to swamp democratic government, as economic power transmutes into political power, and that power further enriches the privileged.

The incentive for CEOs to consider other stakeholders is also far weaker than in George Romney's world. Government and organized labor, the two major sources of "countervailing power" (to use economist John Kenneth Galbraith's famous phrase), once encouraged business leaders to negotiate and seek mutually beneficial compromises.[54] Now unions are almost gone from the private sector, and government leaders are much less willing to use public authority to create beneficial constraint.[55] The business associations that sometimes supported that government role and encouraged a long view and a broader perspective are mostly gone too. In their place are new or reoriented lobbies that cater mostly to the narrow demands of particular sectors.[56] Beneath the high-tech exteriors, much of America's economy has taken on a feudalistic structure, where the barons of Wall Street or health care or the energy sector decide the "corporate" position on the issues they care about most. These structures of corporate power leave little room for George Romney's view that government is an essential partner for generating broad-based prosperity.

If the private sector and the definition of personal success have changed, so too has the character of the Republican Party. It turned out that Goldwater, not George Romney, pointed to the future of the GOP, and George Romney's son would inherit the kind of party that the elder Romney had warned about. The issue that had split George Romney and Barry Goldwater—civil rights—soon split the Democratic Party and reinvigorated Republicans in the South. Even more fateful for George Romney's economic agenda, Goldwater's libertarianism became the lodestar for an economic philosophy centered on tax cuts, deregulation, and hostility toward both government and organized labor. Reagan, who had sided with the Arizona senator over Romney and his allies in 1964 and accused GOP moderates of "betrayal," rejected the latter's model of industrial partnership and political compromise, marking out a rightward path along which his party continues to march.[57]

George Romney's son joined that rightward march. He abandoned
his blue-state positions upon entering national politics as his father had
not. Yet Mitt Romney's effort to cast himself as "a severely conservative
governor" (as he put it in a speech to the Conservative Political Action
Conference in early 2012) quickly proved insufficient. Having moved
toward the conservative pole to run for president in 2008, he moved
further still to capture the Republican presidential nomination in 2012.
As his running mate, he chose the extremely conservative Paul Ryan (an
admirer of the radically antigovernment writings of Ayn Rand). But as
fast as Romney moved right, his party moved faster.

American Motors is just a memory now, swallowed up long ago by much
larger and more globally oriented firms. So, too, is the GOP of George
Romney. And so, too, is the faith in the mixed economy they endorsed
and nurtured. This book explains why.

Part 1 tells the story of George Romney's America: the achievements
of America's mixed economic model and the political balance that made it
possible. This is an American story, but it is not just an American story.
The United States was not alone in crossing the Great Divide, and so we
should resist explanations of American achievements that rest too heavily
on singular features of America's postwar model, effective as it was. America's mixed economy was distinctive, but all nations that catapulted into
affluence had mixed economies of their own—based on some important
but forgotten truths about how markets, and governments, really operate.

Part 2 tells the story of Mitt Romney's America: how and why a once
successful model fell apart and the costs of this disintegration for American society. This is not just an American story either. All rich nations have
had to grapple with the changing contours of advanced capitalism. Yet it
is the United States that has experienced the most concerted attack on the
public foundations of the mixed economy and the most sweeping denial
of prior understandings of what fosters prosperity. And, as we shall see
in the next chapter, it has paid a very high price for this forced forgetting.

The economic challenges that face affluent democracies are well
known: the increase in global competition, the shift from manufacturing to services, the ascent of high-rolling finance as both a powerful
shaper of corporate strategies and a dominant sector of the economy
in its own right. But the social institution of the mixed economy could

have been updated to respond to these changes. The balance between effective public authority and dynamic private markets could have been recalibrated rather than rejected. Instead, the political coalition in favor of such a constructive balance shattered under the pressure of an increasingly conservative Republican Party and an increasingly insular, parochial, and extreme business leadership. The moderate perspective that government and the market needed to complement each other gave way. It was replaced by a destructive insistence that these two centers of power were locked in mortal combat—destructive because so many of those in power rejected adaption in favor of upending, destructive because this insistence so often magnified rather than mitigated the economic challenges faced, and destructive because so few Americans now trust their democracy to do what democracies must do to ensure broad prosperity.

In the book's closing, we make the case that we can and must restore a well-functioning politics that promotes shared prosperity. Yes, the specific arrangements that enabled the American economic model of the last century are dead and buried. But we are convinced it is possible to build a new model for economic success, on new political foundations, to deepen prosperity in the twenty-first century. More than that, we are convinced—and we hope to convince you—that the complex and interdependent knowledge economy of our day offers tremendous opportunities for positive-sum bargains that will strengthen both American capitalism and the health of American society. If we are to grasp these opportunities, however, we need a mixed economy as much as, if not more than, we ever have. For all the changes that have occurred during the fifty-year transition from George Romney's world to Mitt Romney's, that strong thumb of government still needs to assist and constrain those nimble fingers of the market.

Demonstrating government's centrality to our shared prosperity is the main task of part 1. First, however, we must look with clear eyes at the failings of our society that are the predictable and alarming result of forgetting this essential truth.

PART I

* * *

THE RISE OF THE
MIXED ECONOMY

ONE

* ★ ★ ★ *

Coming Up Short

AMERICANS PRIDE themselves on standing tall: rising to the challenge, achieving the once unattainable, raising the bar of social success. Yet as we have faltered in harnessing the enormous positive potential of public authority, we have also fallen behind the pace of social improvement in other rich nations, as well as the pace we set in our own past. In area after area where we once dominated, we are falling down the rankings of social success. In area after area where new threats loom, we are failing to rise up to the challenge. We are not standing tall—literally, we shall see—and our malign neglect of the mixed economy bears a great deal of the blame.

Losing Ground

For much of US history, Americans were the tallest people in the world by a large margin. When the thirteen colonies that occupied the Atlantic seaboard broke from the British Empire, adult American men were on average three inches taller than their counterparts in England, and they were almost that much taller than men in the Netherlands, the great economic power before Britain.[1] Revolutionary soldiers looked up to General George Washington, but not, as often assumed, because he was a giant among Lilliputians. David McCullough, in his popular biography of John Adams, describes Washington as "nearly a head taller than Adams—six feet four in his boots, taller than almost anyone of the day."[2] Those must have been some boots, for Washington was six feet two.[3] At five foot seven, Adams was just an inch below the average for American soldiers and significantly taller than a typical European soldier.[4]

Americans were tall because Americans were healthy. "Poor as they were," notes the colonial historian William Polk, "Americans ate and were housed better than Englishmen."[5] Sickness and premature death were common, of course, especially outside the privileged circle of white men. Still, European visitors like Tocqueville marveled at the fertility of the land and the robustness of its settlers, the relative equality of male citizens and the strong civic bonds among them.[6] J. Hector St. John de Crèvecoeur wrote in 1782 of the American settler in *Letters from an American Farmer*, "Instead of starving he will be fed, instead of being idle he will have employment, and there are riches enough for such men as come over here."[7]

The cause of the American height advantage could not have been income alone. According to most sources, the average resident of the Netherlands or England was richer than colonial Americans but also substantially shorter.[8] Indeed, as the United States matched and then surpassed Europe economically in the nineteenth century, the average height of American men actually fell, recovering back to colonial levels only around the dawn of the twentieth century.[9] These ebbs and flows, which played out in other industrializing nations as well, are a reminder that economic growth and population health are not one and the same.[10] (We shall unravel the mystery of their interdependence in the next chapter.) Nonetheless, Americans remained far and away the tallest people in the world throughout the nineteenth century, and average American heights rose quickly in the early decades of the twentieth.[11] When the United States entered World War II, young American men averaged five feet nine inches—almost two inches taller, on average, than the young Germans they were fighting.[12]

While people know that height is a strong predictor of individual achievement (test scores, occupational prestige, pay), it is also a revealing marker of population health.[13] Height has a lot to do with genes, but height differences across nations seem to be caused mostly by social conditions, such as income, nutrition, health coverage, and social cohesion.[14] Indeed, one reason for the correlation between height and achievement is that kids whose mothers are healthy during pregnancy and who grow up with sufficient food, medical care, and family support tend to be taller adults. An average US white girl born in the early 1910s could expect to reach around five foot three; an average US white girl born in the late 1950s could expect to exceed five foot five.[15] Evolution just doesn't happen that fast.

So it's striking that Americans are no longer the tallest people in the world. Not even close: Once three inches taller than residents of the Old World, on average, Americans are now about three inches shorter. The average Dutch height for men is six foot one, and for women, five foot eight—versus five foot nine for American men and five foot five for American women.[16] The gap is not, as might be supposed, a result of immigration: White, native-born Americans who speak English at home are significantly smaller, too, and immigration isn't substantial enough to explain the discrepancy in any case.[17] Nor can the growing gap be explained by differences in how height is measured. Though some countries rely on self-reported heights for their statistics—and, yes, men tend to "round up"—Americans look shorter even when the only countries in the rankings are those that, like the United States, measure heights directly.[18]

Americans are not shrinking. (Overall, that is—there is some evidence that both white and black women born after 1960 are shorter than their parents.)[19] But the increase in Americans' average stature has been glacial, even as heights continue to rise steadily abroad. To really see our lost height advantage, you have to break the population into age groups, or what demographers call birth cohorts. People in their twenties, after all, are as tall as they will ever be. Changes in average height come from changes in the height of the young (and deaths among older cohorts). And, indeed, the adult heights of those born during a given period provide a powerful image of the living conditions experienced by infants and adolescents at the time. The fall in average heights among those born in the mid-1800s, for example, signaled the costs as well as benefits of the country's industrial and urban shift, which brought increased infectious disease as well as higher incomes, harsher lives for the masses as well as better lives for the elite.[20] (The privileged American men who applied for passports in 1890 were, on average, more than an inch and a half taller than army recruits at the time.)[21]

In general, heights are converging among affluent nations, and the biggest gains have occurred in countries admitted most recently to the rich-nation club.[22] Within countries, younger age groups are generally much taller than older age groups—which makes sense: Older people spent their growing years (including their growth within the womb) in poorer societies with more limited health technology and knowledge.[23] But the United States is a conspicuous exception to these patterns: Average heights have barely budged in recent decades, so young Americans—again, even when leaving out recent immigrants—are barely taller than their parents.[24] Older Americans are roughly on par with their counterparts abroad; younger Americans are substantially shorter. The United States is the richest populous nation in the world. Nevertheless, its young are roughly as tall as the young in Portugal, which has a per capita gross domestic product (GDP) less than half ours.[25]

On Rankings and Ratings

Because height is a powerful indicator of social and individual health, America's relative decline should ring alarms. Our young are coming up short—relative not just to gains in stature of the past but also to gains in stature in other rich nations.

Still, if shorter kids were the only sign of trouble, we might safely ignore the alarms. For all but aspiring basketball players, tallness is not an end in itself. It can even create problems: The Dutch have had to re-write their building codes so men don't routinely smash their heads into door frames.[26] Unfortunately, America's journey from tallest to smallish has played out in area after area. When it comes to health, education, and even income—still our strongest suit, though we're holding fewer high cards than in the past—we are falling down the rankings of social success.

We often miss this, and not just because triumphant cries of American exceptionalism drown out the alarms. Comparing countries on indicators of social health is tricky, and the temptation to stack the deck is strong. Moreover, our standard statistics frequently *understate* how poorly the United States is doing at harnessing the combined energies of government and the market. To get an accurate picture, we have to spend a little time sifting through the best available data, separating the meaningful from the misleading. We also have to focus on the experiences most relevant for understanding not how we've done in the past but how we are doing now—and unless we change course, how we are likely to do in the future.

Put another way, not all performance assessments are equally valid or instructive. Each year brings scores of scores purporting to rank almost every conceivable object of interest—schools, businesses, cities, states, regions, countries—across almost every conceivable category, from college completion, to wine consumption, to online porn viewing. (For the record, Washington, DC, tops US state rankings in all three.) But sensibly comparing states, countries, or anything else requires following a few simple ground rules. The first is to compare apples to apples. Washington, DC, isn't actually that comparable to the fifty states because it's essentially a big city (hence the porn-wine-college trifecta). For cross-national analysis, comparing apples to apples means comparing countries at similar levels of economic development. It also means using indicators that are as close to the same as possible across nations. And it requires transparency: Proprietary data and secret formulas are anathema to serious comparison (but endemic to many special-interest rankings).

So we should compare apples to apples. But which apples should we be comparing? A good place to begin is the three core components of the UN's Human Development Index: health, education, and income. The index captures the idea that development is about "advancing the richness of human life"—to quote its intellectual father, the Nobel laureate Amartya Sen—and not just "the richness of the economy in which human beings live."[27] The index itself isn't all that useful for ranking rich nations. It often sets the bar low (can people read and write?), and it's limited to a few basic indicators available for all countries. Nonetheless, the UN's pioneering investigations provide a solid jumping-off point for asking how well the contemporary United States is doing relative to other rich nations in fostering citizens' well-being.

When asking that question, the issue isn't merely how well we are doing today. It's also whether we are pulling ahead or falling behind. One data point gives us a level; two or more give us a trend. And, in general, it's trends that reveal the most about our relative performance. To be sure, we should be careful not to read too much into short-term fluctuations. Nor should we forget that on many metrics, there is a natural process of "reversion to the mean": Relative to other countries, the highest-performing nations are more likely to fall toward other nations' performances, and the lowest performing to rise toward other nations' performances.

Still, trends matter most. And that means we should be at least as interested in the direction social indicators are heading (and at what pace) as in their level. It also means we should pay special attention to one particular group: the young. Most cross-national analyses look at countries as a whole, comparing several generations of people in one nation with several generations in another. Sometimes that's appropriate. If we want to know which countries are good at getting all citizens flu shots, we are interested in national averages. Usually, however, the experience of the young is most revealing, and not just because the young are most affected by current conditions. The young tell us about trends. If, for example, we're falling behind in getting young adults through college (and we are), looking at the average educational level of the entire population will provide false reassurance. Typically, then, the critical comparisons across nations concern the young. Unhappily, these are also the comparisons where the most troubling image of American performance emerges.

A final issue to keep in mind: Investment (or lack of investment) does not bear its (bitter) fruit immediately. Supporting science, technology, and education, for example, reaps big returns.[28] But it takes time—sometimes a long time—to see the payoffs. As we will see in chapters 2 and 4, the high-tech expansion of the last few decades rested on scientific and technical advances seeded more than a generation earlier.[29] The opposite problem arises in cases of deferred maintenance: failing to upgrade critical infrastructure, for example, or to seed technological advances that will blossom in the future. The costs, though real, won't be fully apparent for some time.

The same can be said about failing to tackle emerging challenges—an area where, we shall see, the United States is doing especially poorly. A generation ago, few worried about how well nations were addressing obesity or global warming. Now we know that the health of our society and the future of our planet depend on effective responses. The low bar for social performance is continuing to meet challenges we've met before. The high bar is doing well where we face new challenges. Unfortunately, not only is the United States having trouble clearing the low bar; it is barely even trying to clear the higher one.

The United States is still a remarkably successful nation. Over the last century, we have achieved unprecedented levels of prosperity, witnessed quantum increases in health and life expectancy, and sought to address problems that once mocked our finest traditions of democracy and opportunity, from vicious racial exclusion to grim elderly poverty to dangerously unclean air and water. And we have continued to gain ground in many of these areas over the last generation. Yet these gains have been halting and slow. Even more worrisome, they lag behind gains in other rich democracies.

Health

Among the big three of health, education, and income, none is more important than health. Those who study the economics of health and longevity find consistently that the value of physical well-being within a society vastly exceeds a nation's total income.[30] But even without such calculations, we all know that health is a precondition for everything else we seek to achieve. When the Declaration of Independence celebrated "life, liberty, and the pursuit of happiness," there was a reason "life" led the list.

When it comes to health—in fact, when it comes to any measure of the well-being of individual members of a society—small differences matter when summed up across large populations. Consider a seemingly trivial example: that dreaded spinning wheel that tells you your computer is spinning its wheels. In his biography of Apple founder Steve Jobs, Walter Isaacson recounts an exchange between Jobs and Larry Kenyon, an engineer whom Jobs had cornered to complain that the new Macintosh took too long to start up:

> Kenyon started to explain, but Jobs cut him off. "If it could save a person's life, would you find a way to shave ten seconds off the boot time?" he asked. Kenyon allowed that he probably could. Jobs went to a whiteboard and showed him that if there were five million people using the Mac, and it took ten seconds extra to turn it on every day, that added up to three hundred million or so hours per year that people would save, which was the equivalent of at least one hundred lifetimes saved per year. "Larry was suitably impressed, and a few weeks later he came back, and it booted up twenty-eight seconds faster," [Apple programmer Bill] Atkinson recalled.[31]

Jobs's point holds more generally: Even small differences in how long we live add up. An extra four months of life expectancy in a country with 321 million residents is 107 million additional years of life. Economists who are comfortable converting lives into dollars generally value a "quality-adjusted life year"—QALY, in economics jargon—in the neighborhood of $100,000 (though estimates range from less than $50,000 per QALY to more than $250,000).[32] That would mean those four months are worth somewhere north of $10 trillion.

Shorter Lives, Poorer Health

So it is more than a little disconcerting that health is also where the United States does most poorly compared with other rich nations. In 2013 the prestigious National Academy of Sciences released a mammoth report with a self-explanatory title: *U.S. Health in International Perspective: Shorter Lives, Poorer Health*. "The United States is among the wealthiest nations in the world," the report began, "but it is far from the healthiest. . . . Americans live shorter lives and experience more injuries and illnesses than people in other high-income countries."[33]

On virtually all measures, according to the report, the United States is losing ground rapidly to other rich nations. At midcentury, American were generally healthier than citizens of other rich nations, and as late as 1980, they were still not far from the middle of the pack.[34] Since then, however, other rich countries have seen rapid health gains. The United States has not.[35]

Take life expectancy at birth—the easiest statistic to track, since death records are generally reliable and consistent across nations. The National Academies study looked at seventeen rich nations. Among these, the United States ranked seventeenth for men in 2011 (life expectancy: 76.3 years, a full 4.2 years shorter than the top-ranking nation). It ranked an equally dismal seventeenth for women (81.1 years, 4.8 years shorter than the top-ranking nation).[36] The United States is home to about 163 million women and 158 million men, so ranking in the middle teens rather than at the top translates into 1.45 *billion* fewer years of life.[37]

Midlife Crisis

The relative decline has been particularly steep for an unlikely group: middle-aged white adults. In a groundbreaking 2015 study, the Princeton University economists Anne Case and Angus Deaton (the latter the recipient of the Nobel Prize in Economics that same year) dug into the mortality statistics to examine how and why the American experience departed so starkly from the international norm.[38] Their startling result: Whites ages forty-five to fifty-four were dying at higher rates in 2013 than they had been in 1999, even as every other rich country had seen dramatic drops in mortality in this age group. Case and Deaton calculated that if this reversal had not occurred—if, that is, the decline in death rates of prior decades had continued—a half million deaths would have been avoided. The only other example of such a shocking loss of life in recent decades is the AIDS epidemic.

The trend was most devastating for whites with a high school diploma or less. In 2013 there were 736 deaths per 100,000 people within this group, up from 601 per 100,000 in 1999. (By comparison, the death rate for people in this age group in Canada fell from around 300 per 100,000 in 1999 to just under 249 per 100,000 in 2011.) But those who had gone to college but not received a degree saw no distinguishable improvement in death rates either—even as, again, such rates plummeted abroad. Only among whites with a college degree did death rates fall substantially over this period. In 2013, white adults in the forty-five- to fifty-four-year-old age group with no more than a high school diploma were more than four times as likely to die as those with a college degree.

As this last troubling statistic suggests, there are also stark disparities in life expectancy across racial, economic, and educational groups—disparities that appear to be far larger than in most other rich nations.[39] Yet nearly every group of Americans—even, as we have seen, whites—fares poorly when compared with its peers in other rich nations.[40] The only area of evident success is life expectancy at age seventy-five, where Americans do quite well. Researchers speculate, however, that this anomaly reflects not just good health care for the aged (who, unlike the young, have universal insurance coverage through Medicare) but also that so many unhealthy Americans die *before* age seventy-five, leaving behind a hardy group.[41]

Falling Behind

To be clear, many measures of health *are* improving in the United States. But they are improving much more slowly than in other countries. One grim statistic commonly used by demographers is the chance that a fifteen-year-old will die before age fifty. For American women, it's 4 percent: four in a hundred women die between fifteen and fifty. The average for other rich nations is around 2 percent, and, on average, death rates in these nations fell below 4 percent almost forty years ago. We are more than a generation behind.[42]

A similar story can be told about infant mortality, or deaths of children before their first birthday. In 1960 infant mortality in the United States was lower than in the majority of other rich nations. In recent decades, however, America has seen limited improvement, while death rates for infants have continued to plummet abroad.[43] In 2011 the average rate of infant death in other rich nations was 1 child for every 300 or so births. In the United States, it was roughly twice that—1 child for every 164 births. That year, the only countries in the Organization for Economic Cooperation and Development (OECD) with higher rates of infant mortality were Chile, Mexico, and Turkey.[44]

This unimpressive performance is particularly striking because the United States spends so much more on health care than other rich nations do—roughly twice as much per person.[45] Of course, medical care is not the only or even the most important determinant of health. But the United States does poorly even where health care matters most. For almost every cause—from injuries to diseases—death rates are the highest or nearly the highest in the United States.[46] And we have the highest rate of what health experts call "amenable mortality": deaths that could have been prevented with the provision of timely and effective care.[47] Despite high spending, we are falling behind other rich nations in reducing such preventable deaths. We don't see our relative decline because we *are* getting better at preventing death. But we're getting better far too slowly for a rich nation.

Education

Another area where the United States was once the undisputed leader is education. As the Harvard economists Lawrence Katz and Claudia Goldin show in their revelatory *The Race Between Education and Technology,* we bolted decades ahead of other Western nations in the spread of elementary and then high schools during the twentieth century, and we were the world leader in college education in the immediate decades after World War II.[48] No more. The United States is now a mediocre performer in international education rankings. And we would look a lot worse if we hadn't done so well in the past. The share of Americans who have completed high school, for instance, remains impressive. Yet this high average mostly reflects our big early lead. Among young adults, high school graduation rates are subpar (though they have risen in the last decade).[49] The United States now ranks twentieth out of twenty-seven OECD nations in the share of young people expected to finish high school.[50]

Losing the Race

This isn't just a case of other countries racing ahead; it's also a story of American stagnation. Graduation rates in the United States have barely budged since the early 1970s, rising from 81 percent to 84 percent. At the same time, more and more kids who are counted as having finished high school actually receive a General Educational Development (GED) certificate.[51] Yet GEDs confer little of the economic and social benefits of graduating from high school. (Many European countries have vocational high schools, but, unlike GEDs, these produce strong outcomes.)[52] Another reason is that young adults behind bars disappear from the statistics. In most rich nations, this distinction makes little difference because incarceration is so rare. In the United States—which incarcerates roughly ten times as high a share of the population (eight in a thousand versus fewer than one in a thousand in most other advanced industrial democracies)—it makes a real difference, especially for demographic groups with the highest rates of incarceration.[53] Indeed, the high school dropout rate for young black men is more than 40 percent higher when we include in our count the incarcerated, wiping out all the apparent gains in their high school completion since the late 1980s.[54] Here again, conventional indicators present an overly sunny picture of our relative performance.

The big story, however, is our relative decline in higher education. The United States has many of the finest institutions of higher education in the world. The problem is that the share of young people getting a degree is rising much more slowly in the United States than in other OECD nations.[55] One reason is the erosion of public support through federal grants and state universities, leaving students and their families much more reliant on loans. Once without peer, the United States has fallen to nineteenth in college completion in the OECD, and the gap in completion between higher-income and lower-income students has widened.[56] Older Americans are the most educated in the world. Younger Americans, not even close.

Skills Slowdown

Indeed, despite the popular image of young Americans as digital wizards, America's youth fare particularly poorly when it comes to numerical and technological skills. The OECD assessed adult skill levels in twenty-three nations in 2011 and 2012. Across the population as a whole, the United States scores about average when it comes to reading ability and close to the bottom when it comes to mathematical ability and the capacity to work with computer technology.[57] Other international tests show us doing even better in reading, but they all show the performance of Americans as a whole to be mediocre or worse in the STEM (science, technology, engineering, math) areas so prominent in our technology-saturated economy.[58]

The truly alarming results, however, emerge when looking across age groups. In all countries, the young are better at math and working with digital technology than the old. But improvements in test scores from one generation to the next are much smaller in the United States than in other rich countries. Older Americans are close to the international average for older adults. Younger Americans, while scoring slightly higher, are years behind their international peers. So, again, American math scores *are* improving—barely. But they are improving far faster in other nations. The same is true of the other skills measured by the OECD: The United States falls further and further in the rankings as you move down the age ladder.[59]

Degrees of Inequality

And if the United States as a whole is in the breakdown lane, some Americans are barely getting on the road. At least as striking as our poor performance among the young is how *unequal* educational opportunities in the United States are. Decades after de jure integration of schools and the famous 1966 Coleman Report on the subpar schooling of the poor, we remain a nation with gaps in educational quality, funding, and outcomes that are far greater than the norm for developed democracies. These gaps not only thwart the upward progress of tens of millions of Americans but hold back our economy overall.

Since the 1960s, the divide in test scores between children from high-income families and those from low-income families has grown by more than a third; it is now twice as large as the gap between blacks and whites.[60] Yet the United States is one of the few nations that finances schools primarily through local property taxes, which magnifies unequal opportunity. As one OECD researcher puts it, "The vast majority of OECD countries either invest equally in every student or disproportionately more in disadvantaged students. The US is one of the few countries doing the opposite."[61]

Inequality of opportunity begins early, and it costs everyone. Good pre-K education, for example, more than pays off in higher growth and tax receipts and lower public costs, from social assistance to incarceration.[62] Yet the United States ranks twenty-fifth in the OECD in the share of three-year-olds in early childhood education, and even lower, twenty-eighth, when it comes to four-year-olds.[63]

Income

Income, the third indicator of the big three, might seem to be an exception to the story so far. Only a few small countries surpass us in national income per head, and American productivity growth has remained comparatively strong.[64] Even here, however, the reassuring averages hide some worrisome trends.

Beyond GDP

Historically, economists have considered national income per capita the best single measure of the standard of living of middle-class citizens. For much of the twentieth century, it was. Since the early 1970s, however, the link has broken. The American economy is more and more productive, and national income has continued to grow smartly (if more slowly than before).[65] But these gains have not translated into substantially higher wages for most Americans. The typical hourly earnings of American workers—adjusting for inflation and *including* the escalating cost of medical benefits—rose only 10 percent between 1973 and 2011. That works out to an annual raise of 0.27 percent.

But American *families* have grown significantly richer, right? Yes and no. Between the early 1970s and the late 1990s, the typical household's income increased from around $49,000 to almost $57,000 (after adjusting for inflation).[66] Yet the wage stagnation of the 2000s and the financial crisis that closed out the decade wiped out all of the gains created by the strong economy of the 1990s, leaving typical households about where typical households were in *1989*. True, families are smaller than they were in the early 1970s, but they aren't appreciably smaller than they were in 1989 and, in fact, have grown since the financial crisis. Moreover, families have shrunk in other rich nations, too. Yet over the past generation, the incomes of working-age people in the middle of the distribution have grown more slowly here than in almost any other OECD nation.[67]

Just as important, the overriding reason the typical family earns a little more today is not more pay per hour but more paychecks per household, as women have moved into the paid workforce. This change isn't because the United States has led the world in female employment. (In 2010 America was seventeenth in the OECD in the share of women in paid employment, down from sixth in 1990.)[68] It's because US workers, both male and female, work many more hours than workers in other countries do—and the gap is growing.[69] More paychecks per household is good in many ways. But given the strains of balancing work and parenting, more hours of work isn't necessarily a positive development. Either way, it's a different story than the one of prior decades, when wages and salaries rose smartly even though the number of hours people worked did not.[70]

America Unequal

Where did all the growth go? The answer, it turns out, is simple: It went to the top, especially the very top. When it comes to inequality, the United States once looked relatively similar to other rich countries. Today it's the most unequal rich nation in the world by a large margin.[71] However else that matters, the increasing concentration of income at the top drives a wedge between overall economic growth and the income gains of most households. When a rising tide lifts all boats, economic growth is a better measure of ordinary Americans' living standards than when a rising tide lifts only yachts.

You can see the disparity even more clearly when you look at wealth: housing, stocks, bonds, and all the other assets that people hold to weather economic shocks and build their future. Americans' *average* net wealth is an impressive $301,000, the fourth highest in the world, behind only Switzerland, Australia, and Norway.[72] *Median* net wealth—the amount held by someone exactly in the middle of the distribution—is another story. The typical American adult has just $45,000, which places the United States nineteenth in the world, behind every rich country but

Israel (including such "economic heavyweights" as Spain and Taiwan).[73] The obvious reason for the difference is that wealth is so unequal across American households. The richest 1 percent own more than a third of the nation's wealth; the top 10 percent, more than three-quarters.[74] No other rich country comes close to this level of concentration at the top.

Broken Ladders

So the rungs of the economic ladder are farther apart. But isn't it easier to climb the ladder in the United States than elsewhere? From Crèvecoeur to Tocqueville to the German sociologist Werner Sombart, descriptions of American society from the Founding through the early twentieth century emphasized the ease of mobility compared with Europe. Indeed, Sombart's basic answer to his famous question *Why Is There No Socialism in the United States?* (the title of his 1906 book) was that the American worker was less disgruntled because "the prospects of moving out of his class were undoubtedly greater . . . than for his counterpart in old Europe."[75] Historians and social scientists have debated Sombart's assertion ever since. But there's little question that the United States— and other settler societies such as Canada—enjoyed a mobility advantage over Europe through the nineteenth century, especially for Americans willing to strike out for the nation's expanding frontier.[76]

Today, however, the frontier is gone, and so is America's mobility advantage. Indeed, the United States now has close to the lowest level of upward mobility in the advanced industrial world: lower than in Tocqueville's France, lower than in Sombart's Germany, and lower—much lower—than in our northern neighbor, Canada.[77] Roughly two in three Americans born in the bottom fifth of incomes either stay there (42 percent) or rise just into the next fifth (23 percent). An American boy whose dad is in the bottom fifth has only a 30 percent chance of climbing into the top half. A Canadian boy has a 38 percent chance. This 8-point difference might seem small, but it's not. With 138 million American men, 8 percentage points represent 2 million boys escaping the bottom fifth into the top half.

The Kids Aren't All Right

Again it's the youngest of the young who are most disadvantaged. The United Nations Children's Fund (UNICEF) has compiled a composite index of the "material well-being" of children in developed countries, which takes into account various measures of childhood poverty and material deprivation (lack of access to regular meals, for example). In the most recent report, the United States ranked twenty-sixth out of twenty-nine developed nations.[78] First in the standings was the Netherlands, where soon-to-be-giants are born. UNICEF has produced its index since the early 2000s. The United States was one of only five nations that were below average at that time yet failed to improve kids' material well-being in the following decade. The other four were Greece, Hungary, Italy, and Spain.

"Prediction is very difficult," the physicist Niels Bohr reportedly said, "especially about the future." But today's young are the clearest vision of the future we have. If they are falling behind—unhealthier than young people in other rich countries, less well educated, more likely to be economically marginalized—we face grim prospects. As two health researchers conclude after reviewing the international evidence on the well-being of American children, "The US stacks up relatively poorly on critical measures of child health. Similarly, the US compares unfavorably to other nations on indicators of governmental investment in children and their families. The picture that emerges is one of a powerful and immensely wealthy nation that, compared with other nations, has made a startlingly modest investment in its children."[79]

Shortchanging the Future

We come then to the last of our alarming grades. Where we once led, we are losing ground. But that's better than we are doing in preparing for our future, especially when it comes to responding to newly emerging challenges, such as global warming and obesity, for which no inheritance of American leadership exists. With regard to these crucial tests of the resilience and innovative potential of our society, we are getting failing marks.

R&D RIP

Consider research and development, or R&D, a key source of fuel for the knowledge economy.[80] Leave it up to the market, and it won't be adequately supplied. That's not because corporations don't value R&D—they do, and they do a lot of it. It's because corporations will underinvest in R&D that aids many firms rather than mainly themselves because they pay the cost but receive only a small fraction of the benefit. This incentive problem is a major reason why government support for R&D became so large and so valuable as the capacities of science exploded in the twentieth century.

Nowhere was this problem addressed more capably than in the United States. Though government promotion and funding of science has a long history, it expanded dramatically during World War II and continued afterward with the National Science Foundation (NSF), National Institutes of Health (NIH), and other public agencies that supported training in science and engineering and financed research in the private sector and academia. In the quarter century after World War II, the United States didn't just lead the world in R&D funding. It owned the field. Well into the 1960s, the federal government spent more than the combined total of all R&D spending by governments *and* businesses outside the United States.[81] The fruits of these investments ranged from radar and GPS, to advanced medical technology, to robotics and the computer systems that figure in nearly every modern technology. Far from crowding out private R&D, moreover, these public investments spurred additional private innovation. The computer pioneers who developed better and smaller systems not only relied on publicly fostered breakthroughs in technology; they also would have found little market for their most profitable products if not for the internet, GPS, and other government-sponsored platforms for the digital revolution.

That was then. Over the last half century, R&D spending by the federal government has plummeted as a share of the economy, falling from a peak of nearly 2 percent of GDP in the mid-1960s to around 0.7 percent in the late 1990s, before rebounding slightly in recent years.[82] Between 1987 and 2008, federal expenditures were essentially flat once inflation is taken into account (rising 0.3 percent a year). The United States now ranks ninth in the world in government R&D expenditures as a share of the economy.[83] The majority of this spending, however, is for defense-related projects, which have fewer positive spillovers than nondefense R&D does. Take out defense, and the United States ranks thirty-ninth in government R&D spending as a share of the economy.

Calculating the effects of R&D spending on productivity is difficult, but the consensus among economists is that the returns to individual firms are large and the returns to society as a whole, larger still.[84] Public R&D expenditures are already at their lowest level as a share of the economy in forty years, and they are slated to fall to their lowest level—0.5 percent of GDP in 2021—since before the great mobilization of science during World War II.[85] If they were instead increased in line with the size of the economy, according to one cautious calculation, the economy would generate more than a half trillion dollars in additional income over the next nine years.[86] And, of course, this alternative scenario—ambitious given current trends—means never going back to the level of investment of just a quarter century ago. To ramp back up to that level would require *tripling* current spending as a share of the economy.

We are not talking just about dollars and cents. We are talking about lives. Consider one chilling example: drug-resistant infections. As America's breakthroughs in antibiotics recede into the past, bacteria are evolving to defeat current antibiotics. For more and more infections, we are plunging back into the pre-antibiotic era. In the United States alone, two million people are sickened and tens of thousands die each year from drug-resistant infections—mostly because private companies see little incentive to invest in the necessary research, and the federal government has failed to step in.[87] Though federal funding for the National Institutes of Health ramped up in the mid-1990s, it has fallen precipitously since, cutting the share of young scientists with NIH grants in half in roughly six years.[88] As one medical professor lamented recently: "In my daily work in both a university medical school and a public hospital, it's a rare month that some bright young person doesn't tell me they are quitting science because it's too hard to get funded. . . . A decade or two from now, when an antibiotic-resistant bacteria or new strain of bird flu is ravaging humanity, that generation will no longer be around to lead the scientific charge on humanity's behalf."[89]

Public Disinvestment

And health research has fared better than most areas. Public investment of all sorts and by all tiers of government has reached the lowest level since demobilization after the Second World War. Until the 1970s, gross investment by the public sector—R&D plus investment in physical capital—averaged around 7 percent of GDP. It fell below 6 percent in the 1970s and 1980s, and below 4 percent in the 1990s and 2000s. It is now at 3.6 percent and falling.[90] The biggest crunch is in infrastructure: roads, bridges, water supplies, communications networks, public buildings, and the like.[91] These are among the most productive investments

governments make, with average rates of return that are probably several
times higher than those of typical private investments.[92] And American
infrastructure was once the envy of the world: The interstate highway
system started under President Eisenhower—a Republican—eventually
stretched over forty-two thousand miles, at a cost (in present dollars) of
$493 billion. But the investment paid off, accounting for almost a third of
the increase in the nation's economic productivity in the late 1950s and
around a quarter in the 1960s.[93]

American infrastructure is no longer the envy of the world. The
World Economic Forum, the Davos-based center of business-oriented
thinking, ranks the United States fifteenth in the quality of railway
structures, sixteenth in the quality of roads, and ninth in transportation infrastructure.[94] The American Society of Civil Engineers estimates
that the United States would have to spend $3.6 trillion more than cur-
rently budgeted just to bring our infrastructure up to acceptable levels
by 2020.[95] China and India are spending almost 10 percent of GDP on infrastructure; Europe, around 5 percent.[96] Even Mexico spends just over
3 percent.[97] The United States has not broken 3 percent once since the
mid-1970s.[98]

Both of us used to live in the Boston area, and since we study American politics, we traveled frequently to the nation's capital. It takes seven
hours to travel from Boston to Washington, DC, on the closest thing the
United States has to high-speed rail, Amtrak's Acela Express. It takes
just over two hours to travel roughly the same distance between Changsha and Guangzhou on China's high-speed rail network.[99]

Not Stepping Up to the Plate

In January 2013 a blackout shut down Super Bowl XLVII for thirty-four
minutes. Blamed wrongly on Beyoncé's halftime show (which was actually powered by a generator), the exact cause is still not known.[100] What is
known is that if the United States had invested in a "smart grid"—energy
transmission guided by digital monitoring rather than the clunky analog
system and manual meter reading from the age of Thomas Edison—the
lights barely would have flickered in the Superdome in New Orleans. A
smart grid wouldn't just be more reliable but also more efficient, eliminating a significant amount of the roughly 150 million tons of carbon
dioxide that's spewed into the atmosphere each year by the United States
just because of power losses at the grid.[101] For some die-hard fans, saving

the Super-Bowl from blackouts might be reason enough to build a smart grid. Helping to save the planet ought to be reason enough for everyone.

The United States is investing in smart-grid technology. The economic recovery bill passed in 2009 contained $4.5 billion in federal grants, which in turn have fostered new opportunities for tech companies to pursue smart-grid projects.[102] Sadly, however, this initiative is far too modest. In any case, it represents the exception rather than the rule in America's halting effort to tackle the mounting threat of global warming. Every year, the estimated future costs of inaction increase, as the risks of extreme drought, intense storms, lost coastal land, heat-induced pandemics and wildfires, and damaged agriculture loom larger. Economists continue to debate exactly how much a robust response would slow the growth of the world economy (with more and more arguing that it would have little or no effect or even spur growth).[103] But it's become increasingly clear that the costs of inaction are so catastrophic that substantial steps must be taken whatever the exact trade-off—the question is only what the most cost-effective and politically feasible steps would be.

And yet the United States, once the unquestioned leader in addressing pollution and other ecological risks, lags behind the rich world on most measures of environmental performance. It emits more carbon dioxide per person than any affluent country besides tiny Luxembourg—roughly twice as much as Germany and Japan, and more than three times as much as France and Sweden.[104] The widely respected Yale Environmental Performance Index, which assesses air and water pollution and other key environmental outcomes as well as measures relevant to climate change, ranked the United States thirty-third in the world in 2014—two spots down from its similarly uninspiring ranking of thirty-first a decade earlier.[105]

Land of the Big

We have seen how far we have to go in tackling the dangerous warming of our planet—a challenge that cannot be addressed without the leadership of the world's sole superpower and second-largest carbon emitter. But consider a very different emerging challenge where lack of an effective response is literally weighing down America's future.

A larger share of Americans are obese than in any other rich country: Defined as having a body mass index of 30 or higher (roughly two hundred–plus pounds for a five-foot-eight person), obesity now afflicts more than one in three adults and one in six children, compared with around one in seven people or fewer in most European countries.[106] Individual medical costs associated with obesity are on par with those of smoking.[107] In the aggregate, obesity accounts for a tenth of health spending in the United States, generating $270 billion in total economic cost due to medical bills, mortality, and disability.[108] When additional consequences of obesity are factored in—lower earnings, lost work time, reduced productivity—the costs are even more staggering.

The basic causes are no mystery: Americans have become more sedentary, and they consume more calories than they once did.[109] Even small differences in activity and diet can add up: One soda a day—a twelve-ounce can, not the megacups that are served at fast-food restaurants (KFC's "Mega Jug" is sixty-four ounces)—adds up to 55,000 additional calories and fifteen extra pounds a year.[110] And once again, adding up all these individual changes across the population leads to enormous effects (no pun intended), such as $270 billion in higher health spending a year. It's often said that obesity is a personal problem. But people's basic biological desire for fat and sugar hasn't changed in the last few decades; their environment has. And American food policy—including federal subsidies for sugar and high-fructose corn syrup—has played a major role in shaping that environment.

Want a vivid image of how American bodies have changed? The average American woman now weighs around 165 pounds. According to the US Centers for Disease Control and Prevention (CDC), that's essentially what the average American *man* weighed in 1960. (Today's average man is around 195 pounds.)[111] Americans were once the tallest people in the advanced industrial world. We are now not just among the shortest but also far and away the heaviest. Where once we towered over others when standing, now we only do so when everyone is lying down.

Still the American Century?

What makes all this the more poignant and pressing is that it wasn't always this way. When Henry Luce, founder of *Life, Time,* and *Fortune* magazines, wrote of an "American Century" in 1941, the United States had by far the highest standard of living in the world across all dimensions. "At least two-thirds of us are just plain rich compared with all the rest of the human family," Luce wrote, "rich in food, rich in clothes, rich in entertainment and amusement, rich in leisure, rich."[112] Americans also had enviably good health compared with citizens of other wealthy nations. And, not coincidentally, they were much better educated, too.

After World War II, this advantage widened, and not just because of the devastation the war wrought in Europe. With the GI Bill and expansion of state and federal support for universities, the United States leapt into a dominant lead in college attendance and completion. Massive public investments in science training, communications, transportation, roads, bridges, and R&D continued after the war, emphasizing civilian as well as defense aims. These efforts supercharged US growth, bequeathing many of the scientific breakthroughs and revolutionary technologies that have driven our economy to this day. The American Century was created, not inherited.

Of course, the United States was not alone on this remarkable journey to prosperity. Instead, it occupied the leading edge of a revolutionary economic transformation experienced by a small club of rich nations. Which raises a natural question: How did this revolution in human well-being happen?

TWO

★ ★ ★

The Great Divide

I N 1912 the prominent Harvard Medical School professor Lawrence
Henderson observed that the United States had crossed a "Great Divide."[1] "For the first time in human history," Henderson wrote, "a
random patient with a random disease consulting a doctor chosen at random stands a better than 50/50 chance of benefiting from the encounter."
American medicine had advanced to the point, in other words, where it
was better to be treated by physicians than to run in fear from them. The
change was surely overdue: Even in the richest and healthiest nation in the
world, life expectancy for men was still just forty-eight years.[2]

Today, a century later, male life expectancy in the United States exceeds seventy-six years—more than an extra quarter century of experience and activity and achievement.[3] The average life expectancy of
American women has risen from under fifty-two years at the beginning
of the last century to nearly eighty years at the beginning of the current one.[4] Of course, the United States was hardly alone in experiencing
this "escape" from ill health and premature mortality, as Angus Deaton
phrases it in his sweeping account of global economic development.[5]
(Deaton is the Nobel laureate economist whose work on mortality we
encountered in the last chapter.) With somewhat different tempos—
America near the lead at first, still a high performer in midcentury, but
then falling behind, as we have just seen—rich nations all saw life expectancy rise and death rates fall, beginning with children and eventually extending to the last stages of life.[6] In 2000 life expectancy in
these affluent nations averaged nearly eighty years, with women living

to around eighty-two.[7] No other period in world history has witnessed such a dramatic improvement in mortality.[8]

We might assume that social progress, like human evolution (or at least our image of it), is gradual and even. If Americans lived half again as long in 2000 as they did in 1900, then they must have lived roughly half again as long in 1900 as they did in 1800. In fact, the improvement in health and mortality was rapid and discontinuous.[9] It shot ahead in the twentieth century. Citizens of the late 1800s had conveniences and inventions and forms of social organization that their hunter-gatherer ancestors could not dream of. But their patterns of health and mortality were much closer to those ancestors' than to ours. As three demographic experts conclude,

> Until the late 1800s, the world's lowest-mortality populations were not far below the observed range of variation for hunter-gatherers around the prime of life (when mortality is lowest), yet a greater than species-level jump in mortality reduction has been made since. Overall, the bulk of this larger gap in mortality between the longest-living populations and hunter-gatherers occurred during the past century. . . . In gross comparative terms, this means that during evolution from a chimp-like ancestor to anatomically modern humans, mortality levels once typical of prime-of-life individuals were pushed back to later ages at the rate of a decade every 1.3 million years, but the mortality levels typical of a 15-year-old in 1900 became typical of individuals a decade older about every 30 years since 1900.[10]

Put more simply, life expectancy increased far more in the last century than it did in the evolutionary leap from chimpanzee to human.

What happened to create such a momentous, positive, and still-progressing transformation? As Henderson's 1912 observation suggests, the main answer is not advanced medical care. Nor, as we shall see, is increased national income the major story. What happened around the turn of the last century was neither a revolution in medical treatment nor a natural dividend of growth. It was the emergence of effective government action to improve the health of citizens. Funded by growing income, spurred by pressures from reformist social groups, and informed by a new awareness of the benefits of public health (and, eventually, new science that explained where disease came from), public authorities stepped in to use government's distinctive powers to push back the specter of premature death that had plagued humanity for millennia.[11] In the process, they enabled us to cross a Great Divide far more momentous than that described by Henderson: a divide that split centuries of slow growth and poor health from one of unprecedented, rapid improvement in the health of humans and the flourishing of their societies.[12]

What happened, in short, is that reform-minded leaders discovered, harnessed, and expanded the healing powers of the mixed economy. If we are to see what we are losing—and, even more important, understand what made such breakthroughs possible, not just in the United States but in all countries that crossed the Great Divide—we need to look back at the forgotten story of progress's visible hand.

The Health of Nations

Adam Smith wrote about *The Wealth of Nations*. Yet it is in the *health* of nations that we can see most clearly why the modern mixed economy of combined public and private initiative represents such a powerful technology of progress. The fortunate constellation of countries able to harness the force multiplier of private markets and public authority experienced nothing less than a revolution in human flourishing. And they did so because government stepped in to translate increased wealth and improved science into rapid and sustained advance in the health of nations.

In many ways, the thirty-year growth in life expectancy experienced by Americans in the twentieth century *understates* just how profound the shift has been. To see more than a 50 percent increase in life span within a society requires truly staggering declines in the chance of death, especially in the earliest years of life. At the outset of the twentieth century, one in every ten American infants died before their first birthday, roughly the same share that die in contemporary Liberia.[13] In some US cities, the ratio was a heartbreaking three in ten.[14] Things were not much better in the countryside. The problem afflicted rich and poor, prominent and obscure alike.[15] Thomas Jefferson lost four of the six children he had with his wife, Martha, who died after giving birth to the last. (Of the two surviving children, the youngest, Mary, died in her twenties—also after giving birth). Lincoln saw two of his four sons die in childhood; a third died at age eighteen, six years after Lincoln's assassination. Three of Rutherford Hayes's seven children died before age two.[16]

By the end of the twentieth century, however, infant mortality in the United States was around 7 in *1,000*, or 0.7 percent—higher than in peer nations, as we have seen, but more than 90 percent lower than a century earlier.[17] And while the decline in infant mortality was the largest driver of improving life expectancy in the early decades of the twentieth century, as the century wore on, death rates dropped sharply for older age groups as well.[18] If you had filled a room with forty-two representative Americans in 1900, the chances were that one of them would have been dead by the end of the year. By the end of the twentieth century, you would have had to pack three times as many people into the room, 125, to have the same chance of someone dying within the year. (To ensure comparability, these figures are adjusted for the changing age distribution over this period.)[19]

This advance deserves to be seen as the greatest positive development of the twentieth century. Monetized as best as we can monetize it, the increase in human longevity over this period, taken on its own, was worth at least as much to society as the spectacular growth of national income. If we could have somehow achieved these longevity increases without becoming a single dollar richer, according to influential calculations by the economist William Nordhaus, Americans would still be at least twice as well off economically, per person, as we were a century ago. Add in the more general increase in health, and the gains implied by a health-to-dollars calculation are staggering. The health of rich nations is worth at least as much as the wealth of rich nations.[20]

Yet even figures like these seem inadequate to convey how much better off we are for our longer lives; how much it means to be able to enjoy life and contribute to society for a longer period; how much more fortunate we are not to lose children in infancy or parents in early life or siblings in middle age. Perhaps more than the monetary total that Nordhaus estimates, the true value of our improved health is conveyed by his observation that had he, born in 1941, "experienced the 1900 life table, the odds are long that this paper would have been written from beyond the grave." And it all happened because of the mixed economy.

Cleanup Time

Infants and young children were the first to benefit. In the first four decades of the century, as the economist David Cutler has shown in a series of pathbreaking essays, life expectancy in the United States increased by sixteen years. Somewhere between four and five of those additional years—more than a quarter of the total—resulted simply from children living past their first birthdays; around the same amount reflected children's reduced risk of dying between their first birthday and their fourteenth. In the first decades of the last century, improved mortality was mainly a story of more and more children living into adulthood.[21]

And this in turn was a story of fewer and fewer children dying from infectious diseases. If you look at the mortality tables of the early twentieth century, what will strike you is how infrequently people died from the causes that kill them now. Cancer, cardiovascular disease, kidney disease, even low birth weight—all of these were remote dangers compared with infectious illnesses such as pneumonia and diarrheal diseases, which alone were responsible for about half of infant deaths.[22]

What did government do to save so many young lives? More than anything else, it cleaned up milk and water. The leading source of deadly infections among children was what infants drank when they did not drink breast milk: water, but especially cow's milk. In the late nineteenth century, public health experts noticed that fewer infants died during wartime sieges—even as everyone around them was at greater risk. The reason was that their mothers were more likely to breast-feed them. Breast milk was not contaminated with bacteria; cow's milk and water were.[23]

This observation was just one among many that bolstered support for what we know now as the "germ theory of disease": the revolutionary idea that disease comes from microorganisms introduced into the body. Though the germ theory was accepted widely only after the initial health breakthroughs, the growing understanding of infection and disease—coupled with increased education and income—helped change private behavior and motivate philanthropic campaigns.[24] But only government authorities with the power to restructure markets and compel behavior could translate this knowledge into sustained social progress.

Though taken for granted today, making milk safe and cleaning up water supplies were herculean efforts, involving massive investments of public dollars and new laws mandating that farmers, milk distributors, and other private actors change their behavior. No city required milk pasteurization at the beginning of the twentieth century. By the early 1920s, virtually all the largest cities did, and many offered "milk stations" where poorer residents could buy clean milk. Infant mortality plummeted.[25]

The change was equally dramatic in municipal water supplies. While cities had made strides in moving garbage and human waste away from urban dwellers, their water systems were pulling that refuse back in: Many cities poured sewage into the same lakes and waterways from which they drew water, and even those that did not failed to clean water before pumping it into homes.[26] Private citizens and entrepreneurs—families, factories, small-scale providers of refuse disposal—dumped human and other waste in water sources as well. Filtration, chlorination, rerouting sewage, and other measures to purge municipal water of contaminants deserve recognition today as (in the words of health economists David Cutler and Grant Miller) "likely the most important public health intervention of the 20th Century."[27] Effective government action saved millions of lives.[28]

This spectacular achievement was not a result of better medical care. The sophisticated medical interventions that define our present era have done much to reduce mortality and morbidity, especially at later stages of life. Yet medicine was not the major factor in the initial huge fall in the chance of death in industrializing nations.[29] More surprising, perhaps, neither was industrialization itself. Contrary to common perception, the growth unleashed in the nineteenth century did not result in significant health gains.[30] Though increased wealth and education were generally good for health, industrial development also brought with it increased concentration of growing populations in crowded urban centers, where, in the words of one historian, communities were plagued by "four Ds": disruption, deprivation, disease, and death.[31] Those frightening infant mortality numbers—three in ten infants dead within a year of birth, higher than anywhere in the world today—suggest just how threatening the four Ds were.

To be sure, the economic growth unleashed by early industrialization created resources for new public and private efforts to improve health. But the plummet in the rate of premature death required a new capacity to harness that increased income to tackle the threats to life lurking all around.[32] When this capacity was realized, however, the results were profound. In cities that cleaned up milk and water, the retreat of death's shadow was sudden, discontinuous, and rapid. People were significantly richer, on average, in cities than in the countryside, but before big investments in public health, death rates were higher in urban centers; afterward, death rates converged.[33] As three economists conclude after a careful review of existing studies, reduced mortality "comes from institutional ability and political willingness to implement known technologies, neither of which is an automatic consequence of rising incomes."[34] In fact, we could say just as easily that improved public health fostered economic growth as claim the opposite. By increasing the size and productivity of the working-age population, the public health measures pursued by government in the early twentieth century were a major cause of the rapid growth that occurred.[35] Effective governance made a huge difference.

The Drugs That Changed the World

If the gains in health engineered by public leaders before the 1940s seem like low-hanging fruit, the next acts in the mortality revolution showed that advanced nations could do much more than reduce disease through sanitation. By promoting medical science, acting on it, and spreading access to its fruits, they could conquer illnesses that had plagued humanity for centuries.

Antibiotics and vaccines are the heroes of this act, but they are misunderstood heroes. Today we think of these as routine drugs, associated with private pharmaceutical companies. In fact, both were largely products of the combined energy of scientists—usually publicly funded—and government agencies. More important, neither would have had the positive effects they did if not for extensive public action and substantial government constraints on individual freedom.

In one form or another, vaccination has been around for a long time. In 1721 the Reverend Cotton Mather (of Salem witch trials fame) urged Boston doctors to deliberately infect patients with mild versions of smallpox to reduce the toll of a major epidemic (roughly 6,000 cases and 850 deaths in a city of just over 10,000 citizens). His slave had told him about the millennium-old practice originating in Asia. In 1799 an English doctor developed the world's first vaccine for smallpox; unlike infection with a live virus (or "variolation"), it involved much lower risk.[36] Almost immediately, European governments and the fledgling American

T-Jeff

Republic pursued large-scale vaccination campaigns. Thomas Jefferson, his life shaped tragically by infectious disease, took such an interest in vaccination that he personally inoculated much of his own family, came up with a means of transporting the virus safely, promoted vaccination as a public health measure, and insisted that Lewis and Clark take vaccine with them to inoculate Indians during their expedition.[37]

It was not until the late 1800s, however, that vaccines began to be developed for a range of deadly and debilitating conditions. Louis Pasteur, the French microbiologist who discovered that boiling liquids reduced bacteria, was a pioneer, developing successful inoculating agents for anthrax and rabies.[38] Others vaccines—for diphtheria, cholera, pertussis, tuberculosis, tetanus, polio, measles, mumps, rubella, and many diseases now all but forgotten—followed. Virtually all were promoted by large-scale public funding of research and development.[39] The exception that proved the rule was the polio vaccine, developed in 1955, which relied on unprecedented philanthropic activism by the March of Dimes. But private drug companies never played a major role, and today they shy away from the area because it is so much less profitable than other fields of drug development.

When it came to vaccines, the free market failed. If John Doe got vaccinated, that was an enormous benefit to everyone he might infect otherwise—yet this enormous social benefit was not one that John had direct personal interest in considering. Perhaps as important, there were the inevitable free riders: people who recognized that if everyone else was vaccinated, they could go without and avoid the small but real risk vaccines posed. But less-than-universal vaccinations meant much higher risk of disease.[40] Some people had to be compelled to be vaccinated. In the United States and elsewhere, they were—most effectively, by requiring that children receive vaccines when entering public school.[41] Public authority, not the market, was key. The same has been true of developing nations in recent decades, as the usually market-championing World Bank concludes: "Had it been left to private markets during the last few decades, it is inconceivable that today some 80 per cent of the world's children would be immunized against the six major vaccine-preventable childhood diseases."[42]

Even more so than vaccines—many of which were developed after the diseases they targeted had declined greatly—antibiotics were responsible for the substantial fall in the chance of death that occurred in the middle of the twentieth century.[43] Their broad use is a now-forgotten story of the public mobilization of science and industry in the midcentury United States.[44]

Today antibiotics are losing ground to drug-resistant bacteria—itself a failure of coordinated action to reduce the indiscriminate use of antibiotics and to develop new drugs as private companies have deserted the field for more lucrative pastures.[45] When they achieved wide availability at midcentury, however, they were a medical revolution. Antibiotics such as penicillin prevented death at all age levels, including among the elderly, who succumbed frequently to influenza and pneumonia. In contrast with the early twentieth century, midcentury gains in life expectancy occurred across the age distribution, reaching old as well as young.

The first class of the new miracle drugs was sulfonamides. Developed in Europe, they were soon overshadowed by penicillin and other broad-spectrum antibiotics, which had fewer side effects. Still, sulfa drugs ushered in the antibiotic era. As it happened, they also ushered in modern pharmaceutical regulation, when faulty manufacturing of sulfonamide led to more than a hundred deaths in 1937 and helped galvanize Congress into greatly expanding the powers of the US Food and Drug Administration.[46]

The role of the federal government in developing penicillin was even more direct. In essence, federal officials created a Manhattan Project for penicillin, comparable in vision, if not scope or secrecy, to the rush to develop the atom bomb during World War II. The effort relied on the free exchange of scientific information, cooperation across scores of public agencies and private companies, public investment in research and development, and even coordinated production of the drug itself. The Scottish bacteriologist Alexander Fleming's famous 1928 discovery of penicillin occasioned no real interest from private companies. It was up to scientists at Oxford and elsewhere to push forward the refinement of the mold into a usable antibiotic. Federal scientists working for the US Department of Agriculture did much of the pioneering research, quadrupling yields in a matter of months. Yet it was the US War Production Board, working with other public agencies and leading private companies, that in the four short years between 1941 and 1945 transformed penicillin from a "laboratory curiosity" into a "mass-produced drug."[47]

In contrast to today's preferred model of drug development, patents were not crucial to what is still the greatest pharmaceutical breakthrough of all time. Fleming himself never patented penicillin, and the US federal government patented many of the production processes and shared them freely with companies.[48] But under this open-source model, private industry thrived. Following the wartime production of penicillin, the firms involved adapted the new production strategies to the creation of new antibiotics, related classes of drugs, and brand-new compounds. As one historian concludes, "The experience and technology garnered from the government-coordinated development of penicillin were significant and vital predecessors to the biotechnology revolution."[49]

Insuring Health

The final act in the longevity explosion in advanced societies began before the second ended. Its hallmark was expanded government efforts to broaden the quality of and access to medical care. Here the landmarks are more familiar: public investments in the infrastructure of care and in medical research and education, the creation of programs of national health insurance, and reforms designed to slow the increase of costs while safeguarding health.

Yet two points about these developments are less well understood. The first is that they, too, have resulted in spectacular gains. The huge amount of waste and inefficiency in American health care—exemplified by our declining performance on key indicators of health even as we spend vastly more than other rich nations—should not blind us to the enormous improvement in the treatment of conditions that once spelled rapid death, most notably, cardiovascular disease.[50] Since the 1960s, the mortality revolution in rich nations has occurred primarily among the aged. Life expectancy at age sixty-five barely budged between 1900 and 1950, but shot upward between 1950 and 2000. In the last few decades of the twentieth century, around three-quarters of gains in life expectancy at birth were due to increasing years of life after age sixty-five.[51]

Some of this improved longevity, to be sure, was due to interventions that helped the young. After all, today's elderly received pre-1950 medical care in their youth, and we know that early life experiences powerfully affect future health. But much of the improvement was due to better medical treatment of the aged when they became sick.[52] What is sometimes called the "medicalization" of health—the development of

new treatments and technologies and improved coordination of and access to care—drove the change as it hadn't before midcentury.

The second underappreciated feature of this third act is that it, too,
was very far from a natural market development. The expansion of medicine's capacity and broadening of access to sophisticated care were results
of private activity stimulated by public authority. This was true even in
the United States, where private funding of medical care remains substantially greater than in other rich countries (but still less than half the
total when you take into account public employees' health benefits and
tax breaks for private health insurance). Consider just a few of the main
US federal policies of these decades: investments in hospital construc-
tion and medical research and development (embodied in the National
Institutes of Health), encouragement of private health insurance through
federally sanctioned collective bargaining and tax breaks worth eventually hundreds of billions of dollars a year, and the passage of Medicare
for the aged and Medicaid for the poor in 1965.[53] In all these ways and
others, improved health after midcentury depended on government.[54]

The fruits of these early and extensive investments are countless. The
MRI (magnetic resonance imaging) emerged from a series of National Science Foundation grants starting in the mid-1950s. The laser, also vital
to medical practice as well as consumer electronics and much else, grew
out of military-funded research.[55] In drug development, a 1995 investigation by researchers at the Massachusetts Institute of Technology (MIT)
found that government research had led to eleven of the fourteen most
medically significant drugs over the prior quarter century.[56] Another
study showed that public funding of research was instrumental in the
development of more than 70 percent of the drugs with the greatest
therapeutic value introduced between 1965 and 1992. (Most of the rest
received public funding and research during their testing in clinical trials.)[57] The same is true of almost all the biggest medical breakthroughs of
recent decades: According to a 1997 study of important scientific papers
cited in medical industry patents, nearly three-quarters of those funded
by American (rather than foreign) sources were financed by the federal
government.[58]

Of course, the United States did not enact national health insurance
in the middle part of the twentieth century, as most advanced industrial countries did. But it followed the model of other rich nations by
constructing its own version of national health insurance for the group

most dependent on modern medical science: those older than sixty-five. And the United States actually led the rich world in educational and regulatory efforts to reduce hazardous health behaviors.[59] The highly successful campaign against smoking was a *public* campaign: Tobacco companies fought tenaciously against efforts to inform consumers about the risks of smoking or shift the societal costs of smoking onto tobacco companies and their customers through taxation and regulation.

Also important to this revolution in public health were broader public efforts to increase economic security and reduce inequality. Though research in this area is fraught with methodological challenges, evidence suggests that job loss and other forms of insecurity reduce life expectancy. According to one careful study, job displacement leads to a 10 percent to 15 percent increase in workers' chance of death for the next twenty years: a worker displaced in midcareer can expect to die about two years sooner than one not displaced.[60] The recent economic crisis has provided social scientists with a chilling new look at how extreme financial events affect the chance that people will take their own lives. The conclusion: Across the American states, suicide rates rose about 1 percent for each 1 point increase in the unemployment rate.[61] For all these reasons, it is not so surprising that, as one analysis sums up the emerging evidence, "the welfare state is good for life expectancy."[62] Big government and long lives go together.[63]

Prosperity Found

What is true of health is also true of other measures of human welfare: income and standards of living; education and scientific progress; reductions in economic hardship, insecurity, and inequality. Indeed, a strong case can be made that the twentieth century witnessed greater progress on key dimensions of social well-being than did all the centuries of human experience before it *combined*.

This claim might seem like hyperbole, or dismissive of the great tragedies of the century. But the point is not that the twentieth century was a magical period in which all nations propelled themselves into peaceful affluence. To the contrary, states and markets did much damage as well as much good, and the gains were far from automatic. They required the right conditions: democratic capitalism that combined publicly responsive state authority open to scientific expertise with well-regulated markets and vibrant voluntary sectors.[64] But where these conditions arose, where the mixed economy came to prevail, the gains were remarkable.

Of Riches and Residuals

Put yourself for a moment in the shoes of an American of the late nineteenth century. You would soon live in the richest nation in the world (the United States was just surpassing the United Kingdom in per capita income), and the first industrial revolution had already occurred.[65] Steam-powered railroads, mass-production factories, and the first forms of mechanized agriculture had brought to a close centuries of anemic growth, during which incomes barely grew fast enough to sustain an expanding population, and periodic plagues and crises wiped out these small gains seemingly overnight.[66] In escaping this Malthusian misery, you could be thankful.

Yet for all this, your life remained precarious and, in all likelihood, grim. Death and illness, we have seen, were all around you. Your job, most likely on a very cash-strapped farm, was probably backbreaking and paid little. Despite increased industrial output and the expansion of cities, the United States was still overwhelmingly rural and agricultural. Most farms barely provided subsistence, never mind a surplus.[67] If you were lucky enough to own a home, as the economist Robert Gordon reminds us, it would be "not only dark but also smoky" from cooking fires, candles, and lamps. It wouldn't have running water, much less indoor plumbing, so you would be making lots of urgent trips outside and hauling lots of heavy water inside. If you lived in or ventured into cities, you would encounter a different but hardly more pleasant problem: streets filled with manure from the horses that were the only practical means of transporting goods and people short distances.[68] And unless you were rich, you would live—by today's standards—in abject poverty. Average income per head in 1900 was around $5,000 a year (in 2015 dollars), roughly the contemporary level for Bolivia.[69]

That all changed in the twentieth century, and quickly. In a handful of decades, the United States was electrified, clean indoor plumbing became nearly universal, whole dwellings could be heated without fire and (by the 1950s) cooled using the same basic technology employed to preserve food, urban mass transit became common and automobiles ubiquitous, farms emptied out while cities and factories filled up. And incomes began to grow and grow and grow.

Before his death in 2010, the British economist Angus Maddison painstakingly assembled data on income levels across the world, going back in some cases to the year AD 1. What these data show is what we see with life expectancy: an almost flat line until (in world-historical terms) the very recent past, when incomes in rich countries suddenly shoot upward. The American data do not go back to AD 1, of course, and there are controversies over the accuracy of particular estimates. But all the sources show the same basic picture: Incomes took off around the dawn of the twentieth century and, with the visible exception of the Great Depression, skyrocketed with little interruption—until the 2008 financial crisis. By the end of the twentieth century, Americans were producing and consuming six times as much per person as they had in 1900.[70]

They were doing so because they were becoming vastly more productive. People with the same basic mental and physical capacities could produce orders of magnitude more in a given amount of time. In the United States in 1870, an average hour of work produced just over $2 in GDP. By the end of the twentieth century, the average amount of GDP produced per hour of work was over $34. In other words, labor productivity increased more than *fifteenfold*, with the strongest growth occurring in the middle of the twentieth century, when real productivity rose regularly by 2.5 percent to 3 percent a year.[71]

For centuries before this great productivity leap, economic thinkers had seen growth as tied to the abundance of fundamental factors of production: land, labor, capital—the fuel, if you will, in the prosperity machine.[72] Growth required increasing inputs of one or more of these factors. In the twentieth century, however, factors of production proved far less important than technologies of production, fuel less important than the efficiency of the machine burning it. Writing at midcentury, the MIT economist Robert Solow made a basic but profound observation for which he would later win a Nobel Prize: The meteoric growth of the first half of the twentieth century could not be explained by the increased use of labor or even capital. It had to be the result primarily of increased productivity—changes that allowed us to get more out of a given input of labor or capital. Solow ascribed this startling rise in productivity to "technological progress in the broadest sense," by which he meant improved knowledge, machinery, techniques, and skills—basically, anything that transformed a given lump of labor or capital into a final product society could enjoy.[73]

A year after introducing this simple model of growth, Solow did some calculations with the best data available at the time and came to a startling conclusion: Between 1909 and 1949, essentially all of the increase in US productivity was due to technological change, broadly understood. More precisely, 12 percent of the doubling of workers' productivity over this period resulted from increased use of capital, while 88 percent reflected technological changes that allowed workers to do more with that capital.[74] It was not even close.

Solow's findings are among the most famous in economics, and his 88 percent estimate even has a name, catchy by the standard of economics: "the Solow residual." Yet the implications remain poorly appreciated even today.[75] What Solow demonstrated is that the main reason we are so much richer than those living in 1900 is not that we work harder or somehow have more capable brains. Nor is it because masters of industry and finance are pouring more capital into the economy. Instead, we have figured out how to produce vastly more with our work and capital. As Solow's contemporary William Baumol expressed it in 2000, almost all of our current output—Baumol calculated 90 percent, a tad higher than Solow's finding—is a result of "innovation carried out since 1870."[76]

What does "innovation" mean in this context, and where does it come from? Here we enter a grey area for economists. Everyone agrees that four factors are crucial: the advance of knowledge (ideas), the transmission of knowledge (education), the application of knowledge (technology), and the political and social structures that make all these work (institutions). But uncertainty remains about what drives the virtuous institutional circle that allows better ideas, transmitted through education and embedded in technology, to progress so rapidly.

One thing is clear: This virtuous circle is fundamentally a social product. Individual investments and inventions are important, but they don't arise without key social institutions that develop and disseminate knowledge and encourage improvements in economic production, from research institutions and educational systems to public economic policies.[77] Decades of research on scientific and technological progress, for instance, has shown that big breakthroughs are typically made by multiple innovators at the same time, often with each innovator ignorant of the others.[78] From the profound (calculus, DNA's structure) to the practical (the steam engine, the polio vaccine)—two or more (frequently many more) people working on their own come upon the same discovery around the same time. One revealing contemporary indicator: Upward of 98 percent of patent lawsuits are not against copycats but against other inventors who claim to have gotten there first.[79]

It's not that *anybody* can come up with a valuable innovation. It's that the conditions have to be right for a certain class of somebodies in the right places with the right skills to do so. Most advances are tweaks of existing ideas and technology. Even the biggest build on an enormous stock of existing knowledge.[80] This stock is precisely what the Solow residual highlights: the prior advance of "technology in the broadest sense." As the economic historian Joel Mokyr captures it, the Solow residual is as close as economic reality gets to a "free lunch"—that is, an "increase in output that is not commensurate with the increase in effort and cost necessary to bring it about."[81] Only it's not free. It is paid for by the collective efforts that make it possible: today and in the past.

The Political Economy of Prosperity

Around the time of America's great growth explosion, a Jewish émigré left Russia in the wake of the revolution. Simon Kuznets came to New York to join his father, but the timing of his arrival in 1922 could not have been more propitious for the breakthrough in economic knowledge that he would soon create.[82] At Columbia University, where he sailed through graduate training in economics, he met Wesley Mitchell, the head of the newly created National Bureau of Economic Research. The NBER was doing for economics what similar institutions were doing for the natural sciences, fostering improved scientific practice (better data, better methods) with an eye toward practical applications (better policy).[83]

The innovation that Mitchell sought—and which Kuznets achieved—was an accurate measure of the size of the US economy.[83] Put more technically, Mitchell wanted to know what our gross national product was, a statistic that could underpin many others: income per capita, the size of different sectors of the economy, the scope of government spending, and so on.

Now that GNP—or, more commonly today, GDP, the total domestic economy—is one of those stand-alone acronyms used without explanation, it is easy to neglect how complex and valuable it is to add up the total value of all goods and services that a nation produces. As late as the 1930s, presidents Herbert Hoover and then Franklin Roosevelt had only a series of incomplete statistics as their compass, from stock market prices to freight car loadings.[85] It may not have been the "economic dark ages," as one recent celebration of GDP puts it, but the light that leaders could use to illuminate a huge and growing national economy that self-evidently required greater understanding and oversight was appallingly dim.[86] The man who ended up brightening that light was Simon Kuznets.

He was hardly alone in his quest. Pioneering thinkers in Britain had made the first intellectual steps toward national income accounts long before Kuznets became involved. In many ways, the development of GDP followed the model of penicillin, albeit on a smaller scale. The NBER did some of the first work. Then the US Department of Commerce commissioned Kuznets to turn these early attempts into official, comprehensive statistics. From 1944 to 1946, a period when monitoring industrial output was particularly crucial, the Russian transplant worked for the US War Production Board.[87] As this close intermingling of public authority and private scholarship suggests, Kuznets's fascination with statistics was not primarily intellectual. It was practical. He wanted to give decision makers the information they needed to manage the macroeconomy more effectively.

A quarter century later, Kuznets won the Nobel Prize. The honor, however, was not for developing the measures for which he is now best known; it came instead for what he *did* with those measures: namely, show that the rich world had entered a qualitatively new economic epoch, the era of what he called "modern economic growth." In his Nobel address, Kuznets described this new reality as a "controlled revolution"—a *revolution* because it featured a massive step-up in growth rates accompanied by unprecedented structural shifts; a *controlled* revolution because ultimately this growth was restricted to a small circle of nations that had come up with social, political, and economic structures that promoted rapid economic transformation.[88]

Kuznets's lifework was figuring out what animated this revolution, so different from the disastrous one he'd left behind in Russia. He believed economists could find the answer only if they looked beyond the economy. In a 1955 address celebrating his presidency of the American Economic Association, Kuznets told his colleagues, "If we are to deal adequately with processes of economic growth . . . it is inevitable that we venture into fields beyond those recognized in recent decades as the province of economics proper. . . . Effective work in this field necessarily calls for a shift from market economics to political and social economy."[89]

A half century later, we understand far more about "the political and social economy" of modern growth. Most recently, the economist Daron Acemoglu and the political scientist James Robinson synthesized and expanded this work in their landmark book *Why Nations Fail*.[90] Though the title focuses on the negative, the argument focuses on the positive: What allowed countries like the United States to become prosperous and productive, while most other nations languished in poverty, sickness, and dysfunction? The switchman in their account is a nation's collective institutions, especially its political system. Political systems where economic and political leaders run the economy like a personal ATM— "extractive" systems—feature high inequality, slow growth, and short lives. Those where ordinary citizens are part of the deal—"inclusive" systems—feature low inequality, high growth, and long lives.[91] Individual talent is necessary, geography helps or hurts, but institutions matter most.[92]

Phrased this way, it sounds like a tautology (successful nations have institutions that promote success), and to a degree, it is. Yet through a series of clever comparisons and case studies, Acemoglu and Robinson show that modern growth rests on the broad distribution of power and opportunity. "Economic institutions shape economic incentives," they conclude. "It is the political process that determines what economic institutions people live under."[93]

But what exactly is it about inclusive institutions that makes rapid growth possible? Here Acemoglu and Robinson have much less to say. In a tantalizing but brief discussion, they make clear that the critical ingredient, paradoxically, is not private freedom but public constraint:

> Secure property rights, the law, public services, and the freedom to contract and exchange all rely on the state, the institution with the coercive capacity to impose order, prevent theft and fraud, and enforce contracts between private parties. To function well, society also needs other public services: roads and a transport network so that goods can be transported, a public infrastructure so that economic activity can flourish, and some type of basic regulation to prevent fraud and malfeasance. Though many of these public services can be provided by markets and private

citizens, the degree of coordination necessary to do so on a large scale often eludes all but a central authority. The state is thus inexorably intertwined with economic institutions.[94]

The Public Foundations of Modern Economic Growth

Acemoglu and Robinson's observation can help us make sense of a paradox. In nations that became rich in the twentieth century, it wasn't just the economy that underwent spectacular growth. The size of government did too. Indeed, it grew even more quickly. At the end of the nineteenth century, government spending (at all levels) accounted for around 1 in 10 dollars of output in the wealthiest nations. By the end of the twentieth, it averaged over 4 in 10 dollars, with the public sector accounting for 6 in 10 dollars of GDP in the highest-spending rich nations.[95] In some ways, these numbers overstate government's size, since much of government spending essentially shifts private income from one person or household to another rather than financing goods or services directly. Yet standard measures also *understate* the size of government, because they don't include many of the ways that government affects the economy: from regulation, to protections against risk, to the provision of legal safeguards. Suffice it to say that for all their imperfections and ambiguities, the numbers capture something real: Government has grown much bigger.

Before looking at statistics such as these, it might be assumed that poor countries have large governments—at least compared with the size of their puny economies—and rich countries, small governments. After all, there are a couple of big tasks that governments have to do just to remain governments: provide at least a modicum of protection against internal violence and protect against external threats. These are the basic minimums for a state to be a state—an organization, as the German sociologist Max Weber famously defined it, overseeing a defined territory with the legitimate authority to use force.[96] And these are pretty much fixed costs, or at least costs that vary with country and population size far more than economic heft. So you might expect that as the economy grows, the relative size of the state shrinks.

But that is not at all what we see in Kuznets's epoch of modern economic growth. The *richest* countries expanded their governments the *most*.[97] Yes, rich countries vary in spending, the structure of government, and the like. But in general, they all look very different from poor countries, and they all expanded their public spending dramatically during the period in which they grew most quickly.

Of course, rich states also do much more than spend: They regulate, they have expansive legal systems, they offer implicit and explicit guarantees to private actors that are costless on paper but almost incalculably valuable in practice (such as serving as lenders of last resort). Modern growth occurred where, and only where, activist government emerged.[98] And therein lies a big clue as to why the Great Divide was crossed.

Grade Inflation

Perhaps the most important thing that big states do is educate their citizens. Modern growth commences when people rapidly increase their ability to do more with less. They can do more because they *know* more; they have mastered skills and technologies that allow them to be more productive. Indeed, economists who have tried to break the Solow residual into its constituent parts have concluded that roughly a third of rising productivity is tied directly to increased education, with most of the rest due to general advances in knowledge.[99]

Yet even this understates the role of education, since improved education gives an enormous boost to those advances in knowledge, fostering a scientific community and educated population capable of contributing to innovation and growth.[100] Formal schooling probably plays the starring role, for instance, in the so-called Flynn effect—the generation-to-generation rise in IQ scores in industrialized societies documented first by the political scientist James Flynn.[101] The machinery of our brains hasn't changed. What has changed is our capacity to use that machinery for higher-level cognitive tasks, especially those involving science and technology. And again and again, studies find schooling to be a major, often *the* major, factor in this transformation.[102] The contribution of education to the rapid growth of the twentieth century is unquestionably much larger than the substantial direct economic returns of additional years of schooling.[103] The sustained prosperity of the West was built, in significant part, on the school ground.

And not just any school ground; the *public* school ground.[104] As one conservative notes ruefully, "Schooling is publicly provided by every nation. Such a unique position is shared only by a very limited range of goods: national defense, courts, police, and roads."[105] To this commentator, the hegemony of public schools is strange because, after all, there are and have long been private schools. But for reasons well understood by generally market-appreciative thinkers from Adam Smith to Milton Friedman, mass schooling has never occurred in the absence of government leadership.[106] The most fundamental reason is that education is not merely a private investment but also a *social* investment: It improves overall economic (and civic) outcomes at least as much as it benefits individuals. Ultimately, only the public sector has the incentive (attracting residents, responding to voters) and the means (tax financing of public schools, compulsory attendance laws) to make that investment happen.

It's no coincidence, then, that nations that became the world's dominant economic powers also led the world in the expansion of schooling—first, elementary institutions, then high schools, and then colleges and universities.[107] Education increases the productivity of workers. No less important, it increases opportunities for those on the periphery of the labor force or outside it altogether. Mass education mobilizes an enormous amount of untapped human talent into the economy; the benefits accrue not only to those who go to school but to society as a whole.

Social Science

What about "the growth of science"? By now, the answer shouldn't be surprising. Yet it is striking how frequently observers miss even the most obvious examples of government's pivotal role. As pointed out by Harvey Brooks, former head of the American Academy of Arts and Sciences, "Government has been a much more important and direct influence on the direction and rate of technological innovation than much of our national ideology and public rhetoric would lead us to suppose."[108]

We have seen already that most major *medical* innovations of the twentieth century relied on public authority. Few medicines have had a greater impact on patients' lives in recent decades than those used to treat hypertension—which emerged out of the Veterans Health Administration.[109] Few breakthroughs in medical research have saved more lives than the identification of smoking's deadly health risks—which again depended overwhelmingly on publicly funded or directed research.[110] A short list of *non*medical technologies that originated in government-funded research or contracts would include semiconductors, integrated circuits, nuclear power, satellite communications, GPS, radar, the microwave (used in communication as well as cooking), jet engines, the radio (and its sister technology, television), and a dazzling range of high-tech materials and innovative methods for making them, from titanium to powder metallurgy.[111]

To these examples could be added countless more. Indeed, it is hard to find a major innovation that did not significantly owe its birth to public support. But consider just two that define our era: computers and the internet. It is hard to imagine our economy without them, in part because they are what Brooks calls "generic technology"—building blocks that create the capacity to do many things more efficiently, catalyzing private-sector innovation. (Think Microsoft, Apple, Google.)[112] Moreover, computers and the internet are also characterized by rapid and increasing—or, more technically, *exponential*—growth in capacity.[113] They're not just fundamental generic technologies, in other words; they enable bigger and bigger leaps in technical capacity long after their initial introduction.

And both owe their origins to government, working with the private sector and scientific institutions during and after World War II. Of the twenty-five biggest advances in computing technology during the critical period between 1946 and 1965—breakthroughs like magnetic core memory, graphics displays, and multiple central processors—the US government financed eighteen.[114] After these breakthroughs, it poured increasing money into computer science and electrical engineering, funding 60 percent to 70 percent of university research in these areas from the mid-1970s into the mid-1990s.[115] Meanwhile, the US Defense Department literally created the internet, setting up its precursor, ARPANET (the network of the department's Advanced Research Projects Agency, or ARPA), in partnership with computing centers at top universities.[116] Until the internet and computers reached a large scale, the private market largely ignored this burgeoning network. ARPA tried unsuccessfully to find commercial operators to spearhead its development; none saw the potential.

This was the pattern for much of the twentieth century. In the United States as well as other rich nations, government funding was the critical catalyst for basic research and its applications in new technologies. Before World War II, this role revolved around improvements in agricultural productivity, mineral and resource extraction, and applied areas of engineering, including aeronautics.[117] During and after the war, government funding poured into both basic and applied research in medicine and advanced technology.[118] At least as crucial, government fostered the environment in which scientific progress could take place, not just by spurring massively increased enrollment in higher education but also by supporting individual scientists, many of whom received private research funding only after foundational work with public dollars.

That you can show that government spurred so many specific breakthroughs is enormously revealing, because these developments are really just the last stage of a process of scientific progress that, we have seen, is deeply tied up with effective state action. Even if not a single application of new knowledge could be linked directly to government, the entire infrastructure of scientific and technological advances in the twentieth century depended heavily on public policy. The foundation of Kuznets's modern economic growth, the roots of Solow's growth residual, was the infrastructure of scientific progress that government fostered.[119]

Paving the Road to Prosperity

We come to the last of the major public foundations of modern prosperity: the physical infrastructure that helped make the scientific infrastructure possible and productive. Even before rich countries came to depend on public investments in science and technology for rapid growth, they depended on public investments in national transportation and communications networks that linked together producers and their suppliers and consumers. Among other benefits, public infrastructure facilitated the rapid flow of materials and people across long distances, allowed manufacturers to benefit from economies of scale that supported modern assembly-line techniques, allowed innovations to diffuse and goods to reach far-flung consumers, and created opportunities for workers to find jobs that matched their skills.

No account of modern growth would be complete without mention of railroads. As one historian puts it, their contribution to economic development "is so large and so obvious as to defy accurate calculation."[120] What is often forgotten, however, is that railroads emerged out of huge public inducements, including grants of land and public loans as well as direct spending. Government was even more centrally involved in the creation of waterways that helped make the movement of goods within and between nations cheaper than ever. In the United States, often caricatured as a laissez-faire economy, most trade flowed through navigation routes created by the US Army Corps of Engineers.[121] In the nineteenth century, the corps even loaned officers to corporations to help with engineering projects—in effect subsidizing *private* infrastructure.[122]

Indeed, government investments in infrastructure lie behind nearly every aspect of what economists call "the second industrial revolution"— the rapid growth from the end of the nineteenth century through the immediate decades after World War II. The economist Robert Gordon has identified five major elements of the second industrial revolution: (1) electricity and its spinoffs; (2) improved transportation, especially the automobile; (3) running water and indoor plumbing; (4) enhanced communications such as the radio; and (5) an enhanced ability to rearrange molecules, including pharmaceuticals.[123] All but the last of these— which had much to do with government policy but less to do with infrastructure—rested on public efforts to encourage and spread technological innovations through modern infrastructure.

Electrification, perhaps the most important effort of all, was a policy achievement of the highest order. As the political economists Gar Alperovitz and Lew Daly put it in their powerful book *Unjust Deserts,* "Our generalized system for producing and distributing power is perhaps what most distinguishes the nineteenth from the twentieth century—and the latter's great 'inventions' and sustained economic growth from the marginal and often reversible gains of all previous periods."[124] Like other profound technological developments, electric power showcases the slow, evolutionary process of discovery. Early acknowledgment of electricity dates back to at least 600 BC. Our modern knowledge of electricity began to develop in the 1600s. These scientific advances culminated in the late nineteenth century with the development of technologies—by multiple inventors more or less at the same time—that made large-scale production and transmission feasible.[125]

Yet it would be several decades before electricity transformed the developed world. Exploiting this extraordinary innovation required the creation of a nationwide system for getting power from generators into factories and homes. And who created (or impelled the creation of) this network? Government. It is impossible to imagine the twentieth-century advance in standards of living without electrification. Nor would it have been possible for innovative firms to produce new products reliant on electricity without the basic infrastructure that government laid down.[126]

On the heels of electrification came another essential form of public infrastructure: modern highway systems. Like consumer products dependent upon a consistent energy grid, the automobile could achieve its transformative potential if and only if there were paved roads going where drivers wanted to go or where goods needed to be taken. Even after automobiles became common, that was frequently not the case, especially in the expansive United States. A young soldier known to his family as "Little Ike" recalled crossing the country in 1919 as part of an army convoy that took sixty-two days to travel from Washington to Oakland.[127] Four decades later, that soldier, by then president, led a bipartisan coalition to pass the National Interstate and Defense Highways Act of 1956, the infrastructure equivalent of the federal government's dramatic investment in science and technology after World War II. The road to mass prosperity was paved by government.

Growing Together

The crossing of the Great Divide is a story of unprecedented progress, of rapidly receding human limitation within the life span of a single human being. "When one looks behind the rather unrevealing economic aggregates," observed Kuznets in a rare bit of rhetorical flourish, "one finds a stream of technological changes representing the application of new inventions and new knowledge—and contributing, when applied, to further learning, discovery, and invention."[128]

Within this stream, however, the institution that bears the greatest credit often gets short shrift: that combination of government dexterity and market nimbleness known as the mixed economy. The improvement of health, standards of living, and so much else we take for granted occurred when and where government overcame market failures, invested in the advance of science, safeguarded and supported the smooth functioning of markets, and ensured that economic gains became social gains. Government did not do it alone, nor were its efforts unprompted. Expanded democracy and civic mobilization were crucial. But government was the pivotal and forgotten partner in the dance of prosperity. It is now time for us to understand why.

THREE

* ★ ★ ★ *

The Trouble with Markets

SOCIETIES CAN be rich or poor, and they can have big governments or small governments. That leaves four hypothetical combinations: rich/big, rich/small, poor/big, and poor/small. Yet as we saw in the last chapter, in the real world, one of these combinations is missing: There are no rich countries with small governments—governments that spend and regulate little, governments that eschew public investment and keep the public sector's reach to a minimum. (Okay, there are a few that are sitting on huge pools of oil.) A big government isn't a guarantee of prosperity, but where we find prosperity, we find big government, too.

We have just seen how the mixed economy propelled wealthy democracies across the Great Divide. But the story of how this happened doesn't tell us why it happened. Why does it take a lot of government to get and keep prosperity?

Here's why: Government is special. Democratic government is extra special. In the journey from poverty to prosperity, it doesn't just come along for the ride or get foisted on already prosperous societies. Effective government makes prosperity possible. It can do so because government has unique capacities—to enforce compliance, to constrain or encourage action, to protect citizens from private predation—that allow it to overcome problems that markets can't solve on their own. These problems are both economic and political; they concern areas in which markets tend to fall short and areas where market actors tend to distort democratic processes in pursuit of private advantage. Economists use the term "market failure" to describe many of these problems, and we'll use it too.

But it's crucial to recognize that some of the biggest problems stem not from the operation of markets alone but from the inevitable *interaction* between markets and politics.

The siren song of "free" markets is simple and catchy. The anthem of market failure is not so hummable, made up of a series of rich but complicated themes. But by countering the siren song, these themes can lead us past many shoals. In this chapter, we consider these themes one by one, showing that in modern economies, trouble with markets is everywhere. That doesn't mean markets should be avoided. It doesn't even mean government should always be brought in (since there are government failures, too). It does mean, though, that if you're trying to foster a flourishing society, you need to consider the best mix with a healthy understanding of what markets alone can't handle. And once you do, you'll find that in virtually any prominent economic activity, you'll want a substantial role for government.

The Truth About Markets

Even the conservative icons of economics such as Milton Friedman and Friedrich Hayek acknowledged that under a wide range of circumstances, markets operating on their own will fail to produce good outcomes. Yet discussions of market failure often seem like mere footnotes to the received story of market triumph. They are not. They are an essential part of the story itself.

Public Goods: Do It Together or Don't Do It at All

Many important goods in a society are "public goods": They must be provided to everyone or no one.[1] The classic example is a lighthouse. Its light is available to all ships navigating a coastline. There is no cost-effective way to limit the lighthouse's benefits to paying customers. So nobody has reason to pay. And if no one pays, markets won't motivate anyone to provide the good.

Public goods of this kind are prevalent in modern life. The biggest, most obvious example is national security, which consumes one-fifth of federal spending. As a practical matter, protection from foreign attack is a service that must be provided to *everyone* within a country. A private firm could not sell that protection to paying customers because a customer's neighbors would be able to "free ride." No one will contribute unless required to, which is why in all modern states, national security is a central function of government. Recall Madison: Government is "an institution to make a man do his duty."

Lighthouses are old-fashioned examples of a broad class of public goods: infrastructure. Sometimes there are ways to limit consumption of these goods to paying customers, but these "toll booths" are often sufficiently costly to construct and maintain that it is more efficient to provide roads, bridges, and other elements of infrastructure as a public service available to all. Like national security, the production of infrastructure (either directly or through subsidy) has long been recognized as a core function of government. As we saw in the last chapter, moreover, it's also a key contributor to growth.

Another public good that often escapes recognition but is essential to the development of prosperity is knowledge. Without employing the language of modern economists, Thomas Jefferson recognized this critical quality of new knowledge: "He who receives an idea from me, receives instruction himself without lessening mine; as he who lights his taper at mine, receives light without darkening me."[2]

Ironically, this marvelous feature of knowledge—that it can be provided to everyone without being diminished—is a huge problem for markets. Private actors may find it difficult to capture the full benefits from investments in knowledge. This is especially true for basic research, precisely because its benefits are applicable to so many things. Even if private actors could expropriate the benefits of basic research (through patent protection, for example), it could be damaging to the overall pace of innovation to let them do so. Left alone, in other words, markets will fail to produce socially desirable levels of investment in new knowledge—the cornerstone, we have seen, of gains in productivity and prosperity.

Externalities: The Good, the Bad, and the Ugly

In the case of public goods, it is difficult to create an effective market. The second big case of failure—and it is *really* big—involves markets that produce large effects on people who are neither buyers nor sellers. Economists call these external effects, well, "externalities." In an unregulated market, a factory owner may spew toxins into the air or water with impunity. Neither he nor the buyer of his goods has a reason to take these external effects into account. Where externalities are present, market prices will not reflect the true social costs (or benefits) associated with the private transaction.

Negative externalities such as pollution are the simplest to understand. And they permeate complex, interdependent economies. But positive externalities are at least as crucial and much easier to overlook. Sometimes private transactions can be good for others as well as for the buyer and seller—as when the vaccine I have purchased makes me less likely to develop a contagious disease.

Why should we worry about such positive spillovers? If a deal between two people benefits some unknown third party, isn't that a good thing? It *is* a good thing, but it is a big problem for markets all the same. Markets depend on incentives for private gain. As Adam Smith famously put it, "It is not from the benevolence of the butcher, the brewer, or the baker that we expect our dinner, but from their regard to their own interest."[3] Yet this powerful feature of markets creates no incentive for buyers and sellers to pay any notice to external benefits, which means markets will produce less of such benefits than we would like. The bigger the share of benefits going to people who aren't parties to the transaction, the more the marketplace will get things wrong—even if the benefits to society are very far-reaching.[4]

Consider education. During the 2012 presidential campaign, a young man at a Mitt Romney campaign event expressed concerns about whether he would be able to afford college. Romney replied: "It would be popular for me to stand up and say I'm going to give you government money to pay for your college, but I'm not going to promise that. Don't just go to one that has the highest price. Go to one that has a little lower price, where you can get a good education. And hopefully you'll find that. And don't expect the government to forgive the debt that you take on."[5]

Shorter Romney: You're on your own. Best of luck. Shop wisely!

Romney was posturing as a tough teller of unpopular truths, but he knew his Republican crowd would love it. They shouldn't have. There are huge social benefits that come from having a more educated workforce: enhanced productivity, lower crime, greater technological progress, stronger democracy. Individuals can't capture these external benefits, and so, left to their own devices, they will systematically underinvest in education.[6] Recognizing this doesn't tell us what the exact mix of policies to promote and improve education should be, but it does tell us that society has an enormous stake in whether young Americans can afford to go to college. The blinkered view expressed by Romney (and shared by many others) helps explain why we're falling behind other rich nations in the educational race.

Of course, externalities can be negative as well: A profitable exchange may impose huge costs on people outside the transaction. Unregulated markets encourage us to treat the air, water, and soil as inexhaustible goods, which they are not. Absent external constraint, the result is a rapid deterioration of their quality as the capacities of capitalist economies grow. A hundred years ago, individuals and companies were free to dump raw sewage into municipal water supplies; it took government's coercive powers to stop the lethal practice.

Environmental externalities can be horrific. In rapidly industrializing India, air pollution is estimated to be taking three to five years off average life expectancy.[7] That the air in American cities does not look anything like Mumbai's reflects a series of federal initiatives dating back to the Clean Air Act of 1970. Since then, the size of the economy has tripled, but average levels of six major pollutants have fallen by more than 70 percent.[8] Among the biggest of these initiatives was the Clean Air Amendments of 1990. In one of the last bipartisan efforts to nurture our mixed economy, Congress focused on reducing exposure to ambient fine-particle pollution, a major health hazard. Compliance with these regulatory requirements is expensive: The US Environmental Protection Agency (EPA) estimates that the annual costs will reach $65 billion by 2020.[9] But that $65 billion turns out to be an amazingly good deal. The EPA projects that in 2020 the Clean Air Act amendments will prevent 230,000 adult deaths from particulate pollution, or seven or eight times the number of traffic fatalities likely to occur that year. The regulations are projected to prevent 5.4 million lost school days and 17 million lost workdays per year. Even from the narrowest economic perspective, the gains will vastly exceed the costs. All told, peer-reviewed scientific evaluation estimates that the benefits that year will be $2 *trillion*, exceeding those $65 billion costs by a ratio of 30 to 1.

Interlude 1:
Why the Richer We Get,
the More Government We Need

We are only beginning our tour of market failure, but it is not too soon to step back and notice something important: Many of the characteristics that trigger market failures become much more prevalent as economies develop. The extraordinary scale, diversity, and productive power of modern capitalism generates two huge challenges for markets. The first is growing *interdependence*. The second is growing *complexity*.

Living Too Close to Town?

Metaphors of the frontier and rugged individuals aside, the reality is that we continue to become ever more interconnected. When George Washington became the first president of the United States in 1789, the population was less than 4 million. That is to say it was roughly equal to the current population of the small state where both of us grew up: Oregon. Only 200,000 Americans lived in urban areas of 2,500 or more. The population of New York City was 33,000.[10]

For most of the next century, rapid territorial expansion offset partially the nation's steady population growth. By 1870, however, the United States—with a population just under forty million—had essentially reached its modern boundaries. Life began to get crowded fast. By the close of the twentieth century, more than seven times as many people would share the same territory. And it wasn't just that there were more people; those people were moving to cities (and, in time, their suburbs). Rich societies are urban societies, and the United States is no exception. While the rural population more than doubled from 1870 to 2000, the urban population increased

75

more than twentyfold. Two-thirds rural at the end of the nineteenth century, the country was 80 percent urban at the end of the twentieth.[11]

We don't live on the frontier anymore. There is a country ballad by the singer Tom Russell that contains the line "If a man can't piss in his own front yard, he's living too close to town." By Russell's standards, almost all of us live way too close to town. Despite his lament, the increased density of American society has been overwhelmingly beneficial for most Americans' quality of life. But it has brought with it a huge change in the character of social interactions.

Coping with this growing interdependence requires a lot of government. With increased density, the likelihood that our actions will be consequential for others—that they will produce externalities—increases dramatically. As we explored in the last chapter, much of the initial push for stronger government in the early twentieth century, with its astonishing benefits for population health, was a response to the new challenges facing increasingly urban societies.

Or consider one of the great health scourges of the mid-twentieth century: lead.[12] Exposure to lead was far greater in inner-city neighborhoods—less because of the prevalence of lead paint than because lead additives in gasoline accumulated in automobile-dense urban areas. The consequences were terrible. At the level experienced by kids in urban communities from the 1950s through the 1970s (the decade that saw the phaseout of leaded fuel), lead exposure causes substantial drops in IQ. It also diminishes impulse control. Substantial evidence now suggests that these effects may have played an important role in driving the epidemic of violent crime that began in the 1960s, as well as rising rates of teen pregnancy.

Once again government efforts were essential to fixing the problem. As federal regulations reduced lead in gasoline and paint, cases of lead poisoning in children plummeted. These declines, lagged by the fifteen to twenty years that it takes infants to reach young adulthood, correlate closely with the big drops in crime rates and teen pregnancy of the past two decades.[13] But even if this correlation proves to be mostly coincidental, we know that lead was an enormous risk to childhood development that we are far better off for having controlled.

Urbanized nations also face increasing externalities related to congestion. Jack's decision to drive makes it more likely that Jill will be stuck in traffic. Traffic jams waste time and fuel. Because they increase exhaust emissions, they also damage human health. In 2000 these hidden tolls added up to $90 billion in economic losses and an estimated four thousand premature deaths.[14]

Density also produces huge *positive externalities*—which largely explains why most people in rich countries live in cities. That the United States became more urban and richer at the same time is no coincidence. Globally, the rise of the city was a central part of the crossing of the Great Divide, and the long-term connections among rising income, improving health, and urbanization are strong.[15] Economists have demonstrated that the much greater density of interaction and exchange in cities makes people more productive. These "agglomeration effects" are especially pronounced in the knowledge-intensive activities that now form the foundation for economic growth.[16] Prosperous societies are urban societies.

Remember, though: Positive externalities are just as much of a problem for markets as negative externalities. Private actors will undervalue and undersupply them. If much of modern economic growth is built around cities, governments must play a central role in promoting their development and nurturing the conditions that help make cities engines of prosperity.

It's Complicated

Modern economic life does not just create increased interdependence. It is also vastly more complex. In modern societies, there are more sites of economic and social activity. Interactions within and across those sites are denser, faster, and more multidimensional than they used to be. Our interventions into the social and physical environment can do much more, much faster, and over a much wider territory. And just like interdependence, this complexity has big implications for the mixed economy. It makes the accumulation and dissemination of knowledge (with its associated market failures) ever more central to social prosperity. And it makes the distribution of information—and the often severe limitations of our cognitive capacities—ever more relevant to social interactions. Just as with externalities, coping with all this complexity typically requires government to supplement and constrain markets.

To get a sense of the spectacular growth in complexity, we need to think like a modern-day Henry Adams. In *The Education of Henry Adams*, published commercially after his death in 1918, the grandson of one president (John Quincy) and great-grandson of another (John) wrote of the "sudden eruption of forces totally new." Writing in the third person, Adams described the cascade of impossibilities that had emerged in his lifetime: steamships, railways, the telegraph, the photograph. These ever more complicated devices reflected and reinforced an ever more complex division of labor: "[H]e had seen the number of minds engaged in pursuing force [that is, science and technology] . . . increase from a few score or hundreds in 1838, to many thousands in 1905, trained to a sharpness never before reached, and armed with instruments amounting to a new sense of indefinite power and accuracy while they chase force into hiding places where nature herself had never known it to be." Adams did not shy from the implications of this unfolding revolution: "If science were to go on doubling or quadrupling its complexities every ten years, even mathematics would soon succumb to unintelligibility. An average mind [that is, Adams's] had succumbed already . . . it could no longer understand [science] in 1900."[17]

Almost a half century later, the scholar Derek de Solla Price sought to track the expansion of human knowledge Adams described. In 1750 there were ten scientific journals in the world. Since then, Price calculated, the number of journals had increased *by a factor of 10* every fifty years. By 1830, with three hundred scientific journals, mankind had crossed another Great Divide. It was no longer possible for any single individual to stay abreast of scientific advances. The innovation of the abstract journal—with brief summaries of research—became necessary. Immediately, the ranks of abstract journals began the same exponential growth. Other indicators of knowledge production—books in libraries, scientific papers published—followed the same steeply rising curve. Price found these measures typically doubled every ten or fifteen years.

Indications of exploding complexity are everywhere, from massive increases in advanced education to the astronomical expansion of information to the proliferation of ever more specialized professions and organizations. Google's former CEO Eric Schmidt observes that the "human race generates more data every two days than we did from the dawn of civilization until 2003."[18]

The scientific advances that helped us cross the Great Divide operate on an ever vaster scale—and require ever greater support. De Solla Price offered his estimates of the growth of knowledge in a 1961 book titled *Science Since Babylon*.[19] It documented the shift of cutting-edge knowledge production to huge organizations. In his day, this shift was evident in the Manhattan Project and other massive undertakings connected to World War II and the Cold War. It continues, however, in projects ranging from the effort to sequence the human genome to breathtaking public and private investments in brain science to the $10 billion, 6,000-researcher-strong search for the Higgs boson, or "God particle" (conducted at the seventeen-mile course of the Large Hadron Collider beneath Switzerland and France).[20] More and more light is being transferred between Jefferson's tapers, relying on more and more public support for the research grounding society's greatest advances.

Information: Why What We Don't Know Can Hurt Us

Next time you are asked to sign off on some agreement before making an electronic purchase, take the time to read through the text before clicking "yes" (as you must if you want to proceed). Just kidding. You aren't going to do that—if we all did, the "compliance costs" would be vastly greater than those that conservatives rail about with major governmental regulations. (Two researchers from Carnegie Mellon University estimated that if we all read *just the privacy policies* on the websites we visit, the cost in lost working time would be $781 billion per year.)[21]

That form you didn't read walked you through an extensive range of contingencies and caveats. And as the conservative majority on the Supreme Court declared in 2013—in one of the most profound legal decisions that almost nobody knows about, *American Express v. Italian Colors Restaurant*—when you clicked "yes," you entered a binding contract. You may also have signed away many of your traditional rights to legal redress, such as the right to join a class action. (Admittedly, as far as we know, the episode in *South Park* where a character inadvertently signs away his body for medical research when he agrees to an iTunes update is fictional.)[22]

The contracts we are asked to sign with a click are a reminder of a crucial reality: Modern economies are complicated. If you look closely, other reminders are everywhere—in the many hundreds of pages of text that are typical of any major piece of legislation; in the organizational charts of any large corporation; or in the labyrinths that face the modern consumer attempting to purchase health insurance or seek reimbursements for treatment, plan for retirement, or figure out the best service for their phone or cable needs.

Traditionally, economists didn't worry much about complexity, assuming that buyers and sellers knew everything they needed to know about potential transactions. This assumption wasn't just convenient for economists' models; it was a reasonable approximation of the nineteenth-century economy. The simple commodities and goods that characterized markets of the time—a pound of flour, an ax—encouraged reasonably good decision making. Consumers often received almost immediate feedback about quality, and they often purchased the same goods over and over again. Psychologists have shown that these characteristics—rapid feedback and repeated experience—are those most conducive to consumers making sensible decisions.

By contrast, many modern market transactions are extremely complicated. The transformation to vastly higher levels of complexity raises a host of concerns. The core point is straightforward: *where informational demands are high, the sources of market failure grow.* These problems take three distinct forms. In the first, "adverse selection," we worry that buyers know more than sellers. In the second, "myopia," we aren't that worried about the sellers; we just worry that the buyers know less than they need to protect their own interests. In the third, "asymmetric information," we worry that sellers know more than buyers.

Adverse Selection: When Consumers Kill Markets

Sometimes buyers know *more* than sellers do. Usually this happens when characteristics of the buyer are relevant to a transaction, but buyers know much more than sellers about those characteristics. Now, since most of us are buyers most of the time, this consumer edge might seem good. It isn't. It is, for example, a huge problem in insurance markets. As we learned in the debate over the Affordable Care Act, the biggest fear that private insurers have is that the only people who will sign up for coverage are those who expect to have high costs. This is why health insurers reasonably insisted on the individual "mandate": If the government was going to require them to take all comers regardless of preexisting conditions, it also needed to require *everyone* to sign up, healthy as well as ill, young as well as old.

When buyers know more than sellers about whether and to what extent they'll need insurance, sellers figure out a host of ways to screen out high-risk buyers or charge them exorbitant amounts for coverage. At the extreme, insurance markets aren't even viable: No one will buy the coverage at the rates that frightened insurers want to charge. More commonly, these markets are inefficient and unstable. Lots of people who would be willing to buy coverage at a reasonable rate don't (with taxpayers all too often ending up with the emergency room bill), and sellers spend lots of money on defensive measures to protect themselves.

Myopia: When We're Our Own Worst Enemies

Even more widespread are issues related to consumer myopia, when consumers know too little or focus on the wrong things or don't look far enough into the future to make wise choices. Broaching this issue reeks of paternalism. But the research is clear.[23] The emerging field of "behavioral economics" incorporates insights from psychologists about the many ways in which actual human decision making falls short—*way* short—of the traditional economics assumption of perfect information, perfectly processed. Work in this vein has demolished old verities in which consumers reach the optimal solutions to economic challenges they confront.

Nobel laureate Daniel Kahneman, whose collaboration with fellow psychologist Amos Tversky brought this field of research to prominence, has summarized its insights in his marvelous book *Thinking, Fast and Slow*.[24] Although our brains are in many respects impressively equipped to process information, they are subject to severe biases:

- We are easily distracted by shiny objects and thus vulnerable to being "primed" to attend to particular aspects of a choice situation— and even to things that actually have nothing to do with it.[25]
- We are overconfident, typically expecting our own experience to be better than average, and cocky about our ability to exercise self-discipline down the road.
- We are biased toward avoiding losses rather than achieving gains.
- We are very bad at assessing risks. We are overly concerned about vivid things that are extraordinarily improbable (such as terrorist attacks), and we are lousy at drawing the important distinction between things that are truly rare and those that are merely unlikely.
- We are prone to inertia. Once we've made a choice, we are highly resistant to changing it, even if the stakes are big, the basis for the initial choice was flimsy, and we're exposed to new information that should lead us to change our minds.

The effects of these biases are often huge. Consider the difference in participation rates for a 401(k) plan depending on whether people have to make an affirmative decision to enroll or are signed up automatically.

Traditional economic reasoning suggests it's essentially the same choice: Do you want to participate in the plan or not? Moreover, it isn't a small choice but an important one, and thus one to get right. It turns out, however, that participation rates are *much* higher when employees have to make an active choice to opt out than when they have to make an active choice to opt in.[26] Myopia is that severe; inertia, that powerful.

Donuts or Spinach?

In a culture that celebrates freedom of choice, the overwhelming evidence of gigantic, systematic lapses in judgment carries uncomfortable implications. As Richard Thaler and Cass Sunstein note in their book *Nudge*, one of the big effects is to distort our consumption in alarming ways. We are lured toward "sinful goods," such as smoking and alcohol, where benefits are immediate and costs are delayed. Indeed, this form of myopia (and its cousin, our feeble capacity to assess risk) is closely associated with many of our greatest public health challenges.[27]

Myopia doesn't just lure us toward donuts; it also pushes us away from spinach. The latter is just as big a problem as the former. Think of a whole series of consumption choices that might be categorized as investments: in your health, in your education and skills, in your savings for retirement. Research results are clear: On their own, citizens will underinvest in all these areas. And this underinvestment is *on top of* the underinvestment that occurs because people don't take into account the social benefits of their individual choices. It's another reason we need government nudges, or even firm pushes, to make sound long-term decisions.

Crucially, the point is not that these misjudgments shift our behavior away from what some paternalistic outsider thinks we should want. The point is that our behavior diverges from what *we* say we want. Given the centrality of many long-term investments to quality of life, cognitive biases related to self-control and delayed gratification pose major challenges. Once again, these are challenges where government has special capacities that often prove invaluable.[28]

A closely related problem is that people systematically underestimate many forms of risk. This tendency is especially common when those risks do not generate headlines because they lack drama, and when we have the illusion that we control our own fates. Kahneman cites a study in which those polled estimated the ratio of deaths from accidents to deaths from diabetes at 356 to 1. The true ratio is 1.4 to 1.[29]

Such misperceptions can be deadly. Many Americans, for instance, believe that air travel is more dangerous than travel by car. Car accidents, unlike plane crashes, are rarely front-page news. And cars give us a reassuring but false sense of control over potential danger. (It doesn't help that we vastly exaggerate our competence: One study found that 88 percent of American drivers thought they were safer drivers than average, which we thought was pretty funny until we learned that 93 percent of professors think they are better-than-average teachers.)[30] In fact, airplanes are quite safe, while automobile travel is the most dangerous activity most Americans engage in regularly. But driving is *far* less dangerous than it used to be—thanks to government.

Safer at Every Speed

If you wanted a symbol of the advance of prosperity in the United States, the car would be a prime candidate. As cars became central to the American way of life, however, they also became central to the American way of death. For all the ingenuity that went into fancier and faster vehicles, automobile companies paid little attention to their safety. In the words of Ford executive Lee Iacocca, "Styling cars sells cars, and safety does not."[31] Meanwhile, the auto industry established effective control over the nation's private traffic safety organizations, steering the conversation toward the "three Es" of (highway) engineering, (driver) education, and (law) enforcement. Notably absent from the list was the safety of cars themselves, and the reality that it was the "second collision"—the one between passenger and vehicle—that often made the difference between life and death.

During the 1960s, 450,000 people died on the nation's roads—roughly eight times as many Americans as were killed in Vietnam. Millions more were seriously injured.[32] The automobile industry had a simple response to this extraordinary carnage: "Let the market decide." If Americans cared about safety, they would signal that through their purchases, and carmakers would respond. But if consumers are myopic about risk—understating its severity, overstating their own capacity to mitigate it—carmakers will not get the right signals, and consumers will be at greater danger than they want or need to be.

Still, automobile companies fiercely resisted stronger safety rules. Famously, General Motors deployed detectives to trail the consumer advocate Ralph Nader in an attempt to sully his reputation. The efforts backfired, intensifying concerns about safety. Starting in the late 1960s, a string of new regulations focused on safety features of automobiles themselves—most prominently seatbelts (required for new cars under 1966 legislation) and airbags (required for new cars under 1991 legislation). Other regulations concentrated on behaviors that could reasonably be described as myopic, including drunk driving and failure to use seatbelts. The impact was dramatic: In the four decades after the first laws, traffic fatalities per mile driven fell 80 percent.[33] The National Highway Traffic Safety Administration estimates that just two of these safety improvements—the use of seatbelts and airbags—saved almost twenty thousand lives in 2007 alone.[34]

The annals of consumer safety see this story repeated again and again: On issues from smoking to auto safety, government regulations faced tenacious resistance from the industries that profited from our myopic behavior. (Today the biggest emerging challenge concerns our unhealthy diets and the rising obesity associated with them.)[35] Protecting profits, as market incentives encourage—indeed, require—them to do, corporations did everything they could to mislead consumers and block or water down public responses. Government was essential in helping citizens address risks and self-destructive behavior that individuals were unlikely to identify or act on effectively.

Buyer Beware

We have noted important cases (such as insurance markets) where sellers lack vital information that buyers possess. By far the more common case in modern economies, however, is the opposite: cases of asymmetric information, where sellers have the upper hand. Buyers are operating alone and juggling many, many activities. Meanwhile, our consumption choices have gotten more complicated, episodic, and singular as we've moved from simple agricultural and industrial products to complex "postindustrial" goods—from services such as education, health care, and finance to complex, networked consumer goods such as software and telecommunications.

Now think about the sellers. For most of the products we buy, the sellers are large organizations. They have armies of specialists and many years of experience in a particular line of work. Sellers generally know what they are doing. If they don't, they won't stay sellers very long. The imbalance looks increasingly like those online "contracts" that are written by huge organizations, backed by teams of lawyers, and "agreed to" through obligatory clicks by solitary consumers who sign away their rights of redress. It is no insult to American consumers to say they will typically know vastly less than those on the other side of most of their major purchases. No insult, but a big problem for markets nonetheless.

Recall Thaler and Sunstein's *Nudge*. They argue that very nonintrusive public policies (nudges) can help citizens do a better job of making the best choices for themselves. But they gloss over a fundamental point (which they have acknowledged in more recent writings). In most markets the nudges come from the *sellers*, which is to say large and very sophisticated corporations. In a market system, moreover, competitive pressures will drive companies to exploit their role as "choice architects" wherever they can. If a company doesn't frame choices to make what is profitable look as attractive as possible (even if that appearance is highly misleading), its competitors will. In the absence of legal constraints, highly competitive markets will often encourage deceptive practices, or what Nobel laureates George Akerlof and Robert Shiller call, using the language of internet scams, "phishing for phools" (the title of their 2015 book).[36] Examples of such "phishing" are legion:

- Consumer costs are moved out of prices (which attract our attention) and into "fees" (which don't). Banks have become masters at this practice, attaching sizable fees to transactions that cost them next to nothing to execute. But retirement accounts may be the biggest offender, because people so underestimate the compounding effect of small differences in returns (due to poor investment advice or high fees). Just requiring that investment advisers avoid and disclose conflicts of interest and that companies disclose fees in easy-to-understand ways would save investors in the neighborhood of $30 billion a year.[37]
- Prices themselves can be made difficult to calculate, as is often the case with phone bills, mortgages, medical bills, and automobile purchases. Sunstein and Thaler discuss research that shows that even highly educated consumers with relevant specialized skills often have a hard time determining which options truly offer them the best price.
- Companies work hard to get consumers to "opt in" to arrangements involving a continuous stream of payments. "Bundled" consumption—such as Apple's product line, or efforts to sell combined TV, phone, and internet services—raises exit costs and locks in inertia-prone consumers. Razors are sold at a teaser price, followed by very pricey razor blades. Cheap printers hook us on expensive printer cartridges.

• Companies prey on our systematic optimism about our future behavior. They like rebates, because consumers are confident that they
will turn in the rebate cards (but don't). They like hefty late fees,
overdraft charges, and high interest rates on balances because most
of us predict we'll pay our bills on time (but won't). Thaler and Sunstein cite estimates that the average American pays $2,000 a year in
credit card interest—at annual rates approaching 20 percent.[38]

Today big businesses can follow the famous edict of a seventeenth-
century French finance minister who defined the art of taxation as "so
plucking the goose as to obtain the largest amount of feathers with the
least possible amount of hissing." Research on our cognitive biases is
now revolutionizing economics, but the basic contours of the story have
long been known to corporate America. It has spent years refining its
feather-plucking skills, getting a big assist from the complexity of modern economies. Or, as Akerlof and Shiller put it, "Free markets produce
good-for-me/good-for-you's; but they also produce good-for-me/bad-for-
you's. They do both, so long as a profit can be made."[39]

How to deal with these problems remains a challenging question.
Governments have to cope with complexity and interdependence, too,
so policy solutions won't inevitably be better than decentralized choices
even when those choices are severely flawed. Still, the information problems faced by policymakers can easily be overstated. The mixed economy
is not about government micromanaging economic decisions. It's about
setting up basic rules, institutions, and policies that correct the market's
most serious failures. Many such corrections are relatively simple: a tax
on carbon emissions, a minimum requirement for bank capital reserves, a
disclosure label on cigarettes. Moreover, government has sources of expertise (scientists, statistics, specialized agencies) that become more capable
as societies become more complex. Increased complexity and interdependence make the case for a capable, informed public sector, not for letting
markets alone deal with these challenges—because markets alone won't.[40]

When the complexity of modern economies, the realities of human
cognition, and the imperatives of the profit motive collide, "Let the market decide" is a toxic prescription. Hundreds of billions of dollars and
hundreds of thousands of lives are saved in the United States every year
because our government has not followed this simplistic bromide.

Interlude 2:
Why All Rich States Are Welfare States

Because governments have chosen to intervene, hundreds of millions of lives are also better protected against ill health and devastating financial risks. In the United States and other rich democracies, the majority of government spending goes to social programs related to health care (Medicare and Medicaid) and retirement (Social Security). These programs are overwhelmingly popular even though they are also, as a rule, highly coercive. We now are in a better position to understand why this is not a paradox.

Social Insurance, Not Socialism

Whenever new health laws are proposed, critics decry "a government takeover of health care," as if the only thing that stands between us and a well-functioning health care market is government meddling. But the health care market isn't a well-functioning one. What critics call a "takeover" is mostly a response to that reality.

If there were no government "takeover" to encourage or require health coverage, few people would get insurance, because of asymmetric information. If there were no government "takeover" to push back against sellers, health prices would (and do) rise to unaffordable levels as consumers agreed to whatever procedures their providers recommended, while having little capacity to negotiate for a better deal. It's no accident that the world's highest-performing health systems all rely on government more than ours does. But even the US system is shot through with government and only works tolerably, if comparatively poorly, because it is.

As with health care, so, too, with retirement. Programs such as So-cial Security are often seen as redistributive. To some degree they are, providing a critical barrier against acute poverty in old age. But Social Security is more like an intergenerational piggy bank. It takes income from individuals during their working years (when they are inclined to overconsume) and provides income during their retired years. This social insurance has guaranteed a modest but secure retirement for tens of millions and has been wildly popular. In recent years, we have given workers more choice by shifting more of the onus onto them to prepare for their own retirement, but we have also expanded the potential impact of myopic behavior. As a result, we now face a looming crisis in which the majority of Americans will reach retirement age unprepared.[41] Here and elsewhere, governments can and do supplement or modify markets in ways that make almost everyone better off, boosting investment in goods that people value but where they are prone to myopia.

The moral case for ensuring that all members of an affluent society have a basic level of material well-being is strong. But we shouldn't gloss over the critical ways in which social programs that supplement markets also drive prosperity. Many programs, for example, support child devel-opment, increasing not just the life chances of individuals but also the growth of long-term productivity. Social protections can also encourage valuable risk taking. Just as the limited liability of the corporate legal structure encourages investors and entrepreneurs to take big chances that may pay off for them and our society, welfare states provide a safety net that makes individuals more willing to invest and take risks. The cushioning effect of social programs is also a major source of modern capitalism's legitimacy. By diminishing the extent to which the system's inevitable volatility inflicts hardship, welfare capitalism has created a durable non-socialist alternative to the harsh laissez-faire that citizens throughout the affluent world have consistently rejected.

Limiting Booms and Busts

Social programs—and government management of the economy more broadly—make another major contribution to prosperity. Market econo-mies are prone to cycles of boom and bust, exuberance and overreaction. Mixed economies have developed a set of critical public policies that in combination can diminish the frequency and intensity of these painful and costly swings. The absence of such policies, as we'll see in the next chapter, was a major cause of the recurrent panics and depressions that plagued the United States before the mixed economy's emergence.

Social programs create an important "automatic stabilizer" that offsets that tendency. Income support programs prop up consumer spending when it is most needed, reducing the risk of a downward economic freefall. When unemployment is high and demand for goods and services low, public spending can prevent a spiral of declining private consumption as people tighten their belts simultaneously. The welfare state's automatic stabilizing effect is just one component of government's larger tool kit of monetary and fiscal policies that reduce the risks of boom and bust. As with all important government undertakings, the specifics of these policies are certainly controversial. But few economists question the critical part that central banks and government budgets have played in diminishing the chronic instability that long characterized capitalism. One such economist, writing in 1948, proposed "A Monetary and Fiscal Framework for Economic Stability" that would automatically run deficits and expand the money supply during downturns to restore economic growth. His name was Milton Friedman.[42]

Active fiscal and monetary policy is not the only way that American government protects against downturns. Restrictions on the financial sector are another—and another coercive policy that is overwhelmingly popular (at least away from Wall Street). Because the financial industry is highly prone to booms and busts, the federal government regulates it heavily. Or, rather, it regulated it heavily during the stable financial era between the mid-1930s and the early 1980s. Then a wave of deregulation pushed by financial lobbyists and free-market enthusiasts unleashed a much bigger, more powerful, more complex—and more unstable—Wall Street.

If anyone needed reminding that markets can fail, the spectacular implosion of our financial system certainly provided it. As the conservative jurist Richard Posner acknowledged in a 2008 speech, "The crisis is primarily, perhaps almost entirely, the consequence of decisions taken by private firms in an environment of minimal regulation . . . We have seen a largely deregulated financial sector breaking and seemingly carrying much of the economy with it."[43] The economic costs of this catastrophe, which spread across the globe and continues to produce widespread suffering almost a decade later, are likely in the tens of trillions of dollars.

As we will see in a later chapter, a variety of perverse incentives led

Wall Street firms to take on way too much risk before the crisis. A crucial
component was what regulators call "systemic risk": that is, risk borne
by all of us, not just parties to the trade. Of course, bankers worry about
whether their investments will go bad. They have no incentive, however,
to worry about the risk that those bad investments might affect *other*
people negatively—that an implosion of their company if things go ter-
ribly wrong might drag other businesses with them into the abyss. This
"systemic" risk is someone else's problem, an externality, and in 2008 it
nearly shattered the American economy.

Power in Markets

The financial collapse was also a reminder of another unpleasant feature
of democratic capitalism: Market actors do not just have strong incentives to exploit our cognitive biases or offload costs onto society. They
also have strong incentives to convert their profits into power and thus
to increase their profits still further.

Conspiracy Against the Public

Since the rise of modern capitalism, the power of large corporations
has been a central challenge. As Adam Smith was keen to point out,
the greatest threat to functioning markets is often those functioning *in*
markets. Capitalists are not natural supporters of competition; indeed,
they tend to see it as an inconvenience. As Smith observed, "People of
the same trade seldom meet together, even for merriment and diversion,
but the conversation ends in a conspiracy against the public or in some
contrivance to raise prices."[44] Smith urged political leaders to look on
the economic advice of merchants with great suspicion, especially when
those merchants were making inordinate amounts of money. Large, sustained profits were not a sign of capitalism's vitality, he argued; they
were a warning that the forces of competition were being impeded.[45]
Smith probably would have nodded knowingly at the private comments
of James Randall, president of agribusiness giant Archer Daniels Mid-
land (revealed in a price-fixing case in the mid-1990s): "We have a saying here . . . that penetrates the whole company. It's a saying that our
competitors are our friends. Our customers are the enemy."[46]

As we will discuss in the next chapter, concerns about the power of
private businesses to conspire against consumers were one of the main

instigators of the push toward a mixed economy in the United States. As industrial capitalism expanded to a national scale, huge corporations came to dominate the landscape, bringing with them the inclination and the capacity to constrain competition. Smith, like other market enthusiasts to follow, argued that the solution to most private conspiracies is increased competition, which requires government policing but not necessarily extensive government regulation. With the rise of modern capitalism, however, this solution was not always available. Consider the railroads, the industry that stitched America together into a truly continental economic power. It made no sense to lay multiple sets of track along the same route. But if one company controlled the tracks, it would use that monopoly to extract excess profits, which, in fact, is exactly what happened in the United States until government helped rein in these "trusts."

Railroads turn out not to be an isolated case. Features of modern technologies often create huge economies of scale (where the larger a firm becomes, the more cheaply it can produce) or involve network effects (where consumers receive greater benefits if lots of others are using the same product) that can trigger rapid consolidation around one or a handful of firms. Many industries, including transportation, electricity, and water, have such characteristics. Tendencies toward monopoly are also evident in central sectors of the modern economy, from telecommunications (phones, cable, and the internet) to the crucial industries of the computer age. Start-up investments are often huge, while the marginal cost of producing an additional unit is essentially zero. Network effects are massive: The benefits of using Facebook—indeed, of using all social media, almost by definition—depend on how many others are in the network.

The history of modern capitalism has seen continuous technological revolution. Yesterday's monopoly may be today's competitive industry. But yesterday's competitive industry may become today's monopoly. Market enthusiasts should be the first to recognize that the lure of profits will attract astute investors to these possibilities. One need look no further than the iconic Warren Buffett, whose investment strategy has favored firms that benefit from substantial barriers to competition. Today business schools teach strategies to construct "moats" around one's business to limit the inconvenience of competition.

Here again, we need government. Sometimes the solution has been to create public utilities, sometimes it has been the establishment of regulatory commissions, and sometimes it has been reliance on antitrust rules and judicial oversight. In all cases, the vital goal is to prevent one or a handful of companies from limiting competition and profiting at the public's expense.

Rent Seeking: From Market Power to Political Power

The specter of monopolies does not exhaust the risks posed by corporate influence. The broader problem is that concentrations of wealth inevitably spill over into politics. When businesses can use their economic power to influence government, they can extract policies that guarantee them returns above and beyond those they would obtain in a competitive marketplace. Such rent seeking is not a "market failure" in the traditional sense, but a failure to maintain political authority that is capable of checking the power of vested private interests.

In contemporary political debate, this dynamic is often described as "crony capitalism." Economists, as we've noted, use their own terminology: They call these extra returns rents and the process of procuring them rent seeking. Where political officials promote the extraction of rents, economists say they have been "captured." When the economists Acemoglu and Robinson (whose work we discussed in the last chapter) speak of "extractive economies," they are talking about political systems where rent seeking permeates politics and government is captured by narrow private interests.

Concerns about rent seeking long predate economists' coinage of the term. They are prominent in Smith's The Wealth of Nations. They motivated the agenda of the so-called Progressive Era more than a century ago, prompting, among other reforms, calls for the direct election of senators. At the time, members were still appointed by state governments and typically well insulated from voters. The result, in the words of prominent journalist William Allen White, was a "millionaires' club," where a member "represented something more than a state, more even than a region. He represents principalities and powers in businesses. One Senator . . . represents the Union Pacific Railway System; another the New York Central; still another the insurance interests of New York and New Jersey."[47]

Conservative economists also worry about rent seeking. Revealingly, however, they have regarded rent seeking as yet another reason for rolling back government, arguing that government regulations typically help privileged companies dig moats around their markets. Historically, certain forms of regulation—such as the midcentury rules that restricted competition in the airline and trucking industries—did fit this stereotype. But in light of what we have already seen about car safety and the Clean Air Act, it seems an odd generalization about government rule making. In fact, looking at corporate influence today, the main vehicle of rent delivery isn't overregulation that limits competition. Instead, it's indirect gifts to companies or economic sectors that seem on the surface to be operating as "free" markets. Most blatantly, huge public resources in land, mineral, and grazing rights (and, in modern times, bandwidth) have been transferred at prices way below market value. Other subsidies come through dubious budgetary handouts to industries (from agribusiness to oil), and, less visibly, through preferential tax treatment, favorable rules on intellectual property, and implicit governmental backing that yields market advantages such as the interest rate edge that "too big to fail" banks get as a result of their unstated but assumed bailout protection from the government.

Indeed, most rent seeking in modern economies takes a form *opposite* of that stressed by conservatives. Nobel laureate Joseph Stiglitz has noted recently that rent seeking by powerful private groups causes many government corrections to market failures to be *much too weak*.[48] Two Harvard political economists, Daniel Carpenter and David Moss, call this "corrosive capture."[49] Its prevalence reflects the growth of externalities and other market failures that warrant regulation in our complex and interdependent modern economies. Examples are endless. The food industry resists efforts to address obesity; oil, auto, and chemical companies fight the removal of lead from gasoline; financial firms mobilize to limit government interventions that would make it more difficult to dupe consumers or to take risks that jeopardize the entire economy. This corrosive form of rent seeking, by far the most common, has been a challenge for all democratic societies. And as we will see later in this book, it is a central feature of the predicament facing the United States today.

Unclean Coal

Nowhere has this tendency been more clear than when it comes to coal. Coal-burning power plants remain the leading source of US electricity. Yet the production and burning of coal leave behind a trail of devastation: blown-up mountaintops, 150 million tons of coal ash a year, and a variety of poisons spewed into our air and water.[50] Coal is the nation's largest source of both carbon emissions and water pollution.[51] Three economists have recently tried to figure out the overall costs and benefits. Focusing only on air pollution, and with a cautious estimate of the costs of global warming, they still conclude that electricity generation from coal is one of a handful of industries that produce *negative* economic value at current prices.[52] It is not just that the absence of appropriate constraints means that private markets overstate coal's true value. Each additional ton of coal we burn makes us poorer.

The industry and its political allies have decried a "war on coal." A more accurate assessment is that the coal industry has been engaged in a war on the rest of us. How can a huge industry get away with producing *negative* social value? It can do so because it is politically powerful, and it uses that power to weaken efforts to use political authority to bring the industry's production and prices in line with what is good for society as a whole. This exertion of private political power is a form of rent seeking. The industry is not just extracting coal from the ground; it is extracting prosperity from the rest of us.

Coal is an extreme case, but private efforts to extract profits by weakening public authority have long been an obstacle to building an effective mixed economy. The early efforts of the Progressive Era focused on political reforms to increase transparency, counteract or expose corruption, and bolster government's capacity to exercise independent judgment backed by expertise. Later efforts have also stressed the need to empower groups representing broad interests, groups that can push back against concentrated economic lobbies—what John Galbraith famously called "countervailing power."[53] From labor unions during the New Deal to consumer and environmental organizations in the 1960s and 1970s, these countervailing forces have proven essential in the ongoing effort to limit the danger that private power will capture public authority.

Government in a Prosperous Society

If you want to read a thoughtful and engaging conservative defense of market capitalism, we recommend Luigi Zingales's *A Capitalism for the People*.[54] Zingales, a professor of finance at the University of Chicago, draws a sharp distinction between defending *capitalism* and defending *business*. He eloquently decries tendencies toward crony capitalism, expressing concerns that the United States is becoming more and more like his birthplace of Italy, with its tendencies toward patronage and corruption.

Like many contemporary conservatives, Zingales portrays much of modern governance as thinly veiled rent seeking. "Government agencies," he states flatly, "tend to be captured and represent the interests of industry."[55] This diagnosis leads to Zingales's preferred solution: much smaller and simpler government. His logic is straightforward: If government does less and is more open about what it continues to do, it will provide fewer opportunities for rent seeking.

Yet Zingales's insistence that the way to cope with crony capitalism is to radically scale back government is a mirage. Like all mirages, pursuit of it is a case of dangerous misdirection.

That misdirection, however, is revealing. Setting out to liberate markets from government, Zingales inadvertently makes a powerful case for a mixed economy with an extensive range of governmental activity. Even in Zingales's market-celebrating account, once you peel away the rhetoric, you see that we need *a lot* of government. His specialty is finance, and in that area, he sees government's necessary role as anything but hands off. He acknowledges that citizens are myopic and subject to serious manipulations, which markets alone will not correct. He worries (rightly) that much of modern finance constitutes rent seeking and, too often, outright fraud rather than a contribution to greater prosperity. He proposes many reforms in financial rules, but his envisioned structures would be no less extensive than today—and probably the opposite.

Zingales also recognizes the need for substantial public authority to counter the threat of monopoly. He notes that extensive provision of education has been central to the growth of American productivity, attributing it to our "democratic (indeed populist) tradition" without noting that this means *the government*. He acknowledges the need for an extensive safety net, and not just as a matter of basic justice. He agrees that such arrangements sustain public support for markets: "A safety net is . . . a mechanism to ensure political consensus for free markets." He accepts that strong safety nets contribute to efficiency by encouraging risk taking, writing that it is "a way to encourage people to invest in their future. The sure way to fail is not even to try, and without a safety net to protect them from the costs of failure, many people won't try."

That's a lot of government. But, of course, even this list is too short for modern realities. Zingales says little about public goods or positive and negative externalities. Nor does he seem to recognize the extent to which the informational problems he sees in finance extend to many areas of modern economies. The oversight is perhaps most obvious in the case of health care. In one of his recent articles, Zingales notes that Americans pay much more for health care than citizens of other countries, before blaming these inefficiencies on government intervention.[56] This argument is odd, since, as noted, all these other countries with much lower costs and better health outcomes rely on government in their health sectors much more than the United States does.

Add it all up, and we are in a position to understand better what conservatives such as Zingales surely find puzzling: Whether you look at the history of individual countries or compare rich and poor countries in the world today, big governments and prosperity go together. The emergence of modern economies capable of generating unprecedented affluence—the crossing of the Great Divide we traversed in the last chapter—has coincided with the emergence of activist government capable of extensive taxation, spending, regulation, and macroeconomic management.

Once you understand why markets are prone to a range of failures, you understand why the rich/big quadrant is full and the rich/small one is empty. All of the largest and fastest-growing sectors of modern economies—health care, education, finance, information technology, energy, telecommunications—are rife with challenges that require government action. All of them require the strong thumb of government to complement and, at times, constrain the nimble fingers of the market.

Because of its powers of coercion and coordination, government can produce public goods and encourage the production of goods with positive externalities. Government can also restrict activities that produce negative externalities. Dumping carbon into the atmosphere has been costless to private actors; put a price on it (with a tax or government auction), and we will all pay more attention to the true costs of our choices. Government can provide nudges of varying strength that combat the dangers associated with our own myopia, and it can work to prevent the predictable efforts of companies to exploit our shortcomings for private profit.

Government does not always work well—indeed, we wrote this book because it is working less and less well. And *when well regulated*, markets often work very well indeed. But there is no recipe for prosperity that doesn't involve extensive reliance on effective political authority. The conservative vision of shrinking government to a size that will make it "safe" from cronyism is the economic equivalent of bloodletting. The cure is far worse than the disease. Prosperous societies need a lot of government. Because they do, the incentives for rent seeking will always be present. Making a mixed economy work requires keeping that cronyism, and the other dangers we have recounted, within tolerable limits—and that requires not less government (or necessarily more government) but effective government.

And here is the most encouraging point: This "Goldilocks" balance *is* possible. In the United States and other rich nations, the mixed economy worked. We crossed the Great Divide. Now, with our eyes opened to the trouble with markets and the promise of public authority, we are in a better position to understand the policies—and the unexpected political coalition—that made America rich.

FOUR

* ★ ★ ★ *

How America Got Rich

THE COVER of *Time* magazine on April 3, 1944, pictured a grey-haired man with blue eyes and a hopeful smile. Below the picture, the caption was short: "In this war, science is G-5."[1] Readers knew the reference. The G-5 was a torpedo boat used against submarines like those that the Nazis had deployed to terrorize Allied fleets. The technology was Soviet, but the Soviets were our allies at the time. And that was the point: Science was our vital ally in the most fateful war the world had ever seen—and in fostering American success more broadly.

The man on the cover was Vannevar Bush, director of the Office of Scientific Research and Development (OSRD), which spearheaded the Manhattan Project.[2] Bush (no relation to the political dynasty) looked the part as well as he played it. Handsome, with wire-rimmed glasses and a pipe in his hand most of the time, the fifty-something civil servant was a distinguished electrical engineer and inventor who had taught for years at MIT and even developed a mechanical precursor to the modern computer.[3] But he would become best known for a federal report laying out the case for massive public investments in science after World War II—a report that would help guide American policy, and spur American prosperity, for decades to come.[4]

The report, *Science: The Endless Frontier,* published in July 1945, defined an unlikely genre. It was a product of the US Government Printing Office that was not just read but also became a national bestseller. Even more unlikely, it was the product of a free-market Republican who lionized Herbert Hoover but worked closely with FDR and whose ambitious plans for big-government science helped inaugurate the National Science Foundation, created in 1950 by bipartisan congressional majorities.[5]

"It has been basic United States policy that Government should foster the opening of new frontiers," Bush wrote in the report's introduction. "It opened the seas to clipper ships and furnished land for pioneers. Although these frontiers have more or less disappeared, the frontier of science remains. It is in keeping with the American tradition—one which has made the United States great—that new frontiers shall be made accessible for development by all American citizens."[6]

Opening the "frontier of science" meant spending money—lots of money. President Harry S. Truman's budget chief joked that the report should have been called *Science: The Endless Expenditure*.[7] World War II had ushered in what Senator William Fulbright later disparagingly called the "military-industrial-academic complex."[8] (Despite frequent assertions to the contrary, there is no hard evidence that Eisenhower dropped *academic*—or *scientific* or *congressional*—from the draft version of his 1961 speech.)[9] Though realized under Truman, the National Science Foundation was conceived under FDR, to whom Bush said he "developed a personal loyalty and liking that was intense."[10] As World War II was drawing to a close, Bush recounted later, "Roosevelt called me into his office and said, 'What's going to happen to science after the war?' I said, 'It's going to fall flat on its face.' He said, 'What are we going to do about it?' And I told him, 'We better do something damn quick.' "[11]

Federal involvement in science was nothing new. From the Founding, America's leaders had sought to expand the nation's scientific frontiers as well as its geographic ones. Thomas Jefferson saw Lewis and Clark's journey as in part a *scientific* expedition, and not only made Meriwether Lewis train with leading scientists but also devoted his own time and intellect to preparing Lewis. In the 1800s, the government standardized weights and measures, carried out research on agricultural productivity, and invested in better medical treatment.[12] Under the Morrill Act of 1862 and its successors, the federal government provided huge swaths of land that states could sell if they wished to set up institutions of higher learning.[13] These land grants—one of the biggest of many giveaways that in essence substituted for the ramped-up spending of fledgling European welfare states—seeded seventy-something institutions that became the core of the nation's scientific infrastructure. Vannevar Bush's MIT was one, as were Cornell University, the University of

California at Berkeley, and the University of Minnesota, not to mention many of the nation's historically black colleges and universities.[14]

Government's role in science expanded dramatically during World War I and then again amid the programmatic flurry of the New Deal. The watershed, however, was the US entry into World War II. In a few short years, the United States became the home (in many cases adopted) of the world's best researchers and theorists.[15] As head of OSRD, Bush had more than six thousand scientists doing the public's work on the public's tab.[16] And though defense technology was the focus, federal largesse was spread across medicine, engineering, agriculture, and basic scientific research. Moreover, much of the defense spending turned out to have civilian uses. This wasn't a coincidence: While in-house scientists did some of the work, the government farmed out the vast majority of it to universities and private research labs, from Bell Labs (of AT&T) to Raytheon to Pfizer—companies eager to nab commerce as well as contracts.[17] *Military-industrial-academic complex* indeed.

As big as the war effort to support science was, however, Bush wanted it to be bigger. "Research within the Government represents an important part of our total research activity and needs to be strengthened and expanded after the war," he argued. "Such expansion should be directed to fields of inquiry and service which are of public importance and are not adequately carried on by private organizations." Science was needed "for the war against disease," "for our national security," and "for the public welfare." "To create more jobs," Bush wrote, "we must make new and better and cheaper products. We want plenty of new, vigorous enterprises. But new products and processes are not born full-grown. They are founded on new principles and new conceptions which in turn result from basic scientific research."[18]

Bush wasn't alone in thinking investment in science was integral to economic prosperity as well as national security. At the close of the war, the only real disagreements were over the character and scale of public investment, not the need for it. These struggles delayed the creation of the NSF for five years. But the final 1950 law, close to Bush's original vision, enjoyed overwhelming bipartisan support as well as Truman's and then Eisenhower's imprimatur.[19] Indeed, the NSF was one among many new federal efforts undertaken just after World War II to spur innovation and job growth at home and meet the Soviet threat abroad: the national highway system, a massive increase in federal aid for education, civilian use of atomic energy, the creation of towering new dams, the Saint Lawrence Seaway (so big it was said to create "a fourth coast"), a national satellite program, and the establishment of the National Aeronautics and Space Administration, or NASA (which, along with the Department of Defense, spearheaded the development of satellite and communications technology).[20]

Nor, as we have seen, was Bush wrong about the positive effects. Taken as a whole, the much more active state that emerged out of World War II was distinctly well suited to building the foundations for future growth. Bipartisan and pluralistic—with government and markets working in tandem rather than in conflict—it was also enormously successful.[21] We have already seen some of the major payoffs: radar, satellites, momentous breakthroughs in computing and medicine, and growth-boosting infrastructure. By far the most consequential, however, was the supereducated population fostered by state and federal support for the nation's rapidly expanding universities.[22] The United States wasn't just racing ahead in the production of cars it was also racing ahead in the production of college graduates. It was a formula tailor-made for goosing the Solow residual, that part of growth explained not by the quantity of inputs but by the capacity to transform those inputs into outputs. In the immediate decades after the war, productivity per hour worked rose at its fastest rate ever.[23]

Looking back today, what seems most remarkable is how unremarkable it all was. Federal backing of organized labor was the great exception—a bitter struggle that, after the war, the antiunion forces dominated. As for the rest, it was all good on Capitol Hill. The NSF had two-thirds or greater support in the House and Senate.[24] And it was one of the more controversial bills: Eisenhower's ambitious highway legislation passed with one dissenting Senate vote (Russell Long of Louisiana, who opposed the three-cents-a-gallon gas tax) and a voice vote in the House.[25]

Of course, Eisenhower and the congressional coalition that backed his initiatives were not European social democrats. Nor, to be certain, were they enthusiasts of state planning. But Eisenhower and Bush were simply not very conservative. The political mainstream flowed toward a mixed economy based on publicly regulated and supported markets and an active, though often decentralized, state role in providing public goods and overcoming market failures. On matters of race and anti-

Communism and organized labor, fierce fights abounded. Yet what *wasn't* fought over was at least as important as what was. Permanent mass taxation to fund big government was the new status quo. So, too, were Social Security and other components of America's budding welfare state. And so, too, was the highly active role for government in supporting science and infrastructure and developing workers' capacities that Vannevar Bush had spearheaded.

The Forgotten Roots of American Prosperity

All of this sounds jarring to the contemporary ear. If you were to ask most Americans why the United States got rich, "effective government"— much less "the mixed economy"—probably wouldn't make the top ten, or even the top hundred. Most would likely start with Americans' famous work ethic. Then perhaps our great inventors and the great inventions they created, our great frontier and the great frontier spirit it fostered, and our great victory in World War II and the Greatest Generation that won it.

The Ten Habits of Highly Effective Economies

If you were to ask those who study economic development why nations get rich, however, you would hear a different story. They would tell you something that is, on reflection, both obvious and true: Effective governance is at the heart of sustained growth. These analysts would come back with a list very different from the idiosyncratic explanations to which most people are drawn. There would be disputes, to be sure, but the following ten factors would make most analysts' lists:

1. private property rights and legally secure contracts backed up by an independent legal system;
2. a well-functioning financial system, including a central bank to provide a common currency, manage the macroeconomy, and serve as lender of last resort;
3. internal markets linked by high-quality communications and transportation infrastructure;
4. policies supporting and regulating external trade and financial flows;

5. substantial public investment in R&D and education;
6. regulation of markets to protect against externalities, such as pollution, and help consumers make informed decisions;
7. public provision of goods that won't be provided at all or sufficiently if left to markets, such as public health;
8. inclusion of all sectors of society in the economy, so that human capital isn't wasted;
9. reasonably independent and representative political institutions, so that elite capture and rent seeking aren't rife; and
10. reasonably capable and autonomous public administration—including an effective tax system that citizens view as legitimate—so that items 1 through 9 can be carried out in relatively efficient and unbiased ways.

What do all these ingredients have in common? They require active, effective government. A libertarian "night-watchman state" that merely provides defense and protects property rights isn't going to cut it. It's not that national defense and property rights aren't important. It's just that they're not sufficient, and even achieving them requires a state much more active than the libertarian vision suggests. As one economist concludes after examining the experience of ninety developing countries, "Too often, policy makers lose sight of how much effort is entailed in creating and sustaining the institutional framework for private enterprise. Big government may be part of the problem, to paraphrase former US President Ronald Reagan, but the solution is competent, not always smaller, government—government that does the jobs where it is paramount."[26]

The "East Asian miracle" of rapid economic growth in nations such as South Korea provides a revealing case study. As one of the most influential analyses concludes, countries that sought "to follow all the advice of the visiting preachers of the free market . . . too often failed to grow."[27] Instead, successful nations were "mixed economies" in which government actively ensured macroeconomic stability, encouraged and directed investment, regulated markets to make them work (especially financial markets, which were "repressed" to discourage speculation), and even created markets where they didn't yet exist. As two economists from Hong Kong—a nation often lauded as the free-market ideal—explain in an article entitled "The Night-Watchman State's Last Shift": "The market needs a strong state to manage it. This means that whether a government is 'big' or 'small' is less important than . . . whether the state is able to ensure high-quality market order. Current policy debates have largely neglected this aspect of the state's role, because Western thinkers take their countries' [market infrastructure] for granted, especially their regulatory and judicial systems, which have benefited from hundreds of years of development."[28]

And remember, these analysts are concerned principally with just one question: How fast does an economy grow overall? But as we have learned, increasing national income isn't synonymous with increasing human welfare. Additional government policies are needed if political leaders are to preserve clean air and water or provide basic social protections against poverty and risk. But even if growth were the only goal, the overwhelming weight of the evidence and theory is on the side of a mixed economy with an extensive state role.

So it would be surprising indeed if America got rich without or in spite of government. Yet that is what we are often told. Here, for example, is Milton Friedman writing in 1980 about the wondrous Gilded Age: "an era of rugged, unrestrained individualism," "an era with the closest approximation to pure economic laissez-faire in American history," "an era in which there was, for most of it, no ICC, no FCC, no SEC, and you pick out any other three letters of the alphabet, and it wasn't there either." "Far from being a period in which the poor were being ground under the heels of the rich and exploited unmercifully," Friedman insisted, "there is probably no other period in history, in this or any other country, in which the ordinary man had as large an increase in his standard of living as in the period between the Civil War and the First World War, when unrestrained individualism was most rugged."[29]

In fact, there *is* another period: the period through which Friedman lived, from the mid-1940s well into the 1970s. The late nineteenth century saw healthy increases in average income, but they were nothing extraordinary by later standards. Friedman penned his paean to "unrestrained individualism" at the end of the tumultuous 1970s—which featured per capita GDP growth a third again as fast as the wondrous 1870s.[30] More important, the late nineteenth century was an era of enormous hardship as well as outsized fortunes, with inequality rising, life expectancy stagnating, and average heights actually falling.[31]

Life for "the ordinary man" improved markedly around the turn of the century—but it did so precisely because "pure economic laissez-faire" (never even closely approximated) lost even more ground. If we truly want to understand why ordinary Americans saw their standard of living skyrocket, we need to remember what four decades of revisionism and government bashing have caused us to forget.

A Revolution in Favor of Government

Milton Friedman was trying to shock his readers when he cast the Gilded Age as the Golden Age. A generation later, however, his revisionism looks mild. Whole books now torture history to show that nineteenth-century American economic development was a lost Eden of unfettered capitalism. In these accounts, the Constitution was meant to create a highly limited government intended primarily to protect property rights and enable market exchange.[32] Only in the twentieth century were Americans cast from the free-market garden as their leaders abandoned these founding ideals.

Calling in the Founders for ideological reinforcement is a long tradition, but not one that displays much commitment to historical accuracy. The Founders disagreed among each other, often fiercely. They changed their views, often fundamentally. They were smart but hardly infallible; public spirited but hardly immune to selfish or blinkered thinking (exhibit A: slavery). Above all, they were operating in a context far removed from our present era. Statements about how they would respond to current challenges are often just restatements of the speakers' prejudices.

So it is with the notion of the Founders as apostles of laissez-faire. Of all the ways to misunderstand their thinking, to see them as protolibertarians may be the most profound. To the contrary, they were enthusiastic state builders whose primary concern was creating a government strong enough to protect and regulate a fledgling nation.[33]

The fifty-five men who gathered in Philadelphia viewed the weak Articles of Confederation, established in the midst of the Revolutionary War, as a disaster. The economy was in shambles—locked in a depression as deep as that of the 1930s—as states pursued beggar-thy-neighbor policies.[34] A federal government unable to tax teetered on the edge of bankruptcy. With no funds except the paltry sums volunteered by the states, the federal government was incapable of mounting a force that could defend itself. At one point, the national army fell to just eighty men. Spain closed the Mississippi River to American commerce, and other powerful nations were positioned to take advantage.[35] To James Madison and his allies, the federal government needed sweeping new powers. Madison did not win on every issue: Opponents defeated his proposal to give the federal government an absolute veto over state laws, for example—a proposal contemporary conservatives who celebrate Madison conveniently overlook. But all the key Founders shared his conviction that the problem was too *little* central power, not too much.[36]

You don't have to review the Founders' deliberations to see how misplaced the celebration of them as free-market fundamentalists is. You can also look at the choices that they made once those deliberations ended. After all, to a degree unique in American history, the men who designed the nation's new institutions were also the men who contested for power and led within those institutions. We do not just have to listen to what they said, in other words. We can also watch what they did.

And here is what they did: They created a stable national currency and central bank; promoted domestic manufacturers; created a national army for external protection and internal expansion; purchased and seized land and laced it with new roads, navigable waterways, and systems of communication, including the world's largest public postal network; guaranteed the expansion of public education by setting aside land to be sold to finance local schooling; expended federal funds again and again to relieve distress from natural disasters and major economic losses; and bound together all these efforts with a national legal system that would eventually give birth to the modern corporation.[37]

As the great American historian Henry Adams wrote in 1879, "A people which had in 1787 been indifferent or hostile to roads, banks, funded debt, and nationality, had become in 1815 habituated to ideas and machinery of the sort on a grand scale."[38]

Jeffersonian Rhetoric, Hamiltonian Policy

Popular histories tell this story today as a grand struggle between two traditions: the friendly-toward-government tradition of Alexander Hamilton and the skeptical-of-government tradition of Thomas Jefferson. Mostly, however, this ongoing "rivalry has been resolved by putting the Jeffersonians in charge of the rhetoric and the Hamiltonians in charge of policy"—as the economist Erik Reinert puts it wryly.[39]

The truth is that leaders in both camps used the state aggressively, if not always visibly, to promote economic development. George Washington's famous indictment of the "baneful effects of the spirit of party" apparently failed to convince America's incipient parties to stop fighting.[40] But his proposals for binding the nation through a better-paid federal workforce, federal support for university education, a national military academy, and federal promotion of domestic industries and agricultural productivity all would be realized in one form or another—under both parties—over the coming century.[41]

Even Jefferson wasn't all that Jeffersonian. He never uttered the famous quote attributed to him: "That government governs best which governs least."[42] And while he did come into office promising an end to Hamiltonian policies, fortunately for the nation's economy, that didn't happen. The new administration cut a few hundred federal workers, and held the line on taxes and spending.[43] Yet as the historian Brian Balogh points out, "Republicans were more than willing to use the latent authority of the General Government once they moved from minority to majority status. Though Jefferson's victory was hailed as a 'revolution,' Republicans eventually embraced a large part of Hamilton's economic policy."[44]

Examples abound: Jefferson's secretary of the Treasury, Albert Gallatin, continued the national bank, Jefferson drew up plans for a national road system, and Gallatin and others successfully advocated a whole host of other "internal improvements."[45] Over the years spanning his presidency, 1801 to 1809, the federal government also expanded the tiny postmaster's office overseen by Benjamin Franklin during the Revolution into the biggest postal system in the world, vital to commerce as well as communication (which, as a federal official, Jefferson used free of charge into his retirement). In the early nineteenth century, the United States had seventy-four post offices for every hundred thousand people. By comparison, Great Britain had seventeen per hundred thousand; France, four.[46]

The greatest example of the Hamiltonian Jefferson is the Louisiana Purchase (which Hamilton, ironically, opposed): a project of federally guided national expansion, launched with ambiguous constitutional authority, financed through complex debt transactions, and bought at a price that, while a steal, was 40 percent larger than all federal revenues at the time.[47]

Jefferson and Gallatin recognized that the public land they acquired could substitute for the public taxes they disliked. It was Jefferson, after all, who had drafted the Land Ordinance of 1785, which set aside land that could be sold to finance local schooling—a provision also included in the better-known Northwest Ordinance of two years later.[48] Gallatin, according to the historian Thomas McCraw, "saw more clearly than most American statesmen that the public lands were by far the government's most valuable asset. Further, he perceived that land could be used for many different purposes, including the raising of money."[49]

Acquire and Distribute, Not Tax and Spend

It was not simply, as McCraw argues, that land "became the keystone of US economic growth, because of North America's rich soil and abundant natural resources." These assets had to be obtained and exploited, and government made that possible. More important, land became the currency of economic statecraft—provided to settlers to encourage agriculture and enterprise (notably in the Homestead Acts of the 1860s and 1870s); to localities to build schools; to investors to finance public projects; to private companies to build rail lines and canals; and eventually to public agencies, such as the US Forest Service and the US Geological Survey, to oversee direct extraction of the nation's resources. To give a sense of the scale of these commitments, a single railroad, the Union Pacific, received free territory equivalent in size to New Hampshire and New Jersey *combined*.[50]

Land was the medium of America's hidden interventionism. Other growing governments mainly took through taxation and gave through spending.[51] Much of US economy policy followed a track far less visible but no less effective—and no less governmental. The federal government exercised its most aggressive power literally at the borders, where new land was seized from native peoples, surveyed, developed, exploited, and sold. Inside these expanding borders, governance appeared localized, decentralized, privatized, and mostly invisible. But government was there nonetheless, forging a national market.

State and local governments got into the game, too. In 1902 the American economist Guy S. Callendar pointed out what few at the time wished to acknowledge—"that this country was one of the first to exhibit [the] modern tendency to expand the activity of the State into industry."[52] Callendar was speaking not of federal policies but of state governments' efforts to aid industrial development through infrastructure investment. All told, according to Callendar's calculations, state development bonds added up to a debt greater than the federal government had ever assumed—"the first large funded debt created by the government of any country for purely industrial purposes."[53]

Besides its infrastructure-linked national market, America's biggest growth advantage was its extensive network of local schools. It's therefore worth remembering that, as the economists Goldin and Katz explain, "the most important features of US elementary and secondary education around 1900 were its public funding and public provision"— which, again, often depended on federal grants of land.[54] While local governments pioneered primary schooling, state governments took the lead on public higher education, with the help of the Morrill Act and subsequent laws providing federal land for colleges and universities.[55]

America's emergence as a world economic power in the latter half of the nineteenth century featured plenty of enterprising citizens seizing on the opportunities for economic advancement the Constitution protected. But the role of the Founders and their political heirs was much more direct. They built a state with the power to tax, spend, enforce, defend, and expand. Once in office, they and their fellow leaders helped create a vast nation linked by infrastructure, governed by a federal legal system, and hosting the most educated workforce in the world, using land rather than spending as their main policy tool.[56] These were the seeds of America's economic flowering, but their budding branches would soon face stiff new winds from concentrated corporate power.

The Laissez-Faire Myth

For much of the twentieth century, America's leaders looked back on the Gilded Age as a cautionary period in American history. In recent decades, however, the era of extremes has received something of a makeover. The critics were wrong, says a growing chorus, to impugn the giants of industry and finance who dominated the period. "Never before—or (arguably) since—have opportunities been so ripe for those capable of mobilizing capital and organizing large enterprises," argues the historian Maury Klein in the conservative Manhattan Institute for Policy Research's in-house journal. "The entrepreneurs who came to dominate this scramble were to the American economy what the Founding Fathers were to the political system."[57] Others have lauded the philanthropic efforts of these titans.[58] The implication is obvious: Laissez-faire works, government doesn't, and today's billionaires uphold a tradition of innovation and generosity pioneered by the captains of commerce of a century ago.

In fact, the era of "opportunities" is a casebook on the limits of markets—and not just because its greatest achievements rested on public foundations. The Gilded Age demonstrated that a modern industrial economy could not function without independent national authority. And no one made the case more powerfully, if inadvertently, than a railroad tycoon named Jay Gould.

America's Most Successful Pickpocket

Gould was the quintessential robber baron, as the muckraking journalist Mathew Josephson would term the economic princes of his day. Like nearly half of the superrich of the era—men with wealth greater than twenty thousand times that of the average worker—Gould was a railroad magnate.[59] Yet his real skill was finance. Ruthless, corrupt, and brilliant, Gould ignored the mechanics of rail and focused on the money.

Gould was not alone. The railroad fortunes that dominated turn-of-the-century America came not from moving goods but from moving securities.[60] They also came from moving politicians and judges with the proceeds. The most famous example—both brazen and emblematic—was the "Erie War" of the late 1860s, fought between Gould and Commodore Cornelius Vanderbilt for control of the lucrative Erie Railway Company.[61] Vanderbilt ran the rival New York Central Railroad. Capturing the Erie would give him a monopoly on railroad traffic from New York westward. Defending Erie against Vanderbilt's hostile takeover, Gould first diluted its stock by printing millions in new securities. Vanderbilt responded by buying off a judge to rule against Gould. Eventually the fight ended up in the New York legislature, where—as a contemporary account puts it—an "open auction" ensued, "which Gould won by paying higher bribes to more legislators."[62] Said the *Railway Times* of another of Gould's more audacious financial exploits, in 1884: "No pickpocket, either ancient or modern, has been more successful."[63]

Later Gould would throw the US gold market into turmoil with a scheme that implicated top public officials in the administration of President Ulysses Grant, as well as Grant's own brother-in-law. Only by selling $4 million in gold did the federal government avert the plot and protect the financial backbone of the national economy. (A Treasury Department insider tipped off Gould, and he got out before the collapse.)[64]

The economic chaos that ensued was a sign of just how unstable the nation's financial system was. Indeed, with the country lacking either deposit insurance or a national bank (abandoned under President Andrew Jackson), financial crises were the norm, not the exception. Major bank panics rocked the nation at least six times between 1873 and 1907.[65] Meanwhile, the country was in a depression or recession in 1865–67 (featuring a 24 percent decline in business activity), 1869–70 (10 percent), 1873–79 (34 percent), 1882–86 (33 percent), 1887–88 (15 percent), 1890–91 (22 percent), 1893–94 (37 percent), 1895–97 (25 percent), and 1899–1900 (15 percent).[66] Deflation—that strange inversion of the normal rule of rising prices—was common, encouraging investors to hoard cash and wreaking havoc on farmers, who turned increasingly toward antibusiness populism.

Today's defenders of the Gilded Age try to divide the barons into good and bad apples. One account, *The Myth of the Robber Baron,* argues that crony capitalists gave the real entrepreneurs a bad name—as if everything would have been fine if the government had just stayed out of the way.[67] Yet all the robber barons depended on government and their manipulation of it. Another railroad financier, Collis Huntington—who, along with Leland Stanford (yes, the founder of the California university), rounded up support for the ill-fated Central Pacific Railroad—managed to see higher purpose in his bribery of politicians: "If you have to pay money to have the right thing done, it is only just and fair to do it."[68]

Rebalancing Democracy and the Market

Trying to separate the good barons from the bad also misses the bigger problem: a massive and growing imbalance between the power of America's new economic elite and the capacities of the public officials who were supposed to defend broader interests. No era in American history featured concentrations of income, wealth, and power as extreme. By 1896, railroads alone accounted for a larger share of the economy than all levels of the US government put together. And ownership and control of these massive resources were increasingly in the hands of a few, as inequality rose to new heights that would not be approached again for a century.[69]

The consolidation of the corporate economy in the late nineteenth and

early twentieth centuries challenged the republican vision of the Founders. Though members of America's upper class, early American leaders
nonetheless saw the broad distribution of wealth (among white men) as
essential not just for economic dynamism but also for democratic equality. Jefferson (a slaveholder) wrote to Madison that "enormous inequality" caused "much misery to the bulk of mankind" and therefore that
"legislators cannot invent too many devices for subdividing property."[70]
John Adams believed that "equal liberty and public virtue" rested on
making "the acquisition of land easy to every member of society," in
part because "a natural and unchangeable inconvenience in all popular
elections" is "that he who has the deepest purse, or the fewer scruples
about using it, will generally prevail."[71] Noah Webster, the writer and
lexicographer who issued influential calls for federal union, lauded the
proposed Constitution because he believed its design protected "the
very soul of the republic" and "the whole basis of national freedom"—
"a general and tolerably equal distribution of . . . property."[72]

America's expanding industrial economy didn't exactly produce such
a distribution. Most of America's corporate giants were companies with
huge economies of scale. In these sectors—such as railroads, steel, oil,
timber, and their affiliated financial arms—the tendency toward monopoly was overwhelming. At their peaks, U.S. Steel controlled nearly
70 percent of its market; Eastman Kodak, more than 70 percent; General
Electric, 90 percent; International Harvester, 70 percent; DuPont, 65 percent to 75 percent; American Tobacco, 90 percent.[73] Strong economic
pressures encouraged consolidation and bigness. Cunning and corruption ensured there would be no government pushback.

To be sure, with cunning and corruption came much creativity as
well. Inventors and entrepreneurs such as Alexander Graham Bell and
Thomas Edison played a critical role, though less critical than suggested
by popular accounts that ascribe technological breakthroughs to a single visionary. The role of such enterprising figures rested on a public
foundation, including the federal patent office.[74] But America's proto–
mixed economy, like the much more advanced version that would follow, depended on private fortune seeking as well as public inducement.
Congress funded the development of the telegraph industry, subsidized
it through the Pacific Telegraph Act of 1860, and nationalized and expanded it during the Civil War.[75] Yet private corporations—eventually,
corporation, with the formation of the Western Union monopoly—ran

the service and laid much of the cable. As it happened, this private mo-
nopolization of publicly seeded innovation allowed Jay Gould to take
over the industry and add to his considerable fortune.[76]

So while the titans of the new industrial age were skillful in ways
both laudable and despicable, they were also just plain lucky. They came
along when national markets were finally possible, benefited from public
land grants and loan guarantees, capitalized on economies of scale that
allowed early movers to bury rivals, and then monetized future profits
(likely or imagined) through volatile and manipulable financial markets.
These fortunate circumstances help explain why "a group of divided,
quarrelsome, petulant, arrogant, and often astonishingly inept men," to
quote one recent colorful description, managed to amass so much economic and political power.[77]

All of which suggests the most important point about the mythical age of laissez-faire: The monopoly capitalism that emerged was
unsustainable—economically, politically, and, though few paid attention to it at the time, ecologically. Government policies were successful
in promoting development. Without them, building the railroads likely
would have taken decades longer, with a huge economic loss.[78] But these
policies fostered concentrated corporate power that the federal government lacked the capacity to govern effectively, and the costs of that incapacity to American society were skyrocketing.[79]

Moreover, increased interdependence brought new social problems.
Workplace accidents soared as industrial and rail work expanded.[80] The
toxic financial assets of the era proved even more toxic than those of
our own, making economic crises the norm. With industrialization came
social and environmental costs that the nation could not ignore for long.
To take one forgotten example, the railroads that Jay Gould and his ilk
commandeered led to massive environmental degradation, especially in
the plains, where bison were driven almost to extinction and replaced
with open-range cattle farming that devastated wild habitats.[81] Courts,
of course, provided little recourse, whether to victims of fraud, monopolies, accidents, or tainted food or medicine. Buying justice was simply a
cost of business for the powerful interests causing harm.[82] And so long as
government sat on the sidelines, the harms just kept multiplying.

It was time for the mixed economy.

Building the Mixed Economy

Theodore and Franklin Roosevelt were distant cousins and very different men. But they shared a conviction that government had to be strengthened to rebalance American democracy and ensure broadly distributed gains. Either could have said what TR declared in 1910: "The citizens of the United States must effectively control the mighty commercial forces which they have called into being."[83]

Theodore Roosevelt would not achieve that goal during his lifetime. The list of major reforms enacted in the first two decades of the twentieth century (under Woodrow Wilson as well as TR) is neither short nor trivial: enfranchisement of women, the direct election of senators, the nation's first income tax, workers' compensation, the Clayton Antitrust Act, the Federal Reserve, the first restrictions on money in politics, the first serious attempts at environmental preservation, and extensive new national regulations, including the Pure Food and Drug Act of 1906, which established the US Food and Drug Administration (FDA).[84] Yet TR died in 1919 on the eve of another decade of financial speculation and runaway inequality, during which public authority decayed while problems festered—until, of course, an economic crisis made continued inaction untenable.

The Long Progressive Era

Despite the interregnum of the 1920s, however, it makes sense to think of the two Roosevelts as bookending a long Progressive Era. It was *progressive* because at crucial moments, nearly everyone in a position of high public leadership came to believe that the American social contract needed updating. It was *long* because challenging entrenched elites is so difficult, and only persistent agitation and huge disruptions to the American political order allowed the translation of these new beliefs into new governing arrangements.

TR's Republicans—heirs to the Hamiltonian tradition—led the charge. Yet, as in the nineteenth century, Democrats often ended up completing the task (and would eventually switch ideological places with their partisan rivals). No wonder conservatives of our time, from Glenn Beck to George Will, so abhor Wilson. With the Federal Reserve, the FTC, the nation's first income tax, the modern estate tax, and other transgressions against the antigovernment creed, Woodrow Wilson signaled more clearly than any economic tract could that the emerging mixed economy was a necessary adaptation to modern capitalism—one that no democrat, or Democrat, could long evade.[85]

Few figures were more important in this intellectual shift than Louis Brandeis. Nominated by Wilson to the Supreme Court in 1916, Brandeis was the first Jewish justice.[86] Yet his appointment was controversial not so much because of the widespread anti-Semitism of his day as because Brandeis was so unpopular among business interests and the politicians closest to them. More clearly than any other legal thinker of the time, Brandeis saw that economic interdependence demanded public action to protect workers from abuse, manage systemic risks, and ensure that big corporations did not dominate politics. He also saw that such action required freeing government from the vise grip of powerful private interests. "We must make our choice," Brandeis famously wrote. "We may have democracy, or we may have wealth concentrated in the hands of a few, but we can't have both."

The question that consumed Brandeis was how to effectively regulate corporations in a national industrial economy.[87] In a 1933 dissent, he lamented that "men of this generation" had acted at times "as if the privilege of doing business in corporate form were inherent in the citizen." Corporations were possible only because of state law, he argued, and it was reasonable to regulate them to limit "monopoly," "encroachment upon the liberties and opportunities of the individual," "the subjection of labor to capital," and, above all, the "concentration of economic power" through which "so-called private corporations are sometimes able to dominate the state."[88]

Within three years of Brandeis's impassioned dissent, the court had sanctioned the New Deal and, with it, the modern mixed economy. Most of us take the results so much for granted that it's hard to grasp the scope of the transformation. But consider just a few of the profound ways in which the United States got a new deal.

An End to Economic Fatalism

The first and most important change was the creation and deployment of effective levers for managing the macroeconomy. Economists are not of one mind about what caused the Great Depression. But most agree that it was worsened greatly by the Fed's failure to expand the money supply. Reorganized by statute in 1935, the Fed became an integral part of a set of national regulations, institutions, and practices that created remarkable new macroeconomic stability relative to the past.[89] These reforms included bank deposit insurance, financial regulations that limited speculation and systemic risk, and, increasingly, the use of fiscal policy (taxes, spending, and deficits) as a counterweight when deep downturns loomed—the prescription urged by the great English economist John Maynard Keynes in his 1936 book *The General Theory of Employment, Interest, and Money*. Virtually overnight, bank failures ended, and an era of moderate economic cycles, rather than wild seesaws, began.[90]

While FDR did not end the Depression, the New Deal did stabilize the economy as its policies reorganized it. Expansionary fiscal policy was abandoned prematurely in 1937, driving unemployment back up. The fiscal sluice gates reopened, but states and localities continued to cut back as tax coffers stayed light, prolonging the downturn.[91] Still, the 1930s and 1940s saw the fastest sustained growth in the productivity of the economy yet.[92] At the same time, the rapid improvement in life expectancy that began around 1900 continued, even accelerating in the wartime 1940s. Between 1870 and 1900, life expectancy increased between one and two years each decade, on average. Starting in 1900, that number rose to between three and six years each decade.

Taxes and spending were used not just for macroeconomic management. They were also used to finance new programs, especially to provide relief and promote development. These efforts included the public works projects that built much of America's infrastructure in the 1930s, the widespread electrification that made modern technological expansion possible, and, of course, the military buildup to fight and win World War II. The Works Progress Administration built more than a half million miles of road, more than a hundred thousand bridges, more than forty thousand miles of sewers and water mains, and more than a thousand airports. It also built places of governance and learning: courthouses, public offices, libraries—a reminder that not all new state activity was directed at recovery.[93] Another reminder: In 1938 Congress transformed the FDA into the powerful agency it is today with authority to review drugs prior to sale, after at least seventy-three deaths from a single adulterated medicine.[94]

Taxes were also a tool of social reform. The national income tax had existed since Wilson's presidency, but FDR and congressional Democrats used it more actively to tamp down extremes of inequality. And inequality did fall—first because so many fortunes vanished in the market crash, then because of Roosevelt's policies, and finally because of the broad labor mobilization and corporate restraint that accompanied World War II.[95] Yet populist rhetoric notwithstanding, taxes on all classes expanded. The Social Security payroll tax focused on blue-collar workers, and the income tax became, for the first time, a "mass tax" during World War II.[96]

America's Insurance-Opportunity State[97]

The mention of payroll taxes brings up the most controversial aspect of Roosevelt's legacy: the American welfare state. States and the federal government were more involved in the provision of social welfare prior to the New Deal than legend suggests.[98] Still, it was only in the 1930s that the United States created a national framework of social insurance, available to workers and their families as a right rather than as charity. This development came later than in most rich democracies, in large part because of the limits on national authority in the United States prior to the Great Depression.[99] But during the 1930s, the United States made up for lost time and was (briefly) seen as a world leader in the development of unemployment, retirement, survivors', and antipoverty benefits, as well as work programs.[100]

The rationale for social insurance was, and is, that private markets cannot adequately insure many of the major risks that citizens face. The Great Depression laid bare the lack of individual savings for unemployment and retirement, and the unreliability of company-based benefits when the economy falters. Indeed, even most contemporary critics of these programs do not argue that such risks can be tackled with voluntary action; instead, they want government to compel individuals to insure themselves (through private Social Security accounts) or subsidize private efforts (with tax breaks for workplace health and retirement benefits). Or they argue that benefits should be less generous. Not even Friedrich Hayek, now a libertarian icon, contended that private insurance could do the job. In *The Road to Serfdom,* written in the early 1940s, he saw no reason "why the state should not be able to assist the individual in providing for those common hazards of life against which, because of their uncertainty, few individuals can make adequate provision." Lest his readers doubt his meaning, he continued, "The case for the state's helping to organize a comprehensive system of social insurance is very strong."[101]

The New Dealers set out to rescue and reform capitalism, not replace it. The academic who oversaw the development of the Social Security Act, Edwin Witte, said of it, "Only in a very minor degree did [the Act] modify the distribution of wealth, and it does not alter at all the fundamentals of our capitalistic and individualist economy."[102] The welfare state softened the sharp edges of capitalism without tight restrictions on economic dynamism. "Necessitous men are not free men," Roosevelt declared in 1936.[103] With protests against the dismal economy rocking Washington, he didn't have to add that necessitous men are not natural supporters of the market, either.

A New Deal for Labor

Among the popular forces pressing from the left was the nation's growing labor movement, the final critical pillar in the emerging mixed economy. As we have seen, the 1930s brought fundamental policy shifts. Yet the long Progressive Era was also about shifting the balance of power, and labor unions were pivotal in this transformation.

The politician most responsible for elevating organized labor was not FDR but another New York progressive: Senator Robert F. Wagner. The four-term senator grew up in the immigrant tenements of New York City. From 1904 until the end of World War I, he served in state government, where he sometimes butted heads with a fellow Democrat named Franklin Roosevelt. While in state government, he investigated the Triangle Shirtwaist Factory fire, the 1911 tragedy that helped galvanize progressive reformers. By the time his former state senate colleague had become president, Wagner was in the US Senate. He would become, in FDR's own words, "the copilot of the New Deal."[104]

With regard to labor law, however, Wagner was mostly flying solo. FDR and his labor secretary, Frances Perkins, did not place as high a priority on new union protections. But as Wagner laid the groundwork for the 1935 law that appropriately bears his name, he won the administration's strong backing.[105] The Wagner Act (formally, the National Labor Relations Act of 1935) contained now-familiar provisions: the National Labor Relations Board (NLRB) and its process for union certification, guarantees of collective bargaining rights, and bans on employer practices that contravened them. But its core message was that workers could band together legally to serve as a countervailing power to corporations and their associations.

The results were dramatic. Unions were struggling at the end of the

1920s, their membership having declined from over 5 million to under 3.5 million in a decade—a tenth of the nonagricultural workforce (roughly where total union membership stands today, though private-sector membership is significantly lower than it was in 1929).[106] By the mid-1940s, with the Wagner Act's protections in place and wartime labor markets tight, unions covered a third of the workforce, and an even larger share of nonagricultural households had a union member in the family.[107]

Most business leaders had little affection for unions. But many would, in time, come to accept and even work with them. With their broad membership in the most concentrated sectors of the economy, unions proved a valuable source of countervailing power to the large industrial organizations of the era, helping to ensure that increased worker productivity translated into rising wages, as it had not during the 1920s.[108]

It would be a mistake, however, to see the effects of unions as limited to union members, much less as purely economic. As a growing body of research shows, unions reduced the sharp inequalities of the 1920s among nonunion workers as well as union members.[109] Even more important, labor unions constituted a unique political movement that, for all its shortcomings—stubborn racism, mob connections, poor leadership—did more than any other organized force in American politics to address the concerns of less affluent citizens. In "the tripartite arrangement of a robust labor movement, an active state, and large employers," explains the sociologist Jake Rosenfeld, unions did not simply "counterbalance corporate interests at the bargaining table." They also served "as a powerful normative voice for the welfare of nonelites" and the "core equalizing institution" during "the 'golden age' of welfare capitalism."[110]

Let's look at the world they helped create.

The Goose That Laid the Golden Age

Vannevar Bush, the conservative who became FDR's national science czar, was never all that fond of organized labor. As an MIT professor, he witnessed the Boston police strike of 1919, and cheered on Governor Calvin Coolidge as he replaced the strikers. But reflecting on Coolidge's presidency at the end of the 1960s, Bush was harsh: "In the late twenties, there was ballyhoo that business was good, and it wasn't. . . . Who would go back to the old days? Perhaps we are overdoing the welfare state. . . . But one cannot view the whole movement without feeling a bit more confident that man is learning how to govern himself, and that a political system with a growing prosperous middle class which knows its power still aims to care for the weak."[111]

Vannevar Bush had a right to feel satisfaction. He had helped create the public-private partnership that fostered that "prosperous middle class." The main contours of this engine of development are now familiar. But let us examine more closely the goose that laid the Golden Age.

Tax and Spend and Grow

Feeding the goose, of course, were taxes—and never before had tax policy changed as much as it did between 1939 and 1943. Before the war, income taxes had brought in no more than 2 percent of national income. By 1943, they raked in 11 percent. Meanwhile, the share of Americans paying income taxes skyrocketed from 7 percent to 64 percent.[112] If, as Adam Smith believed, taxes were a "badge of liberty," many more Americans were wearing that badge after the outbreak of World War II.

Most of the money went to the war effort, of course. But research in universities and industrial labs was among the main beneficiaries, too. Although Vannevar Bush's effort to keep science from falling "flat on its face" ramped up programs and organizational forms already in place, the scale of investments dwarfed what had come before. And it paid off with major advances in medical treatment, computer technology, chemical engineering, aeronautics, communications, and much else. The seed corn for more than a generation of productivity advances and human betterment was stored up.

Crucially, just as scientists flocked to US universities to join in the action, young Americans poured into college with funding from the GI Bill.[113] Science did not just build better technologies and treatments but also better-trained minds capable of capitalizing on and furthering these advances.

Rivaling these investments, both in their impressive scale and their enormous social returns, were vast government outlays for highways, airports, waterways, and other forms of infrastructure that allowed goods and people to move faster than ever. The interstate highway system, the benefits of which were described briefly in chapter 2, began with Eisenhower's 1956 National Interstate and Defense Highways Act, which dedicated over $200 billion (in current dollars) to the cause and authorized a nationwide gas tax for highway financing. Along with continuing refinement of macroeconomic tools, postwar investments propelled the fastest sustained growth in history—which, unlike the rapid growth of Coolidge's day, was shared broadly. Indeed, incomes increased slightly faster among families in the middle and at the bottom than among those at the top.[114]

New Deal programs of economic security expanded as well. With Eisenhower's strong support, Congress extended Social Security to cover almost all Americans and made it generous enough to pull more of the elderly out of poverty, even as disability protections were added.[115] By contrast, national health insurance—proposed by Truman but opposed by the growing private health industry—never made it to the floor of Congress. Nonetheless, wartime price and wage controls that permitted supplemental benefits, the spread of collective bargaining, and tax breaks for health insurance helped push private coverage up to an eventual peak of around three-quarters of Americans by the mid-1970s.[116] The federal government also subsidized and regulated private pensions that built on top of Social Security.[117]

As these tax breaks suggest, the new American state was no unchecked Leviathan. It commingled public and private, direct spending and indirect subsidies, central direction and decentralized implementation. It fostered pluralist competition for funds among researchers, contractors, and private intermediaries, as well as among states and localities. But it was enormously active and enormously successful—and soon its rewards would extend to groups that had yet to feel the warm sun of American prosperity.

Money on the Table

In 1966 a scrappy basketball team from Texas Western College in El Paso made history by winning the National Collegiate Athletic Association (NCAA) Championship over the powerhouse University of Kentucky. Coached by the legendary Adolph Rupp, Kentucky was the overwhelming favorite. The top-ranked Wildcats had won four national titles. The Texas Western Miners—so named because the college had begun as a state mining school—were unheralded.[118] Nobody but the players and their coach, Don Haskins, expected the upset. Certainly not Rupp: He called the Miners "loose-jointed ragamuffins" who were "hopelessly outclassed."[119] Yet the outclassed ragamuffins had a secret weapon that transformed basketball forever.

For those who know sports history, the secret weapon is no secret: The starting lineup of the Miners comprised five black men. Before they took to the court, no major-college team had started five blacks in any game *ever*.[120] Coaches believed that teams had to be mostly white to win—a conviction grounded in powerful currents of racism. The storied Southeastern Conference, where Rupp's teams flourished, did not have a single black player until 1967. That player, Perry Wallace (who went on to become a distinguished law professor), would say later, "Whites then thought that if you put five blacks on the court at the same time, they would somehow revert to their native impulses. They thought they'd celebrate wildly after every basket and run around out of control, [and] you needed a white kid or two to settle them down."[121]

Prejudice was the Miners' powerful advantage. As recounted in the movie *Glory Road*, the Miners' rise becomes a feel-good story of smart coaching and racial progress. Above all, however, it was an indicator of just how much exclusion stifled success. Yes, Coach Haskins had given the black players new skills. But they were good already—they just didn't have a chance to play at the top. Kentucky's president had encouraged Rupp to put an African American on the roster. He refused, complaining to his assistant coach, "That son of a bitch is ordering me to get some niggers in here."[122] Looking at the top ranks of basketball today, one can see that Rupp's racism was ignorant as well as shameful: He was fielding much worse teams than he could have.

We now look back on the 1960s and early 1970s as a turbulent period of redistribution: of rights, of income, of national priorities. But as with the entry of blacks into college basketball, the era also marked a long-overdue recognition of huge social costs that had been ignored or denied. Failure to grant equal rights to racial minorities and to women was not only horribly wrong but also spectacularly inefficient. Failure to give all Americans the opportunity to attend college or a shot at a middle-class life was not only unfair, it also made our nation as a whole poorer.

Expanding Opportunity, Expanding the Economy

In expanding rights for women and minorities—through statutes, through judicial action, and through the government's own example (most profoundly, in the armed services)—the nation was finding money on the table. When future Supreme Court Justice Sandra Day O'Connor graduated third in her class from Stanford Law School in 1952, law firms would consider her only for the secretarial pool.[123] But who can doubt that the blinkered male law partners, like so many others who resisted the rights revolution, were shortchanging their own companies? Arizona Republicans were the beneficiaries: She became the first female majority leader of a state senate.

Government policies also boosted the skills and opportunities of the least advantaged, where the returns on such investments were highest. We forget that most of LBJ's War on Poverty was about expanding opportunity, not lifting poor families' incomes directly.[124] With the move toward integrated schools and increased investment, educational prospects became notably more equal, if still far from equivalent, across lines of race and class. Just as black ballplayers could now achieve their potential, the abilities of more than half the nation's population had a greatly improved chance of being recognized and cultivated. Our society benefited as a result.

The seismic shift can be seen in the changing composition of students at elite universities. As the columnist David Brooks observes, at these bastions of old-money privilege, "admissions officers wrecked the WASP establishment."[125] Before the shift, two-thirds of all applicants to Harvard were admitted—90 percent of all applicants whose fathers were alums—and average SAT scores were dismal.[126] If you came from the right background, you had a ticket. Everyone else, including, most notoriously, many brilliant Jewish students, was out of luck. But as Ivy League schools opened up, talented students from a much broader range of backgrounds had the opportunity to access the best of American higher education. Exclusion had meant mediocrity as well as marginalization. At top schools, SAT scores skyrocketed.

At least as big a change was the expansion and enhancement of public universities. A marker was the elevation of the celebrated labor economist Clark Kerr to the presidency of the University of California system in the late 1950s. Pragmatic and professorial, Kerr was nonetheless passionate about the ability of well-run organizations to foster economic and social progress. He was, in the words of journalist Nicholas Lemann, "a supreme rationalist who believed that a system could always be devised to solve a problem," that "government ought to be the highest, biggest, and best system," and that scientists and their students were needed to "help make it run properly."

"Universities today are at the vital center of society," Kerr proclaimed in his inaugural address in 1958, "We must again concern ourselves with educating an elite—if I may use this word in its true sense, free of the unhappy connotations it has acquired. But this time we must train an elite of talent, rather than one of wealth and family."[127]

To drive home his message, Kerr gave his speech at the university's obscure Riverside campus, a commuter school that was giving California's working- and middle-class young a chance to enter the once-locked gates of higher education.[128] Riverside was just one of the new public institutions rising up on the fast-changing educational landscape: In the twenty years after Kerr's speech, the number of colleges and universities in the United States increased by more than half, the number of professors nearly doubled, and the amount of public spending (both state and federal) on higher education nearly doubled, too. The share of twenty-five- to twenty-nine-year-olds with a college degree shot up from around 5 percent in 1940 to around 25 percent in the mid-1970s (where it largely stayed for the next two decades even as other nations continued to improve, and, in some cases, race past the United States).[129]

Although support for this transformation came from many quarters, the federal government was the crucial catalyst. Starting with the GI Bill in 1944 and continuing through the National Defense Education Act in 1958, federal aid poured into higher education through a series of landmark initiatives that culminated in the creation of Pell Grants in 1972. The average Pell Grant covered all the tuition at an average four-year public university, with some left over for housing and other expenses. (Today it covers roughly half of tuition alone.)[130] And though Claiborne Pell was a Democrat, the legislation was thoroughly bipartisan: Republicans and Democrats voted for it in almost exactly equal proportions.[131] Supporters of the law believed, as Senator Pell put it, that "any student with the talent, desire, and drive should be able to pursue higher education."[132] Our nation is richer for that conviction.

How the American States Got Rich

As the federal government expanded, it did not merely extend opportunities to individuals on the periphery of prosperity. It also extended opportunities to *places* on the periphery of prosperity, injecting assistance and employment, housing and highways, development projects and defense jobs into regions previously left behind by modern economic growth. And nowhere were these enormous federal investments larger and more consequential than in the American South.

In 1938 FDR declared, "The South presents right now the nation's number one economic problem—the nation's problem, not merely the South's."[133] His administration's subsequent *Report on the Economic Conditions of the South* did not mince words: "The low income belt of the South is a belt of sickness, misery, and unnecessary death." "The paradox," the report concluded, "is that while [the South] is blessed by Nature with immense wealth, its people as a whole are the poorest in the country."[134]

The South was certainly poor. When Vannevar Bush was at MIT in the 1930s, his fellow Massachusetts residents had an average income of over $12,000 (in current dollars). By contrast, residents of Mississippi, then and now the poorest state in the nation, had annual incomes of less than $4,000.[135] Among African Americans, poverty in the South was even more extreme—"pathological" was the description of the Swedish social scientist Gunnar Myrdal, who visited the region in the 1940s.[136]

Whether southern poverty was a "paradox" is more debatable. The main sources were no mystery. The South's once impressive wealth came from enslavement and extraction, not innovation. Southern economies mostly missed out on the industrial revolution. With agricultural production reliant on artificially low wages even after slavery's end, the incentives for mechanizing and diversifying production were weak. And without effective political competition in the Jim Crow South, there was little political pressure to expand the scope of opportunity to those left behind—not just blacks, who were brutally excluded from civic life, but also the majority of whites.[137]

By the late 1970s, however, Mississippi had come within hailing distance of Massachusetts in economic terms, with average per capita incomes roughly 70 percent of the Bay State's.[138] Nor was it alone in its rapid movement toward northern standards of living: All of the poorest American states saw dramatic income growth in the middle of the twentieth century.[139] By any economic measure, these were years of remarkable convergence: The rich states got richer; the poor states got richer even faster.

Of course, convergence is what you'd expect in an integrated market with free movement of labor and capital. Yet as Roosevelt's 1938 plea for action suggests, it was far from an automatic process. During and after the New Deal, the federal government invested massively and disproportionately in developing the South. There was rural electrification and highway building; new social programs with benefits that were scaled inversely to personal income; public health, worker safety, and environmental efforts that had their greatest positive effects in the least developed regions; and enormous earmarked funding to bring the poorest states toward a national standard.[140] On top of all this, FDR and later Truman deliberately steered defense spending to the region to promote continued modernization.[141]

Today critics of the federal government often cite the economic success of low-tax states—more specifically, low-tax *southern* states—as an indictment of federal policies and proof of the superiority of limited, localized government. But this assertion is completely backward. Not only do these states continue to trail their high-tax counterparts on many measures of prosperity, they have also relied on immense resources from the federal government to promote their partial catch-up. Though these earmarked investments have declined, the region continues to receive huge net transfers from the federal government, mainly because it still remains comparatively poor. For every dollar that Mississippians pay in taxes, $2.34 comes back in federal spending. South Carolina—like Mississippi, home to some of the nation's most virulently antigovernment politicians—receives over $5 for every $1 its taxpayers send to Washington. By contrast, the five richest states—Connecticut, Massachusetts, Maryland, New Jersey, and New York—receive an average of 77 cents. New Jersey receives less than 50 cents; Delaware, just 31 cents.[142]

Just as America became rich not in spite of, but because of, government, the American states became rich not in spite of, but because of, government. Indeed, the states that are most likely to be held up as exemplars of free enterprise today are those that benefited the most (and continue to benefit the most) from this active federal role.

Attacking Externalities

Even as the mixed economy opened its doors to tens of millions of previously neglected citizens, America's leaders made another vital contribution to the country's rising prosperity after World War II: a revolutionary push to address market failures associated with an increasingly dense, interconnected, and complex commercial society. The most obvious breakthroughs concerned pollution, which rapidly came to be seen as a fundamental threat to the quality of life, requiring vigorous regulation of markets.[143] The federal government also improved protections for worker safety, and in response to the growing profile of activists such as Ralph Nader, it paid greatly increased attention to vulnerable consumers in areas ranging from tobacco to automobiles.[144] Negative social costs imposed on others were only one focus; regulations also sought to address myopic behavior that caused grievous harm to individuals and the nation—and nowhere was this more true than with regard to smoking.

Fifty years after the War on Poverty, many conservatives are quick to declare the effort a failure (though their case is based largely on the failure of our antiquated poverty measure to include most public aid to the poor, such as the Earned Income Tax Credit, also known as the EITC, and supplemental nutrition assistance, aka food stamps).[145] But they are notably silent about another fifty-year landmark that also rankled many on the right at the time: the first surgeon general's report on the health risks of smoking.[146] The silence is revealing. Today no sensible observer doubts that discouraging cigarette smoking is good policy. Yet the major efforts of federal and state governments to reduce tobacco use were opposed at every turn in the name of market freedom.

By the middle of the twentieth century, the accumulating evidence of tobacco's toxicity—much of it revealed by federally supported research—was overwhelming. Yet manufacturers denied the evidence, spewed out misinformation, and insisted that consumers could make their own "informed" decisions.[147] Consumers couldn't. Even after government warnings were slapped on cigarette packs, and the majority of Americans recognized that smoking causes cancer, most adult smokers remained ill-informed about the risks they were taking. Moreover, most smokers start this addictive habit before age eighteen, when the future risk of dying seems even smaller and more distant.[148]

In the half century since the 1964 report, cigarette smoking has caused an estimated twenty million premature deaths in the United States.[149] Today about half a million lose their lives each year—one in five annual deaths in the United States—and smoking-related medical costs and lost productivity exceed $300 billion a year.[150] Yet the toll would be far higher were it not for active government. At the time of the surgeon general's report, over four thousand cigarettes were smoked annually for each adult American.[151] In the decades since, following a ban on broadcast ads, rising federal cigarette taxes, increasingly strong warning labels, repeated FDA actions to promote smoking cessation, and a string of settlements between states and tobacco companies (along with various state-level antismoking policies), annual consumption has dwindled to just over a thousand cigarettes per adult. According to a recent careful estimate, efforts to reduce tobacco consumption over the past half century prevented more than eight million premature deaths, extending average life expectancy by a remarkable one and a half to two years.[152] Whether the 1964 report was a critical catalyst or merely one important contribution to this broad shift in science and policy, it is hard to disagree with the surgeon general's fifty-year assessment: "The epidemic of smoking-caused disease in the twentieth century ranks among the greatest public health catastrophes of the century, while the decline of smoking consequent to tobacco control is surely one of public health's greatest successes."[153]

The 1964 report defined a new model of federal scientific involvement: the independent commission, guided by scientists, seeking to provide recommendations in the best interests of the nation. It was the model that informed and guided the massive investments in medical research made after World War II, as well as the new regulations designed to protect individual health and safety, the environment, and, later, the planet itself. As the fifty-year appraisal concluded, the 1964 report did more than start the nation down a healthier path. It was also "a pioneering step toward anticipating a much larger role for government, in collaboration with scientists, to use science to inform regulatory and other policies."[154]

Vannevar Bush would have been proud.

The Goldilocks Economy

The story of America's rise to richness is a story of an ongoing rebalancing of political institutions and economic realities, of public policies, social knowledge, and democratic demands. But the arc of that history bends toward a more extensive role for government, and for good reason: As the United States has changed from an agricultural society into an industrial society and then a postindustrial society, the scale of economic activity and the interdependence and complexity of that activity have expanded, along with the scope of the harms that this activity can yield. As America's leaders responded to these challenges and to pressures for action and inclusion from below, they came to recognize that making Americans healthier, better educated, and freer to pursue their own dreams—regardless of race, gender, and ethnicity, whatever the circumstances of their birth—made America richer, too. For all the barriers yet to be broken, for all the ignorance and indifference that remains, it is no longer possible to pretend that exclusion is costless.

As far from its origins as it now is, America's mixed economy still bears the marks of its founding: in the ideas, so often misunderstood, of a revolutionary generation that insisted on unified authority that could defend a rising nation and build a national economy, and in the interventionist nineteenth-century republic of bountiful land rather than bountiful spending that built on this foundation. Still, the mixed economy is unmistakably a twentieth-century creation, a modern social technology. And it is arguably the greatest social technology not just of its time but of all time.

Vannevar Bush died in 1974, on the eve of the computer age, but he would not have been surprised by the miraculous technologies his work fostered. In a 1945 article for the *Atlantic Monthly*, titled "As We May Think," Bush wrote of a device with "translucent screens, on which material can be projected for convenient reading," along with a keyboard to control access to that information.[155] Data would be stored in files, each with "trails" (we would now call them links) that would allow vast amounts of knowledge to be sorted and searched at the touch of a button. Scientists could find any article, lawyers any case, doctors any clinical study, inventors like Bush any patent. The "Memex," as he called it, is familiar to us today as the personal computer and the internet. What we too often forget is the enormous public investments that made this technology, and so many other contributors to our productivity, possible.

Near the end of World War II, an aspiring scientist named Doug Engelbart came across Bush's 1945 article while stationed in the Philippines. Inspired, he returned to complete his undergraduate degree at Oregon State (a land-grant university); found a job at a government aerospace lab in California, where he refined his thinking; and then completed a (highly subsidized) PhD at UC Berkeley (another land-grant university). He eventually set up a research group at the university that Leland Stanford founded, with funding from the US Air Force, NASA, and the Advanced Research Projects Agency—the Defense Department arm that would create the predecessor of the internet, ARPANET.[156] Twenty-three years after seeing Bush's Memex in his mind's eye, at a San Francisco conference bringing together more than a thousand of the world's best computer scientists, Engelbert would hold his fellow technophiles in rapture as he showed how Bush's vision could be made real. When Engelbart died in 2013 at the age of eighty-eight, his obituary in the *New York Times* captured the moment:

> For the event, he sat on stage in front of a mouse, a keyboard, and other controls and projected the computer display onto a twenty-two-foot-high video screen behind him. In little more than an hour, he showed how a networked, interactive computing system would allow information to be shared rapidly among collaborating scientists. He demonstrated how a mouse, which he invented just four years earlier, could be used to control a computer. He demonstrated text editing, video conferencing, hypertext, and windowing.[157]

Unlike Vannevar Bush, Engelbart lived to see his futuristic ideas become mass-market products. He never received much money or credit from the companies and CEOs who reaped billions from his vision. But he was not alone: neither did the federal government.

Given that technological breakthroughs are at least as much a result of the right environment as the right person, perhaps it's fitting that neither Vannevar Bush nor Doug Engelbart is much remembered today. Yet we should not forget Bush's legacy: Bush the Republican, conservative, probusiness, free-market advocate was also Bush the apostle of the mixed economy. He was not the only architect of active government who now seems an unlikely advocate. Along America's path to the mixed economy, plenty of leaders within the business community and the Republican Party joined him as well. Undergirding a successful mixed economy was a successful politics.

FIVE

★ ★ ★

"An Established and Useful Reality"

FOR FDR, meeting the youthful and charismatic Eric Johnston in September 1942 came as a jolt. The new head of the US Chamber of Commerce, the nation's largest and most prestigious business association, was not what the president expected. After all, Roosevelt had been feuding with most of the business community for almost a decade. Taking office in the darkest days of the Depression, Roosevelt had received initial support from some big companies and the moderate leadership of the Chamber, especially as he fashioned the big-business-friendly National Industrial Recovery Act. But that had been years ago, before the NIRA fizzled (and then was terminated by a hostile Supreme Court), and before the New Deal expanded beyond its initial emergency measures to incorporate Social Security, more progressive taxation, expanded organizing rights for unions, intensive regulation of the financial sector, and a host of other ambitious federal initiatives.

As the nation crawled out of the Depression and Roosevelt's reformist ambitions grew, the business community reverted to its antigovernment traditions. In 1935, business conservatives staged something akin to a coup at the Chamber of Commerce, until then the bastion of moderation within the corporate community. The year before, the fiercely antigovernment du Pont brothers (Pierre, Irenee, and Lammot) had used the proceeds of their vast trust to bankroll the archconservative American Liberty League, which portrayed the New Deal as an enemy of freedom. The league made defense of the Constitution its rallying cry, but the alternative names it considered—the Association Asserting the Rights of

Property, the National Property League, and the American Federation of Business—indicated its main priorities.

One of the Liberty League's founders, former General Motors chair John Raskob, identified the du Ponts as the cornerstone of their efforts: "No group, including the Rockefellers, the Morgans, or anyone else . . . begins to control and be responsible for as much industrially as is the Du-Pont company."[1] In addition to the du Ponts, the Liberty League's leadership included Alfred P. Sloan, president of General Motors; Edward F. Hutton, the founder of General Foods; and J. Howard Pew, president of Sun Oil. The league's financial and organizational resources soon rivaled those of the Republican Party, and rhetorical fireworks between corporate America and the New Dealers intensified. Liberty League pamphlets attacked New Deal initiatives as fascist, socialist, and un-American, and compared FDR to Hitler, Mussolini, and Stalin.[2]

Roosevelt reciprocated. At the opening of his 1936 campaign, before a crowd of more than a hundred thousand at Franklin Field in Philadelphia, he attacked the "economic royalists" who took "other people's money" and used it to impose "a new industrial dictatorship." At the campaign's close four months later, he told a raucous crowd at Madison Square Garden that "organized money" was "unanimous in their hate for me—and I welcome their hatred. I should like to have it said of my first administration that in it the forces of selfishness and of lust for power met their match. I should like to have it said of my second administration that in it these forces met their master."[3]

Hence the unexpected jolt six years later when Johnston sat down with FDR. The Chamber's new president was eager to change the tone and update the reputation of the association he led. He recognized that the world had changed, and that with these changes came the need for a "new capitalism." Capitalism, Johnston insisted, was "a human institution, vibrant and evolutionary, capable constantly of adjusting itself to new conditions." As he was to tell the Chamber membership the next year, "Only the willfully blind can fail to see that the old-style capitalism of a primitive, free-shooting period is gone forever."[4]

Johnston was a Republican, not a New Dealer. But while he opposed "superstatism," that didn't mean he was opposed to the state. "The role of government must keep pace with change," he said. "The game has become so complicated that government in its legitimate character of umpire has vastly more to do."[5] And it was not just the state's expanded role that needed to be acknowledged. Organized labor, too, was here to stay. Johnston insisted he wanted to move corporate views beyond their "primitive stage" of "illogical prejudices and blind opposition." Collective bargaining needed to be accepted as "an established and useful reality." FDR reportedly exclaimed at their first meeting, "My God, Eric, how did they ever elect you president of the Chamber!"[6]

Johnston did not just talk a good game. He accepted Roosevelt's invitation to serve as one of two business representatives on the administration's new Economic Stabilization Agency. He supported the development of policy expertise within the Chamber, which would facilitate a more vigorous and informed engagement in complex deliberations over modern governance. In time, the influx of economic experts would encourage the Chamber to embrace a cautious version of Keynesianism, the ascendant economic doctrine that acknowledged government's vital role in preventing crashes and promoting growth.

More broadly, Johnston accepted the "established and useful reality" that business could be a central, but not controlling, participant in shaping economic policy. In 1945 he joined with the heads of the American Federation of Labor (AFL) and the Congress of Industrial Organizations (CIO) in signing a labor-management charter that recognized "the fundamental right of labor to organize and engage in collective bargaining" and to "employment at wages assuring a steadily advancing standard of living." As Ralph Bradford, the Chamber of Commerce's general manager, put it, under Johnston's leadership "the Chamber has become a part of what goes on in Washington. . . . We can no more remain aloof from government than from any other element of society."[7] Other business leaders had reached the same conclusion. George Romney, who headed the Automobile Manufacturers Association at the time, used the association to broker production deals with the federal government to aid the war effort.

Johnston's reign was brief. The Chamber of Commerce was a membership-based organization, and at the end of the war, conservatives within the organization regrouped and gained strength. Sensing the shifting winds, Johnston announced that when his term expired in 1946 he would accept a position as head of the Motion Picture Association of America (MPAA), where he was to play a central role in developing the blacklists of the 1950s. Johnston went out in style, continuing to preach moderation in his final address to the Chamber: "We in business must liberalize or face the threat of economic liquidation." Moderation, he emphasized, was a necessity, but it was also an opportunity. It opened a path to sustained prosperity—if, that is, business approached the reality of the new capitalism "stripped of the ancient prejudices against organized labor, government activity, and community planning."[8]

With Johnston's departure, the Chamber of Commerce took a step back toward conservatism. Yet it did not retreat to the staunchly hostile approach to government that had characterized much of its previous history. It accepted grudgingly, for instance, the Keynesian argument that running occasional deficits could help moderate the business cycle.

What was even more striking was that the Chamber's limited step back turned out to be a step away from political relevance. Less intransigent elements of the business community moved to the fore. Within a few years, the Chamber would be scrambling again, with limited success, to find a foothold in politics and a voice in policy making. In the dawning postwar era, it was not progressive figures such as Johnston who were marginalized, but the more conservative elements of the business community.

The period from the early 1940s to the mid-1970s was the heyday of the mixed economy. Not coincidentally, this period also marked the high point of the business community's acceptance of a consensus politics that included organized labor and government officials, and recognized that government, in Johnston's words, "had vastly more to do." Reform elements of the business community had played a significant role in building the mixed economy in earlier decades, especially during the long Progressive Era. But business support for government involvement in the economy now reached new heights. By the 1950s, there were many Eric Johnstons engaging in politics and policy making at the highest levels.

Not all was sweetness and light. Republicans (often backed by southern Democrats) waged battles with northern Democrats over the scope of the federal government. Truman's proposals for national health insurance, for instance, met fierce and successful resistance. Even more significant were conflicts over labor law. The Taft-Hartley Act, passed over Truman's veto with the overwhelming support of southern Democrats, rolled back some, but not all, of the legal gains unions had achieved during the New Deal and World War II.

Crucially, however, the area of consensus during the three decades that followed the end of World War II was broader, and more supportive of a mixed economy, than ever before or since. For roughly thirty years, from the early 1940s to the mid-1970s, the mixed economy of American capitalism was a model of unprecedented achievement, nurturing innovation, sustaining stability, and generating opportunity and prosperity. This successful model rested on a series of social and political understandings, compromises, and accommodations. Given their power in American society, leading business figures were necessarily key participants in this success.

Hence the ascendance of the new breed of business progressives such as Johnston represents a crucial historical puzzle. How did they come to play such a vital and constructive role? Why did they decide that the mixed economy was an established and useful reality?

Overcoming a Legacy of Distrust

America's corporate elites, as the great scholar of business David Vogel puts it, "distrust 'their' state."[9] Even though business interests have long played a leading role in shaping what government does, the political attitudes of business leaders have generally reflected a profound suspicion and skepticism of government.

Some of this distrust flows from deep currents in American political culture that prize individual initiative and question public authority. But, according to Vogel, an even more critical factor is that American business became a formidable, organized national force a generation or more before the modern role of Washington, DC, emerged in domestic affairs. In most of the countries embarking on the road to advanced democratic capitalism, extensive national governments that taxed and spent on a large scale either predated the rise of large corporations or grew alongside them. In the United States, the opposite was true: Large corporations—nurtured and enabled by government, to be sure, but often overshadowing it—arrived first. This sequence led business elites to position themselves inaccurately but effectively as the proud owners of American capitalism. Notwithstanding occasional accommodations, especially during the long Progressive Era, it also made them fiercer guardians of their autonomy and harsher critics of government than business elites in any other industrialized nation.

Business and the New Deal

The period stretching from the Depression through World War II fundamentally challenged this traditional orientation. Not since the Founding
had there been such an opportunity to expand Washington's role. Two
of the biggest sources of resistance, the business establishment and state
and local governments, watched their power dissipate. Business, discredited by the economic cataclysm and the evident failure of traditional
nostrums of market discipline, saw its influence ebb. The Depression also
cost business another long-standing advantage: the capacity to play one
state off against another within what had been a decentralized federal
system. States and localities had long been jealous guardians of their
prerogatives, but they were now desperate for federal help.

In Washington, business faced yet another challenge. Not only did
the Depression devastate the credibility of the business community; its
strongest ally, the Republican Party, had been routed. The winds grew
even stronger after FDR followed up his landslide victory of 1932 with a
stunning triumph in the midterm elections of 1934.

Still, business stood firm. One can find scattered instances of corporate support for the New Deal, but the overwhelming reaction was one
of opposition and hostility. Business anger was especially evident following the "second hundred days" of 1935. In an extraordinary burst
of activity, Congress passed much of the foundational legislation of the
modern mixed economy: the Social Security Act, the Wagner Act, and
progressive tax legislation that hit top earners especially hard, along
with other major enactments such as the Public Utility Holding Company Act, rural electrification, and the Public Works Administration.
Business leaders seethed. The traditionally powerful but now marginalized National Association of Manufacturers feared that Social Security
would usher in "ultimate socialistic control of life and industry."[10] Beginning in 1934, its hard-line president, Robert Lund, positioned the
NAM as a fierce opponent of the New Deal: A survey of thirty-eight
major laws passed between 1933 and 1941 indicated that the association had opposed all but seven. Businessmen rallied to the call, and the
NAM's membership grew from 1,469 firms in 1933, to 3,008 in 1937, and
to 9,418 in 1943.[11]

The Chamber, too, came to staunchly oppose the New Deal. On January 17, 1935, FDR asked Congress to enact a comprehensive social secu-

rity program. The next day, the Chamber's board of directors authorized
a committee "to determine whether such legislation may be demonstrated as leading definitely to the complete socialization of the United
States." With the moderate Henry Harriman ending his term as Chamber
president, enraged conservatives rebelled. By mid-1935, the Chamber of
Commerce had retreated (in the words of economic historian Robert Collins) to "unquestioned opposition to government and adherence to the
verities of the classical laissez-faire business creed."[12]

As Roosevelt's record suggests, however, this seething occurred
mostly from the sidelines. The New Dealers reached out to business interests when they could and drew support from a handful of business
progressives. But power had shifted away from the business community,
and government reformers drew on broad reservoirs of public support.

Even before the 1940s, elements of the business community began
to adjust. There had always been pockets of dissent to the laissez-faire
orthodoxy that dominated business circles. Over the course of the late
1930s, those pockets began to expand. The viewpoints that Eric Johnston brought to the Chamber's leadership after the outbreak of World
War II were becoming more widespread.

The emerging posture of moderation within the business community reflected a reassessment of both economics and politics. Marion
Folsom, treasurer of Eastman Kodak and head of the Rochester Chamber
of Commerce, was one of the earliest and most prominent members of
the liberal business vanguard. As Johnston would do later, Folsom emphasized two points: A more active state was coming whether businessmen liked it or not, and this wasn't a bad thing—again, an *established*
and *useful* reality. In a 1937 address to other business leaders, he argued
that as "our civilization becomes more complex, it is only natural the
government will have a little more to do with it than it had in the past."
Folsom implored his colleagues to be realistic, observing that the "influence of business organizations has been somewhat discredited, and
we have not had nearly as much to do with the writing of this legislation as we should have had. . . . we must adjust ourselves to changed
conditions."[13]

The War

As much as the New Deal did to change the relationships between government and business, World War II did more. The federal government's

capacity—legal, administrative, and financial—increased spectacularly. It emerged from an existential challenge not simply more powerful but also more respected. Citizens accepted more government and expected more from it. Business leaders were brought into increasingly intensive engagement with policy makers and faced further pressure to adapt to the new realities.

The shift to a war footing brought a swift end to the Depression.[14] Not coincidentally, it also swiftly expanded government. The most obvious, visible measure was public expenditure. Federal spending jumped from just under $9 billion in 1939 to just under $100 billion in 1945. In just five years, the federal government spent twice as much on defense spending alone as it had for all purposes over the entire prior history of the republic.[15]

This astonishing transformation required a revolution in public finance—actually two revolutions. The first was an unprecedented willingness to tolerate public debt. By the summer of 1940, John Maynard Keynes had concluded that it was "politically impossible for a capitalistic democracy to organize expenditure on the scale necessary to prove my case—except under war conditions."[16] Events proved him right. With the onset of war, the federal government borrowed like never before; in 1946 public debt reached 129 percent of GDP.[17] When this surge of deficit spending coincided with the rapid disappearance of unemployment, it forced a broad reconsideration of the potential utility of government borrowing during periods of economic slump.

The second financial revolution was, if anything, even more durable. As we saw in the last chapter, war brought unprecedented federal taxation. Indeed, even with all the new borrowing, Washington funded a greater share of the costs of World War II out of current receipts than it had in World War I. For the first time, most adult Americans financed the federal government directly. Most also contributed to war finance through the purchase of bonds, often organized through joint labor-management committees that added automatic withholding of bond purchases to the income taxes collected in American factories.

As the historian James Sparrow observes, war finance "embedded the federal government more deeply within American society." Yet far from provoking revolt, heightened taxation in the context of a clear and immediate threat produced the opposite effect. "Of all the years of the twentieth century," Sparrow writes, "federal legitimacy grew most dramatically during World War II, just when expanding state capacity most burdened the nation's citizenry."[18] The challenge of global war linked support for the federal government to patriotism and the defense of freedom. The new attitude was exemplified by the popular purveyor of gossip Walter Winchell, whose column reached fifty million readers. In a radio address shortly before tax filing day in 1943, Winchell drew a blunt connection between taxation and citizenship: "Attention Mr. and Mrs. United States. . . . Your income tax blank is not a bill from your government. It is your share in America. Our nation is composed of one hundred and thirty million shareholders—shareholders in civilization. . . . Civilization, like money, must be earned. . . . To those who complain that the tax is a heavy burden, remind them that a soldier's pack on his back weighs sixty pounds."[19]

Most Americans agreed. The fledgling Gallup poll began asking respondents whether the income taxes they paid were fair. Fully 85 percent to 90 percent said yes.[20] This new, popularly supported level of finance would permanently lock in vastly higher levels of federal spending. Having peaked in the prewar period at 10.5 percent of GDP in 1936, federal spending would *average* 17.3 percent in the period from 1947 to 1960.[21]

Of course, spending, along with the taxes and borrowing to finance it, represented just the most easily quantified measure of the government's expanded reach. Federal nonmilitary employment grew dramatically as well, and it would remain at levels far higher than those reached in the New Deal and vastly higher than pre-Depression levels (higher, it turned out, than it would ever be again). The extraordinary growth of production during the war—by 1943, the American armaments industry was producing twice the output of Germany and Japan combined—required an unprecedented extension of government involvement through the economy.[22] Washington introduced controls on vital materials, handed out billions in war contracts, and built factories itself when the imperative for immediate production appeared to outstrip the capacities of the private sector. Formulations such as Winchell's, describing "your government" or "our government," seemed more than rhetorical. Citizens could see what Washington was doing and providing.

Business Climbs Aboard

It wasn't just average citizens who were coming to see the federal government in a new way. As Washington's reach and visibility grew, business leaders were brought into much more direct and extensive collaboration with public officials, whether as "dollar-a-year men," who aided the war effort with no public salary, or through deepening public-private partnerships. Kodak's Folsom, one of the chief architects of the business elite's new, more constructive relationship with government, described the war's impact: "The war did an awful lot to business people. Many of the top business advisory people had government jobs during the war, you see, and realized what a tough job it is to run a government. So the businessmen got to appreciate the government and not be so critical of it."[23] Businessmen were learning to trust their state.

By the early 1940s, many business leaders had come to recognize how much the world had changed. Not only had government grown dramatically and come to interact much more intensively with business leaders, but also business itself had changed. Manufacturing was now the heart of the economy. War contracts flooded to the largest firms, which experienced spectacular growth. In 1939, firms employing ten thousand or more workers accounted for 13 percent of the manufacturing workforce; by 1944, they accounted for 31 percent.[24] The scale of these burgeoning industrial enterprises brought them into frequent interaction with government and gave them a greater capacity to cope with its increasing role.

Moreover, most of these large manufacturing firms were now unionized. After the takeoff in union organizing in the second half of the 1930s, union membership doubled again in the decade of the 1940s. In a cycle of mutual accommodation, big firms got contracts, the federal government supported labor organizing, and unions (at least until the end of the war) agreed to wage restraint and avoided strikes.

The Committee to Modernize American Business

The durable organizational embodiment of this reorientation of the business elite was the Committee for Economic Development. Built to advance big business priorities, the CED was simultaneously business friendly and cognizant of new economic and political realities.[25] The CED grew in part out of earlier government-business networks, particularly the Business Advisory Council of the US Department of Commerce, established by FDR to drum up corporate support for New Deal measures. Yet the group had a social base, organizational autonomy, and a depth of sustained engagement with government at the highest level that the mostly ignored BAC never approached.

The CED would play an important role in the postwar period, but its development is also important because of what it says about the shift under way in business-government relations. In contrast to associations such as the Chamber of Commerce and the National Association of Manufacturers, the CED was not a lobbying organization. Indeed, its leaders insisted that while business leaders would be prominent in its ranks, it was not even a business organization. Its internal structure and public pronouncements emphasized the need to find common solutions rather than advance the interests of any particular group. The CED was thus an unusual hybrid: a social network of establishment figures, heavily weighted toward prominent members of the business community, as well as a proto–think tank with a major role for academics. Each side of this symbiotic partnership was committed to spreading the new gospel of the mixed economy, while developing new ideas about how that emerging economy could be managed effectively.

Symbolic of that hybrid structure were the backgrounds of the CED's cofounders: Paul Hoffman, the CEO of Studebaker, and William Benton, a former advertising executive and vice president of the University of Chicago. They surrounded themselves with a leadership roster that was an impressive expression of the midcentury establishment. Among the members of the board of trustees in the late 1940s were the Chamber's Eric Johnston and Charles Wilson (CEO of General Motors). Other prominent figures included Ralph Flanders, the president of the Federal Reserve Bank of Boston; Robert Sproul, president of the University of California; and Milton Eisenhower, another university president and brother of the future president (who also served for a time on the CED board).

Most CED members had direct experience with government. Many were carryovers from the earlier Business Advisory Council established by FDR. Ralph Flanders stressed that the BAC members were "trained in the knowledge of government operations. They were trained in their insight as to working with and in government. They were trained in patience. They were trained in mutual cooperation and understanding with each other."[26]

The orienting ideas of the CED, as the historian Collins puts it, included "a thoroughly modern view of the state."[27] CED leaders embraced Keynesianism, but with a cautious bent. In a sharp break with traditional business thinking, they endorsed the government's central role in macroeconomic policy. Unlike most New Dealers, however, they favored the use of tax cuts and automatic stabilizers such as unemployment insurance during economic downturns, rather than discretionary government spending. Despite this caution, they acknowledged that public spending could play an important role in bolstering the economy.

CED leaders also accepted the role of unions and resisted the push of more conservative business leaders to repeal the Wagner Act. Hoffman, for instance, claimed that moderate views on such issues constituted "enlightened self-interest." The manager would do best who "deals frankly with his employees, pays the highest wages, and promotes the self-interest of the workingman." He accepted that the "personal dignity of the workman and his individual right to plan his own life certainly encompass the privilege of belonging to a union and dealing collectively with an employer."[28] Hoffman also recognized that "our government's" role extended beyond taming the business cycle. "The major emphasis which capitalism places on the individual does not preclude collective activity," he insisted. "As a matter of fact, the interests of the individual can be advanced only through a wide range of collective actions, both governmental and private."[29]

A Positive and Permanent Role for the Mixed Economy

All of these policy positions, as well as Hoffman's rhetoric, reflected a broad embrace of the core principles of the mixed economy. Far from representing "socialism," Hoffman insisted, the mixed economy was distinct from both traditional capitalism and socialism, and represented a superior alternative to either one. CED cofounder William Benton's 1949 speech described the new attitude: "Philosophically, business was [traditionally] committed to the doctrine that, 'that government is best which governs least.' The emerging CED attitude has been that 'government has a *positive* and *permanent* role in achieving the common objectives of high employment and production and high and rising standards of living for people in all walks of life.' . . . The greatest single achievement of CED . . . may turn out to be the clarification it has been developing on the role of government in the economy."[30]

The CED's unusual combination of a sophisticated shop for policy analysis and an elite network made it a powerful incubator of both men (they were all men) and ideas. It also created an astonishing flow of CED personnel into the highest levels of economic policy making. All told, according to Collins, "in the first fifteen years of the organization's existence, thirty-eight CED trustees held public office."[31] Of the cofounders, Republican Paul Hoffman became the administrator of the Marshall Plan, the crucial program to support economic recovery in war-shattered Europe. Democrat Benton went to the US Senate. In Connecticut, in 1950, he defeated Republican Prescott Bush, father and grandfather of the future presidents, and became a leading voice against McCarthyism. Beardsley Ruml, whose 1943 "Ruml Plan" had introduced the system of automatic payroll withholding, served as president of the New York Federal Reserve. Republican Ralph Flanders became president of the Boston Federal Reserve and later represented Vermont in the Senate, where he would introduce a resolution to censure Senator Joseph McCarthy.

Given the presence of not one but two Eisenhower brothers on the CED board, it is not surprising that the organization's imprint on the Eisenhower administration was deep. *Both* of Eisenhower's secretaries of the Treasury, George Humphrey and Robert Anderson, had been board members. Marion Folsom, former chair of the CED, resigned to join the Eisenhower team. He served first as the undersecretary of the Treasury and later as secretary of Health, Education and Welfare. In the latter position, to the consternation of conservatives and the Chamber of Commerce, he helped steer the administration toward a posture of support for Social Security, including its expansion to include disability protection in 1956. Board member "Engine Charlie" Wilson, CEO of GM, became Eisenhower's secretary of defense. Wilson is perhaps most famous for a misquote of his testimony at his nomination hearing. He did not say "What's good for GM is good for the country." He said, "I thought what was good for the country was good for GM, and vice versa"—a neat encapsulation of much of the CED's thinking.

What Happened?

How do we make sense of this fundamental transformation in the behavior of business leaders? Remember, the norms of the business community had long been—and would be again—that government was a hindrance, not a help. Yet three sorts of calculations came together in the 1940s to shift the balance in favor of the mixed economy: advantage, opportunity, and constraint.

Advantage

Advantage is what it sounds like: business leaders coming to regard aspects of the mixed economy as providing a direct, tangible benefit to their companies. As we have seen, there are many, many ways in which government can contribute favorably to the bottom line. Governments provide essential public goods, correct externalities, combat monopolies, reduce the intensity of boom-and-bust cycles in the economy, expand economic opportunity, and promote social stability and the legitimacy of the market economy. As the statements of various corporate leaders in the postwar period suggest, there was growing appreciation of all of these factors—an acknowledgment that government and market could be complementary factors in promoting prosperity.

Advantage can also come from a less cheery source. Sometimes it is not overall gains but relative position that matters most. As a business leader, you may see government as a way to gain an edge over competitors. Perhaps you can afford regulations more than your competitors can because your firm is larger and thus will find it easier to handle the needed administration. Or perhaps your firm is already unionized, so you see an advantage in new government rules that make it easier for unions to organize the workforces of your competitors. Government action may create, or restore, a company's competitive edge.

Opportunity

Advantage isn't the only force that can shift the posture of business leaders. A second possible factor is the presence of slack in an economic setting that allows room for considerations other than profit maximization. Call this *opportunity*. Businesses may find it *easier* to accept government restrictions and requirements under some circumstances than others. Market enthusiasts typically emphasize that what makes companies push relentlessly toward ever greater efficiency is the Darwinian pressure of competition. This incentive is, indeed, a crucial feature of markets, but it is also the case that the intensity and sources of this pressure vary. In certain times and places, important companies may be sheltered to a considerable degree from competitive pressures, whether because of the inherent nature of their markets (as in the monopoly capitalism seen in the last chapter) or the political and organizational relationships among firms. During important periods of American economic development, major markets (such as the auto industry after World War II) have been divided among a small number of firms, often engaging in implicit or explicit coordination of prices.

Another source of opportunity comes from managerial autonomy: Those who run companies may have more or less leeway to pursue their own goals, depending on how their incentives are structured. As we shall explore in the next chapter, demands to provide "shareholder value" beginning in the late 1970s have intensified pressure on corporate executives to fixate on their share price. During other periods, including the immediate decades after World War II, managers have had more slack to pursue other priorities—slack that could be, and was, used to support compromises with other "stakeholders," including workers, local communities, and public officials. During the Progressive Era as well as the postwar period, as the pioneering studies of historian James Weinstein and sociologist Mark Mizruchi show, companies that faced less intense competition were less likely to take sharply conservative views on economic issues, especially with respect to labor unions.[32]

Constraint

Of even greater significance than advantage and opportunity in generating business support for the mixed economy is a third consideration. Call it *constraint*. More than anything else, business leaders bargain and compromise when they *have to*. This constraint is what Eric Johnston meant when he implored employers to recognize labor unions as an "established reality." Compromise happens when a posture of rejection is unsustainable.

The central political story of the New Deal, World War II, and the postwar period is the emergence of genuine constraint—a system of countervailing power. That the postwar era is often described as a "settlement" or "treaty" is revealing. One makes treaties or settlements only when there are other groups with different views and some power to press their case. Most notable, of course, were organized labor and government officials. Unions emerged from World War II with a new level of legitimacy and an unprecedented organizational grasp on the American workforce. Government, too, was a partly independent force, boasting a string of accomplishments that generated new credibility and high expectations. Business leaders found themselves compelled to negotiate and seek mutually acceptable solutions within a system where other voices would be heard.

The constraints on business leaders associated with these formidable rivals for authority were extensive. Examining the private and semi-private ruminations of business leaders, one sees the same pragmatic assessment. Marion Folsom, the business leader so often at the center of efforts to bring corporate leaders into a posture of constructive engagement, reflected on the process in a 1965 interview: "The people in the large companies have got to keep up with the times. They've got to adjust themselves to social conditions whether they like it or not. . . . I've found a great majority [of business people] to be pretty realistic. They might not like some of these things, but they adjust to it and they don't kick. And then they eventually come around to thinking: 'Well, maybe we were wrong. Maybe this is the right way to do things.'"[33] Whatever the merits of laissez-faire traditionalism, more and more business leaders were concluding that this philosophy was a political nonstarter.

The Republican Contribution to Corporate Moderation

"The times" that Folsom spoke of featured newly effective pressure from labor and the left. Yet perhaps even more significant, because it cut off business's traditional escape route from moderation, was another potent constraint: liberal Republicans. It is hard for Americans watching the Republican Party of today to grasp just how moderate much of the leadership of the GOP was between the early 1950s and the mid-1970s. Of course, there were prominent conservatives. And the GOP as a whole often fought hard to roll back aspects of the New Deal and, especially, to contest the role of organized labor. The far right, however, was marginalized in domestic policy and treated as outside the mainstream in political debate. Even the traditionally right-wing National Association of Manufacturers took the step of purging far-right John Birch Society members from its leadership.

The economic moderation of the GOP was a key foundation of the midcentury mixed economy. Then, as now, Republicans not only responded to the business community; they also shaped what corporate leaders believed was politically possible. After all, if you are a business leader, it is much easier to adopt a fiercely hostile stance on regulation, taxes, and other elements of the mixed economy when you can count on the broad support of the business-friendly party in government. It is even easier, of course, if your political allies are winning. By the time of Eisenhower's election, however, the Republican Party had largely made peace with the mixed economy; when it pushed back, it generally lost; and that meant corporate America faced strong pressures to accommodate as well.

Growing in the Shadows

Writing of the Republican Party at the time of the 1960 election, historian Geoffrey Kabaservice portrays it as consisting of four factions: progressives, moderates, "stalwarts" (traditionalists associated with the legacy of the late Ohio senator Robert A. Taft), and the conservatives who would rally behind Barry Goldwater four years later. Of the four groups, the conservatives were the smallest.[34] The stalwarts were the largest. Yet the moderate and progressive factions were substantial as well. Crucially, they were the source of many of the party's most successful national figures. Whether one looks at the two Republicans who won presidential elections during the 1950s and 1960s, or the other leading contenders for the party's nominations, or congressional leaders, or successful governors of major states, the GOP leadership was full of moderates. Goldwater's 1964 nomination looked to observers at the time like an aberration rather than a portent. In 1968, for instance, Ronald Reagan stood out as the only visible conservative presidential candidate (and a marginal one at that) within a field of contenders that included centrists such as George Romney, Nelson Rockefeller, Charles Percy, and John Lindsay. Richard Nixon, too, was viewed as a moderate on economic and social welfare issues. So were most of the vice presidential hopefuls.[35]

As was true for business leaders, GOP moderation stemmed from changing perceptions of what was "established" and what was "useful." Like moderate figures in the business community, many leading Republicans had revised their views in reaction to the experiences of the 1930s and 1940s. They expressed a growing appreciation for government's role in promoting prosperity. Increased enthusiasm for the mixed economy was even more evident within the rising postwar generation of Republican leaders. Dan Evans, a GOP leader in the Washington State House of Representatives and later the state's governor, sought to address modern, mixed-economy concerns: congestion, sprawl, water pollution, and the creation of improved infrastructure to promote Seattle's participation in growing trade with Asia. He had no trouble calling these efforts "progressive," a label he considered appropriate for those, himself included, who "saw a problem and an effective way to handle it, and the idea of a somewhat larger government for a very limited purpose didn't frighten them."[36]

Indeed, by today's standards, many of the GOP's leading postwar figures would be seen as clearly on the left on most issues related to the governance of the mixed economy. Critical once again, however, was their recognition of constraint—in this case, political constraint. Many New Deal programs were popular, and opposition would lead to repeated defeat. The moderation of the postwar GOP emerged not just from idealistic conversions but also from years of electoral pummeling. In 1952, on the eve of Eisenhower's election, the political journalist Samuel Lubell noted that American politics was not then (or much of the time) a contest between two equal parties "of two equally competing suns, but a sun and a moon. It is within the majority party that the issues of the day are fought out, while the minority party shines in the reflected radiance of the heat thus generated."[37] Eisenhower might have been a full moon, but Democrats remained the sun.

Republicans got the first of many political lessons when their 1936 presidential nominee, Alf Landon, called for the repeal of Social Security, declaring that it was a "cruel hoax": "unjust, unworkable, stupidly drafted, and wastefully financed."[38] Crushed by FDR—no Republican candidate has ever won fewer electoral votes—Landon was the last GOP nominee for almost seventy years to challenge Social Security directly.

For good reason: In 1936, Republicans came about as close as a major American party can come to extinction without, in fact, expiring. It was not just Landon's epic defeat. The Republicans lost six seats in the Senate and fifteen in the House. In each chamber, it was the fourth consecutive election in which the GOP had lost ground. The result was the most lopsided Congress, and the smallest opposition party, since Reconstruction. Republicans held just sixteen seats in the Senate and eighty-eight in the House.

The GOP would skirt the political abyss. At the precise moment when Roosevelt seemed unstoppable, the president suffered stinging defeats on his court-packing proposals and plans to overhaul the federal bureaucracy. The New Deal stalled in 1937. Beginning with major victories in the House and Senate elections of 1938 (fueled in part by "Roosevelt's recession," when he made a premature turn toward austerity), the GOP reestablished itself gradually as a viable national party.

More fundamentally, as Ira Katznelson has recently reminded us in his magisterial history of the New Deal, *Fear Itself*, Republicans would soon build an effective "conservative coalition" with southern Democrats. Segregationists increasingly saw the New Dealers as a threat to the "southern way of life"—which is to say, to Jim Crow. This emerging conservative coalition would stymie Roosevelt from 1937 on, especially with respect to labor issues and administrative centralization. Even in the midst of electoral struggle, the GOP's ability to build a coalition with conservative Democrats allowed it to play a critical role in shaping the policy contours of the mixed economy in the postwar period.[39]

Still, the GOP's partial rehabilitation in 1938 was exactly that: *partial*. Republicans would hold the presidency for just eight of the next thirty years; they would hold the majority in the House and Senate for just four. Like business leaders, Republicans moderated because they had little choice.

Moderation in Defense of the Mixed Economy Is No Vice

The most famous adherent to the emerging GOP view that the mixed economy was an "established and useful reality" was the general-turned-politician Dwight Eisenhower. He understood that the Republican Party needed to make its peace with most of the policy achievements of the previous two decades. In 1954 Eisenhower ridiculed privately the desire of conservatives to roll back the New Deal: "Should any political party attempt to abolish social security, unemployment insurance, and eliminate labor laws and farm programs, you would not hear of that party again in our political history. There is a tiny splinter group, of course, that believes you can do these things. Among them are H. L. Hunt (you possibly know his background), a few other Texas oil millionaires, and an occasional politician or business man from other areas. Their number is negligible and they are stupid."[40]

Eisenhower's point was that the mixed economy was an established reality. There was no going back. Despite his own electoral success, he and other Republicans had to accept the new status quo.

An established reality but a useful one, too. Eisenhower's stance was not just a matter of political expediency. He wrote his letter dismissing those who dreamt of rolling back the New Deal to his oldest brother Edgar— who, by all accounts, shared the dreams of the Texas oil millionaires whom Eisenhower ridiculed. But while Edgar sniped from the sidelines, Eisenhower kept him at a distance. ("Edgar has been criticizing me since I was five years old.") He took counsel instead from his younger brother Milton (whom he once described as the smartest one in the family).[41]

Intelligent, pragmatic, and above all moderate, Milton was a prototypical can-do mandarin of the bipartisan era of countervailing power: He worked for the federal government before and during much of the New Deal (including as head of the War Relocation Authority that oversaw the internment of Japanese Americans), was the first chairman of the US National Commission for UNESCO (United Nations Educational, Scientific, and Cultural Organization), and served as president of three universities (Kansas State, Penn State, and Johns Hopkins). His commitment to bipartisan moderation continued in the 1960s. In 1964—in a move seen to signal Ike's tacit support—Milton nominated the moderate William Scranton (governor of Pennsylvania, and a late challenger to Goldwater) at the Republican Convention in San Francisco. In 1968, responding to the urban unrest roiling the country, President Lyndon Johnson selected him as chairman of the US National Commission on the Causes and Prevention of Violence.

It was Milton who personified Dwight Eisenhower's nuanced views of the nation's political economy. There is little doubt that the first Republican president in two decades was deeply suspicious of statism, focused on the dangers of drift in that direction, and sympathetic to the concerns of the business community.[42] Yet President Eisenhower, along with other leading Republicans, embraced the mixed economy. He insisted that "unions have a secure place in our industrial life. Only a handful of unreconstructed reactionaries harbor the ugly thought of breaking unions. Only a fool would try to deprive working men and women of the right to join the union of their choice."[43] It wasn't just rhetoric. Eisenhower surrounded himself with CED men. More important, while maintaining a stance of fiscal conservatism, he pursued a vigorous agenda of mixed-economy initiatives that relied on the federal government. In his 1953 economic address to Congress, he insisted that "the demands of modern life and the unsettled status of the world require a more important role for government than it played in earlier and quieter times."[44]

Eisenhower's domestic policy agenda focused on economic growth. Democrats would criticize him later for his reluctance to rely on Keynesian policy to prime the economy. Yet his administration devoted substantial energy to policies designed to improve the country's long-term economic performance. As the political scientist David Mayhew summarizes the record of Eisenhower (as well as that of his Democratic successor, John F. Kennedy), at its core were "the aims of *growth, development, efficiency* and *productivity*"—themes that "pervade the president's autobiographical account of his first term."[45]

Eisenhower's perspective echoed that of Vannevar Bush. Ike saw virtue in decentralization and private-sector decision making, and worked to strip away vestiges of planning that remained from the New Deal and World War II. Yet just as Bush wanted the federal government to spend much, much more to promote science through these decentralized structures, Eisenhower promoted federal action on a number of fronts: the economic development of public lands; a massive expansion of the federal role in the development of science and technology (including the National Defense Education Act and the creation of NASA in 1958); and, most dramatically, giant public infrastructure projects, such as the interstate highway system, the Saint Lawrence Seaway, and the Colorado River Storage Project.

"Growthsmanship," as the historian Robert Collins calls it, sidestepped some of the polarizing dynamics of the late New Deal period. Eisenhower concentrated legislative energy on areas where agreement was possible.[46] The president's focus on using government power to generate "more" produced a striking run of bipartisan legislation, releasing a host of economic development initiatives that had been stalemated. Almost all of the elements of this pro-growth agenda passed by sizable or overwhelming majorities. Most commanded majority support of both parties in both chambers of Congress.

The (Temporary) Triumph of Moderation

On economic issues, the moderate consensus continued after Eisenhower left office. Although Kennedy famously adopted a more Keynesian stance on the budget (built around business-friendly tax cuts), in most respects his economic policies followed the tracks laid down in the 1950s. When the GOP veered right with Goldwater's candidacy, and LBJ tacked left with the inclusionary policies of the Civil Rights Act and the War on

Poverty, much of the business establishment went with LBJ. His campaign established Republican Businessmen for Johnson, and succeeded in organizing more than three thousand CEOs who supported the president. The relatively apolitical Business Council, made up of CEOs from large companies, responded similarly. In 1960 seventy-three of eighty who contributed to candidates gave their money to Republicans; in 1964 that share dropped to thirty-six of sixty-nine.[47] All told, three-fourths of LBJ's campaign war chest came from the business community.[48]

Indeed, business leaders actually endorsed some of the major Great Society and War on Poverty programs, including the Housing and Urban Development Act and the Model Cities Program. Again, their motivations were a mix of advantage and constraint, self-interest and prudent accommodation. Many of LBJ's programs were designed to appeal to the private sector, providing important investment opportunities. In general, however, business acquiescence reflected an understanding that its clout was limited. When necessary, Johnson was not shy about using his legendary political skills to remind them. In a phone call to Vice President Hubert Humphrey in 1965, he counseled Humphrey on how to deal with the prospect of NAM and Chamber opposition to elements of his Great Society initiative. Johnson told Humphrey bluntly to issue a threat: "[C]ut the guts out of my program . . . I'll cut the guts out of yours."[49]

A clear case of the constrained influence of business was the enactment of, in 1965, Medicare and Medicaid, the biggest expansion of US social policy since Social Security. The goal of covering the aged had consistently evoked opposition from the organized business community from the time Democrats first started pushing for it after the demise of Truman's proposal for national health insurance. Before the 1964 election, the Chamber of Commerce and the NAM were "strong and unequivocal in opposing Medicare." After 1964 that opposition softened. The evidence is clear, however, that this shift reflected a change in circumstances rather than a change of heart—specifically, LBJ's landslide and the huge Democratic majorities that made the passage of Medicare inevitable.[50]

Twilight of the Postwar Consensus

Richard Nixon was one of the last Republican leaders to embrace the mixed economy—and embrace it he did. Nixon's efforts to fashion a new majority involved positioning himself to the right of Democrats on issues of race and crime, but on matters related to the economy, he adopted a moderate, often activist stance. He supported major extensions of the regulatory state, including big new initiatives for environmental and consumer protection. He favored a guaranteed annual income, a huge expansion of Social Security, and health care reforms way to the left of the Clinton or Obama health plans.

As was true of the overall GOP shift, political calculation drove Nixon's moderation. Encouraged by Daniel Patrick Moynihan, one of his leading advisers on domestic policy, he took nineteenth-century British prime minister Benjamin Disraeli's "liberal Tory" stance as a model, and sought to appeal to working-class and middle-class whites with support for social insurance and cautious backing for many of the new regulatory measures coming out of a Democratic Congress.[51] Nixon showed no interest in the antiunion agenda that would soon spread within the GOP. Instead, he pursued support from union leaders such as George Meany. In the assessment of Allen Matusow, the leading historian of Nixon's economic policies, "Meany loomed as the pivotal figure in Nixon's scheme for [political] realignment. . . . Nixon courted no businessman, or even all of them together, as assiduously as he courted the crusty Democrat who headed organized labor."[52] Indeed, administration officials were disparaging of the political clout of business groups, confident in their support because Nixon believed they had no place to go.

No less than Eisenhower, Nixon was comfortable with the mixed economy. He accepted the notion that in a large and complex society, government had a fundamental role to play in fostering economic growth and social prosperity. Nixon never said the line generally attributed to him: "We are all Keynesians now." He said "I am now a Keynesian in economics"—which, while less poetic, better captured the constrained evolution of the GOP.[53] The embrace extended far beyond the macroeconomic management of boom and bust. It incorporated support for collective bargaining, extensive social insurance and a reasonable social safety net, the provision of crucial public goods, and interventions tackling thorny market failures. He—like all nationally successful Republicans of his era and most business leaders as well—was mindful of the balance of political forces that sustained the mixed economy.

A Crumbling Foundation

In March 1969 the recently elected Nixon spoke before the National Alliance of Businessmen, a nonprofit organization established by the Johnson administration to tackle the problem of long-term joblessness. After thanking the chairman of the group, Donald Kendall, CEO of Pepsi-Cola, as well as its former head, Henry Ford II, he praised the three hundred company heads who were part of the effort for the hundred thousand private-sector jobs they had provided to disadvantaged Americans. Concluding his remarks, he signaled that he would soon propose changes in benefits for the poor.

In August the Nixon administration unveiled the Moynihan-designed Family Assistance Plan: the president's ill-fated proposal for a guaranteed minimum income, which would ultimately fail to gain sufficient support from either conservatives or liberals. On Labor Day Nixon issued a special statement touting his new plan, as well as his proposals for expanded job training, subsidized child care, and an occupational health and safety agency. "As we renew our commitment to the general well-being of the working man," he declared, "we also reaffirm our faith in sound collective bargaining. In an increasingly complex society, one in which so many elements depend so heavily on one another, the process of collective bargaining must be strong and effective and exercised with self-restraint on all sides."[54]

Forty years later almost to the day, President Obama delivered his own speech to prominent business leaders. The occasion was a special gathering of the Business Roundtable (BRT) at the St. Regis Hotel on K Street, the avenue that has become synonymous with Washington's vast lobbying empire. Founded in 1972 amid a wave of corporate political organizing, the Roundtable is unique among business lobbies.[55] Its two hundred or so members are not companies but CEOs—the highly paid executives who run the nation's largest corporations. And its stated mission is to work with both parties to improve the health not of individual sectors of the economy but of American capitalism as a whole. In an increasingly polarized and fragmented lobbying world, the Roundtable is the closest approximation to the corporate establishment in Washington these days.

Flanked by the chairman of the Roundtable, Terry McGraw, and the new secretary of education, Arne Duncan, the president praised the assembled CEOs for "taking a broader view of your responsibilities as chief executives. You've looked beyond the bottom line and the next quarter to the long-term health of your company. You've not only served as accomplished leaders, but as engaged citizens—citizens who understand that it is in the interest of both your companies and your country to have a workforce that's highly educated, healthy, and prosperous; to have a market that is free, but also fair; and to live in a nation that's willing to invest in its own future. You understand the public responsibility of private enterprise."[56]

Obama's emphasis on "the long term" and "the public responsibility" of private enterprise was the opening for his big message. The Roundtable had backed the president when he had sought to rescue the financial sector and stabilize the economy; now he wanted the CEOs to stand behind him as he pursued a larger program of reform that would address what he saw as the underlying problem: a generation of shortsighted actions by public and private leaders who had neglected the long-term foundations of economic growth.[57]

A New Foundation

This was a novel pitch. On K Street, Main Street, and Wall Street, the outlook had become increasingly cramped. Politicians locked in a permanent campaign had little opportunity to look down the road. The spectacular increase in lobbying had ramped up pressures to respond to the most mobilized and self-interested. CEOs, naturally attentive to the immediate needs of their own companies, had become ever more narrowly focused.[58] The mounting emphasis on "shareholder value"—backed by omnipresent threats of retribution for subpar performance—encouraged a relentless preoccupation with the next quarterly report.[59] On Wall Street, massive risk taking and self-dealing masked by a fog of complexity had brought the economy to the brink of ruin. The vernacular of texting captured the new mind-set of self-dealing: IBG/YBG. "I'll be gone, you'll be gone."[60]

To the assembled CEOs, Obama called for a different approach: "a prosperity that no longer rests on a bubble but on a firm foundation that will make this country strong and competitive."[61] A firm foundation, according to the president, required new regulations on Wall Street, health care reforms to cover more Americans and address the explosive growth of costs, and serious efforts to rein in greenhouse gas emissions that threatened the planet. A month later, in a major economic address at Georgetown University, the president attached a slogan to this vision: "the New Foundation." Now forgotten, this was the slogan he hoped would brand his administration's efforts, akin to FDR's New Deal or LBJ's Great Society. In making his case, he drew on the Sermon on the Mount:

> Now, there's a parable at the end of the Sermon on the Mount that tells the story of two men. The first built his house on a pile of sand, and it was soon destroyed when a storm hit. But the second is known as the wise man, for when "the rain descended, and the floods came, and the winds blew, and beat upon that house, it fell not: for it was founded upon a rock." . . . We cannot rebuild this economy on the same pile of sand. We must build our house upon a rock. We must lay a new foundation for growth and prosperity.[62]

This New Foundation was what he called on the CEOs to support.

By all accounts, the president's remarks were received with enthusiasm. Chairman McGraw responded with praise: "There's a misperception, I think, in some people's minds that the relationship between business and the Obama administration is like, well, oil and vinegar. . . . [F]rom our standpoint, that couldn't be farther from the truth."[63] In the months that followed, the president continued to press his agenda with business leaders, mixing appeals to long-term thinking with reminders that popular outcry demanded reform.[64] In April he met with thirteen of the nation's top bankers and urged them to back his financial reform agenda. "My administration," the president warned coolly, "is the only thing standing between you and pitchforks."[65]

Backlash

Within a short time, however, it was business leaders and their Republican allies carrying the pitchforks. Over the course of 2009 and 2010, business lobbies spent never-before-seen amounts to defeat or defang the Obama agenda, with Wall Street, the energy industry, and business groups leading the charge. Under its combative head, Tom Donohue, the US Chamber of Commerce launched the largest legislative campaign in its history, spending more than $270 million between 2009 and 2010 on registered lobbying.[66] Business groups and corporate leaders bitterly denounced President Obama's "vilification," "betrayal," and "demonization" of the country's economic elite. Stephen Schwarzman—cofounder of the private equity giant Blackstone Group, and a member of the Business Roundtable—railed that the president had declared "war" by seeking to close a notorious tax loophole allowing some of the nation's wealthiest financiers to pay just 15 percent federal taxes on much of their incomes.[67] In *Forbes*, an astonishingly vitriolic cover story called Obama the "most antibusiness president in a generation, perhaps in American history."[68]

Republican national leaders also went on the warpath. Whether Obama truly believed in the postpartisan vision of his campaign ("[T]here are no red states or blue states, just the United States"), he found scant evidence of it among congressional Republicans. To the contrary, GOP leaders plotted his defeat even before his inauguration, developing a strategy of all-out opposition: no bargains, no compromises, no alliances.[69] At a December retreat of House Republicans, the new minority whip, Eric Cantor, was emphatic: "We're not here to cut deals and get crumbs and stay in the minority for another forty years. We're not rolling over. We're going to fight these guys."[70] Senate Minority Leader Mitch McConnell rallied Senate Republicans with similar words and a similar directive. Ohio Republican George Voinovich, one of the last relatively moderate Republicans in a chamber where they once were decisive, summed up McConnell's message: "If Obama was for it, we had to be against it."[71]

And against it they were. The president's first legislative priority was a major stimulus bill to rescue the free-falling economy. It received not a single Republican vote in the House and just three in the Senate (though not Voinovich's).[72] These three votes that helped stave off economic collapse proved to be the high-water mark of Republican cooperation. For the first two years of the Obama presidency, Republicans presented a virtually unbroken wall of opposition (with a few tiny cracks forming on financial reform as public disgust with Wall Street mounted). Even in the Senate, McConnell was able to "hold the fort," as Voinovich put it: "All he cared about was making sure Obama could never have a clean victory."[73] Obama did have victories, but all of them were ugly—drawn out, convoluted, savaged by Republicans—and it was Democrats who had the mud on them.

As the 2010 midterm elections approached, business organizations and Republican-allied groups spent unprecedented sums to defeat vulnerable Democrats. The Chamber alone devoted in excess of $75 million—

an unprecedented amount for an outside group in a single campaign. Americans for Prosperity, the advocacy organization created by the ultrawealthy conservative businessmen Charles and David Koch, spent at least $45 million.[74] In sector after sector, but especially from the deep war chests of Wall Street, business funds that had flowed to Democrats in 2008 headed to Republicans, helping to administer the "shellacking" (as Obama put it memorably) Democrats received in 2010.[75] That November, as Republicans retook the House and moved within striking distance in the Senate, the window of opportunity for building the president's New Foundation slammed shut.

What Happened?

President Obama found himself a very long way from the world of business statesmen and moderate Republicans that Eisenhower, Kennedy, Johnson, and Nixon had faced. The business and GOP elite of this earlier era had been to the right of (northern) Democrats, but each engaged with them in addressing major social problems and recognized, if sometimes grudgingly, the "established and useful reality" of government's expanded role.[76] In 2009 and 2010, not so much. The most narrow corporate groups attacked relentlessly, the most resourceful business organizations backed them up, and even ostensibly moderate corporate groups such as the Business Roundtable largely sat on the sidelines, eclipsed by the Chamber and the growing network of nonprofits backed by the Kochs and others on the hard right.

To the president's opponents, the cause of all this was obvious: The president had embarked on an unprecedented left-wing campaign. Yet the president's agenda, though ambitious, was hardly the leftist project caricatured by his critics. His first-term economic advisers, for instance, were all highly credentialed mainstream thinkers—Larry Summers, Timothy Geithner, Peter Orszag—establishment mandarins who could hardly be described as scourges of American capitalism. Nor, considering Wall Street's role in a catastrophic financial crisis, was the president's rhetoric particularly strident. Calling bankers "fat cats" in one interview or speaking critically about "millionaires and billionaires" in another is not Huey Long populism, or even the vastly more combative rhetoric of FDR.[77] What's more, the president's most controversial proposals—health care and financial reform and the defeated "cap-and-trade" bill to lower carbon emissions—all sidestepped more liberal alternatives and embodied elements of prior Republican plans. To be sure, they were more sweeping and more liberal than Republicans wanted. But it takes serious exaggeration to describe them as "breathtaking expansions of state power in huge swaths of the economy," as the head of the conservative think tank the American Enterprise Institute (AEI) charged in the run-up to the 2010 midterm election.[78]

The intense backlash against Obama's New Foundation does say something about the president's agenda: for one, that it challenged many of the most powerful rent seekers in the American economy. But it says far more about how the business and political worlds have changed over the decades separating the political careers of George Romney and his more conservative son. Indeed, it is a measure of how much has been forgotten that so many observers see these events as indicators of the president's temperament or ideology or negotiating skills, rather than of the collapse of the political coalition that once supported the mixed economy. In our contemporary climate, it is hard to even remember the bipartisan corporate establishment and moderate Republican wing of the postwar years. It is harder still to recall the terms of debate that prevailed when these dinosaur-like creatures walked the earth. So fundamentally has the American political-economic order changed since the 1970s, that we suffer from a kind of mass historical forgetting—a distinctively American Amnesia.

To see what's changed, then, we have to look anew at the rupture and what it has wrought. We need to perceive with fresh eyes the interwoven transformation of American capitalism and American politics that has played out since a Republican president stood before American businessmen and called forthrightly for an expanded safety net. In the second part of our historical and intellectual journey, we will discover that our present predicament is a legacy of fundamental changes—in the economy, in the beliefs that guide our leaders, in the associations representing American business, and in the Republican Party. And we will learn that these changes have not only depleted the political support needed to sustain the mixed economy but have also undermined effective governance precisely where it's most needed to secure American prosperity.

PART II

★ ★ ★

THE CRISIS OF THE MIXED ECONOMY

SIX

* ★ *

American Amnesia

N O MODERN politician has had a more conflicted relationship with government than Bill Clinton. A southern Democrat who came of age amid states-rights suspicions of the federal government, he admired JFK's bold call for national service. A leader of the Democratic Leadership Council—the party's centrist vanguard—he ran and won in 1992 as a tribune of the middle class, with universal health insurance a top goal. Within two years, his party in disarray and Republicans in control of Congress for the first time in forty years, he declared, "The era of big government is over." Yet Clinton felt the vise tightening from the first days of his presidency. As his grand ambitions were whittled down to a deficit-reduction plan pressed on him by Fed chairman Alan Greenspan and Treasury Secretary Robert Rubin, he vented, "I hope you're all aware we're all Eisenhower Republicans. We're Eisenhower Republicans here, and we are fighting the Reagan Republicans. We stand for lower deficits and free trade and the bond market. Isn't that great?"[1]

To Clinton, of course, it wasn't great. He had argued passionately for increased social investments. He was in favor of health insurance for all. He wanted to be a New Democrat, not a moderate Republican. Still, his invocation of Eisenhower was astute, and not just because his budget was actually quite moderate. The two leaders faced a similar challenge: how to shift governance back toward their party's priorities within boundaries created by an influential predecessor. Just as Clinton had long argued that Democrats had to make their peace with the Reagan

Revolution, Eisenhower had scoffed at members of his party who believed they could "abolish social security, unemployment insurance, and eliminate labor laws and farm programs." The Republicans who thought they could roll back the mixed economy, he had sneered to his brother Edgar, were "negligible" and "stupid."[2]

But there was a revealing difference between the two men's private assessments. Eisenhower had told his brother that if any party messed with the New Deal, "you would not hear of that party again in our political history." It was *voters*, he had suggested, who stood in the way of more sweeping challenges to the reigning order. To Clinton, the problem was not the electorate. The public investments and middle-class tax cut on which he had campaigned were popular. The problem was the *establishment*: those holding power in government and the economy. As he complained to his advisers, "You mean to tell me that the success of the economic program and my reelection hinges on the Federal Reserve and a bunch of fucking bond traders?"[3] Eisenhower had worried about the American public. Clinton worried about American elites.

In their words to the nation, the two men spoke differently as well. Eisenhower's first State of the Union Address in 1953—essentially the same length as Clinton's first in 1993—mentioned "government" nearly forty times, and the overwhelming majority of his references to government were positive.[4] Four decades later, Clinton spoke of government only around half as often, and the majority of his references were negative. On the other hand, Clinton spoke more than Eisenhower had about the deficit and debt and much more about taxes (all of which were lower in peacetime 1993 than they had been in wartime 1953).[5] And Clinton mentioned organized labor only once in passing, while the closing of Eisenhower's speech directly connected labor stoppages by unionized workers and the nation's struggle against Communism: "Freedom expresses itself with equal eloquence in the right of workers to strike in the nearby factory, and in the yearnings and sufferings of the peoples of Eastern Europe."

The gulf looks only greater if we consider how the agendas of these two presidents were received. The "middle way" that Eisenhower staked out gained strong bipartisan support. Forty years later, Clinton received zero votes from the opposition on his highest-priority goals. Under the direction of House GOP leader Newt Gingrich, Republicans waged a scorched-earth campaign against the president's agenda. Within two years, they had brought down the president's health plan, blocked his public investments, and then converted public discontent with Washington into a congressional majority. By then, Clinton probably *wished* he was the popular former general who left office having passed big infrastructure and education bills with broad cross-party backing.

Why did Eisenhower find support for the mixed economy, initiating massive new public investments with broad support within both parties, while Clinton could not? Why was Clinton so concerned about elite opinion and financial markets, while Eisenhower saw the voting public as the biggest restraint? And, most puzzling of all, why did putatively progressive leaders stop talking about government in positive terms? After all, Eisenhower was a Republican who, for all his moderation, was setting out an agenda substantially to the right of his forerunners'. Clinton was a Democrat. For all *his* moderation, he saw himself as a counterweight to an increasingly conservative Republican Party—a champion of middle-class voters, not powerful corporate interests. If Clinton, the Democrat, saw elite opinion as so powerful, and if Clinton, the Democrat, was so reluctant to talk about government in favorable ways, something very profound must have happened. What was it?

This is the question that carries us from part 1 to part 2, from the rise of the mixed economy to its erosion and current crisis. We unpack this puzzling transformation piece by piece, deconstructing and then reassembling the interlocking changes that have compromised our vital capacity to use government to advance American prosperity.

In the current chapter, we explain the parallel rise of two grave threats to the mixed economy: a new economic elite with ideas (and earnings) starkly distinct from the American mainstream and a newly influential economic philosophy that we call "Randianism" (after the radically individualistic thinking of the midcentury novelist Ayn Rand). At the outset, each of these developments—the economic and the ideological—was partly independent of the other. Over time, however, they became more and more intertwined. The increasing dominance of Randian thinking encouraged shifts in corporate behavior and public policy that exacerbated the intellectual and economic distinctiveness of America's new economic elite: the deregulation of finance, the slashing of top federal tax rates, the growing links between the financial and corporate sectors, the upward spiral of executive pay. Most Americans did not buy into these new assumptions, much less embrace their results. But they did share one important belief with those on the winning side of this growing economic and ideological divide: that government could not be trusted to right the balance.

Yet this is hardly the entire story of the eroding political foundations of the mixed economy. Top corporate and financial executives and others at the pinnacle of the economy did not shape politics and policy on their own; in their efforts, they worked through interest groups and political parties. In the next two chapters, therefore, we show that these changes in elite thinking and behavior have been magnified, rather than countered, by two Great Enablers: the nation's large business associations (chapter 7) and a Republican Party that has made a dramatic move to the right (chapter 8). No business group now plays the role that the CED once did of an independent voice for the broad collective concerns of business. Instead, the biggest—the Business Roundtable, the Chamber of Commerce, and the increasingly powerful political network associated with Charles and David Koch—have moved toward stances that place priority on the narrow interests of particular industries and those occupying executive suites, while advancing increasingly antigovernment worldviews.

These hugely resourceful and organized groups are the first of the Great Enablers. They have made common cause with the second: a Republican Party that has embraced and encouraged the Randian turn of the nation's new economic elite. In the process, the GOP has abandoned not just its prior moderate commitments but also its willingness to work constructively with other political actors to update and strengthen the mixed economy. Indeed, the GOP has learned how to win politically by fostering dysfunction, to achieve its policy goals not by brokering agreement but by breaking government. With positive conceptions of government's essential role marginalized and demonized in political discourse—denounced by Republicans and defended feebly by Democrats—Republicans discovered the benefits of the self-fulfilling prophecy: They could simultaneously cater to narrow corporate interests and denounce "crony capitalism," feed political dysfunction and win by railing against it, undermine the capacity of government to perform its vital functions and decry a bungling and corrupt public sector.

In the final chapters of part 2, we survey the grave damage to effective public authority—and hence prosperity—that all this has produced. Chapter 9 examines the ways in which these shifts have enabled corporate interests that profit from imposing costs on the rest of us, enriching American capitalists even as they undermine the long-term prospects for American capitalism. Chapter 10 explores the collapse of effective governance that these interwoven changes have precipitated. We shall see that the mixed economy has not become irrelevant or outmoded. It is instead being steadily undermined by the concerted resistance of its foes and the increasing indifference of so many more, by the unchecked demands of narrow private interests and the increasing barriers to a sensible updating of our policies, and by the willful forgetting of an ideal of effective governance that remains, for all these changes, the key to our long-term prosperity.

The Great Forgetting

The economic model that propelled American prosperity in the twentieth century was more than a political or economic achievement. It was also an intellectual achievement. New conceptions of the economy came to dominate older understandings. John Maynard Keynes's insistence that public spending could soften recessions was part of this new paradigm. Yet the more basic ingredient was an elevated respect for the capacity of government to address problems that the market alone could not. As one of the nation's most prominent economists wrote in 1948, "No longer is modern man able to believe 'that government governs best which governs least.' Where the complex economic conditions of life necessitate social coordination and planning, there can sensible men of good will be expected to invoke the . . . government."[6]

"The Rediscovery of the Market"

The man who wrote these words was Paul Samuelson, and they appeared in an unassuming textbook that would become something close to the nation's economic bible, *Economics*. For three decades—from the first edition in 1948 through the tenth in 1976—Samuelson's introductory economics text was the nation's bestselling textbook. (At last count, it had sold over four million copies.) Samuelson said once, "Let those who will write the nation's laws, if I can write its textbooks."[7]

Within economics, Samuelson (who died in 2009) is best known for bringing mathematical rigor to Keynesian theory, a contribution for which he became the first American economist to win the Nobel Prize.

For a generation of young Americans, however, Samuelson was the muse of the mixed economy—a term he used throughout his textbook. Yes, the United States relied heavily on private markets, Samuelson argued. But it was successful because it constrained and enabled those markets using public authority. "The private economy is not unlike a machine without an effective steering wheel or governor," Samuelson wrote in the first edition of *Economics* before he launched into the "modern man" passage that summed up the postwar zeitgeist.[8]

Yet a funny thing happened on the way from the first edition of *Economics* to the tenth: Samuelson gradually changed his tune. Under fire from conservative intellectuals, he started playing down the mixed economy. The first salvos came from outside the profession: William F. Buckley Jr. ripped into the "collectivist character" of *Economics* in his 1951 *God and Man at Yale*.[9] But by the 1970s, it was Milton Friedman, George Stigler, and other Chicago School economists leading the charge. To them, government was a drag on the economy—animated by ill-considered causes and beholden to special interests. Samuelson had defended postwar levels of taxation: "With affluence come greater interdependence and the desire to meet social needs, along with less need to meet urgent private necessities."[10] Friedman, by contrast, was "in favor of cutting taxes under any circumstances and for any excuse, for any reason, whenever it is possible."[11] Samuelson had the ear of JFK. Friedman had the ear of Barry Goldwater, whose 1960 manifesto *The Conscience of a Conservative* summed up the Chicago School message concisely: "I have little interest in streamlining government or in making it more efficient, for I mean to reduce its size."[12]

Whether Samuelson was responding to the critics or the conservative shift they exemplified, he progressively retreated from the "modern man" passage. In the fourth edition of *Economics*, published in 1958, he made his conclusion more impressionistic: "No longer is the modern man able to believe 'that government governs best that governs least'" became "No longer does modern man *seem to act as if* he believed . . ." In the 1973 edition, Samuelson cut the offending passage entirely. In subsequent editions, he retreated further. Rather than beginning with the various problems with the market that made "perfect competition" relatively rare, later editions *started* by outlining this microeconomic ideal. His publisher explained that the "leitmotif" of the new approach was the "rediscovery of the market."[13] As the historian Daniel Rodgers observes, "Samuelson's mixed economy had fallen into sharply distinct parts: markets and government, rhetorically at polar opposites from each other."[14]

What We Talk About When We Talk About Government

The idea that government and the market were rivals rather than partners represented a profound shift in political discourse. Even before Reagan proclaimed, "[G]overnment is not the solution to our problem; government is the problem," leading intellectuals from the right well through the center were turning toward a vision of government and markets as zero-sum opponents: competitors rather than complements.[15]

We can see this shift in many places: the rhetoric of politicians, the content of legal opinions, the arguments made in leading journals of ideas. But perhaps the most convincing marker of the transformation is the language used in the medium that captures political discourse most consistently over long spans of history: the newspaper.

Using the *New York Times*, the economist David George has charted dramatic shifts in the portrayal of government and markets over the past forty years. In the mid-twentieth century, government was seven times more likely to be described favorably than unfavorably. Words such as *efficient*, *competent*, and *creative* were far more likely to precede *government* or *public sector* than words like *inefficient* and *wasteful*. Between 1980 and 2009, however, the balance shifted—from seven times more positive descriptions to roughly equal numbers.[16] At the same time, references to government fell sharply overall, just as they did between Eisenhower's and Clinton's speeches. What we talk about when we talk about government, it seems, is to not talk about government at all.

Or at least not positively. Over the same period, stories used the term "big government" more and more often, despite the declining mention of "government." Between 1980 and 2009, the phrase appeared roughly twice as often each year as it had between 1930 and 1979—even though, again, less was said about government overall. As the linguist Geoffrey Nunberg observes, "big government" is invariably pejorative, "implying an overweening state that is 'doing something that the market could do better' or 'coercing people into doing what they ought to choose freely.'"[17] This sort of big government is clearly what Bill Clinton had in mind when he declared it to have ended. But whether or not the era of big government is over, the era of decrying big government is going strong.

The *Times* is hardly a bastion of conservative thinking, so we can be pretty sure that these changes don't reflect a sudden infusion of right-wingers into the paper's inner sanctum. Instead, they likely mirror a shift in broader political discussions—one both dramatic and simple: Government was becoming the villain; the market, the hero.

Consider the changing language used to describe government activity. To say government "acts" is neutral; to say it "interferes" or "intervenes" is to endorse the zero-sum relationship between state and market that became prominent in the 1970s.[18] And, in fact, the *Times* data show a growing shift from the neutral to the negative around this period. At the same time, unfavorable descriptions of "regulation" became much more common: From the 1930s through the 1970s, regulation was twice as likely to be described positively as negatively. From 1980 to 2000, the relationship was reversed, with negative descriptions outnumbering positive ones 2 to 1.

A similarly revealing transformation has played out in the words used to describe business. For much of the twentieth century, the most common term for someone who employed others was *capitalist*. Starting in the 1970s, however, another came to rival and then eclipse this traditional word: *entrepreneur*. The transformation can be seen not just in the *Times* but also in the tens of millions of English-language books tracked by Google, and it obviously carries a larger meaning. A capitalist finances production—half of the employer-employee relationship. An entrepreneur invents new products and even new ways of producing—the creative force behind prosperity. Indeed, in the *Times*, the word *creative* came to be associated increasingly with management rather than with workers. Where once workers were more often described as creative, by the 1980s, management was fifty times as likely to be cast as such.[19]

Not surprisingly, as corporate America's stature waxed, organized labor's waned. Even in the *Times*, unions were cast in favorable terms only a quarter of the time after 1980. This was a dramatic decline from previous decades, when positive references outnumbered negative ones.[20] Here again, the *Times* mirrored changes in politicians' rhetoric. In the New Deal era, according to a careful study of the Democratic Party's platforms, "labor was viewed as the advance agent of reform." But as organized labor declined, labor "receded entirely from the party's presidential agenda."[21] Workers and unions, it seemed, were so mid-twentieth century. The future of American capitalism was in the hands of the capitalists.

The rhetorical apotheosis of this transformation might well be "job creator." The phrase would not flower until the mid-2000s, at which point it would become ubiquitous. But the move toward seeing business as the visionary "creator" of jobs rather than the mere "provider" began much earlier. Starting in the 1970s, "job creation"—a phrase used rarely in prior decades—became more common than alternative wordings in the *Times*.

In this respect, the shift in rhetoric from Eisenhower to Clinton signaled far more than each man's idiosyncratic background or inclinations. If you study all presidential speeches from 1947 through the mid-2000s, you see the same trends.[22] On many issues, presidential positions have oscillated left and right based on the party label of the executive. But presidential rhetoric about the political system has headed in a single direction: toward more and more government bashing. The same is true of congressional rhetoric. The most common three-word phrases in the *Congressional Record* in the 1950s and 1960s were mostly nonpartisan and either unrelated to or favorable toward the mixed economy. In the 1970s, however, phrases such as "free enterprise system" and "lower tax brackets" became prevalent, especially on the Republican side of the aisle.[23] In every river of public discourse, the mixed economy was on the rocks.

The Great Persuasion?

To many, this rhetorical transformation is the story of a paradigm shift—*The Great Persuasion*, as Angus Burgin calls it in his sweeping history of free-market thinkers like Friedman and Friedrich Hayek.[24] Analysts in this mold are fond of quoting Keynes's famous declaration that "the power of vested interests is vastly exaggerated compared with the gradual encroachment of ideas."[25]

Others are more skeptical. They like to quote Upton Sinclair's more cynical observation: "It is difficult to get a man to understand something, when his salary depends upon his not understanding it."[26] In this view, ideas carry limited weight unless they align with material incentives. And when ideas conflict with those incentives, it is the ideas, not the incentives, that are ignored.

In the shift of opinion against the mixed economy, however, Keynes and Sinclair were both right. Ideas *were* crucial, especially in the initial right turn. The emergence of "stagflation"—the combination of inflation and stagnation—strengthened the hand of economic thinkers who argued that government couldn't manage the economy effectively. Had there not been vigorous critics of the mixed economy at the ready, had they not wielded a coherent and powerful set of arguments, these economic troubles surely would not have precipitated such a fundamental reversal.

Yet the rapid and durable repudiation of the mixed economy was hardly a "gradual encroachment of ideas." Instead, new understandings swept the field because they intersected with and guided powerful economic interests that were becoming more and more influential within American politics. Facing meager profits and depressed stock prices, business leaders mobilized to lobby Washington as never before. Fatefully, they were also increasingly inclined to accept the diagnosis offered by the new market fundamentalists: The source of their woes was not foreign competition or deindustrialization or hostile financial players; it was government. The changing economy didn't just change the conversation, in other words. It changed who had power and how those with power thought about their priorities.

Once the door opened to the new antigovernment stance, policy and profit-seeking reinforced one another. The free-market movement advocated financial deregulation and tax cuts, and these policies helped fuel a rapid and sweeping shift in corporate America. Companies faced intense pressure to become better integrated into an expanding global economy. Even more important, they faced intense pressure to become better integrated into an expanding financial sector. As corporate America orbited ever closer to Wall Street, it adopted Wall Street's priorities as its own: immediate stock returns, corporate financial engineering, and extremely high executive pay closely tied to share prices. On the other side, the constraint on top management created by organized labor was rapidly weakening, as unions struggled in an increasingly hostile climate.

The result was not just enormous fortunes going to a narrower and narrower slice of executives. It was also an enormous shift in power toward a new corporate elite much more hostile to the mixed economy, much less constrained by moderates in government or by organized labor, and much more in tune with the new celebration of the "free market." Ironically, by the time these changes had flowered fully, many of the industries that helped spark the new thinking and policies would be teetering on the brink or worse. But a new set of economic leaders was ready to carry the antigovernment message—in softer and harder forms—into both political parties.

That '70s Show

The immediate cause of this broader transformation was the economic turmoil of the 1970s. The decade was not the economic wasteland it is often remembered as today. Income growth was actually fairly healthy, and many social indicators, such as college graduation rates, continued their rapid improvement. Still, the decade witnessed a series of destabilizing shocks, none more destabilizing than stagflation—the combination of high inflation and economic stagnation that marked the end of the long postwar boom. It was Paul Samuelson who had coined the term but Milton Friedman who had predicted the outcome. In Friedman's eyes—and the eyes of more and more policy makers—stagflation proved that Keynesian macromanagement was a fool's errand that would inevitably break down in the face of market forces.[27]

In retrospect, the economic tumult of the 1970s looks less baffling than it did at the time. The surge of inflation reflected both singular shocks (notably, the 1973–74 oil embargo by the Organization of Petroleum Exporting Countries, or OPEC) and obvious policy mistakes (Johnson's guns-and-butter spending and Nixon's urging of loose monetary policy to secure his reelection).[28] Meanwhile, productivity growth was slowing, as the burst of economic activity after World War II gave way to the more normal expansion of rich countries at the edge of the technological frontier.[29] At the same time, the United States faced greater competition from its affluent trading partners as they recovered from wartime devastation.[30]

It was inflation, however, that captured the public's attention and drove the increasingly panicked national debate. Throughout the latter half of the 1970s, large majorities of Americans told the Gallup poll that inflation—never before a major response in the survey—was the number one problem facing the nation. In 1980 a peak of 83 percent cited it. (Three decades later, the most commonly identified problem would be "government.")[31] Part of the reason was that income tax brackets were not tied to inflation, so rising wages caused many households to pay higher tax rates even when the purchasing power of their incomes wasn't any greater. Indeed, one of Reagan's first moves upon assuming office was to index tax brackets to inflation, cutting off the automatic (and almost invisible) hike in tax revenues that had helped fuel postwar public investment.[32]

Stagflation raised the profile and influence of the critics of the mixed economy, and it shifted the national discussion from fostering growth to fighting inflation. Under pressure, Carter appointed the prominent inflation hawk Paul Volcker to head the Federal Reserve, where, as expected, he raised interest rates sharply. The move triggered the worst downturn since the 1930s and probably cost Carter the 1980 election.[33] It also decimated the economic reputation of the Democratic Party, paving the way for Reagan to pursue a very different vision of government's relation to the economy.

For all this, however, the challenges of the 1970s did not have to compromise the entire edifice of the mixed economy. Getting macroeconomic policy on track and confronting heightened foreign competition did not require unwinding government's constructive role in ensuring broad prosperity. Nor did popular pressures. Although voters headed right as inflation headed up, the conservative shift in public opinion was short-lived. The elite turn against the mixed economy, however, just kept going and going—and, in fact, intensified through subsequent decades. To understand the scope and persistence of the change, we need to look closer at the new titans coming to dominate the American economic landscape.

Financializing America

Pete Peterson

Nixon's response to the problems of the early 1970s was shaped by a fortysomething ex-industrialist on his economic team named Peter Peterson. A son of Greek immigrants with a knack for salesmanship, Peterson (known to most as Pete) had just stepped down as CEO of film equipment manufacturer Bell & Howell and had already made a name for himself with his acute diagnoses of the nation's changing role in the world economy. In 1972, when Maurice Stans stepped down to run the Committee for the Reelection of the President (soon at the center of the Watergate scandal), Nixon tapped Peterson to become the nation's twentieth secretary of commerce.[34]

Being There

By then, Peterson had seen plenty of the old economy from the inside. His first exposure came after he was kicked out of MIT in 1944 for cheating. MIT offered to expunge the black mark from his record if he went to work in the university's Radiation Laboratory (dubbed the Rad Lab), yet another creation of Vannevar Bush's federal scientific office. The eighteen-year-old Peterson cleared his name by purchasing supplies for the laboratory, unaware until later that he was contributing to the Manhattan Project.

Peterson's expulsion proved to be his first big break. After finishing his degree at Northwestern University (and before moving to Bell & Howell), he went to business school at the University of Chicago, where Friedman and Stigler made an enormous impression on him. "I was shaped by their basic principles from then to now," Peterson would write in his memoir, *The Education of an American Dreamer*. "They have stuck with me and proven far more practical than my Northwestern courses in retail inventory control and retail sales promotion. I often think how different my life would have been had the University of Chicago Graduate School of Business not been so close to my . . . office."[35]

Peterson's second big break was also unexpected: He was dumped by Nixon in 1973 amid Watergate palace intrigues. Fortunately for Peterson, dozens of corporate boards came calling, hoping to gain the prestige and connections that his background offered. He joined the investment firm Lehman Brothers, in part because he knew and liked Lehman principal George Ball, a Democrat who had served as undersecretary of state.[36] It was the first of many bipartisan ventures that would end up serving Peterson, if not the broader public, well.

Peterson was a networker who straddled the worlds of Washington and corporate America. His greatest gift, however, turned out to be his uncanny ability to move to greener pastures just as the last was about to wither. He left Bell & Howell before the bottom fell out of American manufacturing, and the Nixon administration just before it collapsed in scandal. He then went to Lehman, where he pushed the venerable institution to move toward high-risk investments. Weakened by trading losses, Lehman would be sold to Shearson/American Express—just after Peterson was pushed out. Then, in 2008, it would fail spectacularly in an inferno of toxic assets and deceptive accounting.[37]

The sale of Lehman made Peterson rich. He plowed the proceeds into a partnership with former Lehman associate Stephen Schwarzman. The two men pioneered a new model of high-yield investment known as private equity, calling their firm Blackstone. (The name was a play on those of the partners: *Schwarz* is German for "black"; *Petros*, Greek for "stone.") When Blackstone went public in 2007, Peterson and Schwarzman became billionaires. Again, Peterson had gotten out while the getting was good. Within a year, Blackstone's share price dropped 40 percent.[38] By then, however, Peterson had moved on to a new passion: spending his fortune to influence public debate.

On FIRE

Peterson always seemed to ride the wave to its crest, jumping away just as it crashed. But his rising fortune reflected not just excellent timing but also larger economic tides. He entered Wall Street at the beginning of a three-decades-long increase in the share of the American economy devoted to finance—to the buying and selling of assets rather than the production or exchange of goods. This development, often referred to as "financialization," battered workers caught in its disruptions and ushered in financial instabilities once thought solved. It also enriched and emboldened a new class of high-rolling executives—Peterson included—who were far more critical of the mixed economy than were the captains of industry they displaced.

When Peterson signed up with Lehman, manufacturing made up more than a quarter of national economic output. Finance, insurance, and real estate—FIRE, for short—was around 15 percent. By 2001, the two sectors' relative positions had reversed. Even more striking, profits in the FIRE sector had climbed from a fifth of total corporate profits in the 1970s to nearly half in 2001.[39]

The United States isn't the only country with a large financial sector. Yet American finance led the world in broadening and deepening the sector's role in the rest of the economy, and even today it remains unique. What makes it distinctive isn't the amount of financial leverage or the size of capital markets. It's the relationship between the financial sector and the rest of the economy. Starting in the late 1970s, finance became not a servant of larger corporate aims but more and more the driver of them.

At first, this switch was mostly inadvertent. With inflation raging, President Carter and Democrats in Congress lifted interest rate ceilings on Savings and Loans in 1980.[40] The change freed S&Ls to pay higher rates. It also sent them in search of higher returns to finance those rates—a search that would soon end in the nation's biggest banking crisis since the 1930s. But these were baby steps compared with what would come next. By the early 1980s, free-market ideology, Reagan's election, and the increasing sway of Wall Street had started an exuberant wave of financial deregulation that would continue for nearly three decades.

Fomenting the Shareholder Revolution

The first of these new deregulation warriors was a Wall Street conservative with a similar name to his boss's: Donald Regan, Treasury secretary to Ronald Reagan. Fresh from a decade of running Merrill Lynch, Regan declared that his top priority was "deregulation of financial institutions . . . as quickly as possible."[41] Within two years, Reagan and Regan, working with a receptive Congress, wiped out many of the rules that had restrained finance for the previous sixty years. Gone were most of the restrictions on S&Ls. Gone were most of the rules that stabilized the mortgage market. For the first time, the federal government allowed companies to buy back their own shares to raise stock prices. For the first time, the federal government allowed the pooling of mortgages into so-called mortgaged-backed securities—the risky investment vehicles that would eventually destroy Lehman. And for the first time, corporate raiders started taking on established companies, financing buyouts with massive amounts of new borrowing.

Today, when it is routine to buy and sell corporations like commodities, it is hard to convey what a fundamental shift the takeover movement represented. Since the rise of the modern corporation in the late nineteenth century, business financing had presented a public face that conflicted with private realities. On paper, corporations were beholden to shareholders. Yet because most companies were owned by a multitude of diffuse shareholders, the ability of shareholders to direct managers was limited. Moreover, established companies financed their internal investments mainly through retained earnings instead of external sources, which further insulated them from outside pressure. Managers were stewards rather than servants; their job was to look out for the long-term interests of the organization rather than the short-term entreaties of investors. Indeed, Adolf A. Berle Jr. and Gardiner C. Means, in their 1932 classic *The Modern Corporation and Private Property*, went so far as to suggest that corporate ownership and corporate control had become so distinct that executives were largely unaccountable to shareholders.[42]

That all changed in the 1980s. If you were a Fortune 500 executive in the 1970s, you had much to fret about. But you didn't have to worry about hostile takeovers. Now you did: Between 1980 and 1990, one-third of the Fortune 500 ceased to exist. The companies still standing were battle scarred. A third had experienced hostile bids in the prior decade. Two-thirds had adopted antitakeover defenses—designed mostly with the security of top management in mind rather than companies' long-term interests.[43] With all the churning, the tenure of corporate executives was becoming shorter. The imperative of keeping up stock prices—to protect against takeovers, not to mention deliver the big rewards that more mobile CEOs demanded—was becoming greater. Indeed, CEOs were inviting the barbarians into the castle, hiring high-paid Wall Street consultants who could help firms reengineer themselves so that more hostile players wouldn't.

The public rationale for takeovers was that companies had become complacent and needed discipline. Yet the takeover model depended on cashing out, not maintaining control. That was because the enormous returns that corporate raids could yield reflected the enormous amount of exotic debt relied upon by corporate raiders. Just as with a home mortgage, making a small "down payment" on a company and financing the rest through borrowing transformed even small gains into astronomical returns. To make the deal sweeter still, debt was deductible as a business expense under the corporate tax code. For most companies, interest payments on debt were negligible. But for newly acquired companies loaded with debt, such payments could easily exceed earnings, making the deduction a major source of profit—and a major subsidy for takeovers.[44]

Because the purchase was leveraged, returns—and losses—were magnified. A quick payoff was essential to finance the borrowing and avoid potential ruin. For this reason, raiders did not go after struggling companies. They went after companies with undervalued stock and predictable cash flow that could be used to pay off debt.[45] Big conglomerates were a favorite target: They had lots of parts that could be liquidated before the companies were sold to another buyer or taken public again. Companies with "excess" cash and "overfunded" pensions were also attractive. Raiders were less willing to talk about "excess" employees. But along with exotic new securities, the industry developed ever more disingenuous euphemisms for laying off workers: *restructuring, trimming fat, downsizing, delayering,* and, most Orwellian of all, *workforce optimization.*

LBO's

Here again shifts in federal policy were critical. By filling the National Labor Relations Board with appointees hostile to organized labor and then breaking the high-profile strike of air-traffic controllers in 1981, Reagan signaled what had already become clear: Labor was down, business was up, and government had left the field.[46] Unions had pushed for a major rewriting of federal law in 1978 to make it easier for workers to organize as production shifted south and companies adopted more aggressive anti-union strategies. The bill had been defeated by a Senate filibuster—rare at the time—in response to unprecedented corporate political mobilization. The writing was on the wall: From the early 1980s on, workers would increasingly bear the dislocations of adjusting to new economic realities. If the model of the 1950s and 1960s had been "retain and reinvest," the model that replaced it was "downsize and distribute."[47]

The celebrated goal of the new model was "shareholder value," a phrase now so familiar that its radical implications are often forgotten. Business leaders had always seen healthy stock returns as one of the key goals of the corporation. But it was not the *only* goal. At least as important were the long-term growth of the company and the standing of its workers, as well as its responsibilities to its customers and its community. The traditional view was summarized by GE's longtime chairman Owen Young, who led the company from the 1920s through World War II: "Stockholders are confined to a maximum return equivalent to a risk premium. The remaining profit stays in the enterprise, is paid out in higher wages, or is passed on to the customer."[48] As late as the early 1980s, the nation's largest organization representing CEOs, the Business Roundtable, noted that "balancing the shareholders' expectation of maximum return against other priorities is one of the fundamental problems confronting corporate management."[49]

By the 1990s, however, the Roundtable had dropped all references to "balancing" and embraced the constant maximization of shareholder returns. As two economists explain, the new credo signaled "a fundamental shift in the concept of the American corporation": "from a view of it as a productive enterprise and stable institution serving the needs of a broad spectrum of stakeholders to a view of it as a bundle of assets to be bought and sold with an exclusive goal of maximizing shareholder value."[50] The simplistic division of the economy into markets versus government paralleled a view of corporations as bundles of assets, independent from their social context.

This new conception of the corporation also carried profound implications for American understandings of shared prosperity. The valorization of shareholders (even if it was often a cover for the acquisitive aims of top executives or hostile-takeover engineers) challenged the notion that wealth was a social creation that rested on the efforts of multiple stakeholders, including labor and government. Instead, it implied that enhanced prosperity was generated by investors and executives, with their entrepreneurial creativity and investment daring. The Solow residual—the increased productivity due to enhanced knowledge and technical capacity within society—was not, in this view, a collective creation. It was the product of the "job creators" and "risk takers" who were rightly enjoying more and more rewards.

The Rise of the New Economic Elite

LBO = merchant banking

This new world was the one Pete Peterson wanted to be part of when he came to Lehman. Peterson saw a lucrative future in what he called "merchant banking," a polite way of describing leveraged buyouts. The rumpled trader who would oust him, Lew Glucksman, recalls that "Pete . . . was obsessed with the amount of money William Simon made selling Gibson. And he couldn't stop talking about it."[51]

Simon, a former Treasury secretary under Presidents Nixon and Gerald Ford, had bought and sold Gibson Greeting Cards to make over $60 million on a $330,000 investment.[52] (He would go from Wall Street to running the John M. Olin Foundation, a philanthropy now famous for funding the "counter-intelligentsia," as Simon called it, of antigovernment thinkers.)[53] No doubt Peterson thought that he, a former commerce secretary, could do at least as well. In time, he would. He would also reshape the way those around him thought about markets, government, and American prosperity.

Capitalist Tools

In 1982, the year that William Simon bought out Gibson Greetings, *Forbes* magazine published the first of its iconic lists of the four hundred wealthiest Americans. Topping the ranking was an octogenarian shipping magnate, Daniel Ludwig, with an estimated fortune of $2 billion (around $5 billion today, adjusted for inflation).[54] Ludwig was one of only two billionaires on the list. The entire four hundred were worth around $225 billion (in current dollars). Readers seemed impressed. One federal judge, dismissing a lawsuit by a millionaire who wished to stay off the roster, declared, "Money is power, and the wealthy wield great power and influence economically, socially, and politically in this country, and the American public has a right to know who they are."[55]

If money is power, however, that first four hundred were a bunch of weaklings compared with those to come. In 2014 *every* member of the Forbes 400 was a billionaire; indeed, 113 US billionaires were left off the list because they fell below the entry price of $1.55 billion.[56] The combined net worth of the list tickled $2.3 trillion—ten times its 1982 level after adjusting for inflation.[57]

Those who looked closely at the Forbes 400 might have noticed another change: Wall Street increasingly eclipsed Main Street as a generator of outsized fortunes. In 1982 barely one in twenty-five of the Forbes 400 had made their money in the financial sector. Thirty years later, more than one in five had. No other sector—not technology, not retail trade, not media, not energy, not real estate, not consumer goods—had as large a share. Nor had any other increased in prominence as much as finance had, not even that quintessential twenty-first-century industry, computer technology. Finance and computing enjoyed about the same number of spots on the list in 1982. Three decades further into the digital era, finance had about two-thirds more spots. High-tech might have topped the list with Bill Gates, but high finance dominated the rest.[58]

When Pete Peterson left Lehman in 1983, his official salary was $225,000. Year-end bonuses and other perks raised the total to an after-tax equivalent of roughly $5 million. With his 1 percent stake in any future sale of Lehman, as well as equity in the firm and severance benefits, Peterson walked away with $18 million.[59]

Fast-forward to 2007, when Blackstone went public. On the day of the sale, Peterson made $1.9 *billion*, a hundred times what he had upon his departure from Lehman. His earnings in his last year at Blackstone were $200 million. Peterson's partner, Steve Schwarzman, walked away from the deal with nearly $10 billion—after a year in which his take-home pay was almost $400 million.[60]

Mining Corporate America

Schwarzman was Peterson's alter ego. An aggressive deal maker, he was as publicly lavish as the Depression-baby Peterson was austere. A diminutive five foot six next to the six-foot-plus Peterson, he was big in ambition. As a young Lehman partner, he saw the future in Simon's Gibson deal and the even more spectacular 1979 buyout of Houdaille Industries by the private equity firm Kohlberg Kravis Roberts & Co. (Kohlberg made out well; Houdaille, a large conglomerate with almost eight thousand workers, was dismembered, and its core business so saddled with debt that it succumbed to Japanese competition.) Years later, Schwarzman still remembered his reaction to the Houdaille deal: "I read that prospectus, looked at the capital structure, and realized the returns that could be achieved. I said to myself, 'This is a gold mine.'"[61]

Schwarzman found many gold mines. It was he who almost single-handedly brokered the sale of Lehman to Shearson/American Express. It was he who engineered the initial public offering of Blackstone that made Peterson and him multibillionaires. (By then, Peterson was so disengaged from the company that he wasn't made aware of the IPO until six months into its planning.) [62] And it was he who would come to personify the excesses of the financial industry even as he racked up bigger and bigger victories.

On the eve of the Blackstone IPO, Schwarzman celebrated his sixtieth birthday with some friends—friends such as Barbara Walters, Colin Powell, New York mayor Michael Bloomberg, and the chief executives of all the major Wall Street banks. The musical headliner was British rock star Rod Stewart. The warm-up act consisted of soul singer Patti LaBelle backed up by not one but two Harlem choirs. Another opener, comedian Martin Short, joked that the Seventh Regiment Armory, where the event was held, was "more intimate" than Schwarzman's $30 million penthouse on Park Avenue.[63]

Among the new financial wizards, Schwarzman's astronomical earnings were nothing extraordinary. The year of Blackstone's IPO, *Institutional Investor*'s blog, *Alpha*, released its annual list of the top twenty-five hedge fund managers. For the first time, the top three earned more than $1 billion *each*. Combined, the twenty-five managers pulled in $14 billion. "So much for steel, oil, railroads, and real estate—or microchips and software, for that matter," the report announced. Hedge funds were "the best bet for making the biggest bucks the fastest in the postindustrial world."[64] Especially so because of an obscure provision of the tax code dating back to a very different Wall Street. Partners in private equity firms took most of their pay as a share of the investments they oversaw:

other people's investments. But they were allowed to treat these "carried interest" earnings as capital gains subject to a low tax rate. By 2014, Blackstone was rolling in $4.3 billion a year in profits with just 2,300 employees—more than the investment banking giant Morgan Stanley, with 55,000 workers. Thanks to the creative use of the carried-interest tax break, it paid just 4.3 percent in taxes on its profits.[65]

The year of Blackstone's IPO marked another milestone: It was the year that the share of household income going to the richest 1 percent of households equaled that reached on the eve of the stock market crash of 1929, with nearly one in every four dollars accruing to this tiny slice of American society. The gains were even more concentrated than this staggering number suggests, since roughly half of the top 1 percent's income went to an even smaller group: the top 0.1 percent. In 2007 the top 0.1 percent averaged more than $7 million in annual income, its share of national income having increased fourfold over the prior generation.[66]

Who are these fortunate 0.1 percenters? Tax records show that most of them belong to two groups: financial executives (around 20 percent) and corporate executives outside finance (around 40 percent). (By way of comparison, sports and media stars—often singled out in popular commentary on the rich—make up just 3 percent.)[67] In other words, the majority of the superrich are corporate and investment managers. What's more, nearly all of these managers enjoy close ties to Wall Street—and not just because they operate in a business environment fundamentally reshaped by financialization. At the top, most compensation takes the form of stock options and other capital gains. This group looks very different from the business elite described in 1950 by the great management theorist Peter Drucker: "Where only twenty years ago the bright graduate of the Harvard Business School aimed at a job with a New York Stock Exchange house, he now seeks employment with a steel, oil, or automobile company. . . . There is very little room in an industrial economy for international banking, international capital movements, and international commodity trading on which the power and position of the 'capitalist' ruling groups rested primarily."[68]

Of course, the new economic elite isn't a monolithic "ruling group." Those at the top include Democrats as well as Republicans, liberals as well as conservatives. Nor do they operate as some kind of secret cabal, privately coordinating their assaults on the mixed economy. Still, the changing face of the economic elite matters a great deal. As we saw in chapter 5, the moderate elements of the business community were critical to the establishment and legitimation of the mixed economy. The public voices of *this* elite were restrained and engaged—a reflection of wartime experience, regular engagement in national and community affairs, the constraints of labor and moderate Republicans, and the relatively modest economic gap between those at the top of corporate America and rank-and-file workers.

Today's economic elites look very different. They are tied less closely to local production and investment. They are tied more closely to Wall Street. And they have much greater resources relative to the rest of society. They are also, we shall see, much more skeptical of the mixed economy. Again, the views of those at the top are far from monolithic (and if we are to understand fully their engagement with government, we have to consider not just their individual attitudes but also the organized activities of the nation's major business associations—the subject of the next chapter). But on core economic issues, the ideological middle of the new economic elite is far to the right of the postwar business elite, not to mention the midpoint of the contemporary American electorate. Indeed, we can see its two central tendencies in the two men who founded Blackstone: Steve Schwarzman and Pete Peterson.

Masters of the Universe

"Who is John Galt?" That question appears again and again in Ayn Rand's *Atlas Shrugged*. In the book's morality tale of capitalists overcoming government collectivism, Galt is the handsome genius who leads a "strike" by the "producers" that ultimately causes the world economy to collapse. The message of *Atlas Shrugged* is simple: Government destroys freedom; only creative capitalists produce wealth; everyone else is a "looter," a "moocher," an "incompetent," feeding on the elite's innovations. In one of Galt's most memorable speeches, he declares: "The man at the top of the intellectual pyramid contributes the most to all those below him, but gets nothing except his material payment, receiving no intellectual bonus from others to add to the value of his time. The man at the bottom who, left to himself, would starve in his hopeless ineptitude, contributes nothing to those above him, but receives the bonus of all of their brains."[69]

When Rand's book appeared in 1957, it was greeted with savage rebukes by reviewers. "It is probably the worst piece of large fiction written since Miss Rand's equally weighty 'The Fountainhead,'" judged Robert Kirsch in the *Los Angeles Times*. "It would be hard to find such a display of grotesque eccentricity outside an asylum."[70]

A half century later, however, the book luxuriated in the embrace of leading political and economic figures, from Fed chair Alan Greenspan to House GOP budget guru, 2012 VP candidate, and current House speaker Paul Ryan. In 2008, sales of the book reached record highs, and conservative commentators spoke openly about business owners "going Galt." As one *Forbes* column gushed in 2012, "Galt epitomizes all that is glorious of capitalism in its purist form—innovation, self-reliance, and freedom from government interference."[71]

Hard Randianism

Galt also epitomizes a way of thinking that has become much more common among the nation's elite. As already hinted, we call it "Randianism"—or, since we'll soon look at its softer cousin, "*hard* Randianism." The distinctive core of hard Randianism isn't laissez-faire (a very old fancy); it's the division of the world into a persecuted minority that heroically generates prosperity and a freeloading majority that uses government to steal from this small, creative elite.

Within the shifting ideological climate of the post-1980s era, it was perhaps inevitable that the rise of the superrich would foster a new dog-eat-dog mentality. Still, the increasing openness and stridency of these views bear notice. For most of the top 0.1 percent, the incentives to make a public display of affection for libertarianism are limited. Why alienate shareholders and consumers or invite the attraction of nosy and noisy activists? Better to speak softly and spend behind the scenes if necessary.

It was easier to be quiet, however, when only labor unions and the leftmost wing of the Democratic Party questioned the wisdom of financial deregulation or tax reductions for big incomes and estates. In the wake of the 2008 financial crisis—when Greenspan himself felt forced to admit his "model" of the economy was wrong—that was no longer true. Facing increased scrutiny, the investor class now had to explain why it deserved the friendly policies of prior decades.

Steve Schwarzman rose to the occasion. Speaking to a nonprofit board in 2010, he complained of a "war" between President Obama and financial firms such as his. Obama's proposal to eliminate the carried-interest tax break was "like when Hitler invaded Poland in 1939." Schwarzman walked back the remark, but he also became one of the top supporters of Republican presidential candidate Mitt Romney.[72]

Nazi analogies turned out to be popular. Hedge fund manager Leon Cooperman compared Obama's election to the rise of the Third Reich. Billionaire investor Tom Perkins took to the *Wall Street Journal* editorial page to warn of a looming "Kristallnacht" if the "rising tide of hatred against the successful one percent" was not stopped. Asked later if he regretted the remarks, Perkins insisted "the parallel holds."[73]

As extreme as such statements were, they suggested just how deep the sense of grievance ran. Indeed, Cooperman became something of a folk hero within the financial industry by writing President Obama an open letter condemning his and his "'minions' role in setting the tenor of the rancorous debate now roiling us that smacks of what so many have characterized as 'class warfare.'" (Hedge fund manager Anthony Scaramucci told a writer for *The New Yorker* that Cooperman was the "pope" of the industry revolt against the president.) "The divisive, polarizing tone of your rhetoric," Cooperman wrote, "is cleaving a widening gulf, at this point as much visceral as philosophical, between the downtrodden and those best positioned to help them."[74]

Gilded Bootstraps

The complaints of the new superrich embodied two claims. The first was that those at the top fully deserved their riches. In 2012 the top earner on *Institutional Investor's Alpha* list (with $3.9 billion in pay) was Ray Dalio, chief of Bridgewater Associates, the world's largest hedge fund. Among financiers, Dalio was best known for his online business-strategy tract *Principles*. "Self-interest and society's interests are generally symbiotic," declares *Principles*. "Society rewards those who give it what it wants. That is why how much money people have earned is a rough measure of how much they gave society what it wanted."[75]

Before the financial crisis, the head of Citigroup, Sandy Weill, was similarly self-congratulatory: "People can look at the last twenty-five years and say this is an incredibly unique period of time. We didn't rely on somebody else to build what we built."

Weill's up-by-his-bootstraps assertion was obviously false. Before Citigroup became a ward of the state during the financial crisis, Weill displayed a trophy of sorts in his office: a four-foot wide piece of wood etched with his portrait and the words "The Shatterer of Glass-Steagall." The Glass-Steagall Act was the New Deal legislation that separated commercial and investment banks to minimize the risk of bank failures and self-dealing. Without the act's repeal—signed happily by President Clinton in 1999 at the urging of Weill and his partners—Weill could not have built what he built: a megabank that paid him a staggering $785 million over five years.[76]

Nor was Weill alone in benefiting from financial deregulation and other policies friendly to the investor class. From the 1970s through the 2000s, one of the best predictors of rising pay in the financial sector was the pace of deregulation—which explained perhaps half of the difference between what workers in finance earned and what similarly skilled workers in other sectors took home.[77] As we will see in chapter 9, the financial sector also enjoyed many other favorable policies. Most notably, the consolidated institutions that came to dominate Wall Street received a huge implicit subsidy because investors were willing to accept lower returns from them, assuming—rightly, it turned out in 2008—that government wouldn't let them fail if their risky bets turned sour.[78]

Skyrocketing financial pay drove up CEO earnings in nonfinancial companies, too. For one, it raised the benchmark against which all executives' salaries were judged. Even more important, it encouraged CEOs to demand more and more pay in various forms of stock options. The justification was that executives prospered only when the firms that they led did well. The reality, according to many studies, was different: that executives profited more from luck and short-term measures to boost stock prices than from excellent long-term performance.[79] CEO compensation routinely failed to include even basic safeguards against lucky profits, short-termism, and heads-I-win-tails-you-lose deals, even as it hid from public accounting enormous numbers of goodies (company jets, golden parachutes, lavish retirement packages) that might have provoked shareholder or public pushback.

To be sure, many CEOs were enormously talented. Yet talent wasn't sufficient to explain why American CEOs earned so much more than CEOs in other nations or than corporate heads had in the past, or why their marginal tax rates were at least 50 percent lower as a share of their much higher pay than the rates paid by CEOs of the immediate postwar era. To understand these outcomes required looking beyond the workings of the corporate world to the increasingly solicitous American policy environment.

Pity the Rich

The second distinct claim embodied in the complaints of the top 0.1 percent was that government and the public were parasitic on the accomplishments of the economic elite. Cooperman, in his letter to President Obama, wrote that the rich "employ many millions of taxpaying people, pay their salaries, provide them with health care coverage, start new companies, found new industries, create new products, fill store shelves at Christmas, and keep the wheels of commerce and progress (and indeed of government, by generating the income whose taxation funds it) moving." At a public event, he elaborated: "Our problem, frankly, is as long as the president remains anti-wealth, anti-business, anti-energy, anti-private-aviation, he will never get the business community behind him. The problem and the complication is the forty or fifty percent of the country on the dole that support him."[80]

Randian Thinking Tom Perkins complained, "I don't think people have any idea what the one percent is actually contributing to America." He suggested the problem might be fixed with a change in American voting rules: "You don't get to vote unless you pay a dollar in taxes . . . If you pay a million in taxes, you should get a million votes. How's that?"[81]

Wall Street was not the only place that Randian thinking flourished. Even in the more progressive Silicon Valley, similar grumblings could be heard. In a 2009 essay, the young cofounder of PayPal, Peter Thiel, wrote: "In our time, the great task for libertarians is to find an escape from politics in all its forms—from the totalitarian and fundamentalist catastrophes to the unthinking demos that guides so-called 'social democracy.' . . . The fate of our world may depend on the effort of a single person who builds or propagates the machinery of freedom that makes the world safe for capitalism."[82] Along with Patri Friedman—grandson of Milton Friedman—Thiel founded the Seasteading Institute, a non-profit dedicated to creating a floating city in international waters to realize the libertarian dream of a pure free market.[83]

In the origin myth of the top 0.1 percent, globalization had given rise to a new meritocracy with a steep pyramid of value. Executives were no longer managers. They were supertalented entrepreneurs who produced the economic growth on which an ever-expanding public sector relied. American business needed the stern discipline of constant reinvention that only financial markets could provide. And, according to even relatively moderate voices within the new economic elite, so did the American middle class.

A Kinder, Gentler Libertarianism

Randianism was a strong brew—too strong for many in corporate circles. It would be a mistake, however, to ignore the watered-down form of it that was imbibed much more widely. Peter Thiel's blunt libertarianism was an outlier in Democratic-leaning Silicon Valley. But open disdain for government was mainstream. Google's CEO, Larry Page, envisioned a utopian "Google Island" where technologists could innovate free of government's heavy hand. To Chamath Palihapitiya, a tech venture capitalist (and part owner of the Golden State Warriors), "Companies are transcending power now. We are becoming the eminent vehicles for change and influence. . . . If companies shut down, the stock market would collapse. If the government shuts down, nothing happens, and we all move on, because it just doesn't matter."[84]

Never mind that if government had shut down in the decades after World War II, none of the basic components of the iPhone or Google's search algorithm or, for that matter, the World Wide Web would have come to exist. Steve Jobs was well known for his disdain for government's ineptness. Yet he never could have created his pioneering products or made billions without the enormous reservoir of public investment and publicly trained talent that nurtured the innovation hub of Silicon Valley and fed directly into every major element of the technology on which he drew.

The Penny-Pinching Plutocrat

An even better representative of what might be called "soft Randianism," however, is Pete Peterson. No Steve Schwarzman, Peterson is a moderate by the standards of the new elite. For one, he does not flaunt his vast wealth. "I'm not one that really enjoys living large," Peterson wrote in his 2009 memoir. "I have no desire to be a conspicuous consumer. When I see a thirtysomething hedge funder loudly revving up his red Ferrari convertible in the Hamptons, I feel much more contempt than envy."[85]

Yet Peterson has proved happy to spend conspicuously on one thing: building political support for big spending cuts. In the early 1980s, he emerged as one the most vocal deficit hawks in the nation. After becoming a billionaire, he pledged $1 billion to a new private foundation headed by him, his wife, and his son Michael. The aim of the Peter G. Peterson Foundation, in its founder's words, was to tackle "our nation's massive, unsustainable debts and deficits."[86]

Peterson's obsession with the debt began around the time he started at Lehman. His first high-profile article, published in the *New York Times Magazine* in 1982, was titled "No More Free Lunch for the Middle Class." It advocated steep cuts in retirement and health benefits to make these programs a safety net for the needy rather than insurance protections for the middle class.[87] In his memoir, Peterson complained, "I see an indulgent country living almost entirely in the moment, afflicted with an aggravated case of myopia, and a sense of entitlement, one of my least favorite words."[88]

The greatest example of this "indulgence," in Peterson's telling, was Social Security: "a vast Ponzi scheme" that would go "bankrupt subsidizing middle-class and affluent Americans."[89] Social Security was, in fact, restructured substantially in 1983. But Peterson deemed the bipartisan commission chaired by Alan Greenspan a disappointment because it "asked no sizable sacrifice from anyone who would retire for another twenty years."[90] Over the coming quarter century, even as Social Security declined as a source of income for the aged and secure private pensions disappeared, Peterson churned out book after book about how the bipartisan support for Social Security and Medicare was bankrupting the nation.

Peterson's books all had the same conclusion: The middle class was living large, and benefits had to be cut. He had almost nothing to say about how to restrain health costs—the fastest-rising part of federal government, and a distinctively American pathology—beyond cutting benefits. Nor did he see much role for government other than providing a safety net. Peterson derided those who might see "government intervention as a spur to prosperity." He joked, "Perhaps there exists a major 'industrial' policy that actually accomplished its grandiose purposes without baleful side effects. If so, however, the story is a well-guarded secret."[91]

Rise of the Soft Randians

Peterson was hardly a voice in the wilderness. Soft Randians could be found throughout the business world and within both parties. Indeed, as the GOP moved right, the Democratic Party became their natural home. In part, this was because of the tighter and tighter links between the Democratic economic establishment and Wall Street, which we will look at in chapter 9. Many of the key soft Randians were tied to Democratic policy making through financial-executive-turned-DC-insider Robert Rubin. The former cochair of Goldman Sachs served as Clinton's Treasury secretary and, in that capacity, helped push financial deregulation, balanced budgets, and modest new efforts on behalf of the disadvantaged—the triple package that came to be known as "Rubinomics."[92] (Rubin would then take a role as "senior adviser" at Citigroup, the financial conglomerate that Clinton had enabled with Rubin's support; the firm went down in flames amid the 2008 financial crisis but not before Rubin had earned $25 million.)[93]

Other soft Randians included Larry Summers, Rubin's successor as Treasury secretary, an academic economist who also championed deregulation. Shortly after leaving the Treasury, Summers opined: "There is something about this epoch in history that really puts a premium on incentives, on decentralization, on allowing small economic energy to bubble up rather than a more top-down, more directed approach."[94] Summers knew something about incentives: he earned millions by working with hedge funds and other financial institutions after leaving office.[95]

But nobody spent like Pete Peterson. Even by the high-rolling standards of the day, his advocacy set new records. The foundation funded the Peterson Institute for International Economics, the Committee for a Responsible Federal Budget, the Concord Coalition, the Comeback America Initiative, and even a new web-based media outlet, the *Fiscal Times*. Peterson financed a string of youth-oriented organizations and invested in the development of a high school curriculum, "Understanding Fiscal Responsibility." For several years, he funded a series of town hall meetings across the nation that brought together thousands of Americans to hear frightening warnings about the budget.[96] (Apparently not frightening enough: When the meetings were done, 85 percent of participants backed raising Social Security taxes rather than cutting benefits.)[97]

Later, as the United States struggled through the deepest economic downturn since the Great Depression and most Americans understandably focused on the problem of unemployment, these and other Peterson-funded initiatives radiated across the nation. Huge events involving political luminaries such as Bill Clinton captured media attention and helped make the debt the number one topic in Washington. According to an analysis of media coverage by the *National Journal*, stories about the deficit eclipsed stories about unemployment beginning in early 2010—at a time when the unemployment rate was still above 9 percent and long-term unemployment remained at record levels. In early 2011 there were over two hundred stories per month on the deficit in the nation's five biggest newspapers, compared with just sixty-five on the jobless.[98]

The policy impact of this impressive attention to Peterson's cause is difficult to determine. But after the initial recovery package in 2009, overall government policy pivoted rapidly toward austerity. During the steep economic downturn of 1981, public employment rose steadily even during the darkest days. By contrast, after 2009, for the first time in modern American history, it actually fell, as state budgets plummeted and federal employment stagnated. By 2012, the gap between the historical pattern of public job growth and the post-2009 crunch—even without taking into account the expansionary effects of public spending on private employment—amounted to more than one million jobs.[99]

Pain Above Party

The roster of political figures involved in Peterson's efforts came from both parties. In 2011 the major Peterson-backed groups handed out a "Fiscy" Award to Republican budget chair Paul Ryan for his "leadership on confronting our fiscal challenges." Ryan's "leadership" consisted of putting out a budget plan that slashed spending but never specified where those cuts would come from and included so many tax cuts that, even with all the magic asterisks, it contemplated deep deficits for years to come.[100] Apparently, reducing benefits for the middle class was leadership enough.

In 2010 Peterson also funded the staff of an ostensibly federally run commission authorized to come up with a budget compromise. When the commission failed to produce a plan with sufficient support to pass on to Congress, he created a commission of his own and employed the bipartisan duo that had run the federal predecessor: Democrat Erskine Bowles (former chief of staff to President Clinton) and Republican Alan Simpson (an ex-senator from Wyoming). Bowles had spent the last decade earning millions on corporate boards. He raised eyebrows by praising Paul Ryan, who defected from the federal commission's proposal because it countenanced higher taxes. But Simpson earned the greater attention when, in an email to a women's group, he called Social Security "a milk cow with 310 million tits!"[101]

Despite these off-message moments, media coverage of Peterson's initiatives was overwhelmingly favorable. Allying with Peterson was portrayed as an act of statesmanship rather than an endorsement of a specific, contestable viewpoint. When Peterson launched the Campaign to Fix the Debt, in 2012, 127 of the nation's top CEOs signed up, with many donating $1 million of their own money to the cause. One of the enthusiastic backers of Fix the Debt, Jimmy Lee, vice chairman of JPMorgan Chase & Company, likened the nation's challenge to that of a troubled company: "Some companies tinker, just sort of tinker around the edges. Other companies, on the other hand, really recognize the problem . . . and start thinking about the twenty-, fifty-, hundred-year future of the company and spend some time trying to fix it in a really big, material way."[102]

In the corporate parlance that appealed to soft Randians, "fixing things" meant "downsizing"—downsizing government and downsizing the unrealistic expectations of the middle class that government had fostered. "America's lifestyle expectations are far too high and need to be adjusted so we have less things and a smaller, better existence," explained one billionaire, Jeff Greene, who had made his fortune betting against subprime mortgages. Greene spoke in Davos, Switzerland, at the World Economic Forum's annual gathering of top public officials and corporate leaders. Greene had traveled to the forum in a private jet, accompanied by two nannies for his children. He reported he was planning a conference to be held at a fancy hotel in Palm Beach, Florida, titled "Closing the Gap."[103]

Two Americas

At the same time that the complaints of the top 0.1 percent were providing a vivid image of America's changing elite, a more systematic picture was emerging from academic research. And what it found was what

F. Scott Fitzgerald had said long ago of the world of privilege he chronicled: "The rich are very different from you and me."[104]

Thinking Like a Millionaire

Perhaps the simplest question tackled by this new research is also the most difficult: What do the superrich, as a group, think about politics and policy? Difficult, because the very rich rarely show up in opinion surveys. Never do more than a handful get contacted, much less deign to respond—that is, until 2011, when a team of political scientists used an intensive interview strategy to reach a sufficiently large sample of wealthy citizens to chart their opinions. The average wealth of the respondents was over $14 million; average annual incomes exceeded $1 million. And they turned out to be very different from you and me. As the study's three authors—the political scientists Benjamin Page, Larry Bartels, and Jason Seawright—explained,

> Our evidence indicates that the wealthy are much more concerned than other Americans about budget deficits. The wealthy are much more favorable toward cutting social welfare programs, especially Social Security and health care. They are considerably less supportive of several jobs and income programs, including an above-poverty-level minimum wage, a "decent" standard of living for the unemployed, increasing the Earned Income Tax Credit, and having the federal government "see to"—or actually provide—jobs for those who cannot find them in the private sector. . . . Wealthy Americans are much less willing than others to provide broad educational opportunities. . . . They are less willing to pay more taxes in order to provide health coverage for everyone, and they are much less supportive of tax-financed national health insurance. The wealthy tend to favor lower estate tax rates and to be less eager to increase income taxes on high-income people.[105]

Perhaps the most arresting finding was that the richer the respondent, the more conservative he or she generally was on economic issues. This result was more than a statistical artifact: The richest of the superrich were also more likely to be Republicans, but that didn't explain their increased conservatism. At the same time, other differences—age, race, gender, even occupation—mattered little. Upton Sinclair would have been unsurprised. The greater the potential conflict between ideology and income, the larger self-interest loomed.

One Dollar, One Vote

Do these distinctive positions of the affluent make a difference? Apparently so: In a blockbuster study published in 2013, two political scientists, Martin Gilens and the just-quoted Benjamin Page, examined a familiar question: How many of the policies that the public supports become law? But they gave it a novel twist: They separated out the opinions of the bottom, the middle, and the top of the income distribution. (Of course, because these were typical opinion surveys, their definition of the top was pretty broad—survey respondents at the 90th percentile.) They also calculated where major interest groups such as the Chamber of Commerce stood on each of the issues covered by their survey data.[106]

The result? When all these groupings were considered, neither the middle class nor the poor seemed to have *any* influence. Instead, whether policy changed related most strongly to whether those at the top of the economic ladder supported the change. And among major interest groups, it was business groups that were the most influential.

Of course, this upper-class tilt doesn't mean government never passed laws that poor or middle-class voters wanted. When it did, however, they were usually laws that the well off and business groups wanted, too. On many issues, in fact, there wasn't a huge difference in positions across the income spectrum. But when it came to economic policy, the disagreements were often sharp. (And they would have been even sharper in all likelihood if the surveys had separated out the superrich.) The top income group was substantially more conservative—indeed, further from the middle in its views than the middle was from the bottom—and its distinctive views appeared to have the greatest influence on policy.

Furthermore, these striking findings probably *understate* the disconnect. Even though they encompass nearly two thousand survey questions, opinion polls don't ask about many of the low-profile but lucrative policies that favor the top 0.1 percent—policies that are generally crafted behind closed doors, with limited public scrutiny or input. Over these two decades, Americans were never asked about the carried-interest provision that helped Steve Schwarzman pay low federal taxes, or about the various deregulatory changes that enabled Sandy Weill and others to profit from a much riskier and more lucrative financial sector. Yet even on high-profile issues that garner the attention of pollsters (and, presumably, voters), the affluent seem more than capable of holding their own. The results bring to mind the complaint of one of the superrich's most prominent dissenters, Warren Buffett: "There's a class war, and my class is winning."[107]

Still, there was one area where the general public and the superrich were on the same page: They both hated government.

Right Turn?

These new political studies confirm what common sense suggests: Most Americans are far less conservative on economic issues than those at the top. Indeed, students of public opinion have found no evidence of a consistent rightward shift in public opinion since the 1980s. Surveys have only a limited capacity to capture public views in ways that are true to Americans' complex and sometimes contradictory opinions. But nothing in them suggests a fundamental shift in values comparable to the elite turn against the mixed economy. For example, Americans appear increasingly inclined to believe that hard work (rather than luck or help from others) determines success in life.[108] But the change is modest and seems as likely to reflect the economic strains of these decades as any change in underlying attitudes.

True, the antitax fervor of the late 1970s was a mass movement with significant public support, and Reagan's election reflected a notable right turn in public opinion. Within a few years, however, the pendulum swung back. The political scientist James Stimson has assembled an index of the "public mood" that tracks the ideological movement of the American electorate over the past sixty years. Stimson's measure has fluctuated over time, but it hasn't shifted dramatically or consistently to the right (or left).[109] As another political scientist sums up the voluminous data, "There is virtually no compelling evidence that more Americans have actually embraced conservatism since the 1960s."[110]

This basic stability of opinion does not, however, extend to Americans' trust in government. Here the pendulum has swung toward distrust, and stayed there. At the tail end of Eisenhower's presidency, over 70 percent of Americans said they trusted the federal government "to do what is right" most of the time or just about always. In 1980 only 25 percent of Americans expressed that level of trust. The rest—almost exactly the same proportion that had expressed *high* trust in 1958—said government could be trusted only some of the time or never. And while trust in government recovered briefly in the wake of 9/11, it was back at record low levels by the late 2000s.[111]

Experts still debate why trust plummeted in the United States. Nearly all big institutions have lost trust since the 1960s (though with notable exceptions, such as the military). Yet government has earned a distinctive, and distinctively deep, opprobrium. The initial loss of faith seems to have been linked to discrete events—the urban riots of the 1960s, the Vietnam War, Watergate—but the persistent flatlining remains a puzzle. The strongest explanations center on the increased insecurity of middle-class Americans and, more important, the sense that government could do nothing to remedy it. Put simply, many Americans lost confidence in the capacity of government to safeguard economic prosperity and security, and the party of government—the Democrats—paid the price.[112] Once trust fell, it took little time for political entrepreneurs to realize that stoking antigovernment sentiments was a winning strategy. Politicians used to run for Washington; now they ran *against* it.

One thing is clear: Distrust among the public is rooted in different considerations than those animating the aggrieved 0.1 percent. A key complaint, in fact, is that those at the top have undue influence. In 1964, according to the premier academic survey of US voters, the American National Election Studies, more than two-thirds of Americans felt that government was "run for the benefit of all the people." By 2008, only 30 percent felt that way; the other 70 percent believed that it was "pretty much run by a few big interests looking out for themselves." While those at the top complained about politicians' craven responsiveness to the electoral rabble, the rest of Americans complained that the rich ran the show.[113]

Whatever the cause, declining public faith in government pushed in the same direction as the Randian leanings of the economic elite: away from the mixed economy. At the individual level, low trust appears to

weaken liberal leanings among voters. Public support for specific programs that provide direct benefits, such as Social Security, appears largely
impervious to declining trust. Yet when it comes to more distant or prospective benefits—the benefits typical of the long-term investments that
the mixed economy requires—low trust means little willingness to put
faith in public officials or their policies. If waste and incompetence are
rife, if tax dollars are thrown down bureaucratic rat holes, if politicians
are in it only for themselves or those who shower money on them, why
support new initiatives or put faith in existing policies where the benefits are hard to see? "Trust but verify" becomes "distrust and defeat."

The Sound of Silence

The antigovernment wave that formed in the 1970s was a result of political mobilization and rhetorical creativity, the economic shocks of the
decade, and the changes in understanding and advocacy that flowed
from them. The first tremors were set off by stagflation and its ideological
reverberations. But the wave gained power and speed because of the self-
reinforcing economic and policy transformations that were unleashed by
this initial surge—and the dramatic shifts in America's economic elite
they fostered.

These changes did not go unnoticed or occur without pushback. Yet
those who sought to defend or resurrect the ideas under siege found themselves caught in what communications experts call a "spiral of silence." In
such a spiral, opinions become dominant because of acquiescence as well
as acceptance. Even if individuals do not agree with an idea, their sense
that it is shared broadly makes them reluctant to voice dissent. In time,
this anticipation can create self-fulfilling cycles—a "spiral"—in which
conflicting ideas are pushed to the periphery. When alternative understandings are no longer voiced confidently, we collectively forget their
power.

Consider the fate of the label *liberal*. Why did Americans turn away
from identifying with a political tradition that had played a vital role in
defeating fascism and securing postwar prosperity? Two leading political scientists, Christopher Ellis and James Stimson, give a partial answer:

> What changed . . . was that astute politicians on the left stopped
> using the word *liberal* to describe themselves. Before the change,

the public saw *liberal* aligned with popular Democratic pro-grams. . . . This is a curious case where what is individually rational, for individual politicians to avoid the liberal label, may be collectively nonrational, as they become subject as a class to being associated with an ever more unpopular label as it goes undefended. And as popular politicians avoid the liberal label, it provides an opportunity for their conservative opponents to fill the vacuum with unpopular personalities and causes. The asymmetrical linguistic war sets up a spiral in which *liberal* not only is unpopular, but becomes ever more so.[114]

The positive conception of government at liberalism's core became snared in a similar spiral. When President Eisenhower delivered his first State of the Union Address, he drew on a broad reservoir of support for the mixed economy. He took for granted that government made fundamental contributions to our shared prosperity. Those within his party who thought otherwise were marginalized. Business leaders, too, recognized that they had to engage with government and labor as partners. Many genuinely accepted the partnership, but all understood that they had to accommodate it.

Forty years later, when Bill Clinton took the podium, the world looked different. The reservoir of enthusiasm for government was dry, baked away by the relentless attacks on government that politicians of both parties had found were the surest way to national office. Declining public trust eroded support for active government and created a political vacuum that powerful private interests filled. A revitalized Republican Party led the assault, as chapter 8 will make clear. Yet even the party of government—and those like Clinton who led it—found the spiral of anti-Washington sentiment hard to escape, especially as those powerful private interests became increasingly central sources of financial support.

The corporate world had changed as well. The financial restructuring that began in the 1980s reshaped the character, leadership, and culture of American business. Among those favored by these changes, older understandings of what produced prosperity gave way to new conceptions of the relationship between business and government, the process of wealth creation, and the contribution of managers versus workers—conceptions sharply at odds with those supporting the mixed economy.

In the new corporate world, business leaders who praised the active role of government were harder to find. No less fateful, business associations that could engage with political leaders to pursue broad prosperity were harder to find, with profound consequences for the mixed economy that the next chapter will explore.

SEVEN

★ ★ ★

We're Not in Camelot Anymore

I N OCTOBER 1972, a select group of the nation's leading CEOs emerged from a private meeting at New York's exclusive Links Club having agreed to form a new organization, the Business Roundtable. It was an apt name. The fictional roundtable was a powerful metaphor: round, signifying equality among its members, and singular, symbolizing unified attention to shared rather than individual concerns. The BRT aspired to address the most fundamental collective challenges facing America's biggest companies.[1]

The Roundtable was not the only business group to form or expand in the 1970s. As we saw in the last chapter, the simultaneous pressures of falling profits and increasing government activism galvanized corporate America in ways not seen since the 1930s. Just a year before the Round-table's formation, the National Association of Manufacturers moved its headquarters from New York to DC. ("The thing that affects business most today is government," explained the organization's head.) The US Chamber of Commerce, something of a backwater in the 1950s and 1960s, expanded from 36,000 companies in 1967 to around 160,000 in 1980. By every measure—DC public affairs offices (a 400 percent increase in a decade), Washington lobbyists (1,000 percent in less than a decade), political action committees (400 percent in just four years)—corporate America got political.[2]

As big as the increase in business political activity was, the accompanying changes in power structures, political strategies, and policy aims were even bigger. Responding to the shifting contours of American capitalism and American politics, organizational innovators built new sorts of business associations better matched to a more financialized economy, more narrowly focused corporate elite, and more partisan and money-driven political world. In this chapter, we focus on the three most important such efforts: the Roundtable, the revamped US Chamber of Commerce, and—later on the scene—the network centered around Charles and David Koch. In American political history, few groups have assembled more resources or amassed more power than these three, and few have done more to shape the world we occupy today.

Even more important, the development of these three vast organizations provides a window into the broader transformation of America's corporate leaders: their changing interaction with government, with one another, and with their rivals for political power. Just as the Committee for Economic Development offered a portrait of how many corporate leaders engaged with government in the 1950s and 1960s, these three groups reveal how many engage with government today. Be warned: It is not a pretty picture. In the varied trajectories of the Business Roundtable, the Chamber of Commerce, and the growing Koch network, we see the political erosion of the mixed economy in action.

The Rise and Fall of the Business Roundtable

The Roundtable grew out of a merger of several smaller predecessors. The most important was the short-lived March Group, which had brought together leading CEOs from some of the nation's biggest firms, including Alcoa, Ford, GE, Gulf Oil, Procter & Gamble, and Westinghouse.[3] Like the March Group, the fledgling Roundtable was dominated by the nation's industrial core. All but four of the original thirty-four members came from manufacturing and production, and no financial, insurance, or health firms had a seat at the Roundtable.[4]

The group grew fast. Membership was by invitation only, and by 1975, the BRT had 160 members, including 70 from the Fortune 100.[5] Five years after its birth, it had become possibly the most influential business lobby in Washington, elbowing aside such long-standing organizations as the Chamber of Commerce and the National Association of Manufacturers.

Restraining the Mixed Economy

The Roundtable had one primary goal: to defend its members from what they saw as a concerted assault on corporate profits and prerogatives. While the broadest threats emanated from a shifting world economy and changing financial sector, the top executives in the BRT blamed their difficulties mostly on two more easily confronted culprits: the federal government's expanded regulatory role and the demand of organized labor for more union-friendly policies. What united these concerns was high inflation. In the emerging thinking of the Roundtable's leadership, rising prices called for shifting Washington priorities—away from unions with their wage and legislative demands, away from regulations that increased costs, and away from ambitious government programs that, through spending and deficits, overheated the economy.[6]

For all this, the BRT was designed to be nonpartisan. Its two high-profile leaders during its political ascent, John Harper and his successor, DuPont CEO Irving Shapiro, were Democrats. The BRT meticulously refrained from engaging in electoral politics. Instead, the core of its organizational model was to concentrate on personal interactions between those at the apex of the business and political worlds. Lobbying centered on direct contact between CEOs and public officials, especially on Capitol Hill. The BRT's practices reflected the maxim offered by one mid-1970s executive: "If you don't know your senators on a first-name basis, you are not doing an adequate job for your stockholders."[7]

The Roundtable's approach paid off. Following big Democratic victories in the post-Watergate midterm elections of 1974, Democrats recaptured the White House in 1976. Rapid progress on a liberal legislative agenda seemed imminent—until the Roundtable swung into action. CEOs successfully pressured moderates in both parties to buck the Democratic leadership.[8] The lobbying helped block a new consumer protection agency, an increase in the minimum wage, major labor law reform, and progressive tax reform. The stage was set for a conservative resurgence in the 1978 and 1980 elections. With the most conservative administration in a half century taking office in 1980, the Roundtable went on the offensive, pushing successfully for major cuts in taxes and federal spending—the core of Reagan's first-year agenda.

Cracks in the Roundtable

Yet no sooner had the BRT reached the pinnacle of influence than it began heading downhill. The decline was so gradual as to be almost imperceptible. Today, the Roundtable remains a useful stage set for efforts to speak to and for the business community. It also remains a force on a select but narrow set of issues. Yet the idea of a "roundtable," where business elites work together to tackle the most fundamental issues facing American corporations and the nation's economic health, is a thing of the past.

Ironically, the same innovative design that allowed the Roundtable to catapult to prominence proved to be its undoing. It was built around what would turn out to be an obsolescent idea: the CEO as public statesman. Direct lobbying by powerful corporate chieftains was at the heart of the Roundtable's organizational model. Yet the leaders of the BRT failed to appreciate their own dependence on the postwar economic order they were now criticizing. As the industrial heartland declined and finance ascended, the corporate climate that made the BRT possible disappeared.

The makeup of the BRT's executive and policy committees provides a window into these broader shifts. In the 1970s, traditional manufacturing and production firms dominated the Roundtable's top ranks. A decade later, "new" industries came to the fore: finance, pharmaceuticals, telecommunications. By 1988, the closest to an "old" industry represented on the four-member executive committee was IBM. Holding the other positions were the heads of Aetna, American Express, and Pfizer.[9]

Even more important was the change under way in what it meant to be a CEO. As the sociologist Mark Mizruchi recounts in his aptly titled *The Fracturing of the American Corporate Elite*, the men who started the BRT (they were all men) had, for the most part, spent their lives in a single industry, usually at a single firm. The strong competitive position and relative financial insulation of the industrial firms they headed created what we've called "opportunity," allowing executives to devote significant energy to corporate leadership, political activity, and policy.[10] The new breed of CEOs was different. They were more likely to be products of business schools, where they developed more generic and transferable management skills. They were more mobile across firms and industries. Moreover, the broad process of financialization that had transformed the entire economy had increased their focus on the short term. To survive, executives needed to shift their eyes from the horizon to the next quarterly report. At the same time, the personal payoffs for occupying that corner office were skyrocketing. Tenure at the top might be precarious and often brief, but a CEO who was skilled, lucky, or brazen could accumulate a fortune.

In short, the Roundtable's founders had built their entire political strategy around a corporate model that was fast disappearing. In the early 1980s, Shapiro, Harper, and other key leaders passed from the scene, and no one was there to pick up the mantle. "You don't have the same perception now of there being some central figures," said new chairman Ruben Mettler of TRW (an advanced engineering conglomerate acquired by Northrop Grumman in 2002), "because there really aren't."[11] Another key figure in the early BRT described a new "generation of CEOs who were just not that focused on their relationship with Washington and preferred to work on their bottom lines."[12]

(Round)Table for One

Soon the BRT preferred to work on those bottom lines, too. Even while losing its capacity to influence the biggest economic issues of the day, it showed continuing clout in another political struggle: protecting the interests of CEOs. Increasingly, the Roundtable reserved its dwindling power for issues related to preventing "outside interference" with corporate governance, especially those that might impinge on the spectacular growth of executive pay. In many ways, the BRT's activism on management issues was the exception that proved the rule. Working on big, long-term problems no longer fit comfortably with the incentives of corporate leaders. Protecting the turf and compensation of those leaders, however, couldn't fit better.

The first front in the new battle was the fight in the early 1990s over stock options. Federal regulators had a number of concerns with the growing role of stock options in executive compensation, but were especially bothered by the failure of companies to "expense" them.[13] In their accounting practices, firms often pretended their grants of lucrative options to executives were free. The result could be doubly misleading: By hiding what could be sizable future costs, these practices concealed both the true balance sheet of top corporations and the true compensation of top executives. In the early 1990s, the Financial Accounting Standards Board (FASB) began considering new rules that would force companies to incorporate the expected costs of options into their accounting.

Suddenly it wasn't hard to mobilize CEOs. Executives at the Roundtable launching a multipronged attack on the FASB initiative. One prong was an aggressive effort to silence the compensation consultants who were providing the business press and regulators with information about options. The *New York Times* reported that these consultants were on the receiving end of veiled threats from top BRT figures, including Citicorp chair John Reed and H. Brewster Atwater Jr., chair of General Mills. According to Michael Halloran, head of the Wyatt Company's executive compensation practice, the Business Roundtable "let a number of consultants know in no uncertain terms that they would not view this as responsive to clients' needs"—a euphemism for "Your services are no longer required."[14]

The Roundtable also appealed directly to the FASB. The accounting board had tried unsuccessfully in the past to get the BRT's chief executives interested in its work. Yet when the FASB proposed rules for expensing options in 1993, they were suddenly very interested. Lucas and the voting members of the FASB were asked to a private meeting with Citicorp's Reed, chair of the Roundtable's accounting principles taskforce. Upon arrival, they found Reed joined by two corporate giants, GE's John F. Welch and Sanford Weill, the chief of Travelers Group (who would join with Reed to form Citigroup). The research director of the FASB at the time, Timothy Lucas, reported that the message of the meeting was clear: Drop the new standards.[15]

It didn't stop there. CEOs, especially from the tech industry, swarmed Capitol Hill. Arthur Levitt, head of the US Securities and Exchange Commission (SEC), reported that in his first few months on the job, he was forced to devote one-third of his time to this issue, "being threatened and cajoled by legions of businesspeople."[16] The CEOs also sought support among Democrats in the Senate, where Connecticut's Joe Lieberman—backed by California's Barbara Boxer and Dianne Feinstein, who no doubt heard the howls from Silicon Valley—advanced a resolution that threatened to gut the FASB if it went ahead. Faced with the onslaught, Levitt urged the board to back down, a move he later called the biggest mistake of his tenure.[17]

Look Out on Your Right!

It was not just the "CEO as public statesman" that seemed dated now (at least when CEOs' own privileges weren't threatened). The BRT's studied bipartisanship came under growing fire, too. Initially, the Roundtable didn't attack the mixed economy as a whole; instead, BRT leaders argued it had tilted too far toward government. Alcoa's John Harper, who became the Roundtable's chairman in 1973, acknowledged (in the words of historian Benjamin Waterhouse) "that the American people had a legitimate right to worry about things like pollution, product safety, and workplace health, but business leaders could respect those complaints without surrendering operational control to heavy-handed regulatory authorities."[18] Indeed, as the Roundtable built its clout, it also built a reputation for compromise based on bipartisan outreach and relatively moderate stances.

By the mid-1990s, however, this approach, too, looked obsolete. Over the prior two decades, House Republicans had become a much more conservative force—a transformation that the next chapter will explore in greater depth. They had also become much more powerful: From 1994 to 2016, Republicans would hold the House for all but four years. In most respects, the GOP ascendance was fortunate for business leaders. In the turn from the mixed economy, they would gain a Great Enabler, a strong and reliable advocate of deregulation, tax cuts, and other priorities valuable to the nation's economic elite. But this gain came at a price: growing pressure on the business community to build a firm alliance with the right-turning GOP.

The Republican point person on this matter was Tom DeLay, the Texas bug exterminator turned Republican member of Congress turned House majority whip. DeLay wanted interest groups to work through and with the GOP. Rewards would flow to groups that did; punishment to those that did not.[19] If the BRT expected the GOP to be a reliable ally, the GOP expected the BRT to be reliable in return.

The conflict came to a head in a 1997 meeting between the GOP leadership (including DeLay and House Speaker Newt Gingrich) and twenty CEOs (including the then-head of the Roundtable, Don Fites, CEO of Caterpillar). The Republicans expressed displeasure that BRT companies continued to donate to the Democratic Party and the BRT continued to employ Democrats in important staff positions. The *Wall Street Journal*

reported that the GOP offered an ultimatum: "Stop donating so much
to the Democrats and become more involved in partisan politics, or be
denied access to Republicans in Congress."[20] Roundtable members could
be forgiven for seeing this demand as a little churlish—after all, *more
than two-thirds* of donations from BRT companies during the 1996 election cycle had gone to Republicans. But the dispute was not just about
campaign cash.[21] A *National Journal* report added that some "GOP leaders have talked privately about the need either to revamp the Roundtable
or build another big-business group that can be a more reliable ally."[22]

The BRT resisted, but the clash signaled another widening crack in
its foundation. Nonpartisanship had worked well in the 1970s, when the
parties were relatively weak and direct appeals to individual politicians
could be decisive. It worked less well in the 1990s, when the parties constituted warring camps and the pathway to influence ran through party
leadership. As a careful observer of the Washington lobbying scene concluded: "Washington changed, but the Roundtable did not. . . . No longer could a small group of aggressive corporate chieftains march into the
offices of a few key legislators and make things happen."[23]

Reaching for Relevance

By the late 1990s, the Business Roundtable had lost its once preeminent
position. Periodic "comeback" stories appeared, but they repeatedly
turned out to be false dawns. In September 1997 its president, Donald
Fites, wrote a memo outlining a plan to bolster the organization's position by increasing its budget, intensifying its lobbying efforts, and—in
a telling adjustment—moving beyond its traditional focus on elite pressure by building "a stronger and more consistent advertising and grassroots presence on a small number of issues."[24] To finance this plan, Fites
advocated tripling membership dues, which would expand its annual
budget from $10 million to $30 million. The effort backfired, as companies balked at the cost. Membership dropped from 190 to 130.[25] The
BRT then struggled just to maintain its lobbying expenditures, which
were essentially flat at around $12 million a year after 1998. The decline
was substantial after accounting for inflation, but even bigger relative
to other major groups, since total reported lobbying expenditures would
grow from just under $1.5 billion in 1998 to over $3.5 billion in 2010.[26]

After the GOP achieved unified control of the federal government in
2001 (for the first time since Eisenhower), the Roundtable appointed John

Castellani as its new president. Unlike the presidents who had headed the organization in its heyday, Castellani had never been CEO of a major company. Instead, he had worked in government affairs in a number of corporations, as well as for the National Association of Manufacturers. He was in essence a lobbyist, not a corporate statesman. Castellani became more and more the face of the organization, which now lacked the steady presence of prominent CEOs.

Castellani's arrival sparked a new round of "Roundtable resurgence" reports. Under his tutelage, according to observers, the BRT had transformed from "a sleeping giant into a lobbying juggernaut" known for its "aggressive" posture.[27] "Aggressive" apparently meant greater willingness to take sides in tense partisan combat. The Roundtable backed most of the George W. Bush administration's major initiatives. In some cases, such as Bush's huge tax cuts for the wealthiest Americans, that wasn't surprising. Other stances were less obvious, such as its embrace of the administration's risky and unpopular effort to privatize aspects of Social Security.

The turn toward the GOP went beyond policy endorsements. Though maintaining a formal posture of neutrality, the BRT strengthened its organizational ties with the GOP. In 2004 the organization's number two position went to Larry Burton, who had worked for Republicans in both the House and Senate, as well as in the Reagan administration. Castellani, himself a Republican, became a guest at weekly meetings between the Senate Republican Policy Committee and favored lobbyists. Ohio congressman John Boehner, a prominent manager of relations between the GOP and the business community, spoke approvingly: "The new leadership at the Roundtable has done a magnificent job of getting itself better organized and better focused."[28] He didn't have to say the obvious: "better focused on the GOP."

In January 2011—as Boehner, now Speaker of the House, swore in his new GOP majority—the BRT chose John Engler, former Republican governor of Michigan, as its president. Such a partisan appointment would have been unthinkable in the organization's past. Yet Engler was just one part of a broader game of GOP-BRT musical chairs. He occupied the office Castellani vacated when he moved to a lucrative post as the head of the Pharmaceutical Research and Manufacturers of America (PhRMA), the drug industry's lobbying arm.[29] It was not a major shift for Castellani. An ostensibly broad-minded organization, the BRT now looked out mostly for aggrieved CEOs, making it not so different in practice from a lobbying organization that advanced the particular interests of a single sector. In turn, Castellani replaced former GOP congressman Billy Tauzin, who had taken the PhRMA position after helping shepherd the GOP's drug industry–friendly prescription drug bill through the House.

On the surface, the Roundtable doesn't look so different today than it did at the height of its power. It takes stands on a wide range of policy issues, and professes (and frequently practices) nonpartisanship. Many of these stances have been more moderate than those of other business organizations. In the grand struggle over President Obama's health plan, for example, the BRT was "blandly supportive," in the words of one health policy expert.[30] But there is little sign that the BRT has devoted significant organizational energy to any of these broad issues. Instead, the contemporary Roundtable has saved its energy for narrower goals: backing measures that promise a direct short-term boost to corporate profits, and killing those that involve potential threats to the power and pay of the nation's top CEOs.

Indeed, when a rupture between the BRT and the Obama administration occurred in June 2010, it reflected not larger policy disagreements but the Roundtable's preoccupation with protecting short-term business profits and executive perks. Roundtable chairman Ivan G. Seidenberg, CEO of Verizon, accused Obama and congressional Democrats of creating an "increasingly hostile environment for investment and job creation. . . . We have reached a point where the negative effects of these policies are simply too significant to ignore."[31] Castellani identified two issues that constituted the final straw. One was the administration's tough stance on corporate parking of earnings overseas to avoid taxation. The other was a seemingly obscure issue of corporate governance that explains exactly what the BRT stands for today.

A Call to Arms!

"This is our highest priority," the Roundtable's president, John Castellani, announced. "Literally all of our members have called about this." "This," he added, had brought forty CEOs to Washington just the week before and had engaged the personal attention of top executives such as Seidenberg, Steve Odland of Office Depot, and Jim McNerney of Boeing, the world's largest aerospace company.[32]

So just what was "this"? What could spur such activism, reminiscent of the Roundtable's successful mobilizations of the 1970s? The financial meltdown? Global warming? The deficit? Skyrocketing health care costs? Rising inequality? No, "proxy access"—a comparatively small provision in the sweeping 2009 financial reform bill (formally, the Dodd-Frank Wall Street Reform and Consumer Protection Act) that would make it easier for large, long-term shareholders to propose alternative candidates in elections to a company's board of directors. The debate over financial reform had provided an opening for those who argued that corporate boards were often too cozy with a company's top executives, and the SEC had indicated it was favorable toward new rules to diminish the huge barriers to board challengers. As the financial reform bill lumbered forward, both the House and Senate versions contained a provision explicitly granting the SEC the authority to issue such a rule.

CEOs went into overdrive to kill proxy access. Their stated rationale was that activists would capture board positions to advance their narrow agendas. But the discussed thresholds were so high that only the largest institutional investors would qualify. And again, proxy access would just put the challengers *on the ballot*. They would join the board only if they gained broad support from shareholders. It is hard to believe that CEOs had any other motive than a desire to sustain their tight control over the selection of those who determine their pay and review their decisions.[33]

Whatever the motivations, CEOs lobbied the Obama administration hard. Reportedly gaining some support there, they went to work on Senate Democrats, and especially Connecticut's Christopher Dodd, the Democrats' lead negotiator in the Senate-House conference committee then under way. To the dismay of corporate reformers, Dodd led a last-minute push to add new language gutting proxy access. House Democrat Barney Frank (with the strong backing of Speaker Nancy Pelosi) refused to go along. The final legislation gave the SEC clear authority to fashion a rule broadening proxy access.

In the old days, that probably would have been it.[34] The Roundtable had fought and lost. But Washington was changing, and the Roundtable was not done. When the SEC introduced its rule—a cautious proposal with many limits on proxy access—the Business Roundtable, joined by the Chamber of Commerce, filed suit. The action shifted to terrain much more favorable to the CEOs. Their legal advocate would be Eugene Scalia (son of conservative Supreme Court Justice Antonin Scalia), who has developed a lucrative practice in corporate appellate law.

Matters got worse from there. Big regulatory cases like this one go immediately to the US Court of Appeals for the DC Circuit, the nation's second most powerful court. There Republican appointees long maintained a majority, thanks to repeated GOP filibusters of Obama nominees. The SEC drew an unfortunate slate of judges, which included two Reagan appointees. The third judge was George W. Bush's firebrand appointee Janice Rogers Brown, who in a speech to the influential conservative legal group the Federalist Society once said, "In the heyday of liberal democracy, all roads lead to slavery," and referred to the New Deal as "the triumph of our own socialist revolution."[35]

The court's unanimous opinion read like a BRT legal brief. Established precedent suggested that on complex matters requiring technical expertise, courts should show considerable deference to administrative agencies. Reading the opinion, "deference" is not what comes to mind. The judges were scathing, citing the inadequacy of the SEC's twenty-three-page analysis of the rule's economic impact as "unutterably mindless." In substituting the judges' own view of costs and benefits for the agency's, the opinion cited a study offered by "one commenter" that suggested the rule's costs would greatly exceed its benefits. It failed to note that the "commenter" was *the Business Roundtable*, and that it had hired the consultants who produced the study.[36] No matter: The judges got to make the call. Proxy access was dead.

There was one final irony. The decision created a nice opportunity for social scientists to appraise the quality of the judges' reasoning. Analyzing stock returns before and after the decision, researchers estimated that the Appeals Court's decision, by strengthening CEOs' insulation from the preferences of their own shareholders, had wiped approximately $70 billion in value from publicly traded companies.[37]

In an August 2014 interview, President Obama vented his frustration at the difficulty of mobilizing CEOs in support of major economic reforms:

> There's a huge gap between the professed values and visions of corporate CEOs and how their lobbyists operate in Washington. . . . When they come and they have lunch with me—which they do more often than they probably care to admit [*laughter*]—and they'll

say, "You know what, we really care about the environment, and we really care about education, and we really care about getting immigration reform done"—then my challenge to them consistently is, "Is your lobbyist working as hard on those issues as he or she is on preserving that tax break that you've got?" And if the answer is no, then you don't care about it as much as you say.[38]

Nowhere is this gap more evident than in the evolution of the Business Roundtable. It has morphed from an organization that could look at the biggest issues facing American capitalism to one with a much narrower focus. That evolution tracks the transformation of the American corporation itself—from institutions headed by leaders with some opportunity and incentive to address long-term challenges and reach long-term bargains to institutions headed by executives fixated on immediate returns to their companies and themselves. The CEOs who established the Roundtable aspired to be statesmen, and the organization still styles itself as (in the words of its website) "an association of chief executive officers of leading U.S. companies working to promote sound public policy and a thriving U.S. economy."[39] Actions, however, speak louder than words.

The Rise, Fall, and Rise of the Chamber of Commerce

Nothing in the surface history of the US Chamber of Commerce would suggest a turbulent trajectory. For the past forty years, just two men have held the organization's presidency: Richard Lesher headed it from 1975 until 1997, and Thomas Donohue took over when Lesher retired. Yet each man seized the reins at a moment when the nation's oldest major business group was ready to be remade, and each of these formidable figures seized the opportunity.

The Chamber's ups and downs trace the sharply contrasting strategies of two men with strong convictions and powerful ambitions. But those strategies reflect not just their differing temperaments but also the shifting economic and political environments they faced. Like the Roundtable's descent into a CEO lobbying shop, the Chamber's metamorphosis from a consensus-based organization into a hard-right influence machine illuminates a larger story. It is a story of growing business clout, mounting hostility to the mixed economy, and an increasing focus on the promotion of narrow interests.

The Unlikely Compromiser

Richard Lesher became head of the Chamber at a pivotal moment. In August 1971 a top corporate lawyer named Lewis Powell wrote a now-famous memo to business leaders warning that the "American economic system is under broad attack." Just two months later, Richard Nixon would nominate Powell to the Supreme Court. Powell's memo, which did not become public until after he was confirmed, argued that corporate America needed to fight back with every weapon in its arsenal: "It is essential that spokesmen for the enterprise system—at all levels and at every opportunity—be far more aggressive. . . . There should not be the slightest hesitation to press vigorously in all political arenas for support of the enterprise system. Nor should there be reluctance to penalize politically those who oppose it."[40]

Powell's memo ended up being circulated widely, influencing important figures on the right, from beer magnate Joseph Coors to Charles Koch. Yet he had prepared it specifically for top Chamber officials. In the memo, Powell had described the Chamber's role as "vital" because of its "strategic position . . . fine reputation and . . . broad base of support."[41]

Lesher was in many ways an odd choice for such a "vital" role. He had an eclectic, almost directionless résumé: corporate finance teacher at Ohio State University, a gig in "technology utilization" at NASA, and then president of a nonprofit organization researching garbage disposal. He won the job through his evident energy and his conviction that the Chamber had to make a more passionate case for the merits of free enterprise.[42]

More than anything else, Lesher was an ideas guy. A committed supply-sider who argued that low taxes were the key to growth, he sought to build an organization along Powell's suggested lines—one that could make a loud and strong case for market-based policies and mobilize its greatest resource: more than two hundred thousand US companies of all sizes.[43]

The Chamber both advocated for and benefited from the increasing politicization of the business community. By the late 1970s, its membership had quadrupled. As historian Benjamin Waterhouse recounts, the Chamber "dramatically scaled up its direct and indirect lobbying activities, forged lasting ties to other conservative political organizations, and strengthened its networks with local affiliates, trade associations, and individual business owners around the country."[44] Lesher also introduced innovations, most notably the Chamber's litigation project, that became enduring parts of its operation.

By 1981, the Chamber had reached a level of influence it hadn't seen in a half century. Its connections to both large and small businesses gave it "a privileged position" within the Reagan coalition.[45] Lesher was perhaps the most visible business leader in Washington—admired for his successful reinvention of the Chamber, devoted to the cause of tax cuts, and a favorite of the Reagan administration. It would be his high-water mark.

The next year, Reagan made a U-turn. When a deep recession and his big tax cuts yielded massive budget deficits, the president accepted tax hikes to stanch the red ink. Much of the business community, including the Roundtable, went along. Lesher refused, flouting his board. His intransigence divided the Chamber and alienated the White House. Lesher went from insider to outcast. The administration passed word that it was still interested in hearing the Chamber's views, but they should be communicated by someone else.[46]

Lesher never truly recovered. He fended off challenges to his position but couldn't duplicate his early successes. Fund-raising stagnated. Between the early 1980s and early 1990s, the Chamber's budget fell by almost 40 percent after adjusting for inflation. Membership also declined from its peak, and the group now faced poaching from the expanding National Federation of Independent Business (NFIB)—the conservative small-business lobby—which was wooing smaller companies.[47]

Lesher, as always, was bold. Seeking to reinvent the Chamber one more time, he made an unexpected move to the center. When Bill Clinton became the first Democrat to occupy the White House in a dozen years, Lesher was ready to do business. In 1991 he had installed the moderate and pragmatic William Archey in the organization's number two position: vice president for policy and congressional affairs. "The far-right wing considers the Chamber to be its bastion, its home away from home, its mouthpiece," Archey acknowledged. "But we are not a right-wing think tank, and we are not a left-wing think tank. We are a business advocacy institution."[48]

In elevating Archey, Lesher placed his last big bet: that he could revitalize the Chamber by working with those who sought to modernize, rather than overturn, the mixed economy. It was an audacious move for the man who had once attacked Reagan from the right, but it came at a seemingly auspicious moment. After Clinton's election, Lesher established a good rapport with the new administration. In April 1993 he told a reporter it was at least as strong as his relationship with the preceding Republican administration: "We didn't agree with Bush on a lot of things, and we don't agree with Clinton on a lot of things. In fact, I don't agree with my wife on many things. But you have to have a decent working relationship to get things done."[49] When Clinton reached for the center by pushing a big deficit-reduction program that involved a mix of budget cuts and tax increases, the Chamber was supportive. It remained so when Clinton moved forward with his other big domestic ambition: universal health insurance, designed to contain spiraling health costs and including a requirement that most employers cover their workers. The Chamber signaled that the administration would have its backing.

Yet, just as Lesher and Archey were moving to the center, powerful forces in American society were moving ever further to the right. The pragmatic bipartisanship once championed by business organizations was coming to look as obsolete as the Roundtable's CEO-as-statesman model. Ascendant conservatives within the GOP pushed back, with Congressman John Boehner leading the charge. Boehner reportedly declared at a meeting with Archey and Lesher that it was "the Chamber's duty to categorically oppose everything that Clinton was in favor of."[50] House minority leader Robert Michel—long an advocate of compromise but now under fire from his right—sent Lesher a fierce letter, signed by the rest of the House GOP leadership (including the triumvirate of Gingrich and Texas congressmen Dick Armey and Tom DeLay that would soon lead a Republican-controlled House). The letter warned that the Chamber's position on Clinton's economic program was unacceptable and the "ramifications could be quite severe." Describing "a rapidly spreading frustration and anger with the Chamber's failure to take an aggressive posture on the Clinton economic program," the Republican leaders suggested the need for a course correction "before we pass the point of no return."[51]

Lesher responded in kind: "The Chamber is not an arm of the Republican Party but an independent body of 215,000 businesses, about 30 percent of them headed by Democrats." To Boehner's call for unrelenting opposition, he told a reporter, "I would tell him to get real and try to understand that our members care about progress. They don't care about perpetuating partisan gridlock."[52] The Chamber's official response, penned by its chairman, businessman Ivan W. Gorr, was blunt: "We infer from various statements in your letter if we do not adopt positions acceptable to you, we will suffer the 'consequences.' This apparent attempt to dictate to us what our policies should be is deeply offensive." Gorr continued: "Our 215,000 members represent the broad diversity of the American business community . . . unified in their interest in creating and preserving the best business climate . . . whether or not our positions are pleasing to any political party or policy group."[53]

Dictating Chamber policies was exactly what the GOP's leaders had in mind. They appealed both to individual companies and to local chambers, encouraging protest against—and, in some cases, resignations from—the Chamber. The GOP worked in tandem with the ambitious leader of the National Federation of Independent Business, Jack Faris. A former finance director for the Republican National Committee (RNC), Faris embodied the emerging partisan world. After becoming head of the NFIB in 1992, he expanded the organization, ramped up its campaign spending, and aligned it with the GOP and its increasingly conservative agenda.[54] In short, he moved his organization into the space Lesher was vacating. Now he was stealing Lesher's foot soldiers, telling small firms the Chamber had deserted them. Health reform—unpopular among small businesses even though many would have been exempted from the employer mandate—fit perfectly into this pitch. As longtime NFIB lobbyist John Motley put it at the time, "It is amazing that an organization that is in as much trouble in its membership base as the Chamber is has given us this opening."[55] A Chamber official recounted later: "We were getting creamed in the field by NFIB. It was as much a market share, competitive issue as anything else."[56]

Under attack from both GOP leaders and the NFIB, Lesher was stunned: "I've played a lot of hardball as president of the Chamber, and I've had to deal with Presidents Reagan and Bush lobbying my board members from Air Force One. But these people are playing dirty pool and using tactics that have no place in a democracy. I've gone through the most disgusting week in my eighteen years as president of the Chamber. It's just been awful."[57]

It would only get worse. With the Chamber still tentatively backing health reform, both the GOP's pressure and the NFIB's poaching intensified. Boehner and other Republican leaders lobbied local chambers and individual firms to renounce Lesher's stance. Membership rolls fell further. Finally, with his board's support crumbling, Lesher surrendered. The Chamber reversed course, overturning written congressional testimony prepared only days earlier. Clinton and his team were shocked; his most important initiative was crippled. Advocates of the moderate strategy, including Archey, were purged. Lesher himself would survive until 1997, but the great experiment with moderate reformism was over.[58]

"After Donohue"

The *New York Times* article on Lesher's 1997 retirement equivocated on the cause. The reporter detailed Lesher's tensions with ascendant conservatives and noted that the longtime head was only sixty-three. The article also included a sympathetic quote from Thomas J. Donohue, head of the American Truckers Associations and a former Chamber official: "He just wants to smell the roses."[59]

It was an atypically touching sentiment from the hard-charging Donohue. A few months later, after replacing Lesher as the Chamber's new president, he offered comments to another *Times* reporter that were more in character: "Somebody's got to go hit [AFL-CIO head John Sweeney] in the mouth." On another occasion, Donohue described the plans of EPA head Carol Browner as "totally insane."[60]

The pugilistic rhetoric coming out of the Chamber's headquarters signaled a new direction—one that would make the Chamber the most powerful business lobby in American history. A local chamber leader had once complimented Lesher's transformative tenure by saying there was "Before Lesher and After Lesher."[61] It would be even more apt to say there was "Before Donohue and After Donohue."

At the heart of the Chamber's phoenix-like revival lies a revealing paradox. By all accounts, Tom Donohue is fairly nonideological (or at least less ideological than Lesher). Yet he has led the Chamber to a series of increasingly extreme positions and replaced its previous aversion to partisan politics with an intimate collaboration with the GOP. The resolution of this paradox is that Donohue's strategy reflects a shrewd adaptation to the new realities of Washington. Inverting Lesher's ideologue-to-pragmatist transit, the nonideologue Donohue calculated that a formula combining policy extremism and open partisanship would attract increased support from the nation's biggest companies. And that support would increase the Chamber's clout, creating, in his words, "an eight-hundred-pound gorilla"—the biggest, baddest lobbying organization Washington had ever seen.

Donohue, of course, had had a front-row seat for the fateful clash between Lesher and ascendant GOP conservatives. Lesher had zigged when he should have zagged, moving toward the center just as the foundation of bipartisanship collapsed. That foundation was still holding up in the later Reagan years and (less stably) during the George H. W. Bush presidency, yielding pragmatic reform legislation that updated, refurbished, or extended the mixed economy—the Tax Reform Act of 1986, and, in 1990, a trifecta of moderation: the Clean Air Act Amendments of 1990, the Americans with Disabilities Act, and a major deficit-reduction bill.[62] The last of these, however, was the catalyst for a rebellion within the GOP. What Lesher saw as the way Washington worked ("We want to get things done") was a political world receding in the rearview mirror.

Amid the growing partisan rancor, business associations found it harder to stand aloof. In the old days, passing legislation required crafting coalitions from the middle out, building support among moderates in both parties. Now the moderates were gone or on the run, especially within the GOP. When laws did pass, they typically rested on lopsided party majorities. If you wanted things done, you needed partisans who shared your priorities. All of the major political actors in Washington faced growing pressure to pick sides, and the GOP leadership in the House was committed to a logic of reciprocity—or, less generously, of "pay to play." Tom DeLay's K Street Project, a multipronged effort to pressure Washington lobbying firms to adopt Republican positions and personnel, meant keeping track of friends and enemies, and making it clear that GOP leaders would be responsive only to their friends.[63] Like the Roundtable, Lesher had learned the hard way that espousing neutrality put you on the wrong side of the ledger.

Donohue didn't hesitate. As the Chamber expanded its spending, the dollars flowed overwhelmingly to the GOP. By 2014, well over 90 percent of its reported independent spending supported Republicans or attacked Democrats; almost all the rest was targeted to favor one Republican in a primary over another—typically, to maximize the chances of beating a Democrat.[64] Nor was money the only connection between the two organizations: The Chamber's leadership now meshed closely with that of the Republican Party. Its political director, Rob Engstrom, was previously the political director of the Republican National Committee.[65] Former

Bush official Karen Harbert became president of the Chamber's Institute for 21st Century Energy. Margaret Spellings, Bush's secretary of education, became senior adviser at the Chamber in 2009 and later president of the Chamber of Commerce Foundation. Scott Reed, onetime executive director of the RNC, thereafter assumed the title of senior political strategist for the Chamber.[66]

The Chamber has become increasingly integrated with the GOP political apparatus. In the run-up to the fateful 2010 midterm elections, the Chamber's general counsel, Steven Law, met privately with former Bush adviser Ed Gillespie. Law had a long history with the GOP, having served as Mitch McConnell's chief of staff, executive director of the National Republican Senatorial Committee, and deputy secretary of labor under George W. Bush. Law and Gillespie discussed plans for what became American Crossroads, the super PAC headed by Karl Rove that has become a massive conduit for Republican campaign funding. Enabled in 2010 by the Supreme Court's *Citizens United* decision, which shredded traditional federal election rules, Super PACs are not subject to long-standing restrictions on the size and source of political donations even though they act much like conventional campaign organizations. Indeed, the leadership of American Crossroads looks like a shadow Republican National Committee, dominated by former RNC heavies. The Chamber and American Crossroads coordinated their spending and messaging in the 2010 election. Law would soon leave the Chamber to become CEO of Crossroads.[67]

"Show Me the Money!"

At the same time that Donohue was directing more and more spending toward federal campaigns, the Chamber was directing more and more spending elsewhere: toward state elections and organizing, toward lobbying and litigation, and toward an expanded internal policy capacity. Aside from scrapping Lesher's costly media operations, Donohue's Chamber seemed to be doing a lot more of everything. If half of Donohue's new formula was increasing partisanship, the other half was a vast expansion of fund-raising. Fifteen years into Donohue's tenure, the Chamber's once modest budget was closing in on $250 million a year.[68]

Above all else, Donohue was a rainmaker. Where other execs might place a sign on their desk saying "The buck stops here," Donohue's read "Show me the money!" (A former Chamber lobbyist said, "He used to pound his fist on the desk and say, 'Show me the money!' . . . He got his rocks off on it.")[69] Donohue had honed his fund-raising skills at the American Truckers Associations, tripling its revenues in thirteen years.[70] The Chamber gave him a far bigger platform. Lesher had failed to even tread water during his tenure of nearly a quarter century. It took Donohue just five years to double the Chamber's budget and not much longer to come close to doubling it again.

Most important, he overhauled the Chamber's antiquated financial model. Lesher had relied on membership dues, so stagnant rolls meant stagnant revenue. In the early 1980s, small companies had paid average dues of $150. The largest paid $5,000—a microscopic amount for a huge corporation. When Donohue took over in 1997, the Chamber still raised only $600,000—about 1 percent of its total budget—from its largest corporate members. Just seven years later, they would provide at least $90 million.[71]

Donohue excels at "the ask." Red Cavaney, president of the American Petroleum Institute, said, "When it comes to raising money, Tom is about as skilled as anyone gets."[72] He reports making 200 fund-raising visits a year in person, and another 150 over the phone. Still, one has to wonder: What is the Chamber providing that makes these large companies write such fat checks? Donohue and his organization are notoriously secretive, but occasionally unrelated financial or legal records reveal funding sources. A *Wall Street Journal* report in 2001, for example, recounted $1 million in contributions the prior year from Wal-Mart, DaimlerChrysler, Home Depot, and the American Council of Life Insurers. The destination of the funds, according to the *Journal*, was "one of the Chamber's special projects: a TV and direct-mail advertising campaign aimed at helping elect business-friendly judges. . . . Mr. Donohue raised more than $5 million for judicial campaign ads in Michigan, Mississippi, Ohio, Indiana, and Alabama. Many of the targeted judges had rendered verdicts against one or more of the companies contributing to the effort."[73]

Other spending is election related, as when Rupert Murdoch's News Corporation donated $1 million for the Chamber's crucial political operations during the 2010 election. Corporate funds also fuel the Chamber's nonprofit foundation, which directs a range of efforts critical of federal regulation and spending. Together Goldman Sachs, ChevronTexaco, and Aegon (a Dutch-based insurance company) donated more than $8 million in recent years.[74] A *Washington Post* report detailed 2011 contributions of $1.6 million from the Dow Chemical Company, just under that amount from Prudential, and $725,000 from the pharmaceutical giant Merck & Co.[75]

Large as these donations are, they just scratch the surface of Donohue's big-donor strategy. The Chamber's tax forms reveal every donation over $5,000, but not the source. Yet even these opaque documents make clear that, for an organization that claims to represent three hundred thousand companies, the Chamber heavily relies on a very small number of donors. Its 2008 returns, for instance, listed twenty-one contributions exceeding $1 million, including one for $15 million. All told, just forty-five donors gave nearly half of the $145 million in contributions reported.[76]

Donohue has built the Chamber into a political machine operating on a scale unprecedented in American history (though we will see later in this chapter that there is now a rival: the network built by Charles and David Koch). From the outset, he ramped up the Chamber's capacities at least as fast as he raised money. Donohue correctly gambled on a virtuous cycle in which more capacity would attract more revenue, which could be plowed back into more capacity. Tracing this self-reinforcing cycle of money and activity shows how the Chamber and its big donors believe political influence is wielded today.

The Chamber's single biggest bet is on lobbying. Within a few years of his arrival, Donohue had increased the Chamber's lobbying staff from two to eighteen. But this was just the beginning. Since 1998, organizations have been required to file reports on their lobbying activities. By 2014, the Chamber had reported almost $1.1 billion in such outlays— more than three times as much over that period as any other organization and more than *five times* as much as the Business Roundtable.[77] Back in 1998, the BRT reported spending about $12 million to the Chamber's $17 million. Since then, its lobbying expenditures have been flat, while the Chamber's have skyrocketed. In 2010, when the big policy battles on Capitol Hill over climate change legislation, financial reform, and health reform were at their height, the BRT reported lobbying expenditures of just over $11 million. The Chamber? $157 million.

A second Donohue priority has been campaign spending. The Chamber spent over $70 million in direct contributions and outside spending in 2012 and 2014.[78] But at least as important as this staggering sum is how it's used: to elect Republicans and secure a GOP majority. The shift toward the GOP began in the early 2000s, when large donations from the Chamber helped knock off Senate majority leader Tom Daschle of South Dakota. By 2012, the Chamber would endorse just five Democrats for Congress nationwide.[79]

Lobbying and campaign spending are conventional parts of Washington influence machines, even if the Chamber engages in them on an unprecedented scale. A third area of expanded activity is less common and more revealing: efforts to influence the nation's legal system. This new and intense focus highlights the extent to which lawyers who seek to collect damages from corporations in court (the so-called plaintiffs' bar) have become a major target of business activism. It also shows the extent to which the Chamber sees influencing judges as a powerful means of affecting government.

In Donohue's first public statements as president, he identified the plaintiffs' bar as a prime target. In 1998 he established the Chamber's Institute for Legal Reform, arguing that "America has become the lawsuit capital of the world. It's about time we put a stop to that never-ending spiral of frivolous litigation." The ILR rapidly became a central pillar of the new Chamber—"the black box inside th[e] black box," as one of its critics put it.[80] By 2002, the institute was a $46-million-a-year operation, with reported annual lobbying expenditures of $22 million.[81] If the ILR had been a freestanding operation over its sixteen-year history, it would have been the fourth biggest lobbyist in the United States. (The rest of the Chamber would still be number one by a mile.)

More notable still is the ILR's heavy involvement in judicial races for state supreme courts and state attorneys general—races that were once low-profile, local affairs. In 2004 the Chamber targeted sixteen races for state supreme courts and attorneys general; its favored candidates won fifteen. Some of its electoral efforts seem to go beyond judicial politics. In 2008 it gave over $2 million to the Republican State Leadership Committee, and in 2008 and 2009 it gave six-figure donations to the Republican Governors Association. The ILR also spends heavily to back laws restricting tort litigation, sponsors conferences and publications advocating tort reform, and has even created a series of state and local "news" publications that obscure the Chamber's role in funding.[82]

Even more than the Chamber itself, the ILR is a political vehicle for the nation's largest corporations. Tax returns reveal that in 2009 it received twenty donations of $1 million or more, plus another twelve of

$500,000 or more—all told, 84 percent of its revenues.[83] The ILR's 2009 tax returns also reveal a list of independent directors. It includes current or former CEOs, top executives, or general counsel of many of the nation's largest firms, including Honeywell, Caterpillar, GE, Johnson & Johnson, Chevron, Prudential, Wal-Mart, and JPMorgan Chase, along with the heads of PhRMA and the Financial Services Roundtable (the principal lobbying organization of the financial industry). No doubt there is considerable overlap between this list of directors and the ILR's anonymous financial backers.

That's not all. A second extraordinary organization, the National Chamber Litigation Center (NCLC, also known as the US Chamber Litigation Center), complements the ILR. Rather than seeking to elect judges or change laws, the Litigation Center pursues favorable court decisions, especially from the Supreme Court. Unlike the ILR, the Litigation Center isn't a Donohue creation. Lesher established it in 1977, perhaps heeding Lewis Powell's suggestion that "the judiciary may be the most important instrument for social, economic and political change." Yet the NCLC was a modest endeavor until Donohue took over. It once pursued a couple dozen cases a year. Today its annual caseload is over a hundred. Staffed by formidable legal talent, it works closely with top-notch Washington firms. Recent hires typically feature a clerkship with a Republican-appointed justice on their résumés.[84]

The NCLC is active in many domains, including, increasingly, state courts. But it has focused its energies on getting a business-friendly Supreme Court to hear cases that it believes will help its members. This work is rarified, and the NCLC does it very well. Carter Phillips, a prominent member of the Supreme Court bar, says the NCLC has more influence on the court's docket than any group except the US Office of the Solicitor General. The Supreme Court agrees to hear just 5 percent of the certiorari petitions it receives, but in the last few years, it has agreed to hear 32 percent of those supported by the Chamber.[85] The Chamber's "batting average"—the share of accepted cases won—is also unusually high.

The influence of the NCLC and ILR is hard to measure. A series of recent court decisions have weakened plaintiffs' attorneys considerably, and the Chamber—bankrolled by the nation's largest companies—has been by far the most prominent organized advocate of these decisions. One striking victory has been the Supreme Court's acceptance of aggressive corporate action to use those "contracts" we click on or sign to force consumers and employees to renounce their rights to participate in class action lawsuits. The contracts substitute mandatory arbitration arrangements that are stacked in favor of large companies. Binding arbitration requires individual Americans (who may each have lost relatively small sums, even if the total damages to consumers would amount to billions of dollars) to go up against global corporations. If they lose, they may risk a judgment that they must pay the corporation's legal fees. Rendering judgments are paid arbitrators who will never see those individuals again but see the companies regularly and have a financial incentive to stay on their good side. As a private lawyer, John Roberts had unsuccessfully advocated this shift in a case the Supreme Court refused to hear. As chief justice in 2011, he cast the decisive vote in *ATT v. Concepcion*, which leveraged an obscure 1925 statute to execute a remarkable downsizing of consumer rights.[86]

Understandably Donohue has sounded rather pleased about the successful pincers movement constructed by the Chamber's two massive legal organizations. He summed up the strategy when he spoke at the conservative think tank the Manhattan Institute in 2013: "See, we have one group [the ILR] to stop all these ridiculous lawsuits around the country and class action and mass action and all that stuff. Then we've got another group [the NCLC] that sues the government about a hundred fifty times a year. But we believe in balance. [Their] suits are ridiculous, and ours are necessary."[87]

Chamber of Secrets

No private organization in the history of American politics has assembled anything comparable in scope or capacity to today's Chamber of Commerce. It combines first-rate lobbying and litigation capacities with the ability to fund campaigns and fight the trench warfare over popular and elite thinking on fundamental issues. Donohue raised big money from the biggest companies because he put this impressive apparatus at their disposal—"views for dues," they call it inside the Chamber. According to a former Chamber lobbyist, "A large company before [Donohue] arrived would be paying maybe ten to twenty thousand, and overnight would be paying a million dollars. The message was to go after these major companies. . . . In return they got greater influence, and we did more of their bidding, if you will, on the Hill."[88]

Donohue's success also rests on what a 2001 *Wall Street Journal* report called "his most striking innovation": offering "individual companies and industries the chance to use the Chamber as a means of anonymously pursuing their own political ends."[89] In 2008, for instance, the Chamber received a single anonymous donation of $4.5 million. The next year, it reported a single donation of $15.4 million.[90] Essentially, the Chamber has developed a lucrative practice of political money laundering. "I want to give them all the deniability they need," Donohue said.[91]

Reporters ferret out these secret donors occasionally. The *Journal*'s 2001 report chronicled $15 million "raised from pharmaceutical companies, funneled to ads to protect GOP congressmen under attack on the prescription drug issue." In 2010 the *New York Times* discovered that Prudential Financial had given the Chamber $2 million for an ad campaign to weaken proposed financial regulations, while Dow had given $1.7 million to battle proposals for tightened security at chemical facilities. A foundation headed by Maurice Greenberg, former head of American International Group (AIG), passed $18 million to the Chamber's foundation—which a union group charged was used illegally to support Chamber advocacy of interest to the financial sector.[92]

Still, these numbers pale beside the revelation that the health insurance industry, through its trade association, transferred *over $102 million* to the Chamber to fight against health care reform in 2009 and 2010.[93] Even as the nation's largest insurance companies negotiated publicly with the Obama administration, they were silently bankrolling the Chamber's unprecedented effort to defeat the Affordable Care Act through a barrage of ads and "grassroots events." Commentators focused, understandably, on the hypocrisy of the insurers, who were not only playing both sides to make sure they got the most industry-friendly deal but also relying on conduits of "dark money"—unreported contributions that come overwhelmingly from corporations and the nation's wealthiest families—to cover their tracks. Trevor Potter, former chairman of the Federal Election Commission (FEC), noted that insurers "clearly thought the Chamber would be a more credible source of information and advertising on health care reform, and it would appear less self-serving if a broader business group made arguments against it than if the insurers did it."[94]

This practice, which has become standard procedure under Donohue, reveals even more about the modern Chamber than it does about health insurers. The Chamber describes itself as "a nonprofit membership organization representing *the unified interests* of US business before Congress, government agencies, and the courts."[95] Responding to the news about health insurers, union-sponsored US ChamberWatch commented that the "Chamber has given up the right to call themselves the voice of American business; they are the voice of the insurance industry."[96]

The old Chamber didn't do business that way; its procedures required broad consensus.[97] Back in the early Reagan years, a top Chamber official summarized it this way: "We're a great big organization . . . and we only get involved in big issues common to us all. . . . We don't get into special pleading for anyone."[98] Now you'd have to amend the quote: "We don't get into special pleading *for anyone who's not willing to pay*." Those willing to pay apparently include the tobacco industry, where the Chamber has gone global, launching an aggressive effort to fight antismoking initiatives in countries including Ireland, the Philippines, Uruguay, and Moldova.[99] Richard Lesher, recently asked to comment on his successor's practices, agreed that they represented a fundamental change: "Our policy was that . . . we didn't carry the water for single companies or single industries. In fact, we had policies prohibiting that."[100]

This new model, however, is lucrative, not just for the Chamber but also for Donohue, whose compensation is reportedly tied to its revenues. Back in the early 1980s, Lesher received considerable criticism for living large; his salary at the time was $275,000.[101] By 2011, Donohue's salary was reported to be $4.9 million. Even that figure excluded substantial pay and stock from serving on corporate boards—positions that arguably created a conflict of interest for someone who, in theory, wasn't supposed to play favorites among businesses or sectors.

Like the Business Roundtable, the Chamber made a dramatic shift from broad engagement to particularism. For the Roundtable, this meant focusing on the narrow interests of CEOs. For the Chamber, it meant transforming itself into a lobbyist-for-hire. There was, however, a third set of business-oriented organizations that maintained a broad, long-term vision of American capitalism. Unfortunately, it was a vision dedicated to crushing the mixed economy.

The New Liberty League

For anyone who has attended a charity event, the scene will be familiar.[102] The emcee grabs a microphone to announce the fruits of the audience's generosity. He singles out the biggest givers by name—an expression of thanks, but also a standard ploy to ratchet up peer pressure in a room packed with alpha males. In passionate terms, he describes how this collective effort will advance the great cause that brought them together.

Even if you've seen this strategy at work, however, you've almost certainly never seen anything like the event held in Vail, Colorado, in June 2011. For this was no ordinary charity. The man at the center was Charles Koch, CEO of Koch Industries. The group's shared purpose was to assemble the largest private political war chest in American history. The cause was victory in the 2012 election, which Koch called "the mother of all wars . . . for the life or death of this country." No ordinary cause, and no ordinary audience: At the end, Charles Koch announced that he was thanking more than two dozen individuals who had contributed at least $1 million each over the past year. In addition to Charles and his brother David, the list included Richard DeVos (the founder of Amway), Charles Schwab, Cintas Corporation CEO Dick Farmer, billionaire hedge fund manager Paul Singer, half-a-billionaire Foster Friess (who would later bankroll the presidential campaign of Republican Rick Santorum, the former senator from Pennsylvania), and Art Pope (CEO and chairman of Variety Wholesalers). The total haul was estimated at more than $70 million. And this was just one event for a group that meets twice a year. Every year.

We've become increasingly numb to the role of big money in politics. But gatherings like this reflect a sea change. Between 1980 and 2012, the share of campaign contributions coming from the richest 0.01 percent of donors rose from 15 percent to 40 percent.[103] And, of course, these official numbers track only public contributions, not the huge amounts of dark money—like that raised in Vail—that has become much easier to raise and spend since 2010, when the five-justice conservative majority on the Supreme Court issued its decision in *Citizens United*.

America's wealth explosion means America's superrich are ever more free to indulge ever-larger hobbies. One of the "other" Koch brothers, Bill, loves yachting. He devoted $68.5 million of his then $650 million fortune to a successful bid to win the America's Cup in 1992.[104] Bill, however, is a mere billionaire—having lost a vicious family fight for control of Koch Industries to Charles and David. Combine *their* two fortunes, each estimated at $42 billion in 2014, and you have the richest man in the world (individually, they tie for sixth). Their hobby is politics.

The Koch brothers excite passions on both sides of our polarized politics. To invoke their names is to elicit expectations of caricature and conspiracy. Yet if we want to understand the age we live in, the Koch brothers' political efforts cannot be ignored. Starting from the periphery of Washington politics, both geographically (Wichita, Kansas) and ideologically (committed libertarianism), Charles and David have become central to one of the nation's two great political parties. They have brought together many of the country's wealthiest families and built a political infrastructure that rivals—and in some ways surpasses—that of the GOP itself. They have built what the sociologist Isaac Martin calls a "rich people's movement."[105]

Despite their seeming incongruity in a mass democracy, rich people's movements have a long history in the United States. Probably the most famous was the Liberty League, another effort by fabulously wealthy brothers: Pierre, Irenee, and Lammot du Pont. Irenee, the prime mover, saw in FDR and the New Deal a loss of "freedom granted by the constitution" and anticipated that with that loss the country would "rapidly decline in its civilization and happiness."[106] The Kochs' efforts seem almost explicitly to hark back to the Liberty League. In January 2009, as Barack Obama took office, Charles wrote in a newsletter to Koch Industry employees that the nation faced "the greatest loss of liberty and prosperity since the 1930s."[107] In an invitation to one of the brothers' semiannual events, Charles wrote, "It is up to us to combat what is now the greatest assault on American freedom and prosperity in our lifetimes." The Liberty League, founded in 1934, floundered after only a few years, but the Kochs have built something larger and more durable during their extraordinary forty-year journey: an extreme right-wing organization with massive mainstream clout.

Life on the Fringe

Charles and David Koch grew up in an intensely political family. As David recalled, their father, Fred, "was constantly speaking to us children about what was wrong with government and government policy. . . . It's something I grew up with—a fundamental point of view that big government was bad, and imposition of government controls on our lives and economic fortunes was not good."[108]

If this sounds like run-of-the-mill conservatism, it wasn't. Koch the elder's views were on the extreme right edge of midcentury political opinion. In October 1938—in a year that had already seen the Nazi annexation of Austria, occupation of the Sudetenland, and destruction of the Nuremberg synagogue—Fred Koch looked at the future Axis powers with admiration. He insisted that "the only sound countries in the world are Germany, Italy, and Japan." He compared Germany favorably with the New Deal United States: "When you contrast the state of mind of Germany today with what it was in 1925, you begin to think that perhaps this course of idleness, feeding at the public trough, dependence on government, etc., with which we are afflicted is not permanent and can be overcome."[109]

This contempt for America's moral fiber was not an aberration. Two decades later, Fred Koch became a founding and prominent member of the John Birch Society. Birchers raised many alarms, including the threat of world government embodied in trick-or-treaters carrying UNICEF collection boxes. They saw communists under every bed, including the ones in the White House. The society's leader, Robert Welch, called President Eisenhower a "dedicated, conscious agent of the communist conspiracy." Dwight's brother Milton (the quintessential mixed-economy man we discussed in chapter 5) was probably "his boss within the Communist Party."[110] For Fred Koch, the civil rights movement was also a communist plot: an effort to incite a race war, with communists waiting to pick up the pieces.

The Koch brothers grew up with this worldview, and they carried a lot of it forward. Charles always took politics very seriously. He not only joined the John Birch Society but also opened a John Birch Society bookstore in downtown Wichita. When a friend carried a copy of *The Sun Also Rises* to the Koch compound (part of an English assignment), Charles told him that the book could not cross the threshold, since its author, Ernest Hemingway, was a communist.[111] Over time, however, as the brothers pursued animated political discussions with friends in their basement and attended seminars on the outer reaches of the American fringe, they seem to have made one major adjustment in their worldview: They substituted the federal government for Communism.

The Kochs are what we have called hard Randians: believers that the absolute minimum of government is a moral imperative. Their views are conventionally labeled libertarian, and, indeed, David ran for vice president on the Libertarian ticket in 1980. A regular discussion partner with Charles in the 1960s described him as "a very committed libertarian, possibly even what we call an anarcho-capitalist." Ed Crane (who would become the longtime head of the libertarian Cato Institute, for which the Kochs were for many years the leading funders) remembers that when he first discussed politics with Charles, he was surprised to find that "he was more hardcore than I was."[112]

No doubt the Koch brothers' stance was also consistent with the interests of Koch Industries, a company knee-deep in oil. The economic rents that flow to corporations from the absence of regulation are especially great for companies, such as Koch Industries, that engage in the business of extracting, processing, and transporting commodities. If your business model generates huge negative externalities, libertarian governance is profitable.

Yet if the Koch brothers' views were consistent with the company's interests, their political efforts were not geared toward the short-term bottom line. For a company its size, Koch Industries has not invested heavily in lobbying. And aside from David's brief and catastrophic dip into the 1980 campaign (his ticket polled 1 percent of the vote), it would be many years before the Kochs focused on electoral politics. Instead of seeking votes or currying favor in Washington, they promoted their ideas, beginning a decades-long quest to change the way Americans think about government.

"Academic Scribblers"

Charles Koch is an extraordinary businessman. Since taking the helm of Koch Industries in 1966, the year before his father's death, he has overseen the transformation of a successful but small company into a vast industrial and financial empire. Throughout his adult life, he has applied the same energy, determination, and patience to politics. For most of that period, his focus was striking in two respects. First, he and his brother David largely ignored the Republican Party, which was the natural center of gravity for most business leaders. For the Kochs, the GOP and the Democrats were not so different. Even Reagan attracted little enthusiasm. To the Kochs, he was more of the same.

The second illuminating feature of Charles's political activity was his choice of focus: He and David invested substantially and consistently in reshaping the nation's political culture. They weren't alone: Starting in the early 1970s, business leaders and conservative philanthropists poured large amounts of money and organizational energy into the pro-

---

duction and dissemination of ideas. Nearly all of the biggest think tanks on the right—the Heritage Foundation, Cato, the American Enterprise Institute—either began or were greatly expanded during the next decade. In 1986 the journalist Gregg Easterbrook counted at least twenty-nine new "noteworthy public policy groups" that had emerged or greatly expanded—"nearly all . . . antiliberal."[113] Alongside Heritage, Cato, and AEI, the long list included the Manhattan Institute, the Hoover Institution, the Competitive Enterprise Institute, and the National Center for Policy Analysis.

Nobody, however, placed more emphasis on the ideological fight than the Kochs. In a 1974 speech to libertarian thinkers and business leaders in Dallas, Charles explained,

> The most important strategic consideration to keep in mind is that any program adopted should be highly leveraged so that we reach those whose influence on others produces a multiplier effect. That is why educational programs are superior to political action, and support of talented free-market scholars is preferable to mass advertising. . . . And this task is not impractical. As the "Powell Memorandum" points out, "business and the enterprise system are in deep trouble, and the hour is late." But the system can be restored if business will reexamine itself and undertake radical new efforts to overcome the prevalent anticapitalist mentality.[114]

Beginning in the 1970s, the Koch brothers poured tens of millions of dollars into building what Charles called "a well-financed cadre of sound proponents of the free enterprise philosophy." As the most detailed history of American libertarianism puts it, the Kochs have been "the biggest financiers of libertarian causes in the past few decades." More than mere investors, their support amounts to "a labor of love."[115]

The most prominent result of this labor is the Cato Institute, founded in 1977. Charles also spread money to hundreds of other institutions, especially universities. In just a five-year period, 2007 through 2011, the total for programs, conferences, fellowships, and endowed professorships came to nearly $31 million.[116] Prominent among them was the Mercatus Center at George Mason University, a powerful voice for deregulation.

Charles believed in the centrality of ideas. If agreeing with Keynes on nothing else, he would have appreciated Keynes's conviction that those "in authority, who hear voices in the air, are distilling their frenzy from some academic scribbler of a few years back."[117] As one historian paraphrased a longtime Koch aide, the Koch brothers were operating on the belief that "politicians, ultimately, are just actors playing out a script . . . one gets better results aiming not at the actors but at the scriptwriters, to help supply the themes and words for the scripts—to try to influence the areas where policy ideas percolate from academia and think tanks."[118]

"It took years to bring this country around to believing that government could solve problems better than the market," explained George Pearson, a prominent figure in many Koch-linked organizations and the longtime head of the Charles Koch Foundation, "and it will take years to get rid of that destructive notion." Koch, according to Pearson, "did not see politicians as setting the prevalent ideology but as reflecting it. . . . Charles's strategy focused on grooming the intellectual class—through education, research funding, and other efforts—who would in turn shape public opinion and influence lawmakers."[119]

Building a Shadow Party

By the early 1980s, the Koch brothers began to dip their toes into "downstream" parts of the political process. In 1984 they established Citizens for a Sound Economy (CSE), selecting as its first chairman Ron Paul, the libertarian Republican congressman from Texas. The group engaged in agitation around regulation and taxation, drew funding from major industries (including substantial backing from tobacco companies), and often matched its priorities to those of its contributors. Its most successful foray into Washington politics was to organize the winning coalition against Bill Clinton's 1993 proposal for an energy tax—an appropriate scalp for a group with such close ties to Koch Industries.[120]

Citizens for a Sound Economy was a middle-sized enterprise, and it never became a large one. In 2003 its directors chose Dick Armey—the pugnacious and conservative former House majority leader—as its new chairman. Almost immediately, he clashed with the Kochs, who have a well-earned reputation for demanding tight control and falling out with even their closest allies. (In 2012 they would force out Ed Crane, the man they had picked to head Cato, eventually installing an Ayn Rand devotee in his place.)[121] Within a year of Armey's appointment, CSE ruptured.

Armey's faction inherited part of the organization, renaming it Freedom Works. The Kochs took the rest and rechristened it Americans for Prosperity (AFP).

The rupture coincided with a decisive shift in the nature of the Koch political enterprise. Americans for Prosperity had a $2 million budget in 2004. By 2010, its budget was $40 million. During the 2012 campaign cycle, it spent $179 million.[122] And by then, AFP was just one piece of an (intentionally) bewildering web of organizations that formed the Koch network. The network raised at least $407 million during the 2011–12 campaign cycle. By 2014, its estimated budget had reached close to $300 million annually.[123] The following year, the Kochs announced plans to raise an astonishing $889 million for the 2016 election cycle.

The withering array of Koch-related organizations was no Rube Goldberg machine. It was more like an offshore holding company, designed to shield donors and to make it all but impossible to determine whether money designated for "social welfare purposes"—exempt from campaign finance rules—found its way into electoral politics.[124] These funds have been deployed to construct what is essentially a shadow political party. Working with Art Pope (sometimes called the "third Koch brother"), the network spent at least $24 million to develop Themis, the most sophisticated voter database in conservative politics.[125] By the 2014 election, Americans for Prosperity had five hundred field operatives active in thirty-five states—triple the manpower it had in place just two years earlier. The network built specialized organizations for outreach to particular constituencies. For Latinos, it developed the Libre Initiative, based in Mission, Texas. According to the *Washington Post*, it "has full-time staff members in eight states working to convince Latinos that the new health care law and other Democratic policies are harmful to their families."[126] Similar groups target veterans, the elderly, and young Americans.

Two entities acted as "banks" for the broader Koch network: Freedom Partners and the wittily named Center to Protect Patients' Rights (CPPR). Freedom Partners was set up in November 2011, with a board that includes current and former Koch Industries executives. Because Freedom Partners was organized as a business association, contributors could deduct the expense from their businesses. The group soon had over two hundred members. In an instant, it was larger than the US Chamber of Commerce, with $256 million in revenues in its first year.[127]

Yet Freedom Partners was no ordinary business association. According to a spokesman, the organization funds groups "based on whether or not they advance the common business interests of our members in promoting economic opportunity and free-market principles."[128] Between Freedom Partners and CPPR, hundreds of millions flowed to campaigns, including a huge clandestine contribution from CPPR to groups opposing a 2012 ballot initiative in California that raised taxes temporarily to balance the state budget. The groups doled out large sums to other organizations in the right-wing orbit: $3 million to the Chamber of Commerce, $2.5 million to the National Federation of Independent Business, $500,000 to the Heritage Foundation's political arm, Heritage Action for America, and $6.6 million to the National Rifle Association (NRA).[129]

True, the Koch brothers could have financed these efforts themselves. With a combined wealth of over $80 billion, it would have been a hobby funded easily with their fortunes' yearly earnings. But that is not what the Kochs did. They built a rich people's movement. Beginning in 2003, Charles began to form a social network that could intervene in politics directly on a grand scale. According to Richard Wilcke, who ran yet another Koch organization, Council for a Competitive Economy, Charles "wanted more guys like him who would put money into Cato and these different organizations . . . [He was trying to] identify other Charles Kochs" and build "movement-type organizational support."[130]

The beginnings were inauspicious. The first "seminar" held in Chicago in 2003 could have fit comfortably in a largish living room: a group of seventeen, many of them family friends. But the process became self-reinforcing. The bigger and wealthier the network grew, the more desirable attendance at its gatherings became. It turned into a draw for both the donors and the "talent" that participated in the events. The donor audience grew to a hundred and then to two hundred. A meeting in Rancho Mirage, California, in 2011 raised a reported $49 million. One in Indian Wells raised $70 million. The Vail meeting raised more than $70 million.

Another attraction of the Koch seminars was secrecy. As Kevin Gentry, one of the organizers, put it, "There is anonymity we can protect."[131] Sort of. Reporters slip past security. Guest lists get leaked. People leave spreadsheets behind. In addition to those involved at the Vail gathering, the list of those known to have attended the Koch events include Phil Anschutz, billionaire owner of the *Examiner* newspapers and the conservative magazine the *Weekly Standard*; Ken Griffin, billionaire founder and CEO of the hedge fund Citadel; billionaire tech entrepreneur Rob Ryan; billionaire Minnesota media mogul Stan Hubbard; billionaire members of the family of J. Howard Marshall (who had profited spectacularly from an early stake in Koch Industries); John Schnatter, the billionaire founder of Papa John's Pizza; billionaire private equity king Steve Schwarzman; billionaire Home Depot cofounder Ken Langone; billionaire building products tycoon Diane Hendricks; and on and on.[132] If you build it, billionaires will come.

The dazzling donor list mirrors a dazzling list of the GOP's leadership class, each side jostling to meet the other. The list of known attendees of the Koch confabs is long. It includes prominent Republican political leaders past and current, such as Paul Ryan, Eric Cantor, Mitch McConnell, Marco Rubio, Jim DeMint, Haley Barbour, and Tom Cotton; media figures including Rush Limbaugh, Glenn Beck, and Charles Krauthammer; and Supreme Court Justices Antonin Scalia and Clarence Thomas.[133] Mitt Romney, whom David Koch endorsed in 2008, aggressively courted the initially reluctant brothers in the 2012 race, eventually receiving a gala fund-raiser at the younger brother's summer home in July 2012. (An internal Romney campaign memo leaked to the press described his extensive efforts to attract the support of "the financial engine of the Tea Party.")[134] Former Virginia governor Bob McDonnell—viewed as a rising star in the party until he crashed and burned in a scandal—attended at least eight of the meetings. This movement is not at war with the GOP establishment.

Marrying the GOP

To the contrary, the Koch network inaugurated the brothers' effective alliance with the Republican Party. The Kochs weren't the GOP's only big-money backers, of course. Rove's American Crossroads and Crossroads Grassroots Policy Strategies (GPS) followed many of the same basic strategies, with a somewhat less ideological edge. But while rivalries and disagreements sometimes flare between the two giant machines that now dominate Republican finance—Rove's group is seen as closer to "the Establishment," including groups like the Chamber; the Koch network, including Americans for Prosperity, closer to the Tea Party wing—there is enormous overlap.[135] They draw on many of the same superwealthy donors, contribute to many of the same organizations, and back most of the same candidates. In recent elections, they have coordinated their campaigns to avoid duplicating each other's efforts or stepping on each other's messages. Whatever tensions exist, the Koch network has become an integral part of modern Republican politics.

All of this coordination was on display in mid-January 2015. As Republican elites dusted off from the successful 2014 midterm elections and geared up for the marathon presidential race to come, they gathered in the desert outside Palm Springs for the Kochs' semiannual "seminar." An event that twelve years earlier could fit in a living room had now become one of the biggest dates on the GOP calendar. In the words of a *New York Times* reporter, "Perhaps no organization commands more deference in Republican politics nowadays than the sprawling operation established by the Koch brothers."[136]

"What they've built is incredibly impressive," said Phil Cox, recent executive director of the Republican Governors Association (and a former employee of Americans for Prosperity). "The invitation to the seminar is a big deal. It's important entrée to those donors and potential donors." Likely GOP presidential candidates—Ted Cruz, Rand Paul, Marco Rubio—lined up to attend the 2015 event. Others, such as Governors Chris Christie and Scott Walker, had strong connections to the Koch network already. The "invisible primary" had become in part the "Koch primary." In the words of Sheila Krumholz, the executive director of the campaign finance watchdog Center for Responsive Politics, "Everyone is on display, either being courted or being interviewed for the job."[137]

Like Donohue before them, the Kochs have done what the Business Roundtable could not: forge an alliance with Republicans that leveraged their rapidly expanding resources, including their growing network of the superconservative superwealthy. Yet while the Chamber became a lobbying, legal, and electoral juggernaut—often in defense of narrow corporate interests—the Kochs have remained far more focused on spreading their antigovernment message. Old-time libertarians might look at the marriage of the Koch network and the GOP political establishment and worry that the brothers had sold out. In truth, it was more that the GOP had bought in. Charles and David Koch hadn't left the fringe to come to the Republican Party. The Republican Party had come to them.

EIGHT

★ ★ ★

This Is Not Your Father's Party

I N 1993 Columbia Pictures released the film *Groundhog Day*. Bill Murray stars as a jaded TV weatherman, doomed to repeat the same tedious day over and over again. Each morning, he awakes with hopes for a new dawn. And each morning, those hopes vanish when his radio alarm lets loose the first notes of Sonny and Cher's "I Got You Babe."

For many pundits, American politics seems stuck in its own *Groundhog Day*: an interminable cycle of partisan warfare and gridlock. The cycle's beginning can, like *Groundhog Day*, be dated to 1993. Clinton and congressional Democrats met fierce across-the-board resistance from a Republican Party acting with newfound unity and intensity. The epic battles that followed—budget wars, government shutdowns, impeachment of a president—set the tone for the next twenty-plus years. A new meme in American political discourse, "polarization," became the new normal in American political life.

And now it's *Groundhog Day* every day. Elections come and go, at times offering momentary hope that the cycle will end. Dreams of a fresh start, however, give way to a new round of bickering, finger-pointing, and stupefying incapacity to deal with even the most basic problems of governance. It's as if we're all experiencing the daily letdown of Bill Murray's weatherman as those familiar, soul-crushing notes begin.

Groundhog Day was a fairy tale, of course. So, in fundamental ways, is this familiar political narrative. The sense of endless repetition is an illusion. The past quarter century has been a period of radical political change. We discussed the first of those transformations—the growing

power, conservatism, and parochialism of big business and big money—
in the last chapter. This chapter explores a political revolution at least as
consequential: the relentless march of the Republican Party ever further
to the right. Occurring alongside and often in tandem with the organized
business revolt, the GOP's hard right turn has cost the mixed economy
a second vital ally.

The Great Right Migration

Now, saying that the GOP has grown more conservative isn't exactly
news. Still, it is important to appreciate the breathtaking scale of the
transformation. Recall our discussion of the Republican Party from the
1950s to the 1970s, a party that had embraced a strong role for the federal government across a range of activities. The GOP's three presidents
of that era—Eisenhower, Nixon, and Ford—were moderates comfortable
with the mixed economy. So were almost all the other key Republican
figures who rose to national prominence. Occasional combative rhetoric
notwithstanding, their approach to domestic policy was light on ideology and heavy on problem solving.

Today such leaders have vanished from the party's ranks, replaced
by those portraying the federal government in almost purely negative
and often apocalyptic terms. They denounce once accepted policies and
positions (indeed, ones that their own party championed) and promote
stances relegated to the fringes of political discussion just a few years
prior. In other words, they have embraced the hard Randian thinking
that, over the same period, has become increasingly prominent among
America's corporate elite.

This shift has made today's Republican Party our second Great Enabler, echoing and encouraging the new hard-edged opposition to the
mixed economy within the business community. Indeed, the post-1990
Republican Party has posed a double threat. It has proved a reliable ally
of elite economic interests, even when those interests endanger broad
prosperity—the story we tell in the next chapter. The new, hyperconservative GOP has also undercut the effective use of public authority,
abetting the erosion of our national political capacity that is the subject
of chapter 10.

No less important, the GOP has built a formidable position in American politics even while moving far from the center. It now enjoys a near

lock on the House, a strong hand in the Senate, and a dominant position in statehouses across the country. Given these successes, it might be assumed that centrist voters have headed right too, or that the Democratic Party has moved so far leftward that these voters are torn between red-shifting Republicans and blue-shifting Democrats. But neither is true. The polarization of the parties has been asymmetric. Republicans have moved much further right than Democrats have moved left. As for voters, the middle of the electorate—but not, as we will see, its rightmost tail—has mostly stayed put.

Republicans, in short, have managed a feat of political alchemy: turning extreme policy stances into success within a generally moderate electorate. Understanding how they've done it—and how it's tearing down a constitutional order that wasn't designed to cope with a party like the modern GOP—turns out to be critical to grasping why the mixed economy is in crisis.

Yesterday's Conservative Firebrand Is Today's Republican Moderate

In early May 2012, the four-term Indiana senator Richard Lugar went down in a primary, losing by *20 points* to Tea Party favorite Richard Mourdock. (A few months later, this same Richard Mourdock would announce fatally that he opposed legal abortions in cases of rape because the pregnancy "was something God intended to happen.") Following Lugar's defeat, pundits fretted about whether moderates could survive in the contemporary GOP. Yet as political scientist David Karol countered, what moderate?[1] When Lugar joined the Senate in 1978, he was on the *conservative* end of the party—to the right not only of middle-of-the-road Republicans such as Mark Hatfield of Oregon and New York's Jacob Javits but also of Robert Dole of Kansas and Alaska's Ted Stevens, both of whom were considered conservative.

By the time of Lugar's defeat, he was indeed at the moderate end of the party. This had little to do, however, with any movement on the senator's part. The depiction of him as a moderate is akin to that strange sensation—scientists call it vection—you can experience when sitting in a train at a station. When another train pulls in, you feel as though *your* train is moving in the opposite direction, even though you are staying put. So it was with Lugar. He had stayed pretty much in place, but the emerging party around him was a train moving briskly to the right.

You feel political vection a lot these days. Take House Speaker Paul

Ryan: When he stepped in to rescue his predecessor, John Boehner, from the party's recalcitrant right wing in 2015, he was treated as a leading "establishment" figure and regularly lauded as a consensus seeker. ("Establishment" has become the new "moderate," since even most pundits can't quite call Ryan a moderate with a straight face.) Yet Ryan's positions (soon to be dissected) put him well to the right of any modern GOP Speaker. When Mitt Romney picked him as his running mate in 2012, the noted election expert Nate Silver pointed out that he was "the most conservative Republican member of Congress to be picked for the vice presidential slot since at least 1900."[2] At the time, Silver observed, Ryan's voting record placed him very close to Michelle Bachmann, the Minnesota Republican who founded the House Tea Party Caucus, and who took the floor to urge her colleagues to repeal the Affordable Care Act "before it literally kills women, kills children, kills senior citizens," and suggested investigating Democratic members of Congress to determine whether they were "pro-American."[3]

Ryan is certainly more conservative than Boehner, who, by the end of his rocky tenure, was celebrated (and derided) as a deal-making, center-seeking institutionalist. Yet here again, vection was at work. When Boehner moved into the inner circles of GOP leadership in the 1990s, as we saw in the last chapter, he was a member of the GOP's *hard right*. In the post-1994 Congress that made Newt Gingrich speaker—a House majority seen at the time as stunningly right wing—Boehner was among the most conservative members. Relying on those same scores of voting records used to calculate Lugar's moderation, political scientists ranked members of that 1995–96 Congress from number 1, the most liberal, to number 445, the most conservative. (There are 445 because resignations and deaths created some turnover.) Working from left to right, Gingrich himself was number 309, which placed him just about in the middle of the Republican caucus. Boehner's voting record placed him far to Gingrich's right, at number 391. (Other prominent GOP leaders were even more extreme: Tom DeLay and Dick Armey were numbers 421 and 427, respectively.) Sixteen years later, that same score would put Boehner at number 336, right about in the middle of the new, much more conservative caucus (and far to the left of Paul Ryan). Voilà! A centrist is born.[4]

Nor is the evidence that the middle of the GOP continues to march rightward limited to Congress. Extending these sorts of analyses to other offices, you see the same striking pattern. GOP presidential candidates

have become more conservative, while Democratic candidates have not
moved left. Republican vice presidential nominees have become *much*
more conservative in the past quarter century, while Democratic nominees have become slightly *less* liberal.[5] Similar techniques that are used
to place Supreme Court justices on a left-right scale show that current
Democratic appointees on the court are quite moderate by modern standards. In contrast, four of the current GOP appointees—Thomas, Scalia,
John Roberts, and Samuel Alito—are among the six most conservative
justices to serve on the court in the last seventy-five years. The fifth,
Anthony Kennedy, the reliable swing vote and hence predictably considered a "centrist," is one of the ten most conservative justices on the
Supreme Court over that long period.[6]

Yesterday's Great Republican Idea Is Today's Socialist Plot

It isn't just the voting records of Republican leaders that reveal their Great
Right Migration. An even more telling way to track the GOP's movement
is to focus on its positions on core issues of governance, including health
care, taxes, and policies designed to address inequality and ensure opportunity. In each of these areas, one can see a long, steady march away
from the postwar consensus on the mixed economy. Proposals that most
Republican policy makers had once viewed as part of government's constructive economic role are now viewed with hostility—indeed, derided
as socialism.

Health care provides a vivid example. In the debate over President
Bill Clinton's health plan, roughly half of Senate Republicans backed a
competing, market-oriented approach advocated by the Heritage Foundation. It included an individual coverage "mandate" requiring Americans to have insurance, new subsidies to help low-income Americans
afford coverage, and reform of the insurance market to ensure that insurers couldn't deny coverage to those with preexisting conditions. If these
elements sound familiar, they should: The Heritage plan provided the
blueprint for the bill that passed in Massachusetts with the support of
GOP governor Mitt Romney. As late as 2008, Newt Gingrich and many
other leading Republicans continued to support this basic model. Yet
when these same principles became the template for President Obama's
plan the following year, it turned out that the GOP had always been at
war with Eurasia. Every national Republican, including Romney and
Gingrich, denounced it in the most apocalyptic terms.[7]

243

Once, the Republican Party could be counted on to work with Democrats to restrain the growth of federal health spending by using Medicare's bargaining leverage to hold down provider charges. (In fact, Reagan and George H. W. Bush each spearheaded new payment controls, with substantial GOP support in Congress.) Until 1994, that is. Beginning under Gingrich, Republicans renounced these once bipartisan efforts to control costs within the health care industry. Instead, GOP leaders focused their proposals on cuts in benefits, even ones that would in practice have little impact on overall costs. They advocated turning Medicaid into a limited "block grant" to the states, and proposed to transform Medicare into a voucher-style system in which the federal government made a fixed contribution to the cost of private plans. According to expert analyses, the Medicaid proposal was basically a huge stealth cut in benefits, leaving the states to do the dirty work of slashing the program. Similarly, Medicare vouchers promised to shift health costs from the federal government onto beneficiaries but do little to restrain overall health spending or prices.[8] Cost control was now about cutting benefits, not delivering them for less—at least if delivering them for less meant reducing the income of health insurers, drug companies, and other medical interests.

The GOP has also turned right on issues related to taxes and deficits. Ronald Reagan agreed to raise taxes on numerous occasions, maintaining the established bipartisan formula for handling budget deficits: cut spending and raise taxes. After 1990, Democrats continued to accept the same basic approach. Republicans, not so much. They refused to support *any* tax increases in budget packages. In fact, they went further. On numerous occasions, they insisted that "deficit reduction" include (deficit-raising) tax cuts. Clinton's 1993 budget plan—similar to the agreement reached with George H. W. Bush in 1990—received no Republican votes. In the subsequent budget battles between Gingrich and Clinton, GOP budget plans didn't just reject tax increases; they pushed for spending cuts large enough to eliminate the deficit and *cut* taxes.[9]

And not just any tax cuts. From 1994 on, a simple principle seemed to dictate GOP tax stances: the more a particular tax fell on the wealthiest Americans, the more important it was to cut it.[10] Both Reagan and George H. W. Bush had signaled that a progressive tax code remained a priority and, in 1986 and 1990, had supported tax packages based on that principle. But after the Gingrich revolt, Republicans focused increasingly on tax cuts for the highest income groups—cuts in the estate, dividends, and capital gains taxes, as well as the top marginal income tax rate. They did so even though public opinion polls have indicated consistently that voters' biggest complaint about the federal tax system is that the rich do not pay their fair share.[11]

Or consider the shifting GOP stance on the Earned Income Tax Credit, which provides support to low-income *working* households. The EITC grew out of conservative icon Milton Friedman's proposal for a negative income tax. It appealed to liberals because it boosted low-wage workers' earnings and offset those workers' payroll taxes. It appealed to conservatives because it went only to workers, required minimal administration, and entailed limited distortion of market signals. In the late 1970s and 1980s, the EITC became a cornerstone of moderate thinking in both parties about how to reduce poverty. It was made permanent in 1978, and expanded in 1986 and 1990—each time with strong bipartisan support.[12]

Or, rather, with strong but *declining* bipartisan support. When the 1993 Clinton budget included a further EITC expansion, that plan received not one Republican vote in either chamber. By the mid-1990s, Republicans didn't merely resist expanding the EITC; many began calling for cuts, lumping it into the sinister category of "welfare." The main action on the EITC they favored was not upping benefits but clamping down on alleged fraud—and, in particular, increasing tax audits of the working poor, even though independent analyses showed that the Internal Revenue Service would reduce tax fraud far more effectively by focusing on tax avoidance at the top of the income ladder.[13]

Ever since, spurred by well-funded advocacy groups such as Americans for Tax Reform and the Club for Growth, a hard-line stance on taxes has become the GOP's default position. Reduced to haiku, it might read: "Always cut taxes . . . mostly on job creators . . . reduce spending more." This poetic posture culminated (at least for now) in a Republican presidential debate in Iowa in August 2011. *Fox News*'s Bret Baier asked the eight avowed deficit hawks on the stage, "Say you had a deal, a real spending cuts deal, ten to one . . . spending cuts to tax increases. . . . Who on this stage would walk away from that deal? Can you raise your hand if you feel so strongly about not raising taxes, you'd walk away on the ten-to-one deal?"

All eight candidates raised their hands. The GOP crowd roared approval.[14]

GOP Hearts Rand

The turn against the EITC isn't the only example of tough new GOP rhetoric that rejects the mixed economy's moderate combination of public and private responsibility. In a 2002 editorial that went viral, the *Wall Street Journal* clucked about "lucky duckies": those near the bottom of the income distribution who received benefits from government but paid no federal income tax.[15] Calling the poorest working Americans "lucky" was Orwellian; calling them "the nontaxpaying class" was inaccurate, since even the poorest working families pay other federal taxes, including the payroll tax.

But "lucky duckies" was just the opening salvo. Within a decade, the Randian dichotomy between "makers" and "takers" would assume a central place in the Republican rhetorical repertoire. The most famous expression, of course, was Mitt Romney's "47 percent" analysis offered to donors at an exclusive private fund-raiser during the 2012 presidential campaign:

All right, there are forty-seven percent who . . . are dependent upon government, who believe they are victims, who believe the government has a responsibility to care for them, who believe that they are entitled to health care, to food, to housing, to you-name-it. That that's an entitlement. And the government should give it to them. And they will vote for this president no matter what. . . . These are people who pay no income tax. . . . My job is not to worry about those people. I'll never convince them they should take personal responsibility and care for their lives.[16]

Some have shrugged off Romney's off-the-record comments (videotaped secretly by a member of the serving staff) as an awkward attempt to pander to the candidate's well-heeled audience, which, even if true, would be a revealing statement about the GOP's donor class. But Romney's maker/taker frame wasn't just a momentary indiscretion. Since the financial crisis, GOP leaders have used much the same language again and again. In the words of Iowa senator Joni Ernst, "What we have fostered is really a generation of people that rely on the government to provide absolutely everything for them. . . . We're at a point where the government will just give away anything."[17]

Similar rhetoric has been central to the speeches (and appeal within GOP circles) of Paul Ryan, the man often seen as the leading idea guy in the modern Republican Party. The Speaker of the House has warned of a "tipping point" in which the American way of life is "transformed into a soft despotism" keeping "everyone in a happy state of childhood." He has accused the government of designing a "hammock, which lulls able-bodied people into lives of complacency and dependency." In a major address to the American Enterprise Institute, he referred to the "insidious moral turning point" when "we become a nation of net takers versus makers."[18] Ryan later apologized eloquently for this framing, but there is little to suggest that the broad contours of his thinking have changed from a decade ago, when, in a speech to the Ayn Rand devotees of the Atlas Society, he said that "in every fight we are involved in here on Capitol Hill . . . it is a fight that usually comes down to one conflict: individualism versus collectivism." He described Social Security as "a collectivist system" and touted George W. Bush's privatization efforts as part of the broader push to "break the back of this collectivist philosophy."[19]

Denigration of the "takers" had a natural counterpart—a rapturous celebration of the "makers," as well as a new addition to our political lexicon: "job creators." The extent to which these heroic figures came to dominate Republican discourse is hard to exaggerate, but consider a tweet GOP leader Eric Cantor chose to send out on Labor Day 2012: "Today we celebrate those who have taken a risk, worked hard, built a business and earned their success."[20] Yes, because everyone knows Labor Day was set aside to honor America's business owners.

The GOP's exaltation of those at the top reached its zenith (again, for now) at the 2012 Republican Convention. The target was a speech made by President Obama:

> There are a lot of wealthy, successful Americans who agree with me—because they want to give something back. They know they didn't—look, if you've been successful, you didn't get there on your own. . . . If you were successful, somebody along the line gave you some help. There was a great teacher somewhere in your life. Somebody helped to create this unbelievable American system that we have that allowed you to thrive. Somebody invested in roads and bridges. If you've got a business—you didn't build that. Somebody else made that happen. The internet didn't get

invented on its own. Government research created the internet so that all the companies could make money off the internet.[21]

Obama never suggested that individual entrepreneurs did not make fundamental contributions or merit rich rewards. He just highlighted the broader set of social arrangements, including government policies, that create an environment conducive to productive activity. His basic argument seems unobjectionable—an accurate, if inartful, summary of the enormous contribution of government to a prosperous mixed economy.

Not to today's Republican Party leaders. They took a verbal stumble ("You didn't build that") to suggest the president meant that business people didn't build their own businesses. The GOP's "gotcha" moment was panned repeatedly by fact-checkers, but Republican leaders doubled down. They broke new ground in electoral politics by making a response to an out-of-context quote—"We Built It"—the cornerstone phrase for their national convention, complete with a song and banners.

To be sure, the GOP has been tough on government since the late 1970s. Yet even Ronald Reagan's rhetoric was vastly more inclusive than that of the 2012 GOP presidential campaign. In his portrayals of government-supported parasites, Reagan would typically focus on a tiny subset of the population: the "welfare cheats" who were exploiting the rest of us. "Takers" dramatically widened the circle of parasites to include roughly half the population, even as "job creators" radically narrowed the circle of the truly productive to a tiny fraction of citizens. Embracing Ayn Rand's in-your-face elitism is an astonishing move for a party seeking to win mass elections—a move for which there is scant parallel in any other rich democracy.

"Constitutional Hardball"

In 2012, longtime Washington watchers Thomas Mann (of the Brookings Institution) and Norman Ornstein (of the American Enterprise Institute) wrote a hard-hitting book, *It's Even Worse Than It Looks: How the American Constitutional System Collided with the New Politics of Extremism.*[22] What was "worse than it looks" was America's governing crisis, and what was responsible for that crisis, Mann and Ornstein argued, was the scorched-earth tactics of the GOP. These tactics—procedural obstruction, bitter partisan attacks, budget shutdowns—were captured nicely by Harvard law professor Mark Tushnet with the phrase "constitutional hardball."[23] Among the major examples of such hardball, Republicans have led the way and deserve exclusive or primary responsibility for:

- routinized use of the filibuster to block virtually all initiatives of the majority party;
- repeated government shutdowns;
- the impeachment of President Clinton;
- resorting to mid-decade reapportionments (which are traditionally done following the census counts that occur once every ten years) in order to gerrymander House seats;
- systematic efforts to disenfranchise voters viewed as unlikely to support the GOP;
- refusing to allow Senate votes on *any* appointments for statutorily established bodies as a means to prevent those bodies from functioning or to force legislative concessions (what Mann and Ornstein call "the new nullification"); and
- using the periodic need to raise the debt ceiling (to finance spending *already appropriated* by Congress) to extract concessions from Democrats—in effect, taking the full faith and credit of the federal government hostage so as to ransom it for favored GOP policies.

The list is not short, nor are the items trivial.[24] Together they are what led Mann and Ornstein to call the GOP "an insurgent outlier in American politics."[25]

The increasing combativeness of the GOP is amply documented. Consider Republicans who joined the House of Representatives after 1978 (when Gingrich arrived) and later won election to the Senate. The political scientist Sean Theriault has dubbed these politicians the "Gingrich Senators," and he has found that their behavior is systematically different. Gingrich Senators aren't just more conservative than other Republicans (though they are, even when representing the same state). They are more obstructionist. They are more confrontational. They are more allergic to cooperation with Democrats, not only on matters large, such as budget deals, but also on matters small, such as participating in Secret Santa gift exchanges. They are, in short, committed partisan warriors who reject the postwar bipartisan approach to economic policy. And they are the modern GOP.[26]

They Move in Mysterious Ways

The puzzle of the GOP's Great Right Migration has two parts. First, why would the GOP *want* to move so far to the right? Second, and equally puzzling, why *can* it move to the right without paying an unacceptable electoral price? To head so far toward the right pole, Republicans needed both motive and opportunity.

It's All About That Base

Let's start with motive, and particularly the motive created by the GOP's large and intense base of activists and voters. The United States is not a *Right Nation*—as two *Economist* editors wrongly described it after the 2004 election.[27] Though more Americans identify as "conservative" than "liberal," this imbalance says more about the denigration of the liberal label than about any big rightward shift. If you ask people their views on specific issues, they sound pretty liberal, supporting most modern government policies by large margins.[28] And that's true despite the marked decline in public faith in government since the 1960s.

The American political distribution is nonetheless lopsided. Picture a teeter-totter holding two siblings, with the older and significantly chunkier kid at one end. The Republican base—the heavier of our hypothetical siblings—is not just demographically different: older, whiter, more rural, more male. It is also ideologically different. The core of the party is more, well, *ideological*. Republicans are much more likely to perceive politics as a unified struggle between competing worldviews. This tendency makes them less willing to compromise, more likely to swing behind hard-line positions espoused by party elites and conservative media sources, and much more willing to punish politicians who don't seem equally committed.

As the political scientists Matt Grossman and Dave Hopkins have documented, this partisan asymmetry is most pronounced among party activists.[29] Strong Democrats are often motivated primarily by one issue, such as the environment or reproductive rights. Strong Republicans much more often describe themselves as part of a broad cause to roll back government or protect a way of life. Even at the end of the George W. Bush presidency, when the president was intensely unpopular and the Democratic base was at its most combative, strong Democrats said they favored compromise and wanted their party leaders to take moderate positions. By contrast, Republicans indicate consistently that they want their leaders to take *more* conservative positions, and prefer that the party's leaders take principled stances rather than try to reach agreement.

Given this intensity, it is not surprising that self-described conservatives also show up. The participation rates of the strongest Republicans—voting, working for candidates, contributing to campaigns—are higher than those of any other segment of the electorate. These Republicans are also further from the rest of the party's electorate ideologically than strong Democrats are from other Democratic voters.[30] In short, the Republican base generates a much stronger gravitational force that pulls politicians much further from the ideological center.

Does the Base Not See Race?

The size and intensity of the Republican base is a modern development. Indeed, the GOP was not always the clear party of choice for American conservatives. Well into the 1960s, the most right-leaning region of the country—the South—was solidly Democratic.

The Civil Rights Act of 1964 changed that. Within a generation, the GOP represented the nation's most conservative voters, and the geographic epicenter of loyal Republican voters became the Deep South—a region that is both poorer and more conservative than other Republican bulwarks. When Democratic leaders finally demanded the end of Jim Crow, black voters became overwhelmingly Democratic. More gradually, white southern voters became overwhelmingly Republican. The belated Democratic embrace of racial progress was, according to several recent sophisticated studies, probably *the* critical factor in the move of southern white voters into the Republican column—and hence in the genesis of the contemporary GOP.[31]

A more difficult question is how racial antipathies have contributed to the party's continuing rightward march. Racial hostility is often hard to pinpoint. Politicians can use ostensibly race-neutral language to convey racially charged messages.[32] In surveys, people don't always say what they think, but rather what they think they *should* think. And race-based resistance to policies or candidates can coincide with other motives and attitudes in ways that make singling out its independent influence extremely difficult.

Nonetheless, the case is strong that race is a major ingredient in the

GOP's antigovernment cocktail. Careful analyses by political scientists show that the link between racial conservatism and attachment to the GOP is substantial and perhaps growing.[33] Racial resentment seems to play a significant role, for example, in white evaluations of the Affordable Care Act, reinforced by the identification of the law with a black president.[34] Not only is the racial divide on health care far greater today than it was under President Clinton; whites are more hostile to the *same* proposal when it is attributed to Obama rather than to Clinton. Other studies suggest that white concerns about increasing racial diversity contribute to conservative opposition to social programs, as well as a broader us-versus-them mentality.[35] For some who respond to the GOP's increasingly strident rhetoric, "makers" and "takers" have different skin colors.

Organizing for (Red) America

Despite the racial undercurrents of GOP ideology, the prevalence of conservative racial opinion within the GOP hasn't increased. Opinion surveys suggest that in the past generation, Republicans, like all Americans, have become more racially tolerant.[36] Nor has the share of Americans who identify as "conservative" actually grown much—even as the conservatism of the Republican base has increased dramatically. Something extra has given that base a greater intensity and greater focus on government as the biggest threat to American society.

That catalyst is the strength of the organizations that give American conservatism shape, passion, and direction: media outlets, advocacy groups, think tanks, and other mobilizing institutions. It isn't just the GOP's voters who are distinctive, in other words. So are the elite groups that organize Republican politics. And once again, these organizations have no true parallel on the liberal side. Traditional Democratic groups, such as labor unions, have lost membership and are increasingly outspent by other organized actors. On the conservative side, however, the opposite is true. As the center and left have lost ground, the right has built precisely the kinds of organizations needed to turn general support into focused mobilization.

This machinery has three key elements: Christian conservatism, polarizing right-wing media, and growing efforts by business and the wealthy to backstop and bankroll Republican politics. The tight alliance of conservative Christian voters and the GOP—forged over two decades ago but still a central fact of modern American politics—has given the GOP a substantial base of middle-income voters who side with the party mostly for noneconomic reasons. Because these voters generally care more about the party's positions on abortion, gay marriage, and other social issues than about its increasingly conservative economic stances, Republicans have had greater freedom to head right on economic issues without worrying as much about the electoral support of their least-well-off backers. By itself, however, this freedom hasn't pulled the party to the right on economic matters. To understand that pull, we need to turn to the other two powerful drivers of the Republican assault on the mixed economy: the rise of right-wing media and the mobilization of business and the wealthy.

The Republican Noise Machine

Pundits and analysts often point to similarities between partisan media on the left and right. But the differences in scale and organization are profound. The conservative side is massive. Describing its counterpart on the left as modest would be an act of true generosity. And, in part because bulk provides clout, the conservative side is much more integrated into partisan politics and ideological mobilization.

At the heart of the conservative outrage industry is, of course, Fox News. Fox's role as an ideological platform is unparalleled in modern American history. Its leading hosts, Bill O'Reilly and Sean Hannity, reach audiences that dwarf their competitors—triple or more the typical audiences of MSNBC's Rachel Maddow or CNN's Anderson Cooper. The network's role for its audience is also unique. The rest of America's news watchers scatter across a variety of outlets. Conservatives gather at Fox.[37]

Fox is also distinguished by extraordinarily tight connections to the Republican Party. Roger Ailes, the man Rupert Murdoch hired to construct the Fox News channel in 1996 and still its president, came to the job after a career as a consultant to Republican candidates.[38] And while Ailes quit working directly for GOP candidates, he couldn't quit the Republican Party. He has repeatedly placed prominent Republicans on the Fox News payroll. Indeed, as the 2012 election approached, Fox was cutting paychecks to *every* major prospective GOP candidate for president who did not currently hold office, besides Mitt Romney.[39] The ex-governor, of course, had little need for Murdoch's largesse. As former Bush speechwriter David Frum complained, "Republicans originally thought Fox worked for us, and now we are discovering we work for Fox."[40]

Fox is just the beginning. The other citadel of the conservative media empire is talk radio, and if cable news leans right, talk radio has toppled over on its right side. In their informed book, *The Outrage Industry: Political Opinion Media and the New Incivility*, political scientists Jeff Berry and Sarah Sobieraj suggest that talk radio on the right and left can be similarly extreme, flagging some offensive quotes from left-wing shock jock Mike Malloy. Which raises the obvious question: Who the hell is Mike Malloy? It's okay; we didn't know either. Berry and Sobieraj report that he was on thirteen stations nationwide. At the time, Rush Limbaugh was on more than six hundred.[41]

And Limbaugh is just one of a very large cast. As Berry and Sobieraj themselves acknowledge, talk radio is "largely competition between conservative and even more conservative." Conservative on-air minutes outnumber liberal ones by a ratio of at least 10 to 1, and all of the major nationally syndicated shows are conservative. The six biggest talk radio shows in the country include five hard-core conservatives (Limbaugh, Hannity, Beck, Michael Savage, and Mark Levin) and one financial adviser (Dave Ramsey).[42] Moreover, the number of talk radio stations has tripled in the last fifteen years. Just the top three, Berry and Sobieraj report, have a combined weekly audience of about forty million.

This exploding audience doesn't mean millions of new right-wingers just emerged. Rather, it's mainly a product of competitive pressures caused by technological change. Like travel agencies and taxis, radio is a victim of the revolution in information technology. With more people carrying their own tunes, audiences for music stations are plummeting and, with them, so are ad revenues. Talk radio has filled the void. Cheap to produce, it attracts an older audience (which might not be able to identify Bluetooth, much less figure out how to get it to work in their Buicks). Plus, when people listen to talk radio, they *listen* rather than channel surf. Even better, the emotional intensity creates a bond between listener and host that makes it easier for conservative media celebrities to sell products. Glenn Beck can easily segue from warning of the country's collapse to selling gold coins or running ads for "survival seeds" to grow your own "crisis garden."

As technology continues to generate alternatives, and as radio's core audience ages and becomes less appealing to advertisers, talk radio might finally be in decline. But along with Fox, it remains a huge political force.

The impact of conservative media is difficult to calculate. After all, Republicans were moving right even before Fox emerged, and much of Fox's audience consists of people who already have strong political views. Even so, a recent, innovative study by scholars at Emory and Stanford universities finds that Fox exposure added 1.7 points to George W. Bush's vote in the 2000 election—more than enough to reverse Al Gore's position in the key states he narrowly lost.[43] And this bump excludes both the impact of talk radio and Fox's further expansion since 2000. Another major study found that the arrival of Fox pulled *both* Democratic and GOP members of Congress to the right.[44]

The biggest likely impact of conservative media, however, is to isolate and ramp up intensity within the GOP base. A striking feature of right-wing programming is its constant denigration of mainstream media. Listening to talk radio on a daily basis increases media distrust among politically aware Republicans.[45] And, relative to liberals, conservatives make much sharper distinctions between trusted news sources and "lamestream" alternatives. Indeed, attacks on the media have become the surest route to applause at GOP presidential debates.

Right-wing media also mobilize people. High trust, concentrated exposure, and extreme messages get people riled up, and media figures can focus that intensity on partisan targets and activities. Indeed, this capacity to focus and direct attention might be right-wing media's greatest asset to the GOP. In the early days of the Tea Party, all major news outlets covered its major events. But only Fox hyped them in advance, encouraging attendance and touting the participation of the network's celebrities. According to one careful study, "Fox served as a kind of social movement orchestrator, during what is always a dicey early period for any new protest effort."[46] And by mobilizing the base, conservative media keep politicians looking over their (right) shoulders. "If you stray the slightest from the far right," admits former Senate majority leader Trent Lott, "you get hit by the conservative media."[47]

Bankrolling Conservatism

Flanking conservative media is a network of political organizations supported by wealthy conservatives to advance a right-wing economic agenda. Indeed, no cause has benefited more from the growing role of money in American politics. Yes, there are liberal billionaires. But these liberals often have priorities that have little to do with domestic economic issues: gay marriage, gun control, charter schools, foreign aid or military action. Conservative billionaires appear much more focused on conservative economic policies. Political scientist Lee Drutman has examined contributions of the wealthy—what he dubs the "1 percent of the 1 percent." Among liberals, heavy reliance on these superrich donors doesn't seem to pull politicians to the left or the right. On the GOP side, however, Drutman finds that the heavier the reliance on wealthy donors, the more conservative the politician is likely to be.[48]

In any case, wealthy liberals are badly outnumbered. The share of campaign contributions that come from the Fortune 400 of the nation's wealthiest families has skyrocketed, and that money goes roughly 60 to 40 to Republicans.[49] The gap is likely bigger than that since, again, it does not include the huge flows of dark money that come from the well heeled (like those attending the Koch network gatherings) and are almost certainly tilted much more toward the right than open contributions are.[50]

What is true of individuals is also true of the most powerful organizations active in conservative politics. As we saw in the last chapter, the two large and growing networks dominating GOP finances—the Chamber of Commerce/Crossroads network and the Koch brothers network—are a direct outgrowth of rich people's movements. They are joined by other formidable groups, such as the Club for Growth, that invest their considerable resources in enforcing fealty to an economic vision hostile to the mixed economy. These organizations have their disagreements. But all of them support views on taxes, health care, social spending, regulation, and other economic issues that are well to the right of the positions Republican politicians espoused in the Reagan era. And in another indication of the interlinked organizational networks that have energized the GOP base, many of these well-resourced groups have also subsidized right-wing media. The website Politico reports that groups such as Freedom Works and Heritage spent almost $22 million between 2008 and 2012 to sponsor programs by Hannity, Beck, Limbaugh, and other prominent conservative voices.[51]

The Limited Costs of GOP Extremism

We have our motive. The GOP base is big. It is intense. And it is given direction by a politicized media and well-financed organizational infrastructure. Still, half the puzzle remains. What about opportunity? This is the tougher part of the puzzle, because parties that become too extreme on the major issues of the day are supposed to lose. Political scientists call this the "median voter model," and it prescribes a simple cure for persistent extremism—elections. Parties and politicians who wander too far from the median voter find themselves in the wilderness of electoral defeat.

Admittedly, the median voter model looks a little dated (even as it continues to motivate a huge amount of social science research). But, as Eisenhower's dismissal of the conservative fringe of his day suggests, the model seemed to describe pretty well how American politics worked during the heyday of the mixed economy. Today, however, right-heading Republicans are winning even as middle-of-the-road voters remain moderate. What happened to make the pull of the center so much weaker?

The median voter model rests on three pillars: turnout, competition, and accountability. Citizens need to go to the polls, they need to have a real opportunity to affect the outcome, and they need to know what politicians are doing or saying and act on that knowledge. Unfortunately, as the GOP has headed right, each of these pillars has weakened—and the political foundation of the mixed economy has weakened with them.

Some Voters Are More Equal Than Others

The first critical Republican advantage is turnout. If everyone votes, the median voter is the typical American citizen. But not everyone votes. Turnout in midterm elections is particularly low (36 percent in 2014, the lowest since 1942). In the past, however, that low turnout didn't matter as much as it does today. The midterm electorate has always been smaller, but it has not always tilted so sharply Republican. The most reliable voters, such as the elderly, side increasingly with the GOP. Young and minority voters who lean Democratic continue to have the lowest turnout rates, especially in midterm election years.[52]

It's not just turnout that drives a wedge between citizens' preferences and election results. The distribution of voters across states and districts matters, too. In fact, a growing urban-rural split in American party politics is critical to understanding the GOP's ideological evolution as well as its electoral prospects.

For decades, Americans have been moving "too close to town," as that Tom Russell song puts it. Yet urbanization has accelerated in recent decades. In many places, rural populations are both dwindling and aging as births decline and young people depart.[53] These changes have helped make rural areas much more Republican. In Bill Clinton's successful 1992 election, he carried 1,524 counties. Twenty years later, the equally successful Barack Obama won only 690 (fewer, in fact, than Democratic Massachusetts governor Michael Dukakis carried on his way to losing big in the 1988 presidential race).[54]

The reddening tint of rural America doesn't matter much for presidential elections, where (despite the tilt of the electoral college toward smaller states) greater population generally carries the day. In congressional races, however, it matters a great deal, because American electoral rules reward control of particular blocs of territory as well as particular blocs of votes. This is most obviously true for the Senate. Wyoming gets just as many senators as California, even though the Golden State has sixty-six times as many people. (In fact, Wyoming has as many senators as it has escalators.[55]) But it's also true of the House of Representatives, with its more or less equally populated districts—for different but related reasons.

As Americans head toward cities, the relative power of every voter in low-population states grows *and* those voters become more and more Republican. In the nation's most populous states, Democrats have dominated Senate elections for thirty years. Not so in the small states. Even as he lost the 2012 election, Mitt Romney ran an average of 6 points ahead of Barack Obama in the nation's twenty-five smallest states—states that, combined, claim less than a sixth of the nation's population but choose half its senators.[56] Following the 2014 election, the Senate had a 54-to-46 Republican majority, even though Democrats had won a majority of the total votes cast in those senators' elections. Indeed, between 1994 and 2014, Senate Democrats won more votes than Senate Republicans over the three prior election cycles in nine of eleven sessions (senators have six-year terms, with one-third up for reelection every two years). They held the majority of seats in just four (five if you count the switch of the Senate into Democratic hands due to the defection of Senator James Jeffords of Vermont from the GOP in 2001).[57] As writer Jonathan Chait puts it, the Senate "represents an approximation of America that is whiter and more rural than the real thing."[58]

House districts are roughly equal in population, but they nonetheless exhibit the same structural bias. Many pundits blame the Republican edge in the House on gerrymandering. Republicans are indeed pretty good at that, especially as they've done better at the state level (where electoral lines are typically drawn). Nonetheless, the urban-rural split between the parties is a much more important factor. Democratic voters tend to be packed into urban districts, but there are no bonuses for landslides. Winning a congressional district with nine in ten votes gets you no more than winning with just over five in ten. Spread more evenly across congressional districts, Republicans can turn the same number of votes into substantially more seats. In the 2012 election, even as Mitt Romney was losing the popular vote decisively, he received a majority of votes in 226 congressional districts; Obama carried 209. That year, Democrats won 51 percent of the total vote for House candidates but only 46 percent of House seats.[59]

The urban-rural split has less-obvious consequences, too. Rural areas aren't just redder; they're also areas where key parts of the mixed economy model, such as public investment and regulation of negative externalities, look less attractive than they do in the nation's urban core. Most economic growth is generated in cities, which makes it problematic for a knowledge-based economy when a disproportionate amount of political power is generated in rural areas. And the red-rural intensification also makes the ideological echo chamber even more impervious to outside noise: When local electorates lean strongly toward one side or the other, middle-of-the-road voters—so crucial in presidential elections—don't have much traction.[60] With most voters willing to support whichever candidate their team puts forward, politicians see little electoral incentive to moderate. Better to protect oneself against a primary challenge and focus on bringing out the base on Election Day.

To be clear, this structure isn't entirely good for Republicans. Its major demographic groups (whites, rural Americans) are in relative decline, while Democratic-leaning groups are expanding. The urban-rural split gives the GOP a strong edge in the House and Senate. But Republicans have now lost the popular vote in five of the last six presidential elections, going back to 1992.

Yet moderation still seems optional. "Waiting for the fever to break," as President Obama once described his frustrated search for GOP moderates, appears akin to waiting for Godot.[61] And this puzzling reality brings us to the final big reason why Republican politicians feel limited pressure to moderate and back the mixed economy: Republicans have developed a powerful formula for retaining political strength *without* winning over voters to their policy positions.

Shark Attacks, Voters, and the New GOP

In June 2015, film buffs celebrated the fortieth anniversary of Steven Spielberg's *Jaws*. Set in the fictional New England town of Amity and filmed on Martha's Vineyard, the movie was based on true events that took place almost sixty years earlier on the shores of New Jersey. In 1916 a series of shark attacks left five people dead and prompted a media frenzy. President Woodrow Wilson even summoned his cabinet to discuss the events. Not long after the last attack, a local fisherman captured a seven-and-a-half-foot great white shark. The killings stopped, but tourists stayed away. The local economy was devastated.

Four months later, Woodrow Wilson won reelection. In affected communities on the Jersey Shore, however, his vote was down about 10 points. As the political scientists Christopher Achen and Larry Bartels have observed, the lost votes appear to be attributable to the shark attacks and their consequences.[62] Woodrow Wilson didn't just ruin the twentieth century, it seems. He apparently made sharks attack, too.

Although Woodrow Wilson's ichthyological travails might seem absurd and of limited relevance, Achen and Bartels are emphasizing that voters can be distracted by random events. Yet their depressing finding points to something even more worrisome: Imagine what would happen if political actors could *make* shark attacks happen. And imagine if they could also have those attacks attributed to their opponents. Preposterous, right? But our political institutions make something like this possible, and Republicans have figured out how to engineer it. In ways that the Founders could not have anticipated, the GOP has used the power available to a committed antigovernment minority, even an unpopular minority, to evade accountability and gain politically. It has built itself up by tearing down government—and the mixed economy.

"A Transformative Figure"

The two major figures in this transformation were Newt Gingrich and Mitch McConnell. Appropriately for a party geared increasingly not to governing but to making governance impossible, both men rose to prominence as leaders of a congressional minority intent on stopping a Democratic White House and Congress.

Gingrich described himself as "a transformative figure"—and he was.[63] His genius was to recognize that if voter anger could be directed at government and the party that ostensibly ran it, power for the anti-government party would come. Gingrich and his fellow rebels liked to say that they had two main opponents: the Democrats *and* the Republicans. Over prior decades, GOP congressional leaders had learned to work with majority Democrats in an uneasy coexistence that yielded a steady stream of bipartisan legislation. Gingrich's alternative was to go to war: to foment disapproval of the status quo and to associate that status quo ("Washington") with the party in power. In a 1988 speech to the Heritage Foundation, he described a "civil war" with liberals and insisted, "This war has to be fought with a scale and a duration and a savagery that is only true of civil wars."[64] He meant it. A month later, he launched ethics charges against House Speaker Jim Wright, a middle-of-the-road Democrat whom he called part of the "hard left." (Though never charged with a crime, Wright resigned after a yearlong investigation by the House Ethics Committee.) Gingrich escalated conflict wherever he could. Anything that damaged the reputation of Congress was fair game. Most effective was the promotion, in 1992, of a faux scandal involving overdrafts at the House bank. One of the two GOP ringleaders in that episode was John Boehner.

Gingrich used apocalyptic rhetoric. Democrats were "the enemy of normal Americans." His PAC sent out tapes to Republican candidates explaining how to "speak like Newt." As one relatively moderate Gingrich ally recalled, the tapes were "all about how to demonize the opposition, how to use invective and scary language. It wasn't that he trained them to have a better understanding of foreign policy or economic policy. They were techniques in how to wage a nasty partisan war against your opponent."[65] One Gingrich tape, *Language: A Key Instrument of Control*, offered a long list of "contrast words" to be used against Democrats: *betray, corrupt, sick, decay, incompetent, disgrace, traitors, pathetic, obsolete.*[66]

Some moderate Republicans recoiled. Dan Coats of Indiana, an initial Gingrich supporter in the House, described the Georgia congressman's "belief that to ultimately succeed you almost had to destroy the system so that you could rebuild it" as "kind of scary stuff."[67] But many other Republicans admired Gingrich's savvy. As future Senate majority leader Trent Lott said, "Newt was willing to tear up the system to get the majority. It got to be a really negative pit over there [in the House], but that was probably the beginnings of Republicans being able to take control."[68]

Just as important was the second target of Gingrich's battle: Republicans. Gingrich's break with George H. W. Bush over a bipartisan deficit reduction bill that raised taxes as well as cut spending was fateful for the GOP and fatal for Bush's reelection. "The number one thing we had to prove in the fall of '90," Gingrich later explained, "was that, if you explicitly decided to govern from the center, we could make it so unbelievably expensive you couldn't sustain it."[69] To Tom DeLay, a leading ally, "The only way we could take over Congress and be a party of prominence was to have a very clear distinction between the Democrats and the Republicans. The Bush administration muddied that distinction. The Bush administration wanted to work with Congress rather than beat Congress. And so it was contrary to what we were doing. We were trying to build a party and take over the Congress. The Bush administration was trying to run the country and be reelected."[70]

It is worth pausing over this openly stated desire by two of the most powerful Republicans of the last quarter century to take on not just their partisan opponents but also their own party colleagues—colleagues whose sins were seeking to "govern from the center" and "trying to run the country." Openly stated and successful, for Gingrich and his allies took control quickly. Consensus builder Robert Michel retired, and Gingrich became minority leader. Bush's 1992 defeat made a strategy of intransigence and aggression even easier. Now it was a twofer. With a Democratic president, the GOP assault not only weakened an opponent but also made politics and governance look distasteful. Association with Washington became toxic, and the Democrats were the party of Washington.

By the middle of 1994, 60 percent of Americans disapproved of Congress—20 points higher than the norm in the 1970s. Yet this was just the beginning. Any recent Congress would eye that miserable approval rating with envy. Today our nation's legislative branch struggles to keep disapproval ratings below 80 percent, a stunning loss of legitimacy for the institution the Founders saw as the core of the American political system.[71]

The Party of No

The second great innovator in the Republicans' emerging antigovernment strategy rose to prominence on the other side of that once-venerated institution. On the surface, Mitch McConnell—the GOP leader in the Senate since 2007—could not be any more different from Gingrich in style or substance. If Gingrich always sought the spotlight, the owlish McConnell radiated anticharisma. If Gingrich dazzled with audacious pronouncements, McConnell dulled with arcane procedure. When analysts discussed his skills, they focused on his mastery of the complex rules of the legislative institution he'd worked in for over thirty years.

McConnell's mastery, however, went further. He used that procedural acumen to exploit the opportunities that our political institutions provide to block opponents while avoiding blame. Personally devoid of mass appeal, McConnell possessed a rare understanding of the American voter. He knew that voters are generally only dimly aware of the policy positions and legislative actions of politicians (in part because politicians often diminish that awareness). Moreover, voters may have a hard time distinguishing more moderate candidates from more extreme ones (in part because journalists are often unwilling to describe one party or candidate as more extreme than another). And even when voters pay close attention, they often punish and reward politicians for events they have no control over, such as shark attacks, the weather, momentary economic shifts—or, more relevant, the failure of their opposition to play by the norms that once made legislating possible.

McConnell recognized that American political institutions create a unique challenge for voters. Even attentive citizens face a bewildering task of sorting out blame and credit. The complexity and opacity of the legislative process—in which each policy proposal faces a grueling journey through multiple institutions that can easily turn into a death march—makes it difficult to know how to attribute responsibility. And that means skillful politicians have the opportunity to avoid accountability for unpopular positions.

McConnell embraced this opportunity. Facing off against Obama, he worked to deny even minimal Republican support for major presidential initiatives—initiatives that were, as a rule, in keeping with the moderate model of decades past, and often with moderate Republican stances of a few years past.[72] As McConnell confided to a reporter, "We worked very hard to keep our fingerprints off of those proposals. . . . When you hang the 'bipartisan' tag on something, the perception is that differences have been worked out, and there's a broad agreement that that's the way forward."[73]

Fingerprints is a telling word. American institutions, McConnell knew, gave Republicans considerable power to affect governance without attracting attention—especially when their goal was to prevent the government from acting. With Obama in the White House, most Americans viewed Democrats as running the show, even after Republicans took the House in 2010. Most had little understanding of how hard it was to get anything done in the Senate in the face of a concerted minority whose leader was willing to use every tool at his disposal to derail and delegitimate every single item of significance the president or congressional Democrats put forward.[74]

McConnell's use of the filibuster was typical of this strategy. Once reserved for rare occasions, filibusters had become more common since the 1970s. But McConnell took this form of constitutional hardball to a new level. Cloture motions (that is, the procedural decision to end a filibuster, which requires sixty out of one hundred senate votes to succeed) more than doubled after Republicans became the minority under McConnell's leadership in 2007.[75] The Kentucky senator waged filibusters wherever and whenever possible—even on routine and trivial matters, and even on issues or appointments that the Republicans ultimately planned to support. Few developments could have been more harmful to the basic structure of the mixed economy, which requires that government adapt over time to the changing contours of dynamic markets. The persistent gridlock brought on by endless filibusters meant little or no adaptation. It also meant, McConnell recognized, little or no accountability.

For filibusters left no fingerprints. When voters heard that legislation had been "defeated," journalists rarely highlighted that this defeat meant a minority had blocked a majority. Not only did this strategy produce an atmosphere of gridlock and dysfunction; it also chewed up the Senate calendar, restricting the range of issues on which Democrats could progress. McConnell knew proposals lost support the longer they were out there, subject to attack. He knew constant delay would drive down the approval ratings of Democrats. In the case of health care reform, for example, McConnell encouraged a handful of Republicans to "negotiate" for months. According to a close friend of his in the Senate, Bob Bennett of Utah, this was all part of McConnell's plan to smear the bill: "He said, 'Our strategy is to delay this sucker as long as we possibly can, and the longer we delay it, the worse the president looks. . . . We're gonna delay it, delay it, and delay it as long as we can.' . . . We dragged that sucker out until December."[76]

Like Gingrich, McConnell had found a serious flaw in the code of American democracy: Our distinctive political system gives an antigovernment party with a willingness to cripple governance an enormous edge. With the strategic guidance of these two congressional leaders, Republicans launched a self-reinforcing antistatist cycle. First they made government less functional. Then they highlighted that dysfunction to build political support. The capacity to generate and then benefit from voter alienation reinforced all the other potent factors that encouraged the GOP's rightward shift: a large and passionate base, amplified and mobilized by strong organizations, and reinforced by imbalanced turnout and the emerging structural advantages associated with our political system's growing rural bias. Alongside rising voter disgust and mounting political dysfunction, these powerful trends encouraged a sharp and ongoing turn toward the right.

Back to the Center?

In 2010 the Tea Party wave hit Washington. Disenchantment with the economy, combined with the GOP's vigorous pushback, created a huge "enthusiasm gap." Conservatives mobilized; the Obama coalition stayed home. Republicans picked up a stunning sixty seats in the House, along with six Senate seats, and John Boehner became Speaker of the House. The new GOP majority would go on to fight pitched battles with Obama that ground legislative activity to a halt and nearly tanked the economy. Meanwhile, GOP candidates and elected officials looked nervously over their right shoulders. This anxiety was especially on display in the 2012 presidential primary, where all the candidates moved toward the Tea Party position.[77] Even after Obama was reelected, Republicans showed no greater appetite for compromise.

The "Civil War" That Wasn't

Yet by 2014, journalists announced that the fever had broken. The Republican Party had fought a "civil war," and the "establishment" was back. While a Tea Party primary candidate had claimed another high-profile trophy—the number two Republican in the House, Eric Cantor, who had previously been seen as the Tea Party's best friend within the leadership—nonetheless the pundits declared confidently that pragmatism had triumphed.[78]

The Chamber of Commerce and Karl Rove did jump energetically into GOP primary fights, seeking to advance more electable Republicans than those backed by more hardline groups. By election night, the Chamber had put its thumb on the primary scales to the tune of roughly $15 million, mostly in hard-fought Senate battles in Iowa, North Carolina, Louisiana, and Georgia. And in most places, the candidates backed by the Chamber won.[79]

The GOP's internal conflict, however, had more to do with strategy than substance. On a handful of issues, notably immigration reform, the Chamber was at odds with Tea Party groups. (With its strong interest in the quick and easy availability of workers, the Chamber favored such reform, which Tea Party groups opposed passionately.) GOP internal clashes also took place over debt-limit hostage taking and government shutdowns, which the Chamber and its allies saw as a political minefield for the party. As the Chamber's Scott Reed put it, "The only litmus test we have is against those candidates who want to come in and shut the whole damn place down."[80]

Upon closer examination, however, the "civil war" looks more like a family spat—perhaps over whether or not to invite the crazy uncle to Thanksgiving, or over how to at least get him not to embarrass everyone. Explaining the Chamber's strategy, Tom Donohue put it this way: "When the Tea Party first came out with who they were and what they believe, they talked about things that the Chamber very much supports. Then we had a lot of people who came along who had different views, and they tried to hitch their wagon to the Tea Party engine, and those are the people that wanted to not pay the federal debt and to shut down government and to take more radical approaches *to try and get where we all really want to get.*"[81]

At its core, the goal of the "establishment" was not to select moderates; it was to select candidates who could win and wouldn't engage in blatantly self-destructive practices after they did so. In the past two election cycles, the Republican base had pushed truly awful candidates into general elections, costing the GOP precious seats. As the Chamber's Reed observed, "The big takeaway from the [2012] election was that candidates matter—and that means getting involved in candidate selection, including the primaries." As he commented to the *Wall Street Journal*: "Our number one focus is to make sure, when it comes to the Senate, that we have no loser candidates. That will be our mantra: No fools on our ticket."[82]

The reference to "our ticket" is revealing. Reed, the former head of the RNC and chair of Bob Dole's 1996 presidential campaign, made it clear that the goal was to build the strongest GOP Senate caucus possible. By 2014, the last vestiges of nonpartisanship had been tossed aside. As recently as 2008, the Chamber had endorsed more than three dozen Democrats; in 2012, it endorsed only five.[83] And if the Chamber's $15 million spent in primaries was unprecedented, the fact remained that this outlay was a modest allocation toward the Chamber's main goal: strengthening the GOP. Most of the Chamber's campaign spending was still reserved for attacking vulnerable Democrats.

In short, the Chamber-led "establishment" didn't want moderate candidates; it wanted presentable ones. Consider three of the 2014 Senate victors—all touted as evidence of the GOP's rediscovered maturity, and all backed in contested primaries by the Chamber of Commerce:

- Thom Tillis in North Carolina (a "purple" state at the presidential level) moved to the US Senate from being Speaker of the House in North Carolina, where he had been a central player in the state's sharp right turn. A close ally of multimillionaire Art Pope, an arch-conservative and member of the Koch brothers' inner circle, Tillis sits on the national board of directors of the right-wing American Legislative Exchange Council (ALEC), which in 2011 selected him as its legislator of the year.[84]
- Joni Ernst in Iowa (another purple state), touted for her just-plain-folks demeanor and military service in Iraq, also has a record of astonishingly extremist policy positions. During the primary, she called for abolishing the Department of Education, the Internal Revenue Service, and the Environmental Protection Agency, and indicated her support for a proposal that would allow Iowa offi-

cials to nullify the Affordable Care Act and arrest federal officials who tried to enforce it.[85]

- Senator Tom Cotton, who got the Chamber's backing in Arkansas, opposed the 2014 farm bill—because it didn't cut food stamps enough. About the program's beneficiaries, he said, "They have steak in their basket, and they have a brand-new iPhone, and they have a brand-new SUV." He voted to turn Medicare into a voucher program and raise the Social Security retirement age to seventy, and even opposed a resolution of the debt-ceiling crisis, saying that to raise the debt limit would be "cataclysmic," whereas default would create only a "short-term market correction."[86]

Indeed, the party continued to move right even as it made itself more presentable. Based on voting records, the current Republican majority in the Senate is far more conservative than the last Republican majority in the 2000s. And the 2015–16 House majority is the most conservative in modern history, continuing the forty-year march of the House GOP caucus to the hard right.[86] On the major economic issues, what debate there is within the GOP takes place within a space far to the right and far more hostile to modern government than was true a few decades, and even a few years, ago.

Tempest in a Tea Party Pot

In the fall of 2015, the extreme conservatives in the House, now organized as the "Freedom Caucus," claimed their biggest victory yet, inducing John Boehner to resign the House Speakership. As the irrepressible former Democratic congressman Barney Frank cracked, Boehner had been found "guilty of suspicion to commit government."[88] His replacement was Paul Ryan, the only candidate who could unify the fractious caucus. Somehow, many pundits spun this, too, as a victory for the establishment. Vection again. This was the Paul Ryan who unreservedly celebrated Ayn Rand. This was the Paul Ryan added just three years earlier to Mitt Romney's ticket in order to placate the GOP's right wing. This was the Paul Ryan whose voting record in the House was well to the right of Boehner's, or even Eric Cantor's (who had previously been the most rightward member of the House GOP leadership).

The contemporary Republican Party faces intense internal struggles, and it is easy to play up the divides among its factions or to portray its radical wing as a Frankenstein's monster the establishment can no longer control. But these narratives should not distract from the core story of the past generation: the movement of the party as a whole to a stance of near blanket hostility to the core policies and practices of the mixed economy. This profound shift is as evident within the GOP's establishment wing as it is in the Tea Party wing. The divides on economics between the two, while real, are primarily about tactics or marginal policy matters.

If you want to see how little policy substance divides congressional Republicans today, consider the Export-Import Bank of the United States. "Ex-Im" dates from the time of FDR and provides loans to foreign entities purchasing American goods. It has become a cause célèbre for the Tea Party. Opponents see it as a symbol of "crony capitalism"—a "slush fund benefitting mainly politically-connected companies that receive its subsidies," in the words of the Club for Growth.[89] Heritage Action's director of communications, Dan Holler, described it as a "perfect example of everything that's wrong with Washington." Ending it, he said, "would be a huge victory, not only within the context of the Obama era but in terms of efforts to unwind the New Deal."[90]

No, it wouldn't. Ex-Im is a flea on an elephant. It costs almost nothing, does relatively little, and—compared with other government favoritism for business—looks like a halfhearted pat on the back. As Club for Growth vice president Andrew Roth confessed, it is a "tiny little thing."[91] But a "tiny little thing" can loom large when there is huge shared ground between supposedly warring factions within the GOP.

Ex-Im looked almost dead in 2015, but in the convoluted machinations that led to Boehner's fall, Ryan's rise, and a budget agreement with President Obama, it appeared to win a temporary reprieve. It is sure to remain a prominent target for the GOP's Freedom Caucus. For these self-styled radicals, Ex-Im is an outrage because the government provides open subsidies that benefit specific corporations—most prominently, Boeing. Government, they insist, should not be in the business of "picking winners." Yet when the government hands out massive subsidies to whole sectors, Republicans rally in support. The principled Tom Cotton, who could not abide food aid for the poor in the agriculture bill, had no problem with the same legislation's huge subsidies for agribusiness (the mostly wealthy recipients of which probably do have new iPhones and SUVs).[92] Apparently, if you provide huge subsidies to whole sectors of the economy—the modern robber barons we discuss in the next chapter—you are supporting the job creators.

It's a winning formula: cater to elite economic interests while expressing free-market righteousness. And it's one of the reasons the GOP, despite its radicalism, remains a formidable force. Combining ever more extreme positions with remarkable political resilience, the modern Republican Party has made it far more difficult to exercise effective public authority. In doing so, as we shall see, it has also helped make the biggest rent seekers in the American corporate world richer, more powerful—and more harmful to the mixed economy.

NINE

★ ★ ★ ★

The Modern Robber Barons

T HE BANKS of the Rhine are dotted with medieval castles—some just yards from the river, others perched majestically on nearby cliffs. Romantic as they appear, they tell a story of private gain and social pain that remains all too relevant. For these castles once housed the infamous robber barons: princes who took advantage of the vacuum of papal authority in the thirteenth century to extract tolls along Europe's most important trade route. Wrote one English observer in 1269: "Any boat which carried food or goods of any sort on this river was forced by these castles, unless it could avoid them, to cast anchor. Not deterred by the fear of God or king, [the barons] extorted from each and everyone new and intolerable payments, generally called tolls, as a result of which the goods had to be sold at intolerably high prices."[1]

The Rhine had fewer than twenty toll stations at the end of the twelfth century. By the end of the fourteenth, more than sixty flanked the mighty waters. Sailors described seeing the next station soon after losing sight of the last. Along a nearby river, a shipment of sixty timber planks would be reduced to six by the time it reached its destination.

The costs imposed by the robber barons were enormous. Trade fled from waterways to sinuous overland routes that, in the absence of the tolls, never would have competed with river transport. Adam Smith argued correctly that "one of the principal causes" of Great Britain's growing economic advantage was its free internal movement of goods, "every great country being necessarily the best and most extensive market for the greater part of the production of its own industry."

Private efforts to remedy the problem proved partial and fragile: Everyone had an interest in renewing trade but not in paying for the soldiers. It was not until the Congress of Vienna in 1815 that European states finally banded together to stop the robber barons—but not before five hundred years of faster economic progress had been lost.

Roughly a century later, in 1934, the muckraking journalist Matthew Josephson revived the robber baron epithet with his indictment of the captains of industry and finance who had come to dominate America's economic landscape. "These men," wrote Josephson, in his book *The Robber Barons*, "were robber barons as were their medieval counterparts, the dominating figures of an aggressive economic age."[2] Of course, many of these "dominating figures" provided real value to the economy. Like the barons of the Rhine, however, the barons of the new industrial age used their vast reserves of money and influence to extract economic returns much larger than they would have received otherwise.

Today our economy also has barons. They are harder to see and harder to identify with a single name. And yet there are huge sectors of our economy—health care, finance, energy, mining, petrochemicals, defense, agribusiness, key areas of telecommunications and computing, and many more—where a twenty-first-century feudalism reigns. Like the barons of old, those of our day receive extraordinary gains that a less distorted market would not permit. Like them, too, today's barons impose costs on society even bigger than their private gains. Above all, the modern robber barons benefit from the same basic formula exploited by their predecessors: the conversion of undue power into excess profits—into tolls along America's river of economic progress.

As we saw in chapter 2, economists have a name for these tolls: rents—above-market returns that reflect market or political power (or, more often, both). Influential corporations have always been able to obtain some rents. Yet over the last generation, the scale of their gains has exploded—during an era in which many have assumed the American economy has become more competitive and efficient. One sign of the change is the increasing consolidation of many sectors of the economy. In markets for everything from health insurance to home appliances, mergers have reduced competition to just a few dominant companies. According to a recent *Wall Street Journal* analysis, nearly a third of industries now compete in markets that meet the federal antitrust standard for "highly concentrated"—up from a quarter in the mid-1990s.[3]

Even more important, the modern robber barons have become increasingly adept at converting their growing market power into political power. In some cases, the modern robber barons manage to obtain policies that distort markets. More often, they manage to *prevent* government from fixing distorted markets that create above-market returns. With critics of rent seeking focused narrowly on active government policies, these sins of omission are hard to see. But they are frequently far more lucrative than more visible giveaways. Just as papal weakness allowed private extortion to flourish in the thirteenth century, the failure of government to respond to failing markets allows private toll taking to flourish in the twenty-first.

Why have the modern robber barons been able to build so many castles alongside the river of American commerce? The Great Enablers introduced in the last two chapters deserve plenty of blame. Neither contemporary business organizations nor today's Republican leaders have done much to temper the modern robber barons' demands, as moderate corporate groups and GOP leaders once did. Quite the opposite. In their enabling role, they have encouraged and backed those demands and stood in the way of efforts to limit their impact. At the same time, the gravely weakened capacity of the American political system to overcome gridlock (a transformation we will explore in the next chapter) has proved a particular boon for the barons and their enablers. The costs for the rest of us, from higher prices to higher taxes, from lost growth to severe environmental and financial risks, continue to climb.

Although the modern robber barons can be found in many parts of our economy, three stand out: health care, finance, and energy. Other sectors have barons, but none rivals these big three in the scale of the tolls they extract or the scope of their political influence. They have not gone unchallenged: Each sector faced a concerted pushback after President Obama's election in 2008. (Indeed, each was highlighted in his New Foundation speech.) Yet their castles remain standing even as the threat they pose to the mixed economy continues to rise.

Let's meet the new robber barons.

Overcharged

American health care costs a lot. US health spending accounts for one-sixth of the domestic economy, compared with around one-tenth or less in other rich nations. At the personal level, health expenditures per capita (more than $9,000 in 2013) are roughly twice the levels found in our richest trading partners.

These cost differences add up. In 1980 Switzerland and the United States had comparable per capita spending. Yet Switzerland then moved to control costs while universalizing coverage. By 2010, the Swiss were spending about a third less per person than we were, while producing enviably good health outcomes. A third might not seem impressive. Yet had the United States followed the same trajectory, Americans would have saved $15 trillion collectively over these three decades. That remarkable sum could have financed a four-year college degree for more than 175 million Americans. It could also have eliminated all federal deficits over the same period and left a healthy surplus.[4]

Indeed, America's deficit problem is basically a health spending problem. Take out rising medical expenditures, and the federal budget is more or less balanced as far as the eye can see. No other budget item comes close.[5] After the 2010 midterm elections, Republicans made cutting food stamps the centerpiece of their agenda for fiscal restraint, calling for $40 billion in cutbacks over five years.[6] The federal government spends more than that on health care every three weeks.

The Health Care Prices Are Too Damn High

You might wonder if it's unfair that we picked Switzerland as a comparison. It is: Switzerland has about the *worst* cost-containment record in Europe. The gap between US spending and the spending of most other rich democracies is considerably larger. We can see this disparity at every level of spending but perhaps most clearly in American medical prices. Each year, the International Federation of Health Plans, a trade group of insurance companies in twenty-five countries, publishes a list of prices paid by insurers (public and private) for common drugs and services across the advanced industrial world. And each year, the numbers tell the same story: Health care prices in the United States are off the charts.

Suppose you or someone close to you has just had a normal, uncomplicated delivery. On average, US insurers pay over $10,000 when a patient gives birth. Compare that with a standard price of $2,824 in the Netherlands—the country with the next highest share of its economy devoted to health care (12 percent versus the United States's 17 percent). American women who require Cesarean section surgery will be charged an average of more than $15,000. Women who have a C-section in the Netherlands? Their insurance will pay $5,500.[7]

Not only are American prices sky-high, they also vary enormously. In other rich nations, charges are generally standardized. Not so in the United States. Just within Atlanta, for example, hospital and physician charges for a routine colonoscopy range from less than $1,000 in the least expensive tier of hospitals to more than $4,000 in the most expensive. Using a unique dataset of private claims, the health economist Zack Cooper finds almost unbelievable discrepancies across and within regions.[8] If you live in the San Francisco Bay Area, for example, a new knee will cost you more than $100,000, on average. In Fresno, approximately 150 miles away, it will cost you less than $14,000. By comparison, Medicare—which bases its rates on labor and supply costs in a particular region—pays around $22,000 for knee replacements in the Bay Area and around $15,000 in Fresno.

The Elephant in the Operating Room

Within circles of elite opinion, there is much hand-wringing about high health spending. Yet there is extraordinary resistance to the idea that prices are the problem. As the head of one of America's biggest health care foundations, Drew Altman, observes in the *Wall Street Journal*,

> People in the US go to the doctor less frequently and have much shorter hospital stays than people in other countries that spend far less per capita on health care. But health services are consistently more expensive here than in comparably wealthy countries.
>
> So it's interesting that most efforts in this country to address health care costs don't focus on price much at all. Instead, they focus on reforming the delivery of health care and provider reimbursement to reduce the volume of health care Americans use and to weed out unnecessary procedures and hospitals days.[9]

"Interesting" is one way to put it. "Revealing" would be another. Focusing on price means taking on the robber barons, and that appears to be something that most of America's leaders—especially America's Great Enablers—don't want to do.

Consider the most persistent explanation for why we spend so much more: Americans just don't have enough "skin in the game." Senator Rand Paul, an ophthalmologist, never tires of pointing out that LASIK eye surgery—not generally covered by insurance—has gotten more affordable over time. House Budget Committee chair Paul Ryan also frequently cites the LASIK example as proof that market forces would work if insurance just got out of their way.[10]

Never mind that LASIK is an elective procedure that always costs only a small fraction of even a single day in the hospital, or that it usually ends up costing a lot more than the teaser rates on billboards. Never mind that the problem it addresses is never an emergency, or that, in actual emergencies, shopping around for care is prohibitively difficult. There's an even bigger logical hole: Americans actually have *more* "skin in the game" than do citizens of other nations. In cross-national surveys, they are much more likely to put off care because of its cost. Medical bankruptcies are shockingly common in the United States, yet almost unheard of in other rich nations.[11] Whatever the proper level of cost sharing, the huge gap between health prices here and those in other rich nations can't be blamed simply on Americans' greater insulation from medical costs.

More than that, it's fanciful to think that if everyone just paid for care out of pocket, the health care market would suddenly work. We *need* insurance to pay for the biggest costs in health care. And the sickest patients, who incur the overwhelming majority of US health expenditures, need insurance the most. (Half of costs are incurred by the sickest 5 percent of patients; two-thirds, by the sickest 10 percent.)[12] Saying that the market for health care would be more efficient without insurance is like saying the housing market would be more efficient without mortgages.

But let's imagine that insurance is perfectly designed to make people price sensitive without bankrupting the sick. There's still the problem of information asymmetry that we learned about in chapter 3: Patients simply don't know what they need as well as medical professionals do. This asymmetry is why we go to such providers in the first place. But it also gives them the capacity to pursue their own aims, including charging more for services than better policy arrangements would allow.

In short, the normal price mechanism breaks down in health care. In both the public and private sectors, prices are set mostly through negotiations between providers and insurers. The main difference, it turns out, is that public price setting is significantly more effective. The Medicare program has grown substantially faster than the economy, partly because of rising enrollment and partly because of rising costs. Yet, comparing coverage for the same benefits, it has grown substantially slower than private insurance spending.[13] In recent years, private plans' costs have increased by about 4 percent a year, Medicare's by around 1 percent.[14] This comparative edge is all the more remarkable because private plans have adopted many of Medicare's payment techniques. What they lack is its enormous bargaining power.

The Best Health Care in the World?

The second common explanation for why American costs are so much higher is that American health care is just so much better than the rest of the rich world's. In explaining why he wanted to repeal the ACA in 2012, House Speaker John Boehner echoed many critics in claiming it would "ruin the best health care delivery system in the world."[15]

If we have the best health care system in the world, however, we're not doing a very good job of using it. American health outcomes are rarely better and often much worse than those of the best-performing countries. Across regions within the United States, prices have little or no relationship to the quality of care received.[16] They're higher where providers are more concentrated and high-tech equipment and hospital beds are more plentiful.[17] These might be compelling motives for providers to charge more, but they're not very compelling reasons for patients to pay more.

True, higher-income Americans with generous insurance receive care that is very good—and in some situations, yes, the best in the world. The United States performs quite well, for example, with regard to screening and care for many cancers. Even for these services, however, patients are paying much more than they would if US prices were closer to the international norm. More important, the United States often ranks poorly on direct measures of care effectiveness. Our in-hospital fatality rates for heart attacks and strokes, to name two crucial areas, are middling.[18] And remember amenable mortality: deaths that could have been prevented with the provision of timely and effective care? On this measure, the United States ranks last among nineteen wealthy countries.[19]

The *New York Times* reporter Elisabeth Rosenthal has written a series of compelling articles showing just how weakly prices correlate with quality. Among other revealing investigations, she tells the story of a patient who was quoted a price of $78,000 for a hip replacement, not including the surgeon's fee. The patient got the same hip in Belgium, where the total bill was $13,660, including all provider fees, operating room costs, five days in the hospital, a week in rehab, and round-trip airfare. The risks were, if anything, lower than if he'd stayed home, because hospital-acquired infections are less common there. As he told Rosenthal, "We have the most expensive health care in the world, but it doesn't necessarily mean it's the best. I'm kind of the poster child for that." A prominent orthopedist was more pointed: "Manufacturers will tell you it's R&D and liability that makes implants so expensive and that they have the only one like it. They price this way because they can."[20]

And yet like many informed commentators on America's cost crisis, Rosenthal seems baffled by the exorbitant, irrational pricing that she finds. In a 2014 interview on National Public Radio's *Fresh Air*, host Terry Gross pressed her to explain who or what was responsible. Rosenthal replied, "I think it's everyone. And it's partly our expectations in the sense of, wow, we want a private delivery room with good Wi-Fi and great coffee. Some of these hospitals, they're competing the way universities compete. 'We have a great gym.' 'We have room service.' That's not really the essence of health care. So if that's what we demand, we're really tracking our health care dollars in the wrong direction."[21]

Good Wi-Fi and great coffee. The simpler explanation is the one that Rosenthal's stories highlight repeatedly: Those who receive the biggest rents are doing everything they can to preserve them. Again, it's a measure of how reluctant we are to talk about this reality that Rosenthal backs away from her own clear findings. Unfortunately, many don't even probe deep enough to back away.

Political Malpractice

Which brings us to the third common argument about why our health care costs so much: It's all about malpractice. To hear some commentators, the top cost driver is the threat of litigation. Even Steven Brill, the author of a powerful 2013 cover story in *Time* about high US prices, succumbs to the temptation to feign evenhandedness by suggesting that Democrats' failure to curb lawsuits is a major cost driver.[22] Yet this position has no support in the vast research on health spending. Estimates of the amount of defensive medicine vary, but they're always tiny—perhaps

1 percent to 2 percent of total spending.[23] More telling still, Texas and California have both placed significant caps on damages, and their costs have grown just as quickly as costs in states without such measures.[24]

That malpractice is cited as a big cause of runaway spending shows just how unwilling many observers are to understand or confront the real causes. No doubt the United States is doing *something* with the extra trillions that it has poured into the medical sector over the last few decades. On the available evidence, however, what it is mainly doing is paying higher tolls to the robber barons.

Victor Fuchs, a distinguished health economist, puts the point with unusual bluntness: "If we . . . ask why health care costs so much less in other high-income countries, the answer nearly always points to a larger, stronger role for government." In other nations, Fuchs explains, authorities use their buying power to bargain down prices. Even America's less extensive programs cover enough of US medical costs to "confer considerable bargaining power, but the government is kept from exerting it by legislation and a Congress sensitive to interest-group lobbying."[25]

And there is certainly plenty of such lobbying. Since federal lobbying disclosure began in 1998, pharmaceutical manufacturers, medical device makers, health insurers, hospitals, and medical professionals have reported spending more than $6 billion.[26] Only Wall Street rivals the health care industry as a lobbying superpower. On top of hundreds of millions in lobbying each year, it pours hundreds of millions more into federal campaigns and tens of millions more into state and local races. And none of these totals includes the enormous sums spent on political advertising, grassroots (or more often, faux-grassroots "Astroturf") mobilization, and state-level political activity.

For an example of the payoffs, look no further than the fight over prescription drug coverage under Medicare in the early 2000s. With Democrats pushing for the benefit to help seniors cope with soaring drug prices, Republicans took advantage of their control of the House, Senate, and White House to push through their own plan: a costly expansion of a program many had once opposed. Why? Former Reagan adviser Bruce Bartlett offers a frank account:

> Republicans were keen to make sure that the legislation enacted was theirs, because the Democrats were certain to include cost containment for drugs in their legislation. It was widely be-

lieved that if the federal government used its buying power to pressure drug companies to cut drug prices, the cost of providing drugs to Medicare recipients would be substantially reduced.[27]

But forcing down drug prices would diminish the drug companies' profits, and Republicans were adamantly opposed to that. Consequently, despite their oft-repeated opposition to new entitlement programs, they got behind the new drug benefit, now known as Medicare Part D, and made sure there was no cost-containment provision.

Not long thereafter, the chair of the House committee that designed the legislation, Billy Tauzin of Louisiana, retired and became the drug industry's new top lobbyist, with a reported annual salary of $2 million.[28]

Tauzin was not the only beneficiary of Washington's revolving door. In late 2011, the Center for Responsive Politics reported that an impressive 370 members of Congress had become lobbyists for or "senior advisers" to groups seeking to sway public officials.[29] In recent years, more than half the representatives and senators who retire or lose elections have become lobbyists, up from just 3 percent in 1974.[30] (Since the early 1990s, nearly half of senators have also served on at least one corporate board since leaving office—a lucrative part-time job paying, on average, around a quarter million dollars a year.)[31] Congressional staff and executive branch officials are also more likely than ever to lobby. In 2012, forty former staff members of Senator Max Baucus, the Montana Democrat who chaired the Senate Finance Committee during the debate over the Obama plan, were registered lobbyists.[32]

Standing Up for the Barons

The Great Enablers—business groups and the Republican Party—haven't made reigning in health care costs any easier. Since the Chamber of Commerce's reversal on the Clinton health plan in 1993, business groups have rarely challenged the self-interested stances of the major medical interests. Even before Tom Donohue perfected his pay-to-play model, most prominent corporate leaders seemed content to either sit on the sidelines or parrot the medical industry line. Donohue's innovation—exemplified by his dark money lobbying on behalf on the insurance industry during the debate over the Affordable Care Act—was to get paid for the parroting.

To some extent, this is just a collective action problem. Corporations that provide health insurance would benefit from cost restraint, but it's the health care industry that has the biggest financial stake. For the same reason, the medical industry members of business associations such as the Chamber have an outsized influence on those groups' stances on health policy issues. And even when they don't, the general antigovernment leaning of business leaders makes them skeptical of the kinds of public policy solutions that have contained costs in other rich democracies.

But the biggest enablers aren't in the business community. They're in the Republican Party. As chapter 8 discussed, the GOP could once be counted on to work with Democrats to restrain the growth of federal health spending. After 1994, however, it retreated from these bipartisan approaches. "Controlling health care costs" now meant cutting Medicaid and Medicare. To make matters worse, while advocating sharp benefit cuts on the grounds of fiscal responsibility, Republicans began to pursue changes in Medicare that increased, rather than restrained, costs. In particular, they were the driving force behind the growing role of private plans within the program. Although Medicare payments to private plans are supposed to reflect how much it costs to insure beneficiaries who sign up, a combination of aggressive lobbying and sophisticated gaming of the reimbursement formula have resulted in excess payments that, in the aggregate, cost Medicare nearly $300 billion between 1985 and 2012.[33]

Not surprisingly, insurers love this arrangement, and they have increasingly thrown their support behind the GOP. Republicans have repaid the love by defending these lucrative giveaways aggressively. Remember Republican charges that funding the Affordable Care Act would destroy Medicare, which helped them rack up huge vote margins among older Americans in 2010? Remember irresponsible talk of "death panels" that would kill the old and disabled? These accusations were directed at Medicare savings provisions in the legislation that targeted mostly the subsidies for private plans. No one was actually threatened, and no killing was involved—except the private insurance executives making a killing off Medicare.

One has to marvel at the perverse brilliance of this political strategy. Medicare's difficulty controlling costs, Republican leaders argued, proved that the government was less efficient than the private sector. Yet one of the main reasons Medicare wasn't able to do more to control costs—despite, let's remember, outperforming the private sector—was that the GOP was blocking or undoing all the necessary legislative steps to control costs. Republicans managed to make the case for markets by delivering more rents to the rent seekers.

Amazingly, however, health care isn't where the language of markets is most abused. The bigger offender is a financial sector that has sold itself as the height of market rationality and efficiency while charging tolls that would make the Rhine's medieval extortionists blush.

Wall Street: Too Big, Period

Those tolls are now painfully visible. Eight years after the collapse of Lehman Brothers in 2008, economic production and employment remain far below where they would have been otherwise. When an economy persistently falls short of its potential, economists speak of "output losses"—the prosperity we've missed out on because of slow growth. Based on the long-term trend prior to the crisis, UC Berkeley economist Brad DeLong estimates that America's output losses already exceed $13 trillion and could well reach $35 trillion by the time the economy fully recovers—more than twice America's entire GDP.[34] And this mind-blowing number doesn't account for the crisis's enormous human and social fallout, from the emotional toll of persistent unemployment to the social dislocation of broken communities to the lost opportunities and shortened lives that accompany severe economic downturns to the permanent loss of earning power for the cohort of young Americans who unluckily entered the job market during the slump. "Great Recession" doesn't do this damage justice; DeLong suggests we call this decade-plus disaster the "Lesser Depression."

The (Out-of-)Balance Sheet

Against these and other costs of a large financial sector, what are the benefits? What besides bigger financial crises have we gained from trading in the staid financial system of a generation ago? Among political and economic elites, the conventional wisdom prior to the crisis was that finance was all upsides—faster growth, better capital allocation, lower-cost financial transactions—and for a surprisingly large chunk of those elites, it still is.

But the big upsides look elusive. Researchers have dissected contemporary finance every which way. They have yet to find knockdown evidence of large gains. Luigi Zingales, the iconoclastic Chicago School economist whom we met in chapter 3, summarizes bluntly the findings of finance experts like him: "Although academics can offer plenty of evidence that some financial activities benefit society, we cannot assert that all or even most do."[35] Far from it: The more research that's done, the more it seems that Wall Street's most-touted benefits are mostly a mirage.

Start with the biggest potential benefit: faster growth. You might think bigger financial sectors mean bigger GDP (at least when they're not crashing the economy), but economists who have compared financial systems across rich nations have found no convincing evidence that more finance equals more growth. Indeed, the relationship appears to be more like an upside-down U than an upward line. That is, growth increases with the size of the financial sector until a point of diminishing returns, and then it might even turn negative. Where is that inflection point? According to one study, it's where the amount of private credit is about equal to total GDP.[36] America's financial sector is roughly twice that large.

Why might supersizing finance hurt growth? Well, there's the ugly truth that big financial sectors beget big financial crises. Big financial sectors may also divert productive investments in the real economy that could produce faster growth into activities that reward mostly share-holders and executives.[37] For example, over 90 percent of the profits earned by companies that were in the Standard & Poor's (S&P) 500 from 2003 through 2012 went to stock buybacks (54 percent) and dividends (37 percent).[38] That left less than 1 in 10 dollars of profit to be invested in future growth or higher worker pay. Supersized finance might not be so super at getting capital where it's needed for the long term.

And let's not forget about *human* capital. Even if financial activities were net neutral economically, Wall Street would still be sucking some of the nation's best and brightest from science, education, and other fields that clearly make our society more prosperous. We are very far from the corporate world described by Peter Drucker in chapter 6, in which the top college and graduate degree holders shunned Wall Street for Main Street. At Harvard, for example, the share of college graduates entering finance rose from 4 percent in the 1960s to nearly a quarter in recent years.[39] The story is the same or more extreme at other top universities. Even recipients of the Rhodes scholarship, once the quintessential path to public service, have been going into finance at record rates. Observes the American secretary of the Rhodes Trust, Elliot Gerson, "Nothing is wrong with this picture if one believes that changed career paths of a few privileged people is not of any larger significance. Never mind that some have gifts that realistically could be expected to lead to world-changing breakthroughs, cures, or innovations; to greater respect for politics; or to hundreds of profoundly moved and inspired students."[40]

But isn't finance at least successful on its own terms? Surely it's doing whatever it does at a lower per unit cost. The (still fragmentary) evidence suggests otherwise. Finance is certainly better than ever at making money. But according to new research, the cost of financial intermediation—what households and businesses pay for what finance does, such as making loans or insuring against risk—has actually increased over the past thirty years.[41] Indeed, it now appears to be as high as it was in *1900*, before not just computers but modern communications and transportation.

The rents on Wall Street have been rising. American finance isn't just too big to fail. It's too big, period.

Friends in High Places

The best evidence of rampant rents on Wall Street might be the investment strategies of major financial firms. Not their investments in the economy but their investments in the political system. Whenever we see industries or firms spending enormous amounts to sway government, we should suspect strongly not only that rent seeking is taking place but also that its rewards exceed—and likely vastly exceed—the investment. After all, we typically assume that corporations are rational investors when it comes to economics. Why should we think differently when it comes to politics? To find the barons, look for the castles.

Wall Street has built many castles. Between 1998 and 2014, the finance, insurance, and real estate sectors (again, FIRE) spent more than $6 billion combined on lobbying. Campaign spending by PACs and people associated with FIRE exceeded $3.8 billion—placing Wall Street in a league of its own with respect to campaign donations.[42]

That money has gone to both parties. In the 1980s, FIRE leaned heavily Republican. Recall Reagan's first Treasury secretary, Donald Regan, who went from Merrill Lynch to leading the charge against regulation. The top Republican on the Senate Banking Committee, Phil Gramm of Texas, was another warrior for deregulation. He reversed Regan's trajectory, going from government service into a high-paid position in the industry. Politically, backing finance was low risk for Republicans, providing reliable campaign cash and lucrative post-politics employment, with little or no prospect of voter backlash. Because so much of the largesse toward Wall Street was due to increasingly inadequate regulation, Republicans could decry government giveaways even as they gave away the store. And because so many of the policies that aided finance were low profile and complex—including the lowest-profile policy of all: doing nothing—the GOP maintained plausible deniability even as it lent a helping hand to the new robber barons. Once again Republicans got their cake of free-market rhetoric and ate their share of the rents, too.

Starting in the 1990s, however, Wall Street tilted increasingly—if, it turned out, only temporarily—toward the party traditionally hostile to it. By the late 2000s, as Democrats clawed their way back into the congressional majority, the party of FDR enjoyed a small but significant edge in the chase for Wall Street donations. This arrangement was fateful: Friends in high places is good. Friends among your prior antagonists is even better.

The connections were personal as well as financial. The "Wall Street–Washington corridor," as financial experts Simon Johnson and James Kwak term it, is now so well trod and lucrative that it is noteworthy when someone in a top economic policy job has *not* made millions on Wall Street.[43] Take Gene Sperling, the lawyer-turned-policy-insider who headed President Obama's National Economic Council (NEC). He earned respect for his independence from Wall Street because he had received only around $1 million from the financial sector and restricted his main work to Goldman Sachs's philanthropic activities. By contrast, Sperling's predecessor in the job, Larry Summers, made close to $8 million consulting for and giving speeches to financial institutions between his stint as Clinton's Treasury secretary and his return to official Washington.[44]

And Summers was a piker compared with *his* predecessor, Robert Rubin, the crucial soft Randian introduced in chapter 6. Rubin had spent the previous twenty-six years at Goldman Sachs, and he brought to the Clinton White House strong commitments to deficit reduction and financial deregulation. When the head of a financial regulatory agency called the Commodities Future Trading Corporation (CFTC) pushed for tighter supervision of derivatives—the risky securities that Warren Buffett labeled "weapons of mass financial destruction"—Rubin and Summers sidelined the effort and pushed to restrict the agency's jurisdiction.[45]

Rubin left the Clinton administration to become a senior adviser to Citigroup, a megabank that could not have existed before the deregulatory wave. By the time of Citigroup's collapse, he had netted himself more than $120 million.[46]

Along the way, Rubin served as a mentor to many other Democratic economic insiders with strong Wall Street ties, including Gary Gensler (from Goldman Sachs to the Clinton Treasury Department to head of the CFTC), Peter Orszag (from head of the White House Office of Management and Budget to a lucrative post at Citigroup), Michael Froman (from Citigroup to Obama's transition staff, where he helped pick Obama's economic team even while remaining on Citigroup's payroll), James Rubin (Rubin's son, who went from Citigroup to the NEC under Obama), and David Lipton (from Citigroup to the NEC). Beyond Rubin's circle, Obama's acerbic chief of staff, Rahm Emanuel, had gone from the Clinton White House to a Chicago hedge fund to Congress, where he had used his Wall Street ties to help Democrats out-fund-raise Republicans on their way to recapturing Congress in 2006.[47]

The bustling traffic along the Wall Street–Washington corridor has had two major effects. Most obviously, it has encouraged public officials to remain on friendly terms with the industry they are supposed to keep in check. Yet greater than this traditional problem of political capture may be what is sometimes termed "cultural capture": the acceptance of contestable assumptions that justify a hands-off approach. Perhaps the most destructive of these was that "financial innovation" was always beneficial. So long as new products met the market test, they had to be making the economy stronger. Summers even compared financial innovation to the development of jet airplanes. We wouldn't stop jet travel because planes sometimes crash. Why should we stifle financial innovation merely because bigger financial markets sometimes go awry?

Because financial markets are not jet planes. The finance industry is rife with conflicts of interest and information asymmetries that allow insiders to profit at the expense of outsiders. Indeed, a major part of the reason Wall Street developed ever more complex products was precisely because it was so hard for clients—and regulators—to figure them out. As the noted economist Alan Blinder asks, "Didn't anyone remember the KISS principle? (*Keep it simple, stupid.*) The answer is, in fact, simple, and not at all stupid: Complexity and opacity are potential sources of huge profit."[48]

More important, the financial sector poses uniquely large threats to the whole economy. Unlike an airplane crash, the risk of financial crises is borne by all of us. It is a negative externality—a cost society bears that Wall Street firms don't take into full account. The problem is only worse when industry leaders know that government must come to the rescue if things go bad. As the systemic risk created by financial speculation increased in the 1990s and 2000s, large banks received a huge implicit subsidy because they were able to pay lower interest rates to investors who believed they were too big to fail. With banks growing bigger and bigger—by the mid-2000s, the combined assets of the six biggest US banks represented around 55 percent of US GDP, up from less than 20 percent in 1995—these hidden giveaways grew larger and larger.[49] In 2009, according to one calculation, the too-big-to-fail subsidy represented roughly half of the total profits of the eighteen largest US banks.[50]

The distinguished jurist Richard Posner, a founding father of the generally conservative law and economics field, sums up the lesson: "We need a more active and intelligent government to keep our model of a capitalist economy from running off the rails. The movement to deregulate the financial industry went too far by exaggerating the resilience—the self-healing powers—of laissez-faire capitalism."[51]

Inside Job

So why have we not seen more of an organized pushback? As in all economic baronies, the weakness of ordinary consumers and small investors is easy to explain—though we'll see that such broad groups *can* get their act together under the right conditions. But what about corporations that aren't in the FIRE brigade? After all, a big, freewheeling Wall Street poses obvious risks to Main Street. Moreover, many traditional corporations resisted initially the growing aggressiveness of the financial sector, arguing that the increased focus on immediate shareholder returns was at odds with their long-term growth strategies.

Yet after this early pushback, corporations outside the financial sector largely acquiesced to and then actively supported the expansion of Wall Street. Put more bluntly, they joined the party. Between 1980 and the early 2000s, the share of corporate profits due to financial investments ballooned from 10 percent to 40 percent.[52] As nonfinancial corporations went deeper and deeper into finance themselves, they un-

derstandably became less and less eager to criticize the activities they
had once questioned.

Business associations might have proved another counterweight.
In theory, they represent the broad interests of corporate America and
stress the long-term needs of the business community. And indeed, the
Business Roundtable, National Association of Manufacturers, and Chamber of Commerce all entered the 1980s with their dominant membership
alarmed about finance's growing role. In 1984 a spokesman for the Business Roundtable told the SEC: "Hostile takeovers threaten the well-being
of the country by causing corporations to react to intense pressures for
short-term results."[53]

Imagine corporate groups today taking on Wall Street so directly.
You have to imagine it, because today every major business association
is on the other side. The revitalized Chamber of Commerce has become
particularly hostile to financial regulation. The Chamber's Center for
Capital Markets Competitiveness—dedicated to "promoting a modern
and effective regulatory structure that fosters robust and diverse sources
of capital, investment, liquidity, and risk management for our nation's
job creators"—funnels huge contributions from financial firms into targeted legal and political action against federal regulatory oversight.[54]
Like the barons of health care, financial firms have also used the Chamber as a key lobbying arm, quietly slipping millions to the Chamber to
fund attacks on regulation while proclaiming publicly their support for
effective rules. The Chamber and, with even greater focus, the Business
Roundtable, are also energetic defenders of high executive pay without
increased investor or federal oversight—as we saw in the fights over
stock options and proxy access discussed in chapter 7.

And so we come to the final and most important reason that America's
corporate elites backstopped Wall Street: They benefited handsomely
from doing so. As CEO pay increased and increasingly reflected stock
movements, the interests of CEOs grew more aligned with the interests
of Wall Street. This shift was not always good for American corporations,
much less American capitalism. As a rule, compensation packages are
poorly designed to reward CEOs for long-term success. (The way stock
options are designed, for example, tends to reward share price increases
driven by industry-wide trends over which individual CEOs have no
control—that is, by, say, lower oil prices or better exchange rates—
making it "pay for luck" rather than "pay for performance.")[55] Indeed,

companies whose top executives extract a larger share of managerial pay tend to perform worse, not better, on a range of performance measures, including profitability.[56] But there is one group for which these arrangements work very well: top executives. And as those executives extracted more and more, they also grew more and more favorable toward the unrestricted expansion of the financial sector.

The barons of Wall Street brought the world's largest economy to its knees and still had faithful and formidable defenders. The barons of energy have done them one better: They are threatening the very future of our planet, and yet so far have successfully resisted reforms on the scale necessary to restrict the enormous tolls they are charging.

"The Greatest Market Failure the World Has Ever Seen"

Two numbers, 6 and 16, capture the heart of the rent-seeking realities in the energy sector.

The first number, 6, is the estimated value in *trillions* of dollars of fossil fuel reserves that would be "unburnable" if the world committed itself to preventing global temperatures from rising more than 3.6 degrees Fahrenheit. The second number, 16, is the estimated number of degrees Fahrenheit that the earth's temperature could be expected to rise if all these resources were actually consumed.[57]

A sixteen-degree temperature increase is an unthinkable prospect. Even increases below the 3.6 degrees (2 degrees Celsius) that scientists believe is the upper bound of tolerable global warming are worrisome. Beyond that, the climate science community anticipates devastating effects: "cataclysmic and irreversible consequences" for the Earth, as the British newspaper the *Independent* sums up recent scientific reports. Increases far less than a 16-degree temperature rise would render our planet unrecognizable.[58]

But *six trillion* is also a crazy number. Financial analysts now speak of "stranded assets"—private holdings that must be left in the ground, their value written off. No private company wants to see its assets "stranded." Just as that 16-degree temperature rise is unimaginable, so is it unimaginable that private firms will voluntarily forgo opportunities to turn hugely valuable holdings into profits.

The basic story is 16 versus 6. At the beginning of the twentieth century, private actors treated our streets and rivers as open sewers—until someone with political authority told them they couldn't. Today private actors continue to treat the atmosphere as an open sewer, and they will keep doing so until someone with political authority tells them they can't. Without external coercion, private companies will follow the incentives that drive markets. It is, as Nicholas Stern, former chief economist of the World Bank, put it, "the greatest market failure the world has ever seen."[59]

Critics of rent seeking in the coal, oil, and natural gas sectors sometimes focus on tax breaks and special deals (such as cheap access to public lands), which add up to many billions in transfers every year. Just as with the financial sector, however, the big subsidies are the huge rents that stem from *insufficient* regulation. Some of these rents are associated with traditional air pollution from fossil fuels, which remain too lightly regulated despite the large and important steps that governments have taken. An International Monetary Fund study recently estimated the subsidy value to the oil, natural gas, and coal industries of these hidden costs (related largely to local pollution, contributions to wasteful congestion, and global warming) at an astonishing $600 billion a year in the United States.[60] But climate change due to the underregulation of carbon dioxide (CO_2) is in a category of its own. Nothing else so reveals the tragic tilt of our current politics in favor of concentrated private interests—or the mercenary role of the Great Enablers in protecting those political advantages.

Obstruction, Obstruction, Obstruction

Climate change is not a new discovery. In 1965, just one year after the surgeon general's famous report on smoking, President Lyndon Johnson's Science Advisory Committee sent the president another warning. This one concerned carbon emissions: "Man is unwittingly conducting a vast geophysical experiment . . . [that] will almost certainly cause significant changes in the temperature."[61] The committee warned of melting polar ice, rising sea levels, and more acidic oceans. Just three weeks after his 1965 inauguration, LBJ made a special address to Congress, in which he noted, "Air pollution is no longer confined to isolated places . . . This generation has altered the composition of the atmosphere on a global scale through . . . a steady increase in carbon dioxide from fossil fuels."[62]

The issue lay dormant for two decades. First, environmentalists tackled immediate challenges of conventional air and water pollution. (In the process, they unwittingly set the stage for future action on climate change through language in the Clean Air Act of 1970 that gave the EPA broad authority to act.) Then, starting in the mid-1970s, rising energy prices and corporate political resistance discouraged attention to carbon emissions. Still, climate science continued to develop, and the warnings of climate scientists only grew more urgent. By the late 1980s, the issue reemerged on the national policy agenda—and the battle over the energy industry's risky rents was launched.

The conflict reached a new scale in the early 1990s, following the Intergovernmental Panel on Climate Change (IPCC) report of 1990. It then returned in even more intense form following increased attention to the issue in the mid-2000s. In both cases, major legislation (a new levy on fossil fuels known as a Btu tax in 1993; a much more ambitious cap-and-trade initiative in 2009) passed the House but died in the Senate.[63] Since then, the Obama administration has made considerable progress exploiting its authority under the Clean Air Act to regulate carbon dioxide as a pollutant, but its efforts remain contested, and the eventual outcome remains in doubt—vulnerable to legal challenges and potential reversals by a future administration.[64]

Obstruction has relied on a range of now-familiar techniques. Those producing and relying on fossil fuels are among the busiest influence peddlers in America—in the peak year of 2009, oil and gas interests spent a total of $175 million on lobbying, narrowly defined. (ExxonMobil and Chevron alone reported almost $50 million in lobbying expenditures.)[65] These interests have powerful allies in Congress—and not just within the GOP. When a concentrated interest is also a prominent local constituency, its voice will be loud regardless of a politician's party affiliation. Geographically based representation in Congress means that there will be "coal state" and "oil state" Democrats.

Nonetheless, the GOP has long been the primary home of fossil fuel interests, and the centrality of this alliance has grown stronger. When Republicans have controlled the White House, the grip of the energy industry there has been particularly evident—on vivid display in the strong and lucrative attachments to the industry of the first national leaders of the twenty-first century, George W. Bush and Dick Cheney. Climate science had crystallized over the course of the 1990s, but the Bush administration marginalized the issue. Following his election, Bush quickly reneged on the pledge he'd made as a candidate to place a cap on power plant carbon emissions. Instead, he opened the White House to the robber barons, appointing lobbyists from the industry to prominent positions where they could oversee the climate issue.

The biggest industry plant was Philip Cooney. A longtime official from the American Petroleum Institute, Cooney became chief of staff at the White House Council on Environmental Quality. His boss would be James Connaughton, a lobbyist also moving through the revolving door from the power industry. In 2002 and 2003 Cooney rewrote portions of an EPA report on climate change "to exaggerate or emphasize scientific uncertainties."[66] The White House made so many objections to a draft EPA report on the environment that the exasperated EPA administrator, Christine Todd Whitman, dropped the climate change section entirely. When a prominent news story about Cooney's efforts appeared, he resigned—only to resurface two weeks later working for ExxonMobil.[67]

Merchants of Doubt

The industry attacks on climate science have a clear and simple logic. Despite many disputes on the specifics, scientists have reached a broad consensus on key points: Climate change is real, caused largely by humans, and threatens substantial negative effects. If this consensus comes to be accepted widely—that is, if climate scientists are seen as legitimate guides to the key facts—action to constrain carbon emissions is much more likely. Frank Luntz, the GOP messaging expert, captured the essential point in a 2002 memo to potential GOP candidates: "Should the public come to believe the scientific issues are settled, their views about global warming will change accordingly. Therefore, you need to continue to make the lack of scientific certainty a primary issue in the debate. The scientific debate is closing [against us] but is not yet closed. There is still a window of opportunity to challenge the science."[68] Remarkably, even as the scientific evidence accumulated over the next decade, Luntz and his allies would succeed in prying that window wide open.

"Merchants of doubt" have emerged wherever rent seekers resist regulation.[69] But their role was especially heightened in the climate change fight because of several distinctive characteristics of the issue. Not only does reducing emissions require societies to sacrifice short-term benefits to avoid long-term pain, but the costs of action are concentrated on some powerful losers. To make matters worse, we can't see the problem (unlike, say, a bulging waistline).[70] Though some effects have become increasingly manifest—record temperatures, extreme weather events, disappearing ice sheets—the biggest dangers continue to lie over the horizon.

Rent seekers and their supporters recognized these political openings. To undermine the credibility of climate science, they trotted out a range of themes: The scientists and environmentalists were "extremists" or "alarmists" with a secret ("Marxist" or "socialist") ideological mission; they were corrupt because they stood to gain from their efforts; they were elitist hypocrites because they lived lives of carbon-consuming luxury, jetting off to fancy international conferences; or they were simply fools (because "sound science" suggested that warming was not occurring, or took place for natural reasons, or would have minimal or even positive effects). The lines of attack were flexible, but the focus remained consistent: shoot the messengers.

As the Bush administration staggered toward the exit, the critical fight over proposals to limit carbon emissions gathered steam. By this time, however, there was a flourishing counternarrative of "denialism" or "skepticism." That effort involved a range of specialized groups focused on climate change and funded in part by the fossil fuel industry, including the Information Council on the Environment, given the reassuring acronym ICE. The organization operated initially out of the offices of the National Association of Manufacturers, and included as members Exxon, Chevron, and other oil giants, the big three auto companies, and the Chamber of Commerce.[71] A pollster's strategy paper for the group outlined the goal of "reposition[ing] global warming as a theory (not fact)" through efforts targeted at "older, less educated males" and "younger, lower-income women" in districts reliant on coal-generated electricity.

The countermovement involved over one hundred distinct organizations that include expressions of skepticism about climate change as a central part of their agenda.[72] Every one of the major conservative think tanks—including Cato, Heritage, and the American Enterprise Institute—was a part of this effort. So were smaller or more specialized organizations such as the Heartland Institute and the Competitive Enterprise Institute. After the mid-1980s, there was a large increase in books advancing denialist claims; the overwhelming majority of these books were linked to and promoted by conservative think tanks, which provided a veneer of respectability.[73]

Tracing where the money for these efforts came from is difficult. Much of it was given anonymously; even more was channeled through middlemen organizations that created at least some ambiguity about the donors' intent. The fossil fuel industry was a central contributor, especially in the early years. Exxon and the Koch network were prominent and generous supporters, as were some leading conservative foundations, including the Sarah Scaife Foundation (previously, the Richard Mellon Scaife Foundation) and the John William Pope Foundation (linked to Art Pope, the "third Koch brother").

By 2007, some prominent supporters, including Exxon and the Koch network, seemed to pull back. Exxon, in fact, announced that it would no longer fund such efforts. Yet as the sociologist Robert Brulle has documented, it is very hard to tell whether this repositioning reflected a change of heart or just a tactical adjustment to escalating criticism.[74] The decline in outlays by the Koch network, Exxon, and a few other prominent funders coincided with a marked rise in funding from Donors Trust and Donors Capital Fund—third-party, pass-through foundations with untraceable sources of revenue. Brulle demonstrates that by 2010, these two entities alone accounted for a full 25 percent of funding within the countermovement.

A Coalition of Necessity

The sudden reticence of some funders to leave fingerprints was not the only sign of change. The years 2005 to 2007 marked a new peak in attention to global warming. In 2005 Hurricane Katrina left the city of New Orleans flooded and more than 1,800 people dead. The following year Al Gore's documentary *An Inconvenient Truth* was a success at the box office and the Academy Awards. In 2007 Gore and the IPCC jointly received the Nobel Peace Prize for their work directing attention to climate change. By then, belief in the seriousness of the climate challenge reached a new high, with 41 percent of Americans saying they worried a great deal about global warming, up from 26 percent in 2004.[75]

As evidence continued to accumulate, elements of the business community began to adjust. It was not just that traditional obstructionists lowered their public profiles. Most striking was the emergence of the United States Climate Action Partnership (USCAP), a group combining several leading environmental groups and some of the nation's biggest companies. Corporate involvement included giant firms such as General Electric as well as, strikingly, some of the biggest polluters in the world, like Pacific Gas and Electric Company. USCAP launched in early 2007, coming out in favor of mandatory restrictions on carbon emissions, utilizing a version of the cap-and-trade design that (with bipartisan support) had effectively tackled the acid rain problem in the 1990s.

Though some businesses sensed opportunities to profit from carbon reduction technologies, USCAP was more a coalition of necessity than of opportunity. Environmentalists concluded that to achieve bipartisan support—essential given the inevitable defection of some coal- and oil-state Democrats—they needed substantial business backing.[76] And many big polluters could see that regulation was coming. Given this, it was better to try to influence the legislation—better, as they say, to be at the table than on the menu. According to one report, GE's chief executive officer Jeffrey Immelt's interest in USCAP grew when he "met with a group of power executives and asked for a show of hands from those who thought carbon regulation was coming. Most of the hands went up."[77] Among the early converts was Jim Rogers, CEO of Duke Energy, the third largest corporate emitter of CO_2 in the United States. "Legislation is coming" Rogers said. "We can help shape it, or we can stand on the sidelines and let others do it."[78]

This imperative mounted when the Supreme Court issued a 5-to-4 ruling in *Massachusetts v. EPA* in April 2007. The court held that the EPA not only had the authority to regulate carbon emissions but was required to do so if it found (as it surely would) that these emissions "may reasonably be anticipated to endanger public health or welfare." Those worried about regulation could no longer simply obstruct legislation. If they wanted to preempt or channel EPA actions along acceptable lines, they needed to offer an alternative.

False Dawn

The stars seemed to be coming into alignment for a grand bargain. If it had been American politics circa 1987, maybe they would have aligned. But it wasn't. Even as parts of the energy sector toyed with compromise, the GOP's conservative wing doubled down. Tom Donohue swung his organization's immense lobbying capacity into action. Responding in 2008 to the emerging target of an 80 percent reduction in emissions by 2050, Donohue was adamant: "There is no way this can be done without fundamentally changing the American way of life, choking off economic development, and putting large segments of our economy out of business."[79] A year later, the Chamber's vice president for environment, technology, and regulatory affairs, William Kovacs, would notoriously call for a "Scopes monkey trial of the twenty-first century" to put "the science of climate change on trial."[80]

While the Chamber lobbied Congress, the broader movement worked to fortify the base. The allegiance of conservative elites to unfettered markets was intensifying. For many of the GOP's activists and voters, environmentalism was now a form of socialism or a prelude to world government. The alarm about global warming was environmentalism's Trojan horse. Even as Al Gore was applauded from Hollywood to Stockholm, opponents redoubled their efforts. They also redirected them—knowing that Gore and his allies were investing unprecedented amounts in mass persuasion. Gore himself might have raised inconvenient truths, but he was a convenient target for the Republican base.

Cap-and-trade opponents pursued the emerging strategies of conservative obstruction. The new wave of opposition targeted conservatives, largely ignoring the political mainstream. In 2007 the conservative media, especially Fox News, expanded their coverage of climate change, with the twin themes of hypocrisy (Gore) and fraud (the fake "Climategate" scandal, which received saturation coverage).[81]

Conservative concern about global warming collapsed. In 2007 half of conservatives believed that global warming had already begun. Three years later, less than 30 percent did. Of course, polarization was increasing across many policy issues, but on no major issue was the transformation so fast and so sweeping as on environmental policy.[82] Moreover, the new dynamics on the political right relied much less on nudging the less educated than on exploiting the growing power of the conservative echo chamber. Tellingly, among conservatives, education no longer helped the scientists. The more informed that conservatives said they were about environmental issues, the more dismissive they were of climate science. If they were paying attention, they were listening to the skeptics.

With the GOP base moving into strong opposition, the GOP leaders who were not already there followed. John McCain, Newt Gingrich, and Mitt Romney all reneged on previous expressions of interest in regulating carbon emissions. On no other issue was the extreme-outlier status of the modern GOP so evident. As the veteran Washington reporter Ronald Brownstein observed, "[I]t is difficult to identify another major political party in any democracy as thoroughly dismissive of climate science as is the GOP here."[83] When the forces of USCAP would later seek their carefully crafted bipartisan consensus, with the backing of considerable elements of the business community, they would find no GOP takers.

Assault on the Castles

The battle over climate legislation wasn't the only struggle that involved the modern robber barons. President Obama entered office promising to wage the most concerted assault on large-scale rent seeking in modern American history. The targets will be familiar by now: the medical-industrial complex, high-risk finance, and the fossil fuel industry. Between his inauguration and the GOP capture of the House twenty-two months later, a trio of epic battles played out that showed the chinks in the modern robber barons' armor—as well as the formidable defenses they still possessed.

For all the differences in course and outcome, these battles were waged on similar terrain with similar armaments. In each, the robber barons deployed enormous resources to block or divert efforts at reform. In 2009, reported lobbying expenditures—which do not include organization building, public relations campaigns, or election-related activities—ramped up to $3.5 billion and ticked just above this record level in 2010. Leading the charge were general business groups such as the Chamber, which spent over $300 million on its own between the start of 2009 and the end of 2010. But after general business spending, three giant sectors led the way, spending approximately $1 *billion* each on lobbying across the two years. They were health care, finance, and energy.[84]

In each of these epic battles, too, the Great Enablers did what they do best: stand up for the big guys. Republicans presented an almost unbroken wall of opposition, which, given the narrow Democratic edge and the inevitable wavering of cross-pressured Democrats, created a daunting hurdle for the Obama administration and its allies. Not a single Republican voted for the final passage of the health care bill in either house of Congress. Not a single Republican voted for the financial reform bill in the House. And while eight House Republicans crossed party lines in the House to vote for the energy legislation—which still barely passed because of the expected Democratic defections in districts dependent on fossil fuel production—the bill died in the Senate well short of the sixty votes needed to overcome the inevitable GOP filibuster, having failed to gain the committed support of a single Republican Senator.

Throughout, the GOP was almost perfectly united in opposition. The House and Senate Republican leadership fought all three bills tenaciously, hauling in campaign dollars from the threatened industries as they did. Between 2008 and 2014, the share of campaign spending from commercial banks that went to Republicans increased from 52 percent to 72 percent; from securities and investment firms, from 42 percent to 62 percent; from health insurers, from 39 percent to 55 percent; from hospitals and nursing homes, from 38 percent to 52 percent; and from mining, from 71 percent to 93 percent.[85]

The Republican resistance was all the more notable because in two of the reform drives, Democrats designed their opening bids around previous Republican proposals: the cap-and-trade legislation that the 2008 GOP nominee for president, John McCain, had supported; and the proposal for mandatory private insurance that the 2012 GOP nominee, Mitt Romney, had actually helped pass in Massachusetts as governor. McCain's and Romney's stances were not isolated positions. They represented the establishment GOP alternatives to more far-reaching Democratic proposals—not the center of the party, but the expressed preferences of what remained of its more moderate and pragmatic wing. And, in both cases, they were unceremoniously repudiated.

What about finance? In the wake of the financial crisis, even Wall Street–friendly Democrats conceded the need for new rules. Against a backdrop of widespread outrage, the Republican resistance to reform was audacious. GOP leaders pilloried the Democrats' legislation for not doing enough to end "too big to fail." Meanwhile, they courted financial-sector contributions from those too-big-to-fail institutions. In early 2010 John Boehner met for drinks with Jamie Dimon, head of JPMorgan Chase and a longtime Democratic donor. His message was that Republicans had "stood up" to Democrats' efforts to "curb pay and impose new regulations," reported the *Wall Street Journal*, and Boehner said he was "disappointed" that Wall Street hadn't given more to its true allies.[86] A month later, Boehner urged a roomful of bankers, "Don't let those punk staffers take advantage of you, and stand up for yourselves."[87] At the time, over 1,500 lobbyists for the financial sector were swarming Capitol Hill.[88]

For their part, corporate leaders and business associations either deferred to or defended the barons. Even as the big banks expressed some public contrition, they took a cue from the health insurance industry and plowed tens of millions into opposition efforts spearheaded by the

Chamber of Commerce.[89] This spending was secret at the time, which might have helped the banks in their rehabilitation effort if they hadn't also been lobbying against every new rule, or if they hadn't started trying to undo the regulations the second the ink was dry on the law. The Chamber never said a kind word about health care reform; the Business Roundtable, more sympathetic but also much less influential, said barely anything. With regard to clean energy alone, as we've seen, a serious business constituency for reform did emerge, and it was far weaker than the fossil fuel industry that led the opposition.

Yet in each of these struggles, there were also powerful forces pressing for change—a reminder that the modern robber barons do not enjoy unchallenged supremacy. The president and Democratic leaders in Congress mustered outside support among labor unions, environmental groups, and targeted reform campaigns, such as Americans for Financial Reform and Health Care for America Now! (a group that, as the exclamation point implied, really wanted to expand health coverage). These groups had sway only among Democrats, but that was potentially enough. Democrats had the majority in the House, and they had reached the magical number of sixty in the Senate that allowed them to overcome a filibuster—if they stayed united.[90]

Moreover, a strong case could be made in each of these areas that reform would deliver long-term benefits that outweighed the costs. The president insisted, for example, that his health plan would slow the growth of costs enough to offset much of the expense of expanding coverage. Indeed, the Congressional Budget Office concluded (to GOP dismay) that the plan more than paid for itself with a combination of new taxes and lower projected federal spending. The CBO also concluded that the climate change bill would result in modest new costs and even a small benefit for poorer Americans. House Republican leader John Boehner complained, "They didn't factor in the millions of jobs that will move overseas if the United States imposes this tax . . . I don't know what color the sky is in a world where that won't happen, but I'm sure you can ask the unicorns."[91]

Still, reformers faced a steep climb. The rent seekers merely had to gum up lawmaking gears already filled with sand by the Republicans' gridlock strategy. And so a final common element of all three battles was that the president and congressional Democrats made enormous preemptive concessions to the barons. The simplest financial reforms—tight leverage requirements, breaking up the largest banks, restored regulatory firewalls between banking and investment—were also the ones fought most vigorously. The president's team, generally favorable toward Wall Street, pooh-poohed the most ambitious options from the start. But if they'd made it to Congress, they would have faced withering resistance from Republicans, finance-friendly Democrats, and Wall Street's lobbying juggernaut. In April 2009, with the financial crisis still roiling, Democrat Dick Durbin of Illinois—the second in command in the Senate at the time—blurted out on a local radio station, "And the banks—hard to believe in a time when we're facing a banking crisis that many of the banks created—are still the most powerful lobby on Capitol Hill. And they frankly own the place."[92]

As groundbreaking as it was, the health legislation also incorporated concession after concession. Revealingly, most of them stripped out tougher cost controls or moved authority to the states, which were viewed as less threatening to the rent seekers. Whenever the administration tried to put in place serious cost controls, observes the journalist Steven Brill, "They were stopped by the lobbyists. . . . The only way that a bill this big will pass in Washington is if the powers that be decide that it should pass."[93] The powers that be are the modern robber barons.

Before the debate even began in earnest, for example, the White House and congressional leaders brokered a peace treaty of sorts with the health care barons, promising not to regulate drug prices directly or significantly restrain hospital charges. In return, the hospital and drug organizations promised some modest policy concessions, but everyone knew what the real giveback was: They wouldn't use their huge war chests and lobbying arms to take on the health plan. The deal was the parting achievement of PhRMA head Billy Tauzin, who had brokered the Medicare drug legislation that also kept price negotiation at bay. He would soon leave PhRMA, but not before taking home $11.6 million in pay in his final year.[94]

The White House also signaled it would jettison the so-called public option, which would have created a public plan using rates based on Medicare's that would compete with private insurance plans. The CBO had projected big savings from a strong version of the plan, which was popular with the public.[95] But by the end of 2009, it was gone. The news sent health care stocks shooting upward.

Meanwhile, the clean energy legislation came to include so many provisions exempting or "grandfathering in" big carbon emitters that some environmentalists began to question whether the game was worth the candle. The truth was that no bill would pass without such concessions. In energy, just as with health care and finance, reform required considerable compensation to the rent seekers. The initial giveaways were never sufficient, however, and as legislation wended through Congress—to victory in the cases of health and financial reform, and defeat in the case of clean energy—the protections for the barons multiplied. Only financial reform, the cause linked most to the economic crisis, grew stronger between proposal and passage, and even then the tightened law was significantly weaker and more dependent on future regulatory will than Wall Street had feared.[96]

Which brings us to the final similarity: The passage of bills into laws, as difficult and crucial as it was, did not signal the end of the epic battles. The next steps—rule making by regulators, lawsuits and appeals in the courts, struggles in the states—determined whether the new laws would achieve their promise. And these were the kinds of fights the barons knew how to win, grinding down their opponents during the long, low-visibility path from grand ambitions to ground-level achievements.

Nowhere was this guerrilla warfare more evident than in financial reform. Five years after the 2010 law squeaked through Congress, nearly 40 percent of regulations scheduled to be in place were still in limbo.[97] Many—including crucial regulations that would increase the ability of investors to police excessive executive pay—remained tied up in court battles that were likely to end with the rules either weakened or overturned. Meanwhile, the big banks were bigger than ever, and risky practices such as the trading of exotic derivatives by federally insured financial institutions were on the rise.

The Great Enablers had no change of heart, either. As we saw in chapter 7, the Business Roundtable waged a successful war against so-called proxy access rules, which would have allowed institutional investors and other shareholders to challenge corporations' nominees to their supposedly independent boards. The Republicans were even more aggressive. Contributions from FIRE donors ramped up to nearly a half billion dollars in the 2014 election cycle, and the spending, previously split between the parties, tilted dramatically toward the GOP. This friendly financial infusion helped Republicans take control of the Senate and enlarge their House majority. The party's first item of business? Passing a budget that included a provision written by Citigroup to allow insured banks to start trading in derivatives again.[98]

The Rent Is Too Damn High

Health care, finance, and energy represent a substantial share of our economy. But they're by no means the only places where the modern robber barons practice their dark arts. Before we turn to the bigger picture of American institutional dysfunction, let's meet a few more of the people who are robbing us:

- *Got a License for That?* The most noted change in the American labor force is the precipitous decline of organized labor, from over 30 percent unionization in the 1950s to less than 12 percent in recent years—and less than half that in the private sector. But another, less noticed trend has moved in the opposite direction: occupational licensure. Seventy years ago, fewer than 5 percent of workers were licensed. Today roughly 30 percent work in fields that require some kind of certification (almost always state level and generally enjoying bipartisan support, though this is an area where Democrats are arguably the greater enablers).[99] Sometimes there are good arguments for such requirements—we want our surgeons to be well trained—but many forms of licensure are both overly restrictive and costly, preventing more efficient use of workers with lower but sufficient levels of training. For example, nurses, dental hygienists, and paralegals are often prevented from doing work that they could do as well as doctors, dentists, and lawyers—raising prices for consumers, increasing incomes for highly paid professionals, and lowering earnings for these typically less-well-paid professions.[100]
- *We're Number Thirty!* The internet is the great general-purpose technology of our time. And the federal government made it possible. Unfortunately, our leadership role does not extend to making it possible for people to use this resource. American broadband is vastly more costly on a per-megabyte basis than internet access in many other nations. In a recent study, we ranked thirtieth in the world for broadband value, behind such technological powerhouses as Bulgaria, Romania, and Russia.[101] The problem isn't that

we lack the know-how to do better. Nor is it simply that we are a big nation: Speeds aren't much better in dense regions of our country, and Russia isn't exactly tiny. The problem is that the big cable companies have little incentive to invest in better infrastructure or compete on price. Broadband requires physical infrastructure, and the physical infrastructure of the internet is not only private but also controlled by a highly concentrated industry. One way to tackle the problem would be to create public Wi-Fi networks, as cities such as Chattanooga have done, with impressive results. Guess who's against such efforts? Business groups and Republicans.

• *Fat Profits.* Obesity now rivals smoking as a preventable health crisis. In response, policy makers are thinking about creative ways to encourage physical activity and discourage the excess consumption of fattening foods. These ideas, however, have run headlong into the big agribusiness corporations and food manufacturers that reap the greatest profits from our nation's expanding waistlines. Spending on campaigns and lobbying by the food industry has shot up as the issue has risen on the agenda, with most of the money going to Republicans, who insist that obesity is entirely about "personal responsibility." The Obama administration rolled out rules that would reduce salt and sugar in school lunches, which the federal government largely finances. Responding to industry pressure, congressional Republicans (with plenty of Democrats in tow) declared French fries and pizza "vegetables." Twenty-four states and five cities considered a small tax on sodas—a major culprit in the obesity epidemic. But only two, Washington State and the city of Berkeley, overcame the lobbying juggernaut, and the Washington law was overturned in a referendum in which the soda companies spent $16 million, more than anyone had ever spent on an initiative campaign in the state.[102]

• *Crony Colleges.* Chapter 1 reminded us that the United States has lost its lead in the higher-education race, due in part to insufficient state and federal investment. But there's one part of the higher-education sector that has received more and more largesse: for-profit colleges. Almost a seventh of college students are now enrolled in for-profit schools; in 1993 the figure was just 1.6 percent.[103] And for all their emulation of the private commercial sector, these profit-making enterprises are basically creatures of the federal government: The fifteen biggest firms receive, on average, 86 percent of their revenue from the feds.[104] All this would be less troubling if they were revolutionizing education in the ways their rhetoric suggests. But the outcomes are dismal: Fewer than a quarter of students graduate in six years; the median debt of students who actually graduate is $33,000; tuition is twice what public institutions charge; and job market outcomes are bleak, which makes those big debts more of an economic yoke than a smart investment.[105] But the industry has become a major lobbying power in the higher-education arena, and Republicans have garnered most of the industry's campaign donations. Once upon a time, Republicans criticized the for-profits: Reagan's education secretary, William Bennett, rightly called them "diploma mills designed to trick the poor into taking on federally backed debt."[106] Since the mid-1990s, however, GOP leaders—and plenty of Democrats on key congressional committees who have raked in the for-profits' donations—have eagerly backed the rent seekers.

For-profit colleges are mini–robber barons: bottom-feeders in America's rising sea of rents. The biggest of the barons don't need public dollars or the slightly more hidden giveaways of federal loans. They just need the federal government to let them impose tolls on American society. They don't have to ply Washington for visible handouts. They just have to keep Washington tied up in knots. The costs they impose, then, are not just economic. In undermining essential public authority, they threaten effective democratic governance itself.

TEN

★ ★ ★ ★

A Crisis of Authority

I N April 1786, a year before the Constitution's authors gathered in Pennsylvania, an unfortunate tax collector found himself surrounded by a mob near the state's western frontier. The official had come to collect new state taxes on liquor. The protesters had come to teach the official a lesson about the limits of government authority. They cut the hair off one side of his head, dressed him up in embarrassing attire, and then forced him to ride through three counties, with regular stops at local stills to sample the wares. One dismayed observer called it the "most audacious and accomplished piece of outrageous and unprovoked insult that was ever offered to a government."[1]

Audacious and accomplished it was, but not unprecedented. After all, the case for the American Revolution rested heavily on resistance to taxation, as memorialized in the far more audacious Boston Tea Party. Yet the American revolutionaries decried "taxation without representation." The Pennsylvania mob *had* representation. They were resisting authority. To those who would assemble in Philadelphia a year later, it was such resistance—not just by citizens but also by the states themselves—that was the problem.

The leaders of the movement to write a new constitution shared a common diagnosis: The Articles of Confederation were dangerously weak. The federal government needed coercive authority, including authority to tax. As the political scientist David Brian Robertson explains their thinking, "Taxes were the lifeblood of the new national government."[2] The framers refused, for example, to put any constraint on what taxation could be used for, and they explicitly defeated proposals to limit direct taxes on property, sales, and income. Eleven years after the Declaration of Independence denounced Britain for "imposing taxes on us without our Consent," the architects of the Constitution gave their envisioned national government taxing authority even greater than that held by the Crown. As Alexander Hamilton explained in "The Federalist No. 30,"

> Money is, with propriety, considered as the vital principle of the body politic; as that which sustains its life and motion, and enables it to perform its most essential functions. A complete power, therefore, to procure a regular and adequate supply of it, as far as the resources of the community will permit, may be regarded as an indispensable ingredient in every constitution. From a deficiency in this particular, one of two evils must ensue; either the people must be subjected to continual plunder, as a substitute for a more eligible mode of supplying the public wants, or the government must sink into a fatal atrophy, and, in a short course of time, perish.[3]

If the rallying cry of the nation's first revolution was "No taxation without representation," the rallying cry of the second could very well have been "Yes taxation *with* representation."

Less than a decade later, this "vital principle" came into sharp focus when western Pennsylvanians again showed their displeasure with new taxes on liquor: this time a national tax passed by Congress in 1791 at the insistence of Hamilton, now secretary of the Treasury. In the conflict that followed, known by historians as the Whiskey Rebellion, President George Washington led a force roughly as large as the Continental army to put down the insurgency and establish federal authority. The Whiskey Rebellion was "the single largest example of armed resistance to a law of the United States between the ratification of the Constitution and the Civil War," writes the historian Thomas Slaughter.[4] If nothing else, the huge federal response showed that when the Founders said they believed in taxation with representation, they really meant it.

The Second Whiskey Rebellion

Today the federal government faces another antitax rebellion: a destructive campaign of resistance to the federal government's authority to collect taxes owed under law. Only this time it's not led by frontier outlaws. It's led by federal officials.

Meet Senator Ron Johnson: Since his election in 2010 as a Tea Party darling backed by Koch Industries, the Wisconsin Republican has led a successful crusade against taxation with representation, crippling the capacity of our modern tax collectors to carry out their jobs. Johnson has done nothing so crude as shredding documents or dressing up inspectors. He's adopted a much more effective strategy: slashing the IRS's budget.

In 2014 the independent IRS Oversight Board recommended a budget of $13.6 billion for the agency. Congress, led by Johnson and his House GOP counterpart, Florida's Ander Crenshaw, gave it less than $11 billion. That might seem like a modest difference between two big numbers. It's not. With its funding declining since the 2010 midterm, when Republicans captured the House, the IRS has grown more beleaguered and less capable. Even as it administers an ever more complex tax code for a growing population, its employees have struggled with staff shortages, huge cuts in training, stagnant salaries, and increasingly archaic technology.[5]

The biggest costs, however, are borne by those who must deal with the IRS. At some branches, reported *Bloomberg News* in 2015, "Lines of taxpayers seeking assistance have looped around the block. . . . Waiting times have stretched into hours. An estimated six in ten callers to the agency's toll-free lines haven't been able to get through, and those who have could get help with only the most basic questions." The head of the IRS's Taxpayer Advocate Service, Nina Olson, alerted Congress to a "devastating erosion of taxpayer service, harming taxpayers individually and collectively" and creating "compliance barriers and significant inconvenience for millions of taxpayers."[6]

If $11 billion seems like a lot to spend on tax administration, keep in mind that the IRS collects around $3 *trillion* in taxes. More important, every $1 spent on IRS enforcement yields $6 in recovered taxes, as well as at least three times more in indirect gains due to the deterrent effect on tax evasion.[7] (Targeted enforcement efforts that focus on high-income taxpayers produce more than *$47* in recovered taxes for every $1 spent.)[8] Still, the IRS estimates that one in six tax dollars go unpaid—a loss of nearly $450 billion (in 2015 dollars) each year.[9]

Most people pay their taxes not because they fear an audit but because they believe taxes are legitimate and others are also paying their fair share. (For families that rely mostly on wages, automatic withholding

also makes tax evasion inherently difficult.) Audits are essential, however, to send a message that taxes are being paid—and especially that
they are being paid by businesses and wealthy Americans whose income
is mostly exempt from withholding and whose incentive to avoid taxes is
greatest. Yet audits are at their lowest level in a decade, with large drops
for returns filed by corporations and by taxpayers earning more than $1
million.[10] IRS experts and leaders worry that the United States might be
reaching a tipping point beyond which voluntary compliance will start
to fall. "The IRS will never be a beloved federal agency because it is the
face of government's power to tax and collect," explained TAS's Olson.
"But it should be a respected agency."

"The New Gestapo"

Respect isn't exactly what the IRS is getting these days. The Founders
saw the power to lay and collect taxes as the hallmark of the nation's new
democracy. Now those who claim to speak in their name don't just criticize the laying of taxes but also seek to undermine government's capacity
to collect the taxes authorized by popular rule. In an interview with the
Atlas Society—dedicated to promoting the philosophy of Ayn Rand—
Senator Johnson said, "We're all suffering collectively from Stockholm
syndrome. That's where people who have been kidnapped are grateful
to their captors when they just show them a little bit of mercy." In case
it wasn't clear who those captors were, Johnson explained that "the root
cause" of the nation's problems was "the size, the scope, the resulting
cost of the government."[11]

Johnson is an extreme example. He helped erect a statue honoring
Atlas Shrugged in his hometown, criticized CEOs who called for higher
taxes to reduce the deficit as similar to the corporate pawns who enabled
government "looting" in Rand's novel, and called the Affordable Care
Act "the greatest assault on freedom in our lifetimes"—which might surprise African Americans grappling with Jim Crow when the sixty-year-
old Johnson was growing up. When Johnson was asked the differences
between his ideas and those of Rand, he replied, "I'm not sure there are
too many differences."[12] The businessman-turned-politician even compared himself to the novel's Hank Rearden: the brilliant steel baron who
joins the strike of the productive class led by John Galt.

As we have seen, however, Johnson is hardly alone in embracing
Randian beliefs. Nor is he alone in decrying the IRS. In 2012 Maine's Re-

publican governor, Paul LaPage, called the IRS "the new Gestapo." Asked
to apologize, he clarified, "What I am trying to say is the Holocaust was a
horrific crime against humanity, and, frankly, I would never want to see
that repeated. Maybe the IRS is not quite as bad—yet."[13] In South Carolina the next year, the Republican Party sent out a fund-raising appeal
that described the agency as "Obama's Gestapo."[14] The legacy of Pierce
Butler, the South Carolina delegate to the constitutional convention who
described taxes as "distinguished marks of sovereignty," has apparently
faded in the Palmetto State.

Stirring Up (and Making Up) Scandals

To be sure, not everyone compares the IRS to the Gestapo. The moderate view, however, isn't much friendlier. Since the mid-1990s, when
Republicans went on the warpath against the agency, the IRS has been
portrayed as a sort of evil idiot savant—at once horrendously incompetent and devilishly cunning. When, in 2013, the inspector general
of the IRS alleged that lower-level staff had applied special scrutiny to
conservative political groups seeking tax-exempt status, the cacophony
of contempt was deafening. "This is tyranny," said Joe Scarborough, the
House Republican turned MSNBC TV host. *ABC News* correspondent
Terry Moran described the affair as "a truly Nixonian abuse of power
by the Obama administration."[15] The most colorful complaints, however,
came from the comedian Jon Stewart on *The Daily Show*, who described
the incident as "removing the last arrow" in President Obama's "progov-
ernance quiver." "Congratulations, Barack Obama," proclaimed Stewart.
"You've managed to show that when the government wants to do good
things, your managerial competence falls somewhere between David
Brent [the horrible boss on British TV's *The Office*] and a cat chasing a
laser pointer. But when government wants to flex its more malevolent
muscles, you're fucking Iron Man."[16]

The takedown was humorous, but it wasn't accurate. Subsequent investigations showed that the frontline IRS officials who had questioned
the nonprofit designation were acting substantially on their own. Moreover, their net of scrutiny had ensnared liberal as well as conservative
groups; in fact, the only group flagged by the IRS that ultimately had its
tax-exempt status denied or revoked was a *left-leaning* one.[17] After the
inspector general report, the officials responsible were reprimanded and
the federal supervisor of their division compelled to resign. (President

Obama forced the IRS's head to step down as well, even though he had not been in charge at the time; a Bush appointee had been.)

What's more, the underlying issue *was* complicated. The Supreme Court's *Citizens United* ruling had opened the door to new organizations that claimed tax-free status yet acted much like traditional political groups that are taxed. A year later, a Republican-appointed federal judge dismissed all the lawsuits brought against the IRS. What was portrayed as a witch hunt carried out by a partisan agency turned out to be mostly an ill-conceived screening process developed by a short-staffed IRS grappling with ambiguous law. (Thanks to the GOP attacks, however, the IRS would essentially give up policing the increasingly murky lines between charitable nonprofits and those dedicated to political advocacy.) If this showed the IRS's malevolent muscles, Iron Man had nothing to worry about.

Nor was 2013 the first time Republicans had gone after the IRS. In 1997, GOP leaders launched a sophisticated campaign against the agency. Following the advice of Republican strategists, the GOP chair of the Senate Finance Committee launched two years of hearings on the IRS's "Gestapo-like" (Senator Trent Lott) and "out of control" (Senator Don Nickles) behavior. As veteran tax reporter David Cay Johnston described the spectacle in his 2005 book *Perfectly Legal*,

> Over six days in the fall and spring the television networks gave mostly breathless accounts of a rogue agency ruining lives with abandon. . . . The story: Unnamed IRS agents falsely making un-named people pay taxes they did not owe; dozens of criminal investigation agents, brandishing guns, entering peaceful offices and homes as if they expected armed drug dealers; agents issuing subpoenas for no purpose except to embarrass people. There was even testimony that an IRS agent held a gun on a girl, caught in a raid on her parent's home, and forced her to change her clothes while he watched. There was one problem: Most of it wasn't true.[18]

No matter. The IRS was a "frightening concept," explained GOP word guru Frank Luntz. "Perception is reality," he went on. "People are afraid, whether they should be or not. As a child, you are afraid of monsters in the closet. To my knowledge, there has never been a monster found in the closet of a five-year-old, but how many five-year-olds are afraid of monsters? Same thing here."[19] In time, investigative reporting, court proceedings, and an independent government examination all concluded that the most serious charges were false, and that the biggest problems with the agency concerned insufficient staff, inadequate training, and a focus on the easiest cases rather than the biggest or most egregious ones. By then, however, Congress had passed the Internal Revenue Service Restructuring and Reform Act of 1998—which upended the IRS, requiring that the agency jump significant new hurdles without significant new funding or personnel. In the next fifteen years, the IRS would lose twenty-four thousand employees.

The Antistatist Spin Cycle

If the ongoing GOP assault hasn't illuminated the IRS's real challenges, it does say a lot about how effective governance has been eroded. The cycle of ginned-up scandals and destructive policies follows a recurrent pattern: Antigovernment critics make inflated or fabricated charges. Fox News and other conservative sources sensationalize them. Most of the rest of the news media follow—until the charges are shown to be false, at which point the mainstream press loses interest. Leading Democrats who might have counseled balance stay quiet. No one stands up for a government that works, and so government comes to work less and less well.

For antigovernment forces, this is a win-win proposition. With their two-decade-plus campaign against the IRS, Republicans have mastered the self-fulfilling critique: Say the government isn't doing its job, make it harder for the government to do its job, repeat. Far from paying a price for their exaggerated or false claims, Republicans have used the issue to gain valuable political ground. And from that ground, they have hobbled the enforcement powers of the IRS—particularly when it comes to businesses and higher-income taxpayers. Under Ronald Reagan's IRS, one out of every fifty returns was audited. By 1997, it was one in sixty-six, and after the 1997–98 hearings and legislation, it fell to less than one in a hundred.[20]

Revealingly, there was one group for which audits didn't fall: the working poor. After Republicans captured Congress in 1994, a major agenda item was cutting the Earned Income Tax Credit, which GOP leaders claimed was rife with malfeasance—"the federal government's fastest growing and most fraud-prone welfare program," as Senator Nickles put it. In response to congressional pressure, audits for the EITC rose to record highs for the poor even as they fell to record lows for the rich.

Americans understand that taxes are a civic obligation.[21] Their biggest complaint is not that federal taxes are illegitimate or excessive, but that wealthy Americans don't pay their fair share. Yet Republicans generated enormous support for a crusade that offered increased benefits to affluent tax evaders and increased hassles for ordinary taxpayers, especially the most disadvantaged. After all, everyone distrusts the government.

Forgetting the Founders

The successful attack on the IRS is not an isolated story. It is emblematic of a destructive assault on the capacity of government to carry out its most basic tasks. American government does have a big problem: It's increasingly incapable of doing what it needs to do to ensure a prosperous and safe society. Across nearly every area of domestic government— managing the nation's finances, regulating the market, protecting the environment, delivering basic services, investing in the future—we see decay and destruction, stalemate and subversion, efforts not just to reduce government's capacity but also to undermine the legitimacy of (and hence voluntary compliance with) federal law itself. The tragic irony is that this assault is being waged in the name of a Constitution that was designed with precisely the opposite intent.

Hip-Hop Hamilton

As taxpayers snaked around the block at IRS offices, theatergoers jostled to see the "hottest ticket in New York City": *Hamilton*, the story of the nation's first Treasury secretary, told through contemporary music and dance, with a largely nonwhite cast. The musical dwelled less on Hamilton's thinking than on his modest roots and outsized ambition. Still, there was something incongruous about hordes of fans going to see a show with a hero whose resolutely progovernment stance ran so against the grain of contemporary debate. (At times, the incongruity was hard to ignore: After seeing the musical, Fox News founder Rupert Murdoch tweeted, "Fabulous show! Musical of Alexander Hamilton, great acting, dancing, singing. Historically accurate with lives of Washington, Jefferson, etc.")

It's understandable why a popular musical would give Hamilton's philosophy of government less attention than his illegitimate origins or spectacular demise. Yet we should not forget that, from his first days in public life until his ill-fated duel with Aaron Burr, Hamilton fought for a vigorous, effective national government. Liberty was essential, Hamilton believed, but it could thrive only in the context of effective authority. As he declared in his address to the New York State ratifying convention,

> In the commencement of a revolution which received its birth from the usurpations of tyranny, nothing was more natural than that the public mind should be influenced by an extreme spirit of jealousy. To resist these encroachments and to nourish this spirit was the great object of all our public and private institutions. The zeal for liberty became predominant and excessive. In forming our Confederation this passion alone seemed to actuate us, and we appear to have had no other view than to secure ourselves from despotism. The object certainly was a valuable one, and deserved our utmost attention. But, sir, there is another object equally important and which our enthusiasm rendered us little capable of regarding; I mean a principle of strength and stability in the organization of our government, and vigor in its operations.[22]

More than any other leader of his day, Hamilton worked to construct a modern administrative state, with the ability to impose order on society. The Whiskey Rebellion was a direct outgrowth of his plan to create a functioning fiscal system that could manage intranational and international commerce and borrow to finance military actions and other pressing needs. The crisis of the articles, Hamilton understood, was a fiscal crisis that threatened the very capacity of the fledgling nation to survive. Taking over the debts of the states, creating a common currency, issuing bonds—these were what would make the United States capable of promoting commerce and fighting war. What's more, they would bind the financial elite (what Hamilton called "the moneyed interests") to the federal government rather than to the states. Today's chorus of conservative criticism of active monetary policy—Ron Paul demanding an end to the Fed; former Texas governor Rick Perry accusing the GOP-appointed Fed chair of "treason"; leading Republicans pressing for legislation to "audit the Fed"—turns all these Hamiltonian notions on their head.

Of course, the authors of the Constitution had no way to grasp how dramatically governance would change in the centuries to come. And no matter how many books (or musicals) about these men get produced, it is impossible for us to comprehend fully the task they saw before them in Philadelphia. But one thing is clear: The conservative commentators and antigovernment politicians who call themselves "constitutional conservatives" are espousing a vision of government that those who wrote the Constitution were dedicated to defeating. Tea Partiers are fond of quoting *The Federalist Papers*—without acknowledging that these were propaganda pieces that put a good face on messy compromises and played down their authors' enthusiasm for a strong national government. But if they could somehow be transported back to 1787, they would not be Federalists. They would be anti-Federalists. They would not be the people who wrote the Constitution. They would be the very people whom the authors of the Constitution hoped to marginalize.

Misremembering Madison

Hamilton, of course, has been the bugbear of small-government conservatives for more than two centuries. Of the key drafters of the Constitution, it's James Madison they embrace. "Madison was the most profound thinker among the Founders," writes George F. Will, criticizing today's active national government as "hostile to Madison's Constitution."[23]

In a different sort of celebration, the libertarian social scientist Charles Murray has recently created an activist organization in Madison's name to finance litigation and public relations campaigns against government rules. The goal of the Madison Fund, as detailed in Murray's 2015 book *By the People: Rebuilding Liberty Without Permission*, is to refuse voluntary compliance with federal laws so as to make it excessively costly for government to enforce them. "I want to pour sugar into the regulatory state's gas tank," Murray explains. Regulators will sometimes win the resulting battles, he acknowledges, but "Goliath cannot afford to make good on that threat against hundreds of Davids." To finance his fund honoring the father of the Constitution, Murray is looking for a few of the many "billionaires," "centimillionaires," or even "mere millionaires" who are "principled advocates of limited government."[24]

Yet on the key questions of public authority, Madison was aligned fully with Hamilton. To Madison, the precondition of effective government was a single center of authority that could compel obedience. The "fatal omission" in the articles was its lack of coercive power. The James Madison who described government as "an institution to make people do their duty" does not deserve to be associated with Murray's crusade.

Nor were Madison's emphatic words mere rhetoric. He came to Philadelphia with a proposal to replace the Articles of Confederation: the

Virginia Plan. The plan would have given the federal government an absolute veto over state laws, a power that Madison saw as "indefinite," available "in all cases whatsoever," and "absolutely necessary to a perfect system." Lest those at the convention doubt its centrality, he compared it to gravity within the universe: "the great pervading principle that must control the centrifugal tendency of the states, which without it will continually fly out of their proper orbits and destroy the whole harmony of the political system."[25]

Indeed, Madison advocated a governing structure much closer to a parliamentary democracy than to our current system. In the Virginia Plan, Congress chose the executive, and during the convention, Madison proposed that members of Congress be able to serve in the executive branch—an outline for British-style cabinet government that lost by the narrowest of margins. More important, the Virginia Plan established an upper chamber that, like the House, was based on population, with its members selected by the House rather than by the states. Just as he insisted on federal supremacy over all state laws, Madison never wavered from his conviction that the Senate should mirror the House in representing people, not states. Madison's plan shattered on the rocks of fierce opposition from the less populous states. Only after the population-based Senate was scuttled did Madison swing toward a stronger executive to check state power in the Senate and formulate his famous defense of the separation of powers and federalism.

In other words, the Constitution that many scholars describe as "Madisonian" was hardly a direct translation of Madison's ideas into institutional design. It was a compromise in which Madison had to give up the stronger and more streamlined national government he wanted. No less than Hamilton, Madison believed that states should be subordinate to the federal government and that coercive national authority embodied "the great vital principles" of an effective political arrangement. Today's self-appointed defenders of the Constitution—or "the Constitution in Exile," as constitutional conservatives sometimes call it—hold views that are anything but Madisonian. Instead, their views look a lot like those of the Constitution's original opponents.

Madison, Hamilton, and the others who sought a new constitutional democracy wanted a government that could act. Their immediate fear was not, to recall the quote of James Wilson of Pennsylvania during the convention, a government that "governed overmuch" but one that "governed too little."[26] For all the adjustments in context and content that a journey across three centuries requires, our present crisis bears an unfortunate resemblance to that which the Founders endeavored to overcome: chronic stalemate, eroding government capacity, weakened accountability, declining trust, and increasing accommodation of the narrow interests that flourish when effective public authority withers.

State of Disrepair

In August 2011 Standard & Poor's downgraded the credit rating of the United States for the first time in the agency's more than 150-year history. "The political brinksmanship of recent months," the nation's oldest ratings agency wrote, suggested that American governance had become "less stable, less effective, and less predictable." Everyone knew what S&P meant by "political brinksmanship": Republicans had used an obscure and once routine requirement that Congress raise the upper limit on federal borrowing periodically to pressure President Obama to accept steep cuts in spending.[27] They did so even though failing to increase the so-called debt ceiling could bring about catastrophic economic effects. In essence, Republicans had taken the US economy hostage, demanding huge budget cuts that they couldn't achieve otherwise as ransom.

The strategy was straight out of the Gingrich-McConnell playbook: Find a leverage point no one had dared use before and exploit it ruthlessly, whatever the toxic effects. At the height of the debt-ceiling fight, McConnell argued, "The Constitution must be amended to keep the government in check. We've tried persuasion. We've tried negotiations. We've tried elections. Nothing has worked."[28] McConnell knew a default would be terrible, but he was willing to threaten it—and many of the GOP rank and file looked more than willing to go through with it. As McConnell explained to the *Washington Post* at the end of the ugly fight, "I think some of our members may have thought the default issue was a hostage you might take a chance at shooting. Most of us didn't think that. What we did learn is this: It's a hostage that's worth ransoming."[29]

The ransom was high. Republicans insisted that federal spending be slashed—even as they insisted the still-sputtering economy was too fragile to increase taxes. As consumer confidence fell and job growth ground to a halt, congressional leaders struggled to forge a deal. Yet talks foundered on the shoals of Republican resistance to any increase in taxes.

Democrats floated the idea of reducing subsidies for oil corporations and corporate jets as a small part of a deficit-reduction package. Republicans abandoned the negotiations.

In what he would later admit was a major miscalculation, Obama tried desperately to reach a "grand bargain." With billionaire spending hawk Pete Peterson's antideficit empire cheering him on, the president appeared willing to accept major cuts in Social Security and Medicare. Yet he insisted that higher taxes on the wealthy be part of the bargain. With just days remaining, House Speaker John Boehner made clear the GOP stance: "The American people will not accept, and the House cannot pass, a bill that raises taxes on job creators."[30] Ultimately, the president agreed to cuts in discretionary spending so deep that he believed they would force Republicans back to the table to reduce the hit on the discretionary defense budget. The strategy didn't work. Dreams of a grand bargain evaporated.

There was once a bipartisan formula for deficit reduction: when the economy was on stable ground, a mix of tax increases and spending cuts, with an emphasis on weeding out rents paid to robber barons. That formula, however, was no longer viable. Now grand bargains meant that only one party was going to bargain. It wasn't just that taxes were off the table. Restricting the rent seeking that drove up public spending with little public benefit also seemed to be off-limits.

To make the situation even more vexing, it wasn't clear that GOP leaders knew how to keep their most conservative members from "shooting" the hostage. Major struggles within the party between the hard right and the harder right portended more crises to come. And indeed, the government shut down its nonessential operations for more than two weeks in October 2013 when House Republicans insisted (futilely) that the budget cut funding for the Affordable Care Act. The shutdown ended up being just five days shorter than the epic struggle between Newt Gingrich and Bill Clinton in the mid-1990s that marked the ascendance of today's hyperpolarized politics.[31]

Broken Budgeting

Shutdowns and debt-ceiling crises are just the highest-profile examples of how difficult it has become to get anything done in Washington. It's always hard to do hard things. Now it's hard to do easy things. Our nation's infrastructure lies in disrepair even as the interest rates we would pay to finance those investments are near record lows.[32] Discretionary spending caps have ravaged R&D investment and starved health care research that could produce the next great treatments. Federal Pell Grants for low-income students now cover only a modest fraction of college costs, when they once defrayed most of the expense.[33] Federal agencies struggle to carry out their essential tasks for want of funding, personnel, and congressional direction.

Judged by the number of laws passed, the 112th and 113th Congresses—spanning 2011 through 2014—were far and away the least productive since World War II. The "do-nothing" 80th Congress that Harry Truman ran against in 1948 passed more than nine hundred laws. The 112th and 113th averaged fewer than three hundred.[34] The best that defenders could muster is that Congress had spent a record amount of time developing and debating bills with no chance of getting signed, including more than fifty repealing, in whole or part, the Affordable Care Act. Playing off the popular children's book, the journalist Ezra Klein called the 112th the "very bad, no good, terrible Congress."[35] And he was probably more positive than most Americans, who gave Congress the lowest ratings in the history of modern polling. Among the things more popular than Congress in opinion surveys: cockroaches, zombies, and making the United States a communist state. (For the time being, Congress remains more popular than serial killers.)[36]

The budget process—central to effective governing—is so dysfunctional that the parties in Congress no longer bother to offer plans with a chance of passage. Instead, Congress relies mostly on what are called "continuing resolutions" to limp along from one year to the next. Failure to pass timely, long-term, or comprehensive budgets is not costless. Contracts and grants go unwritten or unfulfilled, federal hiring languishes, agencies are left in limbo, and our military and civilian personnel waste time scrambling to get by when they should be doing their work.

On the other hand, it is often better than what Congress does eventually. Unable to agree on broader budget priorities, lawmakers have repeatedly imposed harsh austerity on discretionary spending for nondefense aims—the small but vital part of the federal budget that finances science and energy investments, health care research, education and training, law enforcement, and all of the vital aspects of day-to-day governance. In the late 1970s and early 1980s, such spending equaled 5 percent of the economy. Today it's around 3 percent—the lowest level since such data became available in 1962. Nondefense discretionary spending is slated to fall to just over 2 percent by the 2020s.[37]

These numbers are so catastrophic that commentators often have a hard time believing anyone would let them occur. Writing about the GOP's latest budget plan in 2015, former OMB director Peter Orszag scoffed that it envisioned "a path so unrealistic, no serious person could defend it with a straight face."[38] As Orszag noted, the plan proposed that the federal government spend the same amount on all discretionary functions in 2025 as it had in 2008—*before* adjusting for inflation. That does seem unrealistic: not a dollar more for the FBI, the National Institutes of Health, the FDA, the Transportation Security Administration (TSA), and most other government agencies over a period in which prices will likely rise between 30 percent and 40 percent. Yet when Orszag was writing, Republican leaders were defending this horrific outcome with very straight faces.

Orszag's reaction, however, is typical of many centrist commentators. Among seasoned Washington watchers, the tendency is to see extreme positions as mostly position-taking: At some point, the "adults in the room" will step in and do what needs to be done. But those adults are becoming less numerous and even less influential. And while the sanguine centrists are busy reassuring us, they are not consistently calling out extremism, much less articulating the positive case for government that extremists attack. When, for example, Washington mandarins celebrated the 2015 budget deal that partially undid the sequester's devastating cuts, few stopped to note that *even with the deal* nondefense discretionary spending would be almost one-eighth lower in 2016 than it had been in 2010—after adjusting for inflation and despite population and economic growth. By 2017, under the deal, nondefense discretionary spending would fall to its lowest level as a share of the economy ever recorded (with data going back to 1962).[39]

Potholes on the Road to Prosperity

To see what this budget dysfunction means, just look down the street— or, more accurately, down *at* the street. As we saw in chapter 1, American infrastructure is crumbling. According to the American Society of Civil Engineers, bringing US infrastructure up to acceptable levels by 2020 would require $3.6 *trillion* in additional spending.[40] A startling 610,000 bridges in the United States—about one in nine—are structurally deficient.[41] Yet for years, Congress has been kicking the infrastructure can down the road. Since 2009, it has passed a dozen stopgap measures, including one that lasted just a week, making it all but impossible for states and localities and their private-sector partners to pursue the long-term planning that serious infrastructure projects require. (In 2015, Congress finally passed a five-year transportation bill that modestly increased anemic funding levels for highways and transit systems. As big a political lift as this was for the contemporary Congress, the legislation fell well short of estimated spending needs, relied mostly on one-time sources of revenue and budget gimmicks, and did nothing to create permanent funding sources for long-term investment.)[42] The Federal Highway Trust Fund is vastly underfunded relative to historical standards or future needs. The reason: It's financed by a tax on gasoline that is pegged neither to inflation nor gas prices. The last time it was raised was 1993—a year before antitax Republicans took control of the House.[43]

The consequences aren't just economic. When infrastructure fails, people get hurt. We hear about the high-profile tragedies: a deadly bridge collapse in Minnesota, a horrifying Amtrak derailment. But the biggest effects are mostly invisible. Poor public transportation means more cars on the road, which means poorer air quality and more traffic accidents. Congestion steals people's time as well as their health—a huge uncounted cost. Failing to upgrade infrastructure also means forgoing the chance to employ the latest insights about how to design roads to reduce auto accidents, including accidents involving pedestrians. The United States used to have the lowest auto accidents per capita of any rich nation. But while America has improved its safety record since the 1970s, other affluent democracies have continued to make the necessary investments, and have brought down accident rates much faster. Now the United States and South Korea enjoy the dubious distinction of being the most dangerous countries for drivers in the advanced industrial world.[44] According to the US Department of Transportation, obsolete road designs and poorly maintained roads contribute to fourteen thousand traffic fatalities a year. Another study estimated the medical costs of injuries from poor road conditions at $11.4 billion in 2013.[45]

What's happened with infrastructure has happened with other pillars of American prosperity, too. Federal investment in medical research, digital innovation, and other breakthrough technologies, for instance, has plummeted. The fallout is hard to see, because R&D spending takes years, even decades, to pay off. But the fallout is real.

The fragmentation of American political authority has always made governance challenging. But the challenges have multiplied as our traditional checks and balances have collided with the growing antigovernment intensity of the GOP. Our political institutions were not built to handle a highly polarized struggle in which one side is openly hostile to the system itself. No less important, many of the broader social institutions that once reduced the inherent centrifugal tendencies of American politics—a labor movement spanning a third of the private workforce; a dense fabric of mass membership organizations; high levels of civic trust and participation—have fragmented and crumbled, too.[46] What remains is a thin shell of governance around a thickening core of dysfunction.

We can see this in many areas: Programs and agencies hobbled and compromised; elected officials with limited incentive or capacity to achieve positive-sum compromises; and narrow interests filling the vacuum. But we should think first about what we can't see: the toxins in our food that are getting more dangerous even as the government we need to protect us is increasingly hobbled.

The Government That Governs Least . . . Governs Pretty Badly

Each year, roughly 48 million people are sickened by foodborne illness—1 in 6 Americans. Of this total, approximately 128,000 end up in the hospital and 3,000 die. According to the CDC, roughly 1 million Americans a year will suffer from chronic illness as a result of food poisoning, including heart and vascular disease, neural and neuromuscular dysfunctions, kidney and thyroid diseases, and reactive arthritis. And these are effects related just to food poisoning. Other dangerous substances in our food—pesticides, chemicals, mercury—also pose risks, though the extent is much less clear.

What is clear is that the main agency charged with protecting us against these risks is overwhelmed. Congress created the FDA in the wake of Upton Sinclair's 1906 novel The Jungle, with its grim depiction of meat factories churning vermin and filth into food. Inspection remains one of the agency's principal and most demanding responsibilities. Over the last generation, the FDA has been required to inspect more and more facilities—more and more of which are overseas. But while the need for inspections and the number of foodborne-disease outbreaks have increased, the FDA's capacity has not. Between 1972 and 2007, domestic inspections conducted by the agency fell by 81 percent. In 2008, according to the FDA's own data, fewer than one-quarter of food facilities under its jurisdiction were inspected. Indeed, more than half of facilities were not inspected at all over a five-year period. At US borders, across which more and more food transits to Americans' tables, only 1 percent to 2 percent of imports are examined.[47]

By 2010, the problem had grown so bad that Congress passed a law updating the FDA's enforcement strategy. Unfortunately, the funding to implement the new law was slashed. Fierce lobbying by the food industry meant that user fees proposed by the FDA were a political nonstarter. Meanwhile, Congress appropriated less than half the total that the Congressional Budget Office said the FDA needed. "We have good plans for moving forward," said a top FDA official in 2015. "The problem is we don't have the money."[48] Nor does it have the manpower. Nearly half of the job openings in its crucial overseas offices remain unfilled. And while the number of workers in domestic food safety offices has risen from its nadir in 2007, it remains well below historical levels.

Regulators Gone Timid

As grim as the FDA story is, it's actually sunny by the standards of federal agencies today. Since the 1970s, the federal workforce has declined dramatically relative to the American population. When Eisenhower took office, there was one federal worker for every 78 Americans. By 1989, the ratio was one for every 110. Now it hovers around one federal worker for every 150 Americans.[49] The biggest decline has occurred in defense-related employment. Yet the drop has been sharp in domestically oriented agencies as well. In a country where the population and economy keep on expanding, the federal workforce has been caught in a time warp.

Assume that the number of federal workers had risen in line with the US population since the late 1970s. By 2009, in this alternative reality, the Agriculture Department would have employed 83 percent more workers than it did. The US Department of Health and Human Services—the agency responsible for two of the nation's fastest growing programs, Medicare and Medicaid—would have employed 60 percent more. Treasury (which certainly has its hands full, too) would have employed 39 percent more.[50] All told, to get the employment-population ratio back to its pre-1980 levels, the federal government would need to increase its workforce by around 80 percent over the next twenty years.

Yet the loudest voices in Washington are calling for the opposite. After the 2010 midterm, GOP leaders vowed to cut the federal workforce by at least a tenth within five years.[51] Not content with that goal, two Republicans in the House introduced the Federal Workforce Through Attrition Act, which would limit new federal hires to one worker for every three who left government. "Real, productive job creation takes place on Main Street America, not in the bloated federal government," declared one of the bill's authors, Wyoming Republican Cynthia Lummis.[52] On the campaign trail in 2015, the Republicans' most moderate major candidate for president, Jeb Bush, endorsed a similar plan.

Recent GOP budget plans have also demanded sharply higher contributions for federal workers' health insurance and retirement benefits—on top of a three-year freeze in federal pay agreed to in the 2011 deal to raise the debt ceiling. Though it is widely believed that federal workers are overpaid, careful studies indicate that the most educated and skilled workers—who make up a much larger share of the federal workforce than the private-sector workforce—receive substantially less than they would in comparable private jobs.[53] Not surprisingly, federal employee satisfaction has fallen dramatically, relative both to the recent past and to private-sector workers.[54]

The dirty little secret is that essential government responsibilities don't disappear when federal workers do. They just get farmed out to private contractors or pushed down to lower levels of government. Study after study has concluded that excessive reliance on outside contractors magnifies complexity, reduces performance, and impairs accountability.[55] For the federal government's most complicated tasks—guiding scientific inquiry, managing medical payments, overseeing complex financial transactions—talented public workers are vital. "Today's federal civil service is not bloated," concludes John Dilulio, the public administration scholar who worked on George W. Bush's faith-based initiatives. "It is overloaded."[56] To be effective, he argues, the federal government needs to hire one million new workers—a 50 percent increase in its workforce—in the next twenty years. Dilulio might still be working on faith-based initiatives: It will take divine intervention to achieve that goal.

Loaded Revolvers

Those whose job it is to serve the public have more to do and less with which to do it. The same is not true of the private industries they are regulating. Over the last generation, as the capacity of government had eroded, the organizational and financial capacity of narrow private interests has exploded. The typical public worker lives in a world of scarcity. The typical lobbyist lives in a world of abundance: lavish salaries, PR wizards, mercenary experts who can provide just the favorable finding or legislative language needed. No wonder the federal government has hemorrhaged talent.

Once, it was rare for those working in government to move into paid advocacy. Today more than half of lobbyists have crossed through the proverbial revolving door between government service and professional advocacy.[57] And no wonder: The median congressional staffer makes around $50,000. Even top congressional staff are in the $100,000 range. By contrast, the average lobbyist is making around three times that. Moreover, those working in Congress and the executive branch are facing greater pressures than ever before.[58] The number of congressional staff has declined roughly in tandem with the shrinking of the federal civil service. Many of Congress's nonpartisan sources of expertise—the Office of Technology Assessment (OTA), the US Government Accountability Office (GAO), the Congressional Research Service (CRS)—have been cut back sharply or canned altogether. (The OTA was an early victim of the "Gingrich revolution.") The House Committee on Science, Space, and Technology—created in 1958 to oversee rapidly expanding federal R&D spending, particularly in astronautics—has gone from writing and overseeing the laws that foster America's scientific leadership to spending much of its time investigating scientists and scientific institutions for their alleged biases (especially the biases that make them think that global warming is serious and caused by humans). Stagnant pay, dwindling in-house expertise, greater outside demands, fewer fellow staff, less respect for evidence-based policy making—these aren't ideal conditions for holding on to workers.

The problem isn't just that talented personnel pass through the revolving door. The prospect of outside employment shapes what people do even before they start the door spinning. Sometimes, the effect is salutary: A government lawyer who wins cases is going to be more sought after than one who loses them. But there's nothing guaranteeing this happy alignment and, indeed, lots of reason to believe that the main effect is to make public servants too solicitous of outside interests. The revolving door creates a modified H. L. Mencken rule: It's hard to get a man to believe something when his future salary depends on his not believing it. No less important, the revolving door creates a network of personal connections between those within government and those outside pursuing narrow ends. For example, former congressional staff who become lobbyists experience major drops in their lobbying income when their former boss resigns or goes down to defeat.[59] Their connections are suddenly worth much less.

The root of the problem is simple: a growing mismatch between the enormous outside pressures on government—more and more organizations in Washington spending more and more to shape policy—and the weakened capacity of government to channel and check those pressures. "More than three decades of disinvesting in government's capacity to keep up with skyrocketing numbers of lobbyists and policy institutes, well-organized partisans, and an increasingly complex social and legal context," argue the political scientists Lee Drutman and Steven Teles, have created "a power asymmetry crisis."[60]

In other words, weak government doesn't mean efficient government. It means government that gives away the store to the rent seekers far too often. It also means government that must confront the most vital challenges facing it—facing us—with one hand tied behind its back.

Unhealthy Politics

Ebola is scary. The virus, discovered in 1976 and centered in West Africa, has a 50 percent fatality rate. Its symptoms include vomiting, diarrhea, organ failure, and internal hemorrhaging—though not, in most cases, the external bleeding that makes the disease so vivid in the public mind. There is no proven treatment and, as late as January 2016, no approved vaccine.

So it was big news when, in September 2014, Thomas Eric Duncan, a Liberian visitor to the United States, was admitted to Texas Health Presbyterian Hospital in Dallas with symptoms of the deadly virus and died shortly thereafter. A few weeks later, another case came to light: a New York doctor named Craig Spencer, who had traveled to Africa to treat Ebola patients stricken by a major ongoing outbreak in Liberia, Guinea, and Sierra Leone.[61] What followed was a case study in how American politics has gone bad: a combination of shallow, alarmist news coverage, ugly right-wing recrimination, and GOP sabotage that suggested the body politic might be even sicker than the Manhattan doctor.

RUUUUUN!

Let's start with the media frenzy. As frightening as Ebola is, it's difficult to transmit: Infection requires direct contact with the body fluids of a person exhibiting symptoms, which is why medical personnel are at such elevated risk. And while the 2014 outbreak in West Africa was the most serious since Ebola's discovery, within the United States only a handful of cases and just one death, Duncan's, had come to light by mid-October.

You wouldn't have known that, however, from watching the news. Hysterical stories suggested that Ebola was a grave and present danger, playing off, and feeding, public fears about immigration and terrorism. Calming words from experts confronted skepticism from news anchors and outright derision from talking heads. Among the many self-styled authorities who appeared on cable programs: Donald Trump, the novelist Dr. Robin Cook, and Gene Simmons of the rock band Kiss. (To be fair, Simmons does have some experience spitting blood.) One longtime media observer summed up the coverage as follows: "You will personally eject blood from your anus and eye sockets! RUUUUUN!"[62]

The spasm of media attention produced lots of anxiety but little understanding. In October Ebola made it onto the Gallup poll's list of top health concerns, beating out obesity and cancer. Even more striking, it debuted on Gallup's list of the "most important problem facing the nation," ahead of terrorism, poverty, race relations, and crime.[63] Yet most Americans were unaware of even basic facts about the disease. Nearly 60 percent believed it "very likely" that Ebola could be caught from a sneeze or cough; 75 percent said that sufferers were infectious before they began to show symptoms.[64] Not surprisingly, given these false beliefs, a quarter of Americans considered Ebola a "major" public health threat, and even more said they were avoiding air and train travel for safety. Revealingly, those following the story most closely had the lowest levels of knowledge: The more they watched, the less they knew.

And then, suddenly, it was over. For a few weeks after the Texas patient died, evening broadcast and cable news couldn't cover Ebola enough, running nearly a thousand segments in just four weeks. Once the threat had passed, and it was clear that federal officials had been right to urge calm, Ebola disappeared from the news. When Gallup asked the public about the nation's most important problem in early 2015, Ebola didn't register at all.[65]

At least one American, however, remembered the hysterical coverage. At the 2015 White House correspondent's dinner—an annual ritual in which the president entertains the nation's top reporters with lighthearted shtick—President Obama brought his "anger translator" onto the stage to convey what the famously cool president was really thinking. For those who haven't seen the "anger translator" routine on the comedy TV show *Key and Peele*, the translator is named Luther (played by Keegan-Michael Key), and his job is to put into words what Obama is too restrained to actually say.

Here is what Obama said to the gathered journalists: "We won't always see eye to eye." And here is Luther's translation:

And CNN, thank you so much for the wall-to-wall Ebola coverage. For two whole weeks, we were one step away from *The Walking Dead*. Then y'all got up and just moved on to the next day. That was awesome.

Oh, and by the way, if you haven't noticed: You don't have Ebola![66]

Pin the Blame on the Donkey

The wall-to-wall Ebola coverage didn't convey much information. But it did carry at least one clear message: Government can't save you. "Ebola is a serious threat," wrote Ron Fournier, a senior columnist and the editorial director at the *National Journal*, "but it's not the disease that scares me. What scares me is the fact that we can't trust the institutions that deal with such threats, and we can't trust the people who run them."[67] The columnist and Fox talking head Charles Krauthammer, writing in the *Washington Post*, opined that "Ebola has crystallized the collapse of trust in state authorities."[68]

And these were the *moderate* voices: Within hours of Thomas Duncan's diagnosis, talk radio and Fox News filled up with right-wing commentators spouting ever more outrageous conspiracy theories. Glenn Beck suggested that Dallas, Texas, was the first US city to experience the disease because it leaned Republican. According to Rush Limbaugh, Obama and the left "have this attitude, 'Well, if they have it in Africa, by God, we deserve to get it because they're in Africa because of us and because of slavery.'"[69] Not to be outdone, Michael Savage—whose show, *The Savage Nation*, has over five million listeners—said Obama's actions regarding Ebola rose "to levels of treason; it actually exceeds any level of treason I've ever seen...." "Obama wants equality, he wants fairness," Savage continued. "It's only fair that America have a nice epidemic, or two or three or four, in order to really feel what it's like to be in the Third World."[70]

Conservative celebrities are in the outrage industry, of course. But it was a strikingly short distance from their apoplectic warnings to the criticisms lobbed by prominent GOP politicians. With the 2014 midterm looming, leading Republicans—including presidential hopeful Rand Paul (a doctor) and former Massachusetts senator Scott Brown, who was locked in a tight race for governor in New Hampshire—warned that a disease centered in West Africa and never seen before in Latin America would soon cross the Mexican border. Paul and other top GOP politicians also claimed that President Obama's decision to provide US military support for efforts to fight the disease in Africa would lead to mass infection of American troops. Raising the specter of a "whole shipload of soldiers" infected with Ebola, Paul suggested the CDC had "understate[d] the transmissibility" of Ebola, and "political correctness" was standing in the way of "sound, rational, scientific decisions."[71] Yet political correctness apparently did not stand in the way of widespread calls by Republicans for travel bans on affected countries—an unworkable policy that, experts warned, would not only prevent foreign medical personnel from reaching patients but also increase the incentive for those infected to evade screenings or lie to health officials.

Perhaps it's no surprise, then, that in the 2015 Gallup poll that showed Ebola disappearing from the public's list of important problems, the problem offered most often by survey respondents was "dissatisfaction with government."[72]

Preventable Illness

The biggest and most telling tragedy of the Ebola scare is that it might well have been avoidable. Over the prior decade, funding for the National Institutes of Health declined by $5 billion after inflation—a drop of almost a fifth in the NIH's budget.[73] Even more striking, the CDC's budget for disaster preparedness, always small, was slashed in half over the same period. These cuts amid the economic downturn contributed to more than forty-five thousand job losses within state and local health departments just between 2008 and 2012.[74] And the cuts continued after the Ebola scare: The so-called sequestration legislation that ended the debt-ceiling standoff put in place tough automatic cuts in discretionary spending (again, the kind of spending that finances many of the most vital investments in American's future, such as infrastructure, medical research, and education), further squeezing the NIH and the CDC.[75]

Bill Gates has argued recently, with justification, that the most dangerous "global threat" today is not terrorism or nuclear weapons but a global pandemic. You might think that a billionaire philanthropist would be unworried about budget cuts. But Gates has publicly opposed sequestration, calling its effect a "crisis" that undermines the effective coordination of public expenditures and private philanthropy. And he has scoffed at those who think the market will step in, arguing that "the flaw in the pure capitalistic approach" is to think that profit-seeking firms will invest sufficiently in cures for dread diseases with inadequate consumer demand, such as malaria.[76]

In retrospect, the most shortsighted cuts were for funding of a vaccine to prevent Ebola (which, at the start of 2016, looked finally to be on the horizon). Since 2010, the NIH's spending to develop a vaccine dropped by half. Indeed, Francis Collins, the head of the NIH, claimed that were it not for the "ten-year slide in research support, we probably would have had a vaccine in time for this that would've gone through clinical trials and would have been ready." Collins said that other treatments, too, "were on a slower track than would've been ideal, or than would have happened if we had been on a stable research support trajectory. We would have been a year or two ahead of where we are, which would have made all the difference."[77]

In the end, the measures pushed by federal authorities—airport screening, self-reporting, specially equipped hospitals, and support for action in Africa—worked. The two people who became sick in the United States recovered, and no new cases of the disease occurred here. As the health reporter Jonathan Cohn noted, "The Ebola response turned out to be a clear public health success—a model for effective, responsive government action."[78] Nonetheless, that response would have been much more effective and perhaps even unnecessary had the capacity of the federal government not been so eroded over previous decades. And yet nobody paid a political price for this erosion. No one paid a price for alarmism or extremism. Indeed, when it became clear that government policy had proved remarkably successful despite these obstacles, no one seemed to notice.

Capitol Hill Calvinball

If you were a fan of the comic strip *Calvin and Hobbes*, you know about "Calvinball": the chaotic game of ever-changing rules that six-year-old

Calvin plays with his stuffed tiger Hobbes. The only consistent rule in Calvinball is that you can never play it the same way twice. But the essence of the game is simple: Calvin makes up the rules as he goes along in whatever way advantages him most. If that means players must wear a Lone Ranger mask and hit a badminton shuttlecock with a croquet mallet, that's what the rules say—until, that is, Calvin changes them again.

Washington has its own version of Calvinball. As we saw in chapter 8, politicians follow two sorts of rules: a set of formal rules that prohibit certain moves and a set of informal, long-observed boundaries that politicians feel compelled to respect. In the decades after World War II, these hazier boundaries loomed large. Opponents didn't filibuster every piece of legislation that came up in the Senate—not because the formal rules prohibited it but because it simply wasn't done. Nominations by the president to fill court vacancies were generally approved quickly and only occasionally with significant dispute—not because Congress couldn't tie them up for months or turn every candidate into a defining ideological fight but because it simply wasn't done outside of unusual circumstances. Congressional deference was even greater for nominations to the executive branch, which the president has the greatest authority to oversee. And when big legislative fights were over, they were over. Sure, sometimes the losers would head for the courts or start mobilizing to rewrite the law. But if the courts didn't come to the losers' defense—and the norm was for them to stay out of big legislative fights—the losers had to lick their wounds, regroup, and head back through the legislative gauntlet. That was how the system worked.[79]

Or that was how the system *once* worked. In Capitol Hill Calvinball, the formal rules remain the same, but it's still possible never to play the game quite the same way twice. The informal rules—the norms once policed by the Washington establishment—turn out to allow plenty of leeway to make up the rules as you go along. And as the gap between the parties has increased, the incentives to play Capitol Hill Calvinball have, too.

The New "Rule of Sixty"

In previous chapters, we have examined the transformation of the filibuster from a rare parliamentary tactic into a routine weapon. Republicans were the innovators here: first in the early 1990s, as Gingrich's Senate allies pushed for a more confrontational stance, and then in the late 2000s under Mitch McConnell. Republicans filibustered popular as well as controversial legislation—bills that would pass unanimously as well as those that would just squeak through. Sight unseen, the GOP response was obstruction.

One way to measure the prevalence of filibusters is to count the number of cloture motions to end them. From 1917 until 1970, there was a grand total of 58 cloture motions—roughly 1 per year. From 1970 until 1990, there were 365—approximately 18 per year. But then the new GOP strategy kicked in. Between 1991 and 2006, there were 563 cloture votes to end filibusters—just over 35 per year. That might have seemed an upper limit, but when Democrats took back control of both houses of Congress in 2006, the GOP Senate minority upped the ante. From 2007 through 2014 (when Democrats lost the Senate), there were 644 cloture motions—or more than 80 per year. When Republicans have raised the stakes, Democrats have stayed in the game. After Republicans captured the Senate in 2014, for example, Democrats staged more filibusters than they did the last time they were in the minority. But it is Republicans who have consistently rewritten the rules.[80]

So normal has this sharp historical change come to seem that the news media barely report on filibusters anymore, making them even less costly for those who launch them. During President Obama's first two years in office, news stories focused relentlessly on the president's ability to attract the support of the last few Democratic senators who constituted the party's fleeting sixty-vote majority. Left unsaid was that these senators' votes were needed only because of the unprecedented obstruction of the GOP. Now it was just taken for granted that the Senate operated under the "rule of sixty."

The filibuster proved beneficial to Republicans not just because it allowed them to block or shape legislation but also because it made the Democrats look so bad. Serial filibusters stymied Congress and took up valuable time that otherwise might have been used to advance the majority's agenda. The tortured efforts of Democratic leaders to rally the troops made them look disorganized and ineffectual. It also created incentives for individual Democrats to hold out for special deals—which, when granted, simultaneously weakened legislation and gave Republicans fresh material for their attacks.

Gridlock, in short, wasn't just a policy win. It was a political win as well. With their committed campaigns of obstruction, Republicans severely compromised both Clinton's and Obama's early legislative drives. Yet far from paying a price for their intransigence, in 2014 they ended four years of minority obstruction in the Senate with majority control of both houses of Congress.

Unpacking the Courts

If gridlock has made Congress less important, it has made the federal courts more important. When Congress is silent, courts become louder voices in lawmaking—not just because political actors turn to the courts to resolve disputes that Congress can't or won't, but also because those courts are more likely to have the last word.

Which means that who is on the courts matters more, too. Federal judges are nominated by the president with the "advice and consent" of the Senate. For much of the twentieth century, presidents consulted with key senators and then made nominations that were approved quickly. As recently as the early 1980s, virtually all presidential nominees to the federal courts were confirmed, usually within a matter of weeks.

That has changed. The big shift came after Bill Clinton brought to an end twelve years of Republican control of the presidency. Confirmation rates for judicial nominees fell to under 70 percent in the mid-1990s, with the average time from nomination to confirmation increasing to around six months toward the end of the Clinton presidency.[81] Although Clinton tried to accommodate the GOP by nominating moderates, Republicans barraged the White House with an unprecedented number of filibusters and "holds" (when individual senators delay consideration of a nominee with the implicit threat of a filibuster—another informal practice once used rarely). Once again Capitol Hill Calvinball had a new set of rules.

While both parties played by the new rules, rewriting them was mostly a Republican project. This became apparent when Obama took office in 2009. Presidents typically have greater success with their nominees when they control the Senate. Yet Obama's Democratic majority did little to temper GOP resistance. In Ronald Reagan's first two years in office, he had a GOP Senate, and around 95 percent of his nominees were confirmed. In Obama's first two years in the White House, he had a Democratic Senate—and only around 55 percent of his nominees were confirmed.[82] In Reagan's first term, the median number of days between nomination and confirmation was 28 days. In Obama's, it was more than *215* days.[83] These numbers are all the more notable because, when Obama entered office, the federal courts had an unprecedented number of vacancies—including a record forty-nine openings considered "emergencies" by the Administrative Office of the US Courts.[84]

That GOP obstruction was the problem became undeniable when frustrated Democrats changed the rules governing nominations in 2013. Using their authority as the majority party, Democrats voted to allow confirmations of federal judicial nominations with a simple majority, except in the case of nominees to the Supreme Court. Many moderate Democrats had long resisted this rule change, fearing they would lose the leverage the filibuster gave them. Moreover, all Democrats worried about what would happen if and when Republicans regained control of the Senate. But the breakdown of the confirmation process overrode these doubts, and after November 2013, appeals and district court nominees could no longer be blocked by the GOP minority. In 2014 Obama successfully nominated 89 new judges. Federal vacancies fell from record highs to historical lows, with only 7 of 179 seats open within the federal appeals courts and 31 of 677 within the federal district courts.[85] Apparently, the main obstacle standing in the way of fully staffed courts was congressional Republicans.

The New Nullification

The final example of Capitol Hill Calvinball might be the most troubling—because it strikes so centrally at the legitimacy of democratic governance. In their 2012 book *It's Even Worse Than It Looks*, Thomas Mann and Norman Ornstein describe a set of obstructionist strategies they call "the new nullification." The phrase comes from the ugly history of state resistance to federal laws. Yet Mann and Ornstein apply the term to a range of contemporary tactics that opponents use to cripple democratically enacted laws. These include coordinated assaults on those laws' constitutionality, denying funds necessary for their implementation, and "blocking nominations, even while acknowledging the competence and integrity of the nominees, to prevent the legitimate implementation of laws on the books."[86]

Consider the fight over the Consumer Financial Protection Bureau, an agency designed to put consumers on a slightly more level playing field with those offering complicated financial services. When the CFPB was included in President Obama's financial reform legislation, the Chamber of Commerce and Wall Street tried desperately to kill it. The head of the Chamber's Center for Capital Markets Competitiveness vowed to "spend whatever it takes" to defeat the proposal.[87] Despite all the spending, however, the opponents lost—which would usually mean the agency would go into operation. Yet Republicans refused to confirm a head to the CFPB unless President Obama agreed to changes that would weaken it greatly. When Obama refused, Republicans threatened a filibuster to block the intellectual architect of the bureau, Harvard law professor Elizabeth Warren, from becoming the agency's first director. (They might have been better off letting her go through, since she would go on to knock off Massachusetts's GOP senator, Scott Brown.) Obama then nominated Richard Cordray, a former Ohio attorney general. Republicans acknowledged that he was qualified, but they did not budge from their nullification stance: no changes in the agency, no head of the agency.[88]

It is worth pausing here to consider just how audacious this demand was. The CFPB was law. Republicans didn't have the votes to repeal it. Yet the GOP still felt it could win the war by refusing to carry out its constitutional role of advise and consent. Nor was this fight the only example of the new nullification at work. The other appointments that Obama made during the Senate's sort-of-recess were to the National Labor Relations Board, an eighty-year-old agency with around 1,700 employees charged with adjudicating private-sector labor disputes. When Obama entered office, the five-member board had only two members—too few to issue binding rulings. Though Obama followed tradition and nominated Republicans alongside Democrats, the GOP threatened to filibuster several of his nominees and refused to act on any of them. It took a first set of recess appointments in March 2010 (one Democrat and one Republican) to get the board running again.[89] But with the GOP vowing to block future nominations to fill pending vacancies, the agency's viability remains in doubt.

Again, the NLRB was established by law to play a specific role. Again, business lobbies and Republicans disagreed with that role. And again, unable or unwilling to change the law through the normal democratic process, they threatened to make the agency dysfunctional. After a complaint against Boeing in 2011 by the NLRB's general counsel (who acts independently of the five-member board), Senator Lindsey Graham of South Carolina vowed to block all nominations to the board. "The NLRB as inoperable could be considered progress," he declared.[90] The complaint was dropped, but GOP resistance continued—even after Obama's reelection. In July 2013, Mitch McConnell made clear the basis of GOP objections by making a remarkable demand: He would support Obama only if he agreed to a board with a Republican majority. Nullification or capitulation—those were the choices.

A similar intransigence has crippled the Federal Election Commission. Created in the wake of Watergate, the FEC is charged with policing violations of campaign finance law. With money pouring into politics from a growing range of legally questionable organizations, policing seems like it should be a priority. For roughly a decade, however, the FEC hasn't been able to do much at all: Between 2008 and 2012, the number of FEC enforcement cases collapsed from 612 to 135.[91] The commission is required to have three Democrats and three Republicans and can act only with four votes. But Republican commissioners have refused to act on all but the most egregious violations—and maybe not even then: In 2008, in what seemed a simple case, a wealthy friend of Mitt Romney's spent $150,000 to fly Romney campaign workers to a fund-raiser. The legal limit on such "in-kind" donations is $2,600. The committee deadlocked 3 to 3.[92] The Democratic chair of the commission, Ann Ravel, admitted in 2015, "The likelihood of the laws being enforced is slim. . . . People think the FEC is dysfunctional. It's worse than dysfunctional."[93]

Even when nullification isn't the goal, the contentious, drawn-out confirmation process impairs governance. In his first year in office, fewer than 65 percent of Obama's nominees to the executive branch were confirmed, compared with just over 80 percent in George W. Bush's first year.[94] The forced vacancies included scores of high-ranking officials whose job was to assist the Treasury secretary in dealing with the financial crisis. A host of critical offices went without heads for months, from US Customs and Border Protection to the National Highway Traffic Safety Administration to the Centers for Medicare and Medicaid Services (which by 2012 had not had a confirmed head in six years). Over three national elections, from 2010 through 2014, the US Election Assistance Commission—created to help voters after the contested 2000 election—lacked a single commissioner.[95] Not surprisingly, Obama ended his first term with a higher share of vacancies in Senate-confirmed positions than either Bill Clinton or George W. Bush.

Some effects are easy to see: It took nearly a half year for President Obama's 2014 nominee for US attorney general, Loretta Lynch, to receive Senate confirmation.[96] Yet as Mann and Ornstein note, the most profound effects are more hidden: "Citizens offering to serve their country, often at significant personal and financial cost, are forced to put their personal lives on hold for many months. With the stress this puts on their careers, marriages, and children, will really talented people remain willing to subject themselves to such indignity? The government that we want to be more effective is crippled."[97]

It's Even Worse Than It Looks

Mann and Ornstein meant their critique as a good-government salvo against the breakdown of American politics—one that spoke the truth that too many Washington insiders were afraid to say. As they wrote in the book's most powerful paragraph:

> However awkward it may be for the traditional press and nonpartisan analysts to acknowledge, one of the two major parties, the Republican Party, has become an insurgent outlier—ideologically extreme; contemptuous of the inherited social and economic policy regime; scornful of compromise; unpersuaded by conventional understanding of facts, evidence, and science; and dismissive of the legitimacy of its political opposition. When one party moves this far from the center of American politics, it is extremely difficult to enact policies responsive to the country's most pressing challenges.

The book was a broadside against Capitol Hill Calvinball. "The argument we're making is that our politics will never really get better until the Republican Party gets back into the game, instead of playing a new one," Mann said after the book came out. "We want a strong, conservative Republican Party—but one with some connection with reality."

What they got instead was a sharp rebuff from the media that had once made Mann and Ornstein go-to political analysts in Washington. After the book's publication, they were no longer quoted in mainstream news stories or invited to the public affairs shows on which they had appeared regularly or, for that matter, discussed by the parts of the news empire set up to examine its own practices. "What the fuck is an ombudsman doing if he's not writing about this?" Ornstein complained to *Huffington Post* in late 2012. Mann lamented, "I can no longer be a source in a news story in the *Wall Street Journal* or the *Times* or the *Post* because people now think I've made the case for the Democrats, and therefore I'll have to be balanced with a Republican."[98]

To Mann and Ornstein, the problem was the continuing insistence that both Republicans and Democrats were equally to blame for government dysfunction. Mann marveled at the degree to which the well-funded campaign by Pete Peterson and others to elevate the deficit as the nation's number one concern had led many journalists to conclude that American government was overextended—and Democrats, in denial about this alleged reality, at least as complicit as Republicans in the failure to address the problem. "The Peterson world, I think, has given journalists the material to keep doing what they're doing," said Mann.

Seeing both parties as equally at fault seems hardheaded and superficially suggests objectivity, but it's an abdication of responsibility. "If voters are going to be able to hold accountable political figures, they've got to know what's going on," explained Ornstein. "And if the story that you're telling repeatedly is that they're all to blame—they're all equally to blame—then you're really doing a disservice to voters, and not doing what journalism is supposed to do." This responsibility is not journalists' alone. But as other sources of truth telling have eroded or been sucked into the partisan vortex, the abdication of the news media has become more damaging. There is no bipartisan Washington establishment anymore, nor the dense network of mass-membership organizations that once helped citizens figure out what Washington is up to, nor much deference to scientific authority that conflicts with what partisans or powerful private interests insist is true. If one side is tearing down government, it's a deep problem when those writing about American politics are convinced that the mess is thoroughly bipartisan.

The breakdown of American governing authority involves a vicious cycle. Those who cripple governance pay little price. To the contrary, they gain when trust in government falls. They gain when government can't regulate or tax the narrow private interests they support. And they gain when it becomes harder and harder to make the case for the effective public authority that Hamilton and Madison both embraced. If we are to break the vicious cycle, we need to understand who is to blame. We also need to know what to do—the focus of our final chapter.

CONCLUSION

* ★ ★ ★ *

The Positive-Sum Society

We have some good news and some bad news.

The last few chapters have been gloomy, so let's start with the good news: The mixed economy remains a spectacular achievement. Over the past century, we leapt across the Great Divide. We broke from the entirety of prior human existence, in which life was nasty, brutish, and short for almost everyone, and entered an era in which most Americans could look forward to long lives, a real education, and previously unimaginable material comfort. By combining the power of markets with a strong dose of public authority, we achieved unprecedented prosperity. However serious the challenges we face—and we wrote this book because we believe they are very serious—we should not forget how much the mixed economy has achieved, continues to achieve, and will achieve if we can rediscover the forgotten roots of American prosperity.

Try this thought experiment: Imagine you could get into the time machine built by the genius toddler Stewie on the animated series *Family Guy* and go back to any prior point in American history. But the catch is that unlike the family dog Brian, who can go back to fetch a bone he buried in the front yard, you have to stay there *permanently*. Where would you go? The answer to us is evident: Don't get in the time machine! This answer seems especially clear-cut for members of those groups who historically suffered from intense discrimination (and still do, but to a diminished degree). But we think the conclusion applies quite broadly. Yes, there are Americans who might benefit from taking the time machine back a decade or two. But looking at our society as a whole, we really have never had it so good.

Of course, there are some big challenges to grapple with. As we saw in chapter 1, we are coming up short in the most important domains of social achievement, failing to build on our prior successes or to match the most successful rich democracies. And yet even this alarming development offers something positive. Precisely because we have failed to seize so many opportunities for enhanced prosperity in recent decades, we have no shortage of attractive options today. Just as in the 1950s and 1960s, a wide range of valuable social investments beckons to our leaders: in infrastructure, in R&D, in human capital. Moreover, despite the enormous progress toward racial and gender equality, our economy still underperforms because of unequal opportunities—at enormous cost. (If women had equal representation in the paid workforce as men, according to a recent study by the McKinsey Global Institute, the economies of the United States, Canada, Australia, and New Zealand would be roughly a fifth larger in ten years on average than they would be given current trends. A similar analysis, also by McKinsey, suggests that the educational achievement gap between black and Hispanic students and white students costs the United States 3 percent to 5 percent of GDP every year, "the economic equivalent of a permanent national recession.")[1]

If we rebuild our roads, bridges, and transportation networks, if we redouble our commitment to science in service of the public good, if we ensure that all kids have good early childhood education and the chance to finish college, we will not just live in a fairer and more contented society; we will be enormously richer for our efforts. And if we also take on the modern robber barons of health care, finance, energy, and other sectors, we can generate even bigger benefits—from slower growth of health spending to lower pollution, from longer lives to stronger financial security, from increased educational opportunity to decreased economic hardship.

In short, *there is money on the table just waiting to be picked up.* At a time when so many argue that we live in an age of inherent limits, we have something truly exciting to aim for: We can make our already prosperous society much more prosperous. And in doing so, we can also get our troubled democracy back on track. Right now American politics is dominated by narrow interests and riven by zero-sum conflicts. If we can start picking up the money on the table—if we can, as President George W. Bush once declared memorably, "make the pie higher"—we have a real chance of forging the sort of broad positive-sum bargains that made our mixed economy possible. Indeed, that might be the best news of all: If we start using government successfully again to enhance prosperity, we *can* fix our broken politics.

There Is No Magic Bullet

Now for the bad news: It won't be easy. It will be hard, and it will take time. Ask political experts how to repair American democracy, and you will often be told that if we did one big thing, all would be well. Don't believe it. Some of those big things aren't realistic. (Sorry, we're not going to adopt a parliamentary system.) But even the most plausible of them—campaign finance reform, improvements in our electoral process, a concerted push to bring politicians back toward the center—are not going to fix the system on their own. *There is no magic bullet.* The problems are too complex, too interdependent, and too entrenched to make any single "solution" plausible.

While understandable, the search for a magic bullet carries two great dangers. First, it is a recipe for disillusionment—a quality that our political culture already produces in abundance. Second, it blinds us to a more realistic possibility: that serious but not sweeping changes, guided by the right diagnosis, can cascade into larger transformations. There are some big reforms to rally around: For example, we will make the case for a major campaign to restore and expand the right to vote. But while we need a serious course correction guided by lofty goals, restoring America's mixed economy is going to require movement on multiple fronts over time, with each making the next more likely.

The history of American political reform follows this pattern. There was no single master innovation in the long Progressive Era, or in the postwar efforts that further developed the mixed economy. There was no single decisive breakthrough in the struggle for expanded opportunity in the 1960s, or in the expansion of protections for our environment and our health and safety in the 1970s. Trial and error, small and large victories that enabled subsequent advances—that's how progress happened, and that's how it will happen today.

Moreover, while there's no single solution, we do believe there's an overarching and inspiring aim: restoring the capacity of our democracy to express and act upon the interests that large numbers of us share in common. Political scientists refer to these as "diffuse interests": goals such as addressing climate change, moderating health costs, and diminishing dangerous financial speculation. These are concerns that matter to tens or hundreds of millions of citizens but are the highest priority of very few. In the rough-and-tumble world of long-term political combat, such interests are often severely disadvantaged. They have trouble organizing and assembling adequate resources, and they frequently lack the staying power or persistent focus necessary to gain an edge and hold it long enough to make a real difference.

By contrast, "concentrated interests"—a genus exemplified by the modern robber barons—have much greater incentive and ability to organize. As Adam Smith recognized, it is much more likely that the folks who sell milk will conspire to keep prices high than it is that the folks who drink milk will organize to ensure low prices. Democracies are at constant risk of being overwhelmed by intensely organized minorities who distort, immobilize, or dismantle government to advance their own interests.

We have spent the past four chapters exploring why it has become so difficult to govern on behalf of diffuse interests—indeed, why we have almost forgotten that such governance is possible. To recap, the power of business has grown even as sources of countervailing power have declined. The new economic elite and the nation's major business associations (the first of our Great Enablers) have greater motives and opportunities to pursue narrow short-term advantages. Meanwhile, the Republican Party (the second of our Great Enablers) has made a fateful alliance with these forces. In the face of these developments, American political institutions have proved highly vulnerable. Our system's complexity and fragmentation make obstruction easy and accountability hard. Antigovernment ideologues (aka hard Randians) face little consequence for their destructive actions, especially because today's so-called centrists (aka soft Randians) offer little defense of public authority. The result is a downward spiral of popular distrust and alienation. So deep has our crisis of authority become that even defenders of government often reluctantly join the spiral of silence, concluding that the best defense of our government's diminishing capacity is not to talk about government at all.

To reverse this spiral, we must reestablish a government with the capacity to foster broad prosperity. We need to ensure that ordinary voters and diffuse interests are capable of triumphing over concentrated interests. And we need to rescue the ideal of the mixed economy from the mists of American Amnesia. Many changes have swept the American economy since the 1970s. Yet our biggest problem is not a lack of attractive policy options. Our biggest problem is our politics. The mixed economy is as necessary as ever—indeed, in a world of increased inter-dependence and complexity, *more* than ever. And despite all the changes of recent decades, it is still within our grasp. We need better policies to restore its potential. But above all, we need a better politics.

A Government That Can Govern

As everyone who has read *The Federalist Papers* knows, the Founders feared a system corrupted by narrow interests—what James Madison termed the "mischiefs of faction." Madison spoke for all the delegates when he explained that elected representatives had to rise above any group whose goals were "adverse to the rights of other citizens, or to the permanent and aggregate interests of the community."[2] Yet the Found-ers' proposed remedy was not just to divide authority, as we are told so often. It was also to create effective national power. In "The Federalist No. 51," Madison argued that strengthening the federal government—creating what he called an "extended Republic"—would empower dif-fuse interests over narrow ones: "In the extended Republic of the United States, and among the great variety of interests, parties, and sects which it embraces, a coalition of the majority of the whole society could seldom take place on any other principles than justice or the general good."[3] Al-though the compromises needed to pass the Constitution watered down Madison's preferred solution, he and his allies continued to argue for strong national institutions to ensure that elected representatives placed diffuse interests over narrow ones.

Those institutions, however, are showing their age. The Founders were brilliant statesmen who valued strong public authority far more than is typically acknowledged. Still, they anticipated neither the vast demands of modern governance nor the rise of today's hyperpolarized parties. The intense fragmentation of American political institutions—which makes our system an extreme outlier among rich democracies—poses substan-tial and growing barriers to those seeking prosperity-enhancing compro-mises. It hinders public officials from responding to pressing problems. It empowers well-organized minorities, particularly if they simply want to block action. And because it makes lines of accountability so fuzzy, it undermines the power of voters. Instead of helping citizens guide what government does, the ballot morphs into a "mad as hell" button that voters push intermittently and mostly without useful effect (or don't even bother to push because they're so alienated or think government is so irrelevant).

For angry citizens, pushing the Mad as Hell button might be momentarily satisfying—much as pressing those elevator Close Door buttons that apparently don't do anything is momentarily satisfying. But like jabbing buttons that aren't wired, jabbing individual politicians who are responding simply to the incentives of today's politics has little effect. As in the long Progressive Era, the problem isn't bad political apples so much as a bad political orchard: a set of political institutions matched poorly to current governing conditions and a political elite that has figured out how to game those institutions. To make American politics work better, we need to make American political institutions work better.

Making the System More Majoritarian

We can start by scaling back the power of entrenched minorities to foster endless stalemate. Federalism, the separation of powers, and the advantages enjoyed by small states are all hard-wired into our Constitution. But that doesn't mean we cannot make our system more majoritarian. Many of the biggest sources of gridlock aren't inherent in our constitutional order but instead reflect rules, external organizations, and routinized behaviors that have been grafted on top of our fragmented system.

The most obvious and effective change in rules would be further reform of the Senate filibuster. Not a part of the Constitution—and, indeed, sharply at odds with the Constitution's careful restriction of supermajority requirements to a few specified areas (treaties, constitutional amendments, the overriding of presidential vetos)—the filibuster has morphed from an intermittent speed bump into a gigantic and expanding sinkhole. Today's "rule of sixty," requiring a supermajority to pass any legislation besides the budget, simultaneously thwarts the majority, tarnishes its reputation, and obscures the role of the obstructionists.[4] It is hard to imagine an arrangement more corrosive to effective governance.

Thankfully, unlike fundamental features of the Constitution, the filibuster rests on a fragile institutional foundation. Reformers recently eliminated the capacity of a Senate minority to block presidential appointments, with the exception of Supreme Court justices.[5] Further restrictions, which at a minimum would restore the pre-1980s practice of reserving filibusters for rare occasions, would increase the capacity of majorities to govern.

To be sure, filibuster reform—by facilitating legislative drives by the contemporary radicalized GOP—could also boost the Great Enablers' attacks on the mixed economy. Ultimately, however, the status quo of gridlock and dysfunction favors those who wish to make it hard to govern and thrive from acting in the shadows. Over time, restricting the filibuster would reduce the leverage of powerful concentrated interests that specialize in preventing robust exercises of public authority. By forcing obstructionists to come out in the open, filibuster reform would also empower ordinary voters, simplifying their vital role of punishing or rewarding governing majorities based on how well they represent shared interests.

Rebuilding Government Capacity

In addition to increasing the capacity of majorities to act, we also need to increase the capacity of *government* to act. The social world has grown more complex, and the organization and resources of concentrated interests have expanded. Yet the ability of elected officials to obtain reliable independent expertise and the capacity of government agencies to carry out their essential tasks have both atrophied. American government is suffering from an acute case of "political decay," to use the phrase of the Stanford political scientist Francis Fukuyama.[6] It has become more reliant on information provided by the most partisan and self-interested political actors, and it has become less capable of carrying out courses of action effectively and consistently over the long term.

The decay is most notable in America's Congress. The world's most powerful legislature is now a punch line. At the peak of its productivity in the 1960s and 1970s, Congress achieved an impressive record of bipartisan problem solving. Not coincidentally, congressional leaders expanded the institution's capacity to draw on in-house expertise, boosting the size of congressional staffs, the role of specialized committees, and the number and resources of analytic institutions such as the Congressional Budget Office and Congressional Research Service. Since then, however, Congress has squandered or destroyed many of these assets.[7] Republican congressional leaders in particular have slashed staff and committee resources, and cut back or eliminated many of the body's expert advisory organizations. These changes haven't simply made Congress less capable; they have also made it more reliant on narrow private interests. Members of Congress let lobbyists write bills not just because they get rewarded for doing so but because they have so little in-house expertise of their own.[8]

What's happened in Congress is an extreme version of what's happened throughout American government. At a time when we face significant challenges demanding long-term vision and technical skill, talented individuals are less likely than ever to seek public employment. And even when they do go into government, they are less likely than ever to stick around long enough to gain the expertise and experience necessary to make a difference.[9] Too many able young people come to see government as something to avoid or a way station to the real goal: a lucrative job serving powerful private interests. Such imbalanced incentives do triple damage. They make it harder for public officials to do their job, they make those officials more solicitous of private interests, and they damage public trust in governing institutions.

The solution is as simple as it is difficult: We need to invest more in government. Fortunately, doing so doesn't require much money. As the political scientists Steve Teles and Lee Drutman remind us, "In 2013 the funding for the entire Senate was about $820 million. The funding for the entire House was about $1.16 billion. That $2 billion a year is considerably less than any number of Pentagon project overruns—a problem, by the way, that could be significantly reduced with better legislative oversight driven by an expert staff."[10]

Even hiring more federal workers—recall John Dilulio's recommendation of at least a million more federal civil servants—wouldn't cost us much relative to what we spend now on inefficient contracting and poorly implemented policies that could be prevented by a better-staffed government. Moreover, it's not necessary that we equalize the pay or resources between the public and private sectors. People *want* to work in organizations looking out for diffuse interests: In the battle between the coal industry and scientifically guided regulators, it's the regulators who hold the moral high ground. The key is to make the distribution of political resources less radically imbalanced than it is now.

To do this, we need to increase the clout of another embattled partner in good governance: the American voter.

Power to the People

In February 2015 singer John Legend addressed a vast Academy Awards audience. Holding the Oscar for Best Song for his and the rapper Common's anthem to the civil rights movement, "Glory," from the film *Selma*, Legend declared, "Selma is now. The struggle for justice is now. The Voting Rights Act that they fought for fifty years ago is being compromised right now in this country."[11]

Millions of Americans celebrated the lessons of *Selma* in movie theaters. At the same time, however, millions of Americans face growing obstacles to exercising their right to vote. Like Legend, we believe the imposition of these barriers is morally wrong. But at least as important, we believe they threaten to distort further a political system already insufficiently responsive to ordinary voters. One half of this worsening problem concerns the weakening sway of citizens; the other half concerns the growing sway of dollars.

Guaranteeing the Right to Vote

Few features of our recent turn against effective governance are as disquieting as the rise of concerted efforts to make voting more difficult. During the 2014 midterm election, voters in twenty-two states faced tougher election rules than they had in 2010; in fifteen states, those rules had been established in just the previous two years. The nonpartisan General Accounting Office studied the impact of the Kansas and Tennessee voter ID laws on turnout in the 2012 presidential election, and concluded that they had reduced voter turnout by about 2 percent—meaning more than 120,000 lost votes in just two small states.[12] The spread of these restrictions is likely to result in millions of lost votes nationwide.

The claim that legitimate concerns about fraud drive these initiatives is absurd on its face—the laws' ostensible purpose is to restrict the (virtually nonexistent) practice of people committing a felony by impersonating other voters.[13] It is a ridiculous pretext for depriving so many citizens of rightful access to the polls. That this rationalization continues to get a respectful hearing is another sign of the media's willingness to condone extremism in order to sustain a posture of impartiality.

There is nothing partisan about observing that voter restrictions are partisan. Republicans have spearheaded these initiatives, and they and their organized supporters have trumpeted a mythical narrative to justify them. A recent statistical analysis by two University of Massachusetts Boston researchers concludes that the proposal and passage of voter restrictions "are highly partisan, strategic, and racialized affairs." New restrictions are more likely where there is a large minority population, where minority turnout has increased, and where Republicans control legislatures. These findings, the authors conclude, "are consistent with a scenario in which the targeted demobilization of minority voters and African Americans is a central driver of legislative developments."[14]

Already the United States has the most class-biased turnout of any rich democracy. In the decisive 2010 midterm, turnout was 62 percent among those making over $150,000, and just 27 percent among those making under $10,000.[15] Partly as a result, the views of those who go to the polls are considerably more conservative than the views of those who do not, especially in low-turnout elections.[16] As with low-turnout midterm elections, the disparity between those who go to the polls and those who don't (or are discouraged from doing so) has grown.[17] Making it harder to vote will only make this disparity worse.

Voter identification laws have added a particularly sordid encumbrance to an election system that should be a national embarrassment. Citizens often have to wait hours at the polls to participate in our nation's core act of political membership. In 2012 many hundreds of thousands of voters likely gave up in frustration. The obstacles they faced were not distributed randomly. Latinos are 50 percent more likely than non-Hispanic whites to face long waiting lines. Blacks are *twice* as likely to face long lines. And Democrats are significantly more likely to face long lines than Republicans are.[18]

As John Legend said, "The struggle for justice is now." National legislation to ease voter registration and ensure access to the polls—even a constitutional amendment, if necessary—should top reformers' priority list. We know what effective policy looks like: automatic registration, mail-in ballots, voting holidays, and other measures that ensure everyone is registered and voting is easy. Now is the time to guarantee every single American the right to vote.

Mobilizing to ensure the right to vote is a prototypical momentum-generating reform. It will not be enough on its own, but it can provide a focal point for multiple activities that strengthen diffuse interests, including campaign finance reform, efforts to revitalize organized labor, and organization building aimed at engaging broader groups of citizens (all to be discussed shortly). Together these initiatives can create the kind of virtuous circle that has characterized previous periods of political revitalization. If more people go to the polls, politicians will have greater incentive to address their concerns. If government majorities have better prospects of governing on the basis of competent expertise, voters in turn will likely see greater reason to participate. And since the well organized thrive where voters are scarce, higher turnout will also dilute the clout of concentrated interests—the antipole of voter power to which we now turn.

Don't Show Me the Money

Money has always been part of US politics. Never before, however, has so much money come from such a narrow slice of our society. Americans across the ideological spectrum think this spending is corrosive, and they're right. The last dollar spent on a high-profile campaign might have little or no impact. But the flood of money into every corner of American politics—especially corners it has never reached before—has pervasive negative effects, shaping who runs for office, what positions they adopt on the way, and what they do once there. Public officials who troll for dollars among the nation's superrich, who see lobbyists everywhere they look, who encounter organizations financed by multi-billionaires at every turn, who know that angering one of these lobbying juggernauts or billionaire political hobbyists will give them more trouble than disappointing voters will—these are not natural allies of diffuse interests or the mixed economy.

   Nonetheless, reducing the sway of money is a tougher issue than getting more Americans to the polls. Even if one rejects the Supreme Court's equation of money with speech (as we do), reducing the influence of deep-pocketed individuals and narrow interests won't be easy. Campaigns attract only a small fraction of the money that flows into politics. Block that channel, and it will seek others. There are just too many ways to use money to win friends and influence people. So while we share the view that political spending worsens the overrepresentation of narrow interests, we are skeptical that crackdowns on campaign funding and advocacy dollars should be the primary focus of reform. Sensible limits on campaign spending, "cooling-off" periods before moving from government service into lobbying, full disclosure of all donations and their sources—yes, yes, and yes. But we shouldn't assume that such reforms will be transformative, at least not without additional changes.

Rather than trying to stifle big money, the more promising strategy is to weaken its impact. Rather than trying to level down, in other words, we should be mobilizing up, making sure that when money talks, there are powerful voices to answer.[19] We have already discussed creating a true right to vote, and, in a moment, we will discuss encouraging broad organizations that can serve as a countervailing power to narrow interests. Other promising ideas include matching small contributors' dollars to increase their clout and creating public financing systems that give all voters the ability to direct some money to candidates of their choice (a proposal that two law professors call "patriot dollars").[20] Ensuring transparency in *all* political spending—an unachieved premise of the Supreme Court's 2010 *Citizens United* decision—would also enhance countervailing power. One thing big money typically lacks is credibility, which is why those who deploy it work so hard to cover their tracks. In referenda campaigns, for example, once voters can identify the role of concentrated interests in financing one side, they often treat that side's blandishments with heightened skepticism.

As with enhanced government capacity, moreover, you don't necessarily need to match corporate spending dollar for dollar. You do need to bring that spending into the open and ensure that there are resources that allow alternative voices to be heard. And in American politics, no resource is more important—and currently more imbalanced between concentrated and diffuse interests—than organization.

Organizing for America's Diffuse Interests

In the fall of 2011, the least active Congress in recent history nonetheless stood poised to enact major legislation. It was preparing to pass the motion picture industry's highest priority: an effort to crack down on online piracy. The industry's lobbying arm, headed by former senator Chris Dodd, a Connecticut Democrat, had attracted a wide and impressive set of sponsors from both parties. The Obama administration had signaled it would not stand in the way. The Stop Online Piracy Act (SOPA) looked unstoppable.[21]

In a matter of days, however, SOPA was DOA. On January 18, citizens going to Google's search page found an online petition; on Wikipedia, they found a blackout page, along with a message about the threat that SOPA would create for an open internet. Over 160 million people viewed that Wikipedia page, and the online encyclopedia reported that 8 million US visitors looked up information about congressional representatives (perhaps to forward a message). Four and a half million people signed Google's protest petition.[22] Twitter reported 2.4 million tweets on the legislation in a sixteen-hour period.[23] It was the largest internet-based protest in American history. In its wake, powerful figures in Washington who had indicated support for SOPA raced to announce their opposition. The bill that had once seemed inevitable never made it to the floor of the House.

The story shouldn't be overdrawn. It was not exactly *Mr. (Cyber) Smith Goes to Washington*. The Motion Picture Association of America confronted powerful adversaries within the tech world who feared that SOPA would put them on the hook for penalties if they inadvertently facilitated piracy.[24] Yet the saga shows something vital: Politicians can respond quickly if they sense that voters care and are paying attention. Demonstrating a capacity to mobilize millions of people gave the MPAA's opponents instant clout.

The SOPA soap opera is a reminder that even in today's politics, there are areas of governance where diffuse interests get a serious hearing or even prevail. Yet in too many cases, such interests have too little organization or influence. Since the 1970s, narrow interests have increased their organizational presence in Washington greatly. But the groups that once brought ordinary Americans into politics—most notably, organized labor—have lost ground, and new organizations have not filled the void. Reversing these trends must be a top priority.

Productive Labor

When the mixed economy was most effective, there was one diffuse-interest organization that loomed over others: unions. In the decades since, powerful economic forces, concerted employer resistance, and increasingly outdated labor laws have made it much harder for workers to organize. Today, while labor unions remain the most important organized defender of Americans' broad economic concerns, they represent only a modest countervailing force. And as their membership shrinks, unions are inevitably devoting a larger share of their resources to rearguard efforts to protect their most immediate and narrow interests. If organized labor is going to champion the mixed economy again, it needs to rebuild membership and support.

That won't be easy. Robert Wagner's breakthrough act of 1935 is now almost defunct, the NLRB a hollow shell of its former self. Company-by-company unionization through the traditional legal process is at best a strategy for stemming the tide, not reversing it. Historically, big extensions of unionization have come in short bursts, bubbling up in ways that are difficult to predict.[25] Right now the most promising strategy for this sort of burst is the social-movement approach often referred to as "alt labor," which describes forms of worker mobilization that are more fluid, community based, and social-media oriented than the traditional route of getting workers to sign up for a union. At one end of the spectrum are limited campaigns to ensure that workers have at least a minimal amount of voice and that poor labor practices get called out. At the other extreme are full-fledged protest movements that involve grassroots actions and sustained pressure on companies to respond to worker concerns. In between are more traditional alternative-labor arrangements, such as work councils and worker centers, that do not involve the adversarial process of union certification but can still deliver important services to workers, including representation in the workforce and advocacy in struggles over law and policy.

Though new to the scene, alt-labor initiatives can point to some striking successes. The "Fight for $15" campaign featured fast-food workers—among the least organized part of the workforce—successfully pushing the issue of low wages onto the national agenda. Similarly, union-backed groups placed significant pressure on the notoriously low-wage retailer Wal-Mart to raise wages and benefits using protest and social suasion.[26] The most important point in favor of alt-labor strategies is their consistency with the way that citizen movements have been built in the past: in waves rather than through piece-by-piece organizing, and through morally grounded appeals rather than through targeted attempts to advance a narrow interest. Yet to truly catalyze diffuse-interest organization, these movements will have to seek legislative reforms as well as ground-level breakthroughs. And that won't happen unless traditional organizing strategies are married to new digital technologies—technologies that create both dazzling opportunities and distinct risks for those seeking to revitalize countervailing power.

You and What Army?

Maybe this has happened to you: You leave a cab only to discover you've forgotten something important—your phone, your laptop, your wallet. By the time you realize what's happened, your item is gone, and there's no way to get it back.

About a decade ago, just such an unfortunate event befell a New Yorker who left her $300 phone in a taxi. We know: big deal. People leave valuables in cabs all the time, never to see them again. The New York cabbie who returned a bag containing thirty-one diamond rings to a woman who had tipped him 30 cents on an $11 fare is the heroic exception. But that phoneless New Yorker had a secret weapon: When the phone turned up in the hands of a tough-talking Queens resident who made clear she wasn't giving it back, the phone owner's friend, a computer programmer, set up a web page and reached out to his online social networks. The page and its cause became a sensation, pressuring the New York Police Department to arrest the girl and return the phone. The girl's mother marveled, "I never in my life thought a phone was going to cause me so many problems."[27]

But, of course, it wasn't the phone. It was the use of new technology. Thanks to the internet and technologies that build on it, it's never been so easy for individuals to identify and communicate with those who share a common interest. These platforms can be challenging to build. But because sharing data is virtually free, the marginal cost of scaling them up is low compared with traditional organizations. For someone doing door-to-door canvasing, the cost of going to a second house isn't much lower than the cost of going to the first. But like publishing additional copies of an e-book, the cost of adding additional people to an e-network is near zero.

The expansion of electronic organizing is a major transformation, captured nicely in the title of Clay Shirky's 2008 book *Here Comes Everybody: The Power of Organizing Without Organizations* (which opens with the lost-phone story).[28] Perhaps inevitably, the shift has been the subject of breathless hype that has far outpaced actual developments. Yet we are still early in the evolution of organizations built around these new technological possibilities. In the next stage of this evolution, digitally empowered organizations with the crucial start-up backing of foundations and other "patrons" could become a powerful weapon for diffuse interests.

So far these possibilities have been realized mostly in electoral campaigns and movements that mimic the rally-the-troops orientation of election contests. The 2008 Obama campaign, for instance, defeated two opponents—Hillary Clinton and then John McCain—in significant part because of its proficiency in using technology to mobilize millions of Americans. Similarly, the SOPA case showed that orchestrated internet-based political mobilization of a diffuse population can produce rapid shifts in political outcomes. Perhaps most significant, durable organizations such as the progressive advocacy group MoveOn.org have succeeded in building a large, ongoing presence in American politics. They have found that social media doesn't just create opportunities to identify and interact with communities of shared interest. It helps groups learn about their members' greatest concerns, the kinds of appeals that are most effective, and the strategies that best encourage long-term political engagement. In other words, new technologies aren't good just at mobilizing followers; they are also potentially valuable for disciplining and informing leaders so that they truly represent the shared concerns of broad groups.

These innovative forms of political mobilization also have substantial limitations. Online participation can be thin and sporadic. One of the big advantages of internet-based mobilization—the flexibility to move rapidly from one issue to another—can also be a big disadvantage if the technology is used merely to create "flash movements" that hop on whatever issue is hot at the moment. No less troubling, internet-based political organization is (like almost all forms of mobilization) badly skewed toward the educated, affluent, and extreme—not so much because of gaps in access to the requisite technology as because those with the intensity to devote their energies to online movements often have more privileged backgrounds and more extreme views. Organizations such as MoveOn.org face a constant tension between responding to the concerns of their most active supporters and building the broader coalitions needed to achieve lasting political success.

Nonetheless, there will be substantial rewards for organizations that master the new digital world. Groups will still need staff and headquarters, but they can potentially engage circles of support far wider than anything seen in Washington today. The key is finding targeted issues that link up to a broad reform agenda with evident moral appeal: Climate change and voting rights reform seem the most likely candidates at the moment. Also key, if less openly discussed, is the need for the financial contributions of like-minded organizations with interest in promoting diffuse-interest causes. Conservative foundations and groups have been much more willing to invest in long-term organizational development than more moderate or liberal backers have been. But it is now center-left patrons who need to step up, particularly nonprofit foundations. Success builds membership, and membership builds success. But climbing the initial steep slope of collective action is almost impossible without outside support.

Once over that slope, organizations do not need to be gigantic to survive and make a difference. Even the most vibrant social movements have active memberships far smaller than the share of the population that supports their aims. Their main role is not to mobilize all sympathetic citizens. Their main role—a very powerful one—is to make otherwise neglected issues salient, to exert consistent pressure on behalf of diffuse interests, and to help supporters learn which public officials deserve their support or contempt. Political change occurs when there are both pushes from below and adjustments from above, when ordinary citizens express their grievances to those in power and those in power become more inclined to moderate in response. Encouraging that second development is a major part of the challenge, too.

Building a Coalition of the Willing

No reform coalition will succeed over the long term without some backing from within the nation's financial and corporate elite. As we saw in chapter 5, the postwar development of the mixed economy was grounded not only in pressure from below but also in support from those at the top who recognized (if frequently out of political necessity) that government had a vital role in developing and sustaining prosperity. Huge and complex societies will always have elites. The question is whether or not those elites are responsible and responsive, seeking inclusive solutions rather than exclusive ones.

Sadly, today's economic elites are not. Even business "moderates" typically fall into the soft Randian camp—not radical free-marketeers, but only grudging supporters of government at best. For too many of them, government is a regrettable reality and something of an afterthought rather than an essential good. They are not aware of, much less feel moved to trumpet, the fact that effective governance is essential for the future of American capitalism.

What's Good for America Is Good for Business

As we have argued, these attitudes reflect real shifts in the American economy. The financialization of corporate activity and the rise of Wall Street have encouraged CEOs to focus narrowly on sustaining their stock price over a time horizon that does not exceed their own tenures at the top. Meanwhile, globalization has strengthened the hand of corporate leaders in their bargaining with labor and loosened the degree to which they see the fate of their companies as tied to the fate of American citizens—or even of American capitalism.

Still, it is easy to overstate the degree to which business can go it alone in the global economy. Yes, many corporations have more readily available exit options, and yes, rich countries are competing more fiercely to attract multinationals (with, for example, low corporate tax rates). But companies need access to wealthy economies too, which gives rich nations leverage to insist that these companies play by a shared set of rules. These nations can also and often do work together to limit corporate free riding—especially when the United States uses its still-considerable clout to encourage them to do so. In recent years, for instance, the United States has led an effective crackdown on banking secrecy centered in Switzerland, forcing one resisting bank to shut down and generating compliance from the rest eventually.[29] Similar efforts can and should be directed at corporate tax-avoidance practices that involve pretending to be based in, or shifting profits to, countries with low corporate tax rates—some of them little more than offshore tax havens, with no real indigenous economic activity.

Moreover, in many sectors of our economy, companies don't really have an attractive exit option. As their fierce resistance to measures to control costs or reduce negative externalities suggests, some of the biggest rent extractors in the American economy are inherently local. Neither health care providers nor coal companies nor power plants are in a position to relocate overseas if political leaders choose to limit the burdens they impose on American society.

Crucially, the same is also true for many of our nation's most competitive companies. It turns out the world isn't so flat, after all. The knowledge-intensive sectors that are key motors of contemporary capitalism are, in many ways, the opposite of footloose. In New York, San Francisco, Los Angeles, Boston, and elsewhere, they are drawn together into tight networks of highly skilled workers and innovative firms located within urban centers. In these knowledge-intensive sectors, talent seeks proximity to other talent, and highly profitable and innovative companies want to be where the action is.[30]

Nobody loves being taxed or regulated, certainly not profit-seeking companies. But businesses don't want to be where their costs are lowest and regulations most lax. They want to be where they can make the most money. The attractiveness of investment involves a mix of factors, including the availability of skilled labor (and the amenities that attract it), high-quality infrastructure, access to markets, clear and predictable legal structures, and political stability. Absent these draws, low taxes and weak regulations are not a magnet for investment—if they were, the distribution of capital in the world would look very different than it does.

And within the United States. The rise of the South, propelled by federal investments, brought it into America's economic mainstream. But many parts of the Old Confederacy continue to lag behind other regions in fostering the dense hubs of innovation that produce the highest corporate and individual earnings. Indeed, southern states are no longer consistently converging with the richest of the states, as they did from the 1930s through 1970s (as discussed in chapter 4).[31] If the only recipe for prosperity was low taxes and limited regulation—a model that southern leaders tend to advocate, if not always follow—you would think they'd be doing a lot better.

Texas, for example, is touted endlessly by conservative commentators as a "red state" beacon for the nation. Yet despite a strong record on employment (driven in considerable part by its energy industry), Texas has not been able to produce large gains in personal income. In fact, since the early 1980s, its income per capita has fallen sharply relative to that of its "blue state" polar opposite, Massachusetts—from a peak of around 96 percent to around 75 percent today.[32] To be sure, the cost of living is lower in Texas, but not *that* much lower; on average, according to the US Bureau of Economic Analysis, regional prices are around 90 percent of those of Massachusetts.[33] Nor does Texas have a meaningfully larger foreign-born population. (The two states with the largest shares of immigrants in their population are California and New York; Texas and Massachusetts are seventh and eighth, respectively.)[34]

And none of this mentions how poorly Texas—and, indeed, all of

the South—performs on broader measures of economic and social performance, such as educational attainment and health. Here, Texas and
other southern states consistently end up in the bottom of the rankings.[35] That may be as much a consequence of the region's continuing
economic troubles as a cause. But it suggests that as-small-as-possible
government is no sure ticket to innovation-driven prosperity. It turns
out the United States isn't flat either.

Globalization and the increasing footloose character of private capital create distinctive challenges. But they don't create an insoluble
conflict between the well-being of American citizens and the vibrancy
of American capitalism. To the contrary, eliminating inefficiencies in
the health care and financial systems, attacking climate change, making the American workforce healthier and better educated, expanding
R&D with all its associated positive externalities, improving the quality of American infrastructure—all these steps would greatly increase
the prospects for profitable investments in the United States. Taken as
a whole, business stands to benefit substantially from these and other
positive-sum solutions.

Amplifying Moderate Corporate Voices

The rub is that what might be good for American capitalism might not
be good for individual American capitalists, especially in the short run.
CEOs and corporations have enormous incentives to let others shoulder the costs of producing long-term collective benefits. As the former
chairman of the marketing firm Young & Rubicam wrote candidly in the
New York Times, "Today, too many corporations reduce investment in
research and development and brand building"—then, if these efforts
hurt company growth, "buy back their stock . . . and thus artificially
boost earnings per share." The ex-chairman describes a classic collective-
action problem. Many CEOs believe things need to change, but they
"need more support from their boards, from prominent business leaders,
from the media, and even from the government, to combat the intense
market pressure to maximize short-term shareholder returns."[36]

In principle, this is a place for business associations to step in. Broad
business groups should be well placed to think about the interests of
American capitalism as a whole. In practice, however, they have become Great Enablers, catering to the private needs of CEOs (the Business
Roundtable), to the concentrated interests of the modern robber bar-

ons (the Chamber of Commerce), or to extreme "free market" views that in the name of igniting liberty would incinerate prosperity (the Koch Brothers network).

Still, some hopeful signs can be found. One is the recent decline of ALEC, the formidable American Legislative Exchange Council. ALEC has relied on broad and extensive business backing to advance an aggressively conservative agenda in state legislatures. In recent years, that aggressive posture (with missteps, including its forays into "stand your ground" gun legislation and extreme stances on global warming) has triggered a backlash. Critics of ALEC have used digital technology to track its activities, and business leaders have often been appalled at what they've seen. Resignations have included Amazon, Coca-Cola, General Electric, Kraft Foods, McDonald's, Wal-Mart, and a slew of other major companies. In the first half of 2013, internal ALEC documents revealed that it had lost sixty corporate members and one-third of its funding, as well as more than four hundred state legislators (almost a fifth of its total).[37] In 2014 Microsoft pulled out of ALEC, citing objections to the organization's actions on climate change. It was followed by Google. The company's CEO, Eric Schmidt, was scathing. Google, he said, "has a very strong view that we should make decisions in politics based on facts—what a shock. . . . And the facts of climate change are not in question anymore. Everyone understands climate change is occurring, and the people who oppose [doing something about] it are really hurting our children and grandchildren and making the world a much worse place. And so we should not be aligned with such people—they're just, they're just literally lying."[38]

ALEC's troubles suggest real limits to corporate support for extremism. Or at least real limits to *open* support for extremism. When such support is unlikely to be made public, corporations are much more likely to push the envelope. Hence the importance of making such financial connections visible, requiring, for example, that political groups disclose their large donors and companies supporting such groups defend these expenditures to their shareholders.

In addition to discouraging extremism, we also need to encourage moderate elements of the business community to go to bat for the mixed economy. Even now, it is possible (if far too difficult) to assemble ad hoc coalitions on issues such as climate change, infrastructure, immigration, and higher education. In these and similar areas, many corporate

elites have already sided at least nominally with reform, though generally without much commitment of energy and resources. Issue activists
and political leaders could and should encourage deeper and broader
mobilization around these issues—through targeted pressure on corporations involving both carrots (good PR, investment opportunities) and
sticks (naming and shaming, shareholder challenges).

But in a conflict where the vital capabilities of governance are at stake,
single-issue support isn't enough. We need a broad, committed push
from those with the independence to take a long view. Someone needs to
play the vital role that the Committee for Economic Development played
in the postwar development of the mixed economy, to stand up for the
constructive use of government to enhance American prosperity.

As elusive as this goal might seem today, it is not a fanciful prospect. Even in our age of narrow short-termism, we have seen scattered
instances of rich and prominent Americans willing to say that vigorous
capitalism depends on effective governance. Here, for instance, is Bill
Gates speaking on the Fox Business Network in 2011: "A bigger estate
tax is a good way to collect money when the government is going to have
to raise more taxes. . . . Very rich estates that have benefited from the
rules and stability of this country, if you had a choice to be born here or
be born somewhere else knowing that you had to pay an estate tax, you
would still pick the benefits that our system provides. Warren [Buffett]
and I are great examples of what the system can do for us."[39]

Buffett and Gates might be the sort of leaders who build a modern
version of the CED. They will need many more allies, however, and potential allies remain few and far between. The wealthy are generally cir-
cumspect about airing their political views, but new research on the
attitudes of the affluent suggests that the moderate outlook of Buffett
and Gates is far from the norm. Compared with those lower on the economic ladder, as we saw in chapter 6, the rich are considerably more
conservative on economic issues: more skeptical of regulation, less supportive of public programs, and more opposed to progressive taxation.

As in the past, a widespread change of heart among the nation's economic elite is likely to be driven first and foremost by external forces.
The shared experience of World War II and ongoing pressure of the Cold
War encouraged a sincere commitment to corporate social responsibility
in the 1950s and 1960s. But the Committee on Economic Development
was less a product of individual enlightenment than of economic and

political constraint—from organized labor, from Democrats, and from moderate Republicans. When corporate leaders must take into account the claims of other stakeholders, members of the economic elite who are open to moderate, positive-sum initiatives are likely to become even more open. They are also likely to become more influential among their peers.

Here again, the links among the various reforms we have discussed come into view. Moderation among business elites will spread when they face political challenges, and they will face political challenges when we increase government capacity, limit powers of obstruction, expand voting, and empower diffuse interests. Building a political system that is more capable, transparent, responsive, and accountable will make it more likely that significant elements of the business community will embrace reform. It will also make those business leaders more persuasive as they press their colleagues for moderate and balanced changes that upgrade our mixed economy. Recent (partial) successes in health care and finance, as well as the initially less successful legislative initiative on climate change, show this essential political dynamic at work. Lowering the obstacles to government action will lengthen the menu of possible policy and political reforms, encouraging private interests to seek compromise rather than simply resort to obstruction.

Facing the Modern GOP

What of the other Great Enabler—the increasingly conservative Republican Party? Here the demands of honesty and propriety collide. The sad reality is that all the reforms suggested here—for a weakening of obstruction, for increased participation by ordinary citizens, for improved public administration, for a reduction in the sway of big money, and for a renewed commitment among economic elites to ensuring the long-term preconditions of shared prosperity—are sure to face tenacious opposition from today's GOP. Some will take that as proof that our agenda is narrowly partisan; others will take it as proof that the only thing that needs to be done is to vote Republicans out of office. We think it is instead a regrettable testament to what the Grand Old Party, over the past generation, has become.

American political institutions ensure that we will have two parties, and that they will both play a continuing central role in our politics. Political competition is essential to effective democracy, and clashes of ideas essential to social progress. The constraints that made the mixed economy work came both from effective public authority and from true contestation over who, and whose ideas, would guide that authority. Eisenhower was not FDR, nor was Vannevar Bush. Their support for a mixed economy marked by pluralism and respectful of markets—and, indeed, the support of an entire generation of Republicans with genuinely conservative commitments but also genuine respect for government's role—was a vital contributor to America's economic success.

Nothing would do more to restore the political foundations for such a mixed economy than a reconsideration within GOP circles of the party's increasingly virulent and destructive antigovernment stance. In the 1980s, the Democratic Leadership Council (with strong business backing) pulled the Democratic Party in a more centrist direction.[39] Today the emergence of a formidable Republican Leadership Council that accepted and sought to update the mixed economy could similarly transform our politics.

At the moment, sadly, nothing like this is in the offing. Quite the contrary: In the immediate future, the prospect for advancing sensible reforms to address our political dysfunction is likely to depend on a series of GOP electoral defeats. Where today's hyperconservative Republican Party holds sway, meaningful reform will not happen. Realistically, the hope must be that strengthening our democracy in the ways we have discussed will gradually force ambitious, farsighted Republican leaders who wish to hold office and want the GOP to thrive to reevaluate their party's most extreme antigovernment positions. In other words, reducing the *opportunity* to adopt extreme positions will encourage Republicans to reevaluate their *motives* for doing so.

Let's not allow Democrats off the hook, either. Many of the same forces that have pulled Republicans to the right—conservative media, business lobbies, billionaire donors—have also shaped where Democrats stand, albeit in a different way. While Republicans have been emboldened by these forces, Democrats have generally been cross-pressured, torn between their less affluent constituencies and their traditional attachment to organized labor on the one hand and their need to attract campaign dollars and avoid antagonizing powerful lobbies on the other. Democrats may have been late arrivals to the financial deregulation party, but as we saw in chapter 9, they became enthusiastic participants. Fortunately, increasing the pressure on Republicans to moderate should also reduce the cross-pressures on Democrats, allowing them to take positions more in line with those casting votes as opposed to those spending dollars.

Before that virtuous cycle begins, however, we must face a final problem. Positive-sum opportunities might abound, but most Americans do not believe that government is capable of seizing them. In short, they do not believe in the vast potential of effective government revealed by economic history and theory. To restore the mixed economy, we must break free of American Amnesia.

Recovering from Our Amnesia

At the beginning of *The Book of Laughter and Forgetting*, Czechoslovakian novelist Milan Kundera describes events that took place on a snowy day in Prague in 1948. Leading communists were addressing a crowd. One, Vladimir Clementis, placed his fur hat on the head of his bald companion, Klement Gottwald. When Clementis was later purged and executed, the party's propagandists erased him from the photograph. All that was left was his fur hat.[40]

The enabling role of government is like that fur hat. Today we see only tiny reminders of a much bigger reality. We know government built a road or a school but too often fail to recognize the many ways in which it built prosperity. To the contrary, an increasingly vocal movement insists at every turn that it is "big government," not private market failures or weak public policies, that stands between us and a better future. Yet in the United States, as elsewhere, building prosperity has always required a constructive, if sometimes contentious, partnership between markets' deft fingers and government's strong thumb. Markets bring extraordinary dynamism. But it is a dynamism that must be constrained and supplemented through public authority. On their own, markets will not ensure clean air or water. They will not invest adequately in education or research and development. They will not provide high-quality infrastructure, or health care that's affordable and accessible, or sufficient preparedness for retirement. They will not discourage predatory practices that damage consumers. They will not deliver a relatively stable macroeconomy—or a livable planet.

It isn't just the hard Randians who have distorted government's role. Soft Randians, perhaps progressive in their sympathies, have too often done the same. There just isn't much of a percentage in giving government its due. Steven Spielberg's 2015 film *Bridge of Spies* provides a good recent example. It offers a great if conventional Hollywood yarn: the independent and indefatigable everyman who sticks to his principles and wins out over the narrow-minded and conventional organization men (including cold and unimaginative government bureaucrats). Real life, however, was more complex than Spielberg's version—and, truthfully, more interesting.

Spielberg's hero, James Donovan, wasn't "just an insurance lawyer." He didn't just accidentally end up defending a Soviet spy and then negotiating with the Soviets and the East Germans during one of the tensest moments of the Cold War. The film drops a hint and then hurries on: Donovan had worked for the chief United States prosecutor at the Nuremburg trials following World War II, Supreme Court Justice Robert H. Jackson. There's more: He got *that* job because, during the war, he had been general counsel of "Wild" Bill Donovan's Office of Strategic Services, precursor to the CIA. He got *that* job because he had been associate counsel at the Office of Scientific Research and Development, where he had worked with Vannevar Bush and had crafted secret research contracts for the Manhattan Project. In short, the real Donovan was no novice to espionage, and he was no everyman. Like so many from the Greatest Generation, he was a mixed-economy mandarin. In artfully managing the extraordinary events that Spielberg portrays, Donovan could draw on his experience working at the highest levels of government. But tellingly, that story—a mixed-economy story—is less compelling to a twenty-first-century American audience. So government's role is airbrushed out.

Hard Randians are not going to change their minds. More vital to our future is the thinking of soft Randians, who too often have joined in the collective forgetting of government's invaluable contribution to our prosperity. The cultural dynamic is often subtle, but it is everywhere—and it has to change.

In many specific areas, of course, Americans still believe that the public sector has a vital role. They support government regulation of the environment and government funding of education. They strongly endorse Social Security, Medicare, and most other social programs. They believe that political leaders have a responsibility to manage the economy.[41] What has changed is that voters have become profoundly skeptical that government has the capacity or inclination to foster broad prosperity, especially when doing so requires it to take on new or newly intensified challenges. To build a mixed economy for the twenty-first century, a critical mass of citizens—and their leaders—have to believe once again that government can address their most pressing concerns.

Beyond Cynicism

Distrust in public institutions is a broad cultural trend. It is whipped up by popular entertainment and reinforced by a news media that sometimes seems to relish treating every person and organization as equally venal. Distrust in government is also, however, spread systematically, deliberately, and relentlessly—by GOP leaders who gain politically by "destroying the village to save it" and by powerful interests that have profited from the confusion and disaffection that widespread distrust feeds.

Consider the biggest threat facing our planet: global warming. Sowing doubt about climate change has proved a huge and hugely successful enterprise. Indeed, the fossil fuel industry deserves some special prize for chutzpah: In its propaganda, the bad guys aren't carbon-emitting corporations trying to preserve trillions in dirty assets but instead *climate scientists* supposedly ginning up a false crisis to get research grants. The modern GOP has joined the industry in its endorsement of whatever egregious defense seems most effective at the moment. Although the first lines of resistance ("Global warming isn't happening"; "It is, but for natural reasons") have more or less crumbled, and "I'm not a scientist" doesn't seem likely to work for long, either, there are plenty of additional trenches to retreat to: "Reform won't work." "It will be too expensive." "It is pointless absent efforts by other countries." "We want reform, just not this one—or the next one." In the meantime, the fossil fuel industry continues to book huge profits, and atmospheric carbon dioxide levels continue to rise.

The marketplace of ideas is of great value. But just as in the actual marketplace, we all need help deciding which products are reliable and which are not. Yet in our hyperpolarized political world, institutions recognized as credible sources of independent knowledge continue to lose ground. Take the news media. As much as the decline of broadcast and print news has hurt independent journalism, the media remain the main means through which people learn about the broader world. Too often, however, reporters structure stories to create controversy or convey catastrophe. Indeed, one basic PR problem of the mixed economy is that it has all the narrative elements that make most journalists recoil. Picture this headline: "Things Are Getting Better, Slowly, Because of Government Policy." Your eyelids are probably drooping. Journalists are attracted to controversy, not cooperation; decline, not improvement; people, not policy. The basic story of this book—that governments and markets, working in tandem, have steadily increased human welfare (if, of late, far too gradually)—offers no hook that will excite reporters.

What's more, even when journalists cover important policy debates, they tend to fall into the trap of "he said, she said" reporting on political conflict. Simply recounting the claims of both "sides" in a debate—each debate having exactly two sides—imparts a potentially misleading message of unresolved controversy and false equivalence. When the weight of the evidence is in fact on one side, the "he said, she said" approach provides journalists with a safe posture of neutrality that, in practice, advances particular agendas and makes it harder for readers to understand events. We have enormous respect for journalists, and could not have written this book without the work of many excellent reporters who combine a deep knowledge of American politics with a strong commitment to informing their audience. But we also find that too often reporters lack the expertise or willingness to assess competing claims or to aid readers in making reasonable judgments. We would be the last to question the contributions of dissenters from conventional wisdom. But the collective assessments of leading knowledge institutions are not just one side in a controversy. When rent seekers and credentialed experts disagree, it is the experts whose views should be granted the greater legitimacy.

And here we have some more hopeful news. Internet journalism, while producing a lot of junk, has also provided an important check on self-interested claims, fact-challenged arguments, and sloppy reporting. The internet's rise has encouraged the development of deep and data-driven journalism, both through new web-based platforms such as Vox and FiveThirtyEight and through efforts attached to conventional news outlets (*Wonkblog* at the *Washington Post*, *The Upshot* at the *New York Times*). Evidence-based analysis can now go toe-to-toe with soft punditry, as when Nate Silver's online election analysis revealed serious limitations in traditional coverage of campaigns. Nonprofit foundations have also played a role, intervening to finance time-intensive reporting on important issues. Readers have new opportunities to learn credible interpretations of public issues and to distinguish such interpretations from hyperbolic postures.

Now the stakes need to be raised. Too often, public figures and anointed experts pay no reputational price when they shill for private interests or state things that are patently untrue. Regurgitating industry talking points or echoing political hacks is simply considered "part of the game." But enhancing our prosperity is not a game, and access to public platforms designed to inform citizens is not a right. Journalists and other thought leaders in the nonprofit and business worlds need to restore basic norms of naming and shaming. They need to be more assertive in identifying and shunning so-called experts who are repeatedly and demonstrably wrong or whose association with vested interests raises questions of ethics and credibility. Reforms that redistribute power can help, by increasing the pressure on media outlets to resist "he said, she said" reporting that protects narrow interests. But journalists and the institutions that train, support, and guide them need to do more to support the basic ideal of evidence-based policy making that the current media environment does too little to encourage.

In Government We Must Trust

The framing of "government versus the market" has become so ubiquitous in our culture that most of us simply take it for granted. In discussing this book with different audiences, we have been struck repeatedly by how often thoughtful and informed people slip into describing government as if it were little more than a vehicle for redistribution. Some favor that redistribution; others oppose it. But what is missing is an understanding that most of what government does is not about redistribution at all; it is about addressing a wide range of problems that markets alone are ill equipped to tackle.

Our discourse about government has become dangerously lopsided. The hostility of the right is unceasing and mostly unanswered. Eloquent leaders defend individual programs but defend too rarely the vital need for effective governance. Politicians facing electoral pressures participate in a spiral of silence. Chastened by government's low standing, they reinforce rather than try to reverse it. In our nation's deafening political debate, the divide is ultimately over what government can and should do. But as the journalist Michael Tomasky asks, "What kind of debate about this have we had? We've had one side relentlessly attacking government as incompetent to evil, and the other side saying nothing, being too cowed to stand up and say that government is, and does, good."[42]

Rhetoric is only one part of the problem. Cowed policy makers also design programs that send much the same message. The political scientist Suzanne Mettler has documented the increasing tendency to "submerge" policies so that the role of government is hidden from those who receive benefits.[43] These subterranean policies include tax breaks for private savings for education and retirement, as well as reliance on private companies and contractors even where these proxies are less efficient than public provision. These submerged benefits are usually bad policies. More important, they are even worse politics. Voters who don't recognize government are not likely to appreciate what government does. Nor are they likely to form an accurate picture of government's role, seeing only its visible redistribution but not the vast numbers of ways in which it enables prosperity.

Making Government Work Better

Frustration with contemporary governance is understandable. American government *has* become less effective. The lawmaking process *has* become dysfunctional. Public policy *is* more beholden to narrow and deep-pocketed interests. Political attacks and pervasive public distrust make government less capable, which in turn provides fodder for more attacks and greater distrust. That this vicious cycle has been pushed along by smear attacks and sabotage campaigns does not make it any less real. We face a profound crisis of authority—not because government is out of control but because it is not in control in the places where it matters.

Nonetheless, our assessment of government has declined far more than has actual performance. When, in 2014, Princeton University Press published a book entitled *Why Government Fails So Often: And How It Can Do Better*, hardly anyone bothered to question the premise.[44] Yet the book, by law professor Peter Schuck, never justifies its scathing title. It leans heavily on one thin source covering only a narrow range of policies. It concedes that Social Security, the largest single domestic program, is an unquestionable success (as were the GI Bill and the interstate highway system). Perhaps most important, it falls into the common trap of comparing government policies with standards of efficiency and value that many markets fail to approach. The book complains, for example, that Medicare is more costly than it should be (which is certainly true), but it fails to even mention that it has lower and slower-growing costs than private insurance does, or that other countries that rely on the public sector more do much better.

Government often performs tasks less well than it could or should. That doesn't mean, however, that we would be better off without government performing those tasks. In fact, the net benefits of modern government are enormous—at the level of major programs and, even more clearly, at the level of governance as a whole. We should be critical of government performance when it falls short, as we should be critical of big corporations and the functioning of private markets when they do. But we should be *appropriately* critical. Government sweats the big stuff: the hard challenges that decentralized private action can't solve, the essential investments that market actors won't make, the vexing choices that individual minds don't handle well. It must be judged with an understanding of that role and with an appreciation of why it is so difficult and so vital to carry out.

Consider the most maligned policy of recent years: the Affordable Care Act. Even as the law has expanded health coverage while moderating costs, critics continue to spew disinformation and insist their direst predictions have come true (and get a respectable hearing from the news media). They claim millions are losing good insurance despite a historic *expansion* of coverage. They claim costs are skyrocketing despite a historic *slowdown* of medical inflation. Among soft Randians such as Pete Peterson, who warn loudly of our impending fiscal collapse, the huge decline of medical inflation should be a major cause for celebration. Instead, deficit hawks have been largely silent. They seem insistent on waiting for the right kind of cost containment—that is, the kind that limits citizens' benefits rather than the kind that diminishes the modern robber barons' rents.

Given all this, it's no surprise that Americans know strikingly little about the most important social policy breakthrough of the past half century. Asked how the actual cost of the law compares with estimates prior to enactment, roughly 40 percent admitted they had no idea. Another 40 percent thought costs were *higher* than predicted. Only 8 percent knew that costs were substantially lower than anticipated.[45] Here, as in so many areas, voters have a limited understanding of government performance, receive scant guidance from the media, and are encouraged by a barrage of negativity to assume the worst. In the 2014 election campaign, anti-ACA ads outnumbered favorable ones by a ratio of 13 to 1.[46]

The point is not to be uncritical of the public sector. There are clear examples of government overreach: The national security state has

threatened our liberties as well as protected them, and our criminal justice policies impose enormous burdens on poor and minority communities that are disproportionate to the benefits for community safety. Rent
seeking is not only a corporate pursuit, even if business rent seeking
has the highest price tag. Labor unions in the public sector, particularly
within our essential but underperforming education system, have too
often stood in the way of sensible reforms that would bring American
practices in line with those of the most successful systems. The US pro-
clivity for what the political scientist Robert Kagan calls "adversarial
legalism"—highly contentious and complex processes for adjudicating
societal disputes—carries undeniable costs for our economy even as it
benefits some sections of the legal profession along with those they represent.[47] Sometimes better governance will mean more expensive government, but in many cases, more effective government could cost less,
especially in the long run. We should be committed to rooting out rent
seeking and remedying government missteps in all their forms.

But we should also recognize just how valuable the mixed economy
is, how fundamental the role of government is within it, and how badly
we are served by the misleading juxtapositions that dominate public
debate: markets versus the state, freedom versus tyranny, free enterprise
versus big government. From a more realistic and historically grounded
starting point, we can have vigorous, reasoned, fact-based debates that
reflect the diversity of our values and priorities as well as the inevitable
uncertainties about the best ways to tackle complex problems. We can
seek positive-sum bargains and broad consensus about how to improve
the mixed economy and address new challenges, learning over time how
to adjust the nimble fingers of the market and the strong thumb of government to best grasp our future.

To get to that more realistic starting point will require a serious and
prolonged investment in ideas. The crisis of public authority is a consequence of orchestrated, persistent efforts to tear down government and
a long spiral of silence in response. To shake free of that amnesia and rebalance our national conversation will take leadership and activism over
many years to rebuild the intellectual and organizational foundations of
effective public authority. The idea that one visionary figure can restore
a more balanced politics is alluring but illusory. We need such men and
women, but as President Obama's experience suggests, even the nation's
most powerful politician requires a strong coalition to transform rhetoric

into reality. Reform must be a multifront, interdependent effort of the sort that we have been discussing, in which robust but realistic reforms steadily build trust and momentum toward a revitalized mixed economy.

In any battle of ideas, organizations are at least as important as individuals; scripts as important as speakers. When conservative business leaders such as Charles and David Koch invested in Cato, Heritage, the American Enterprise Institute, and all the other intellectual weapons of the right, they were playing the long game. When Republican political leaders like Newt Gingrich and Mitch McConnell developed new strategies for tearing down American government to build up GOP power, they were playing the long game. Those like us who believe we can and must build a mixed economy for the twenty-first century—they need to play the long game, too. And they need to speak not just on behalf of individual policy goals. They need to speak on behalf of effective public authority.

A government that effectively promotes human flourishing is a government worth fighting for. More than ever, the problems we face demand a sustained and principled defense of a vital proposition: The government that governs best needs to govern quite a bit. Americans must remember what has made America prosper.

ACKNOWLEDGMENTS

We didn't build this. At least not without enormous help both big and small.

First among those we wish to acknowledge are the extraordinary teachers who sparked our love of discovery. So many have inspired and instructed us over the years that we can only list a special handful. Jacob thanks Elga Brown, Megan Schrogs, Ann Woeste, Jack Citrin, Liah Greenfeld, Mark Peterson, Andrew Martin, and David Mayhew. Paul thanks Harriet Wilson, Marcia Colish, Marc Blecher, Harlan Wilson, Charles Lindblom, David Cameron, and Robert Dahl. Both of us have shared the generous and vital mentoring of Peter Hall, Ted Marmor, and Theda Skocpol.

Our next thanks go to the many hundreds of extraordinary scholars and journalists we relied on in writing this book. In striving to understand the workings of the mixed economy and the mystery of its slow unraveling, we had to range well beyond our intellectual comfort zone. We are grateful to our guides, though, of course, they are blameless for any cases where we ranged too far. Behind just about every endnote is someone who worked hard to uncover or better understand something important. We have strived to make good use of that hard work, and we are profoundly grateful for the imagined conversations we enjoyed along the way.

We are also profoundly grateful for the many real conversations we had with friends and colleagues that deeply influenced our thinking. With advance apologies for the all-too-certain omissions, we thank Neil Fligstein, Jake Grumbach, Rodney Hero, Nicholas Lemann, David Karol, Amy Lerman, Suzanne Mettler, Terry Moe, Hans Noel, Bruno Palier, Ruth Bloch Rubin, Eric Schickler, Theda Skocpol, Damon Silvers, Joe

Soss, Paul Starr, Daniel Stid, Kathleen Thelen, Rob van Houweling, David Vogel, Vesla Weaver, Margaret Weir, B. Dan Wood, Daniel Ziblatt, and Nick Ziegler.

We also received invaluable feedback from early presentations of our ideas at the Wayne Morse Center at the University of Oregon, Queens University, the University of Montreal, Harvard University, and the University of Maryland. We are especially grateful for extensive and stimulating discussions with members of the Canadian Institute for Advanced Research's Successful Societies Program, directed by Peter Hall and Michele Lamont.

A generous and intrepid group of wonderful scholars went the extra mile, reading drafts of particular chapters: Angus Deaton, Lee Drutman, Peter Gourevitch, Peter Hall, Tom Mann, David Mayhew, Mark Schmitt, and Steve Teles. Their detailed and wise feedback provoked further thought and rescued us from many unforced errors. They deserve no responsibility for any mistakes or muddled thinking that remains, but they do deserve our heartfelt thanks.

A happy few, spurred on not only by curiosity but also by the bonds of family, ran the whole marathon. Oona Hathaway, Kit Pierson, and Mike Pierson took a lot of time from their own busy lives to give us copious amounts of tough (and very smart) love. We are lucky and grateful.

Helping us sift through mountains of information was a team of great research assistants on both ends of the country. Berkeley's contingent included Pierre Bourbonnais, Greg Elinson, Sean Freeder, and Jalel Sager; Yale's included David Brent, Stuart Craig, Dan Feder, and Michael Sierra-Arevalo. Not a research assistant but a partner on a related intellectual endeavor, Nate Loewentheil, also deserves great thanks. All of these able individuals did much more than chase down facts. They brought their own knowledge and intellectual curiosity and, through their sustained engagement, helped shape our thinking and motivated us to push harder.

That was especially true of William McGrew, a brilliant Yale undergraduate who took on the Herculean task of straightening out our endnotes. Whether it was closer to cleaning out the stables or slaying a nine-headed hydra we will leave to him to decide. We do know that all these able researchers were able to assist us only because of the support we received from our home institutions, Yale University and the University of California at Berkeley, as well as the Institution for Social and

Policy Studies at Yale University, which Jacob directs. At Yale, Pamela Lamonaca, Victoria Bilski, Limor Peer, and Ella Sandor deserve special thanks for their support and guidance. Paul also acknowledges the generous support of the Canadian Institute for Advanced Research.

And then there are those who helped make all this work into the book you hold in your hands. Our agent, Sydelle Kramer, was once again a source of steady support as well as expert guidance. We have been reminded again and again of the "Sydelle rule": The best plan is always to do what Sydelle advises. One of those pieces of advice was to work again with the wonderful professionals at Simon & Schuster. Jonathan Karp joined the press just as we became Simon & Schuster authors, and we feel fortunate for his engaged leadership, as well as that of Richard Rhorer. Ben Loehnen is the perfect editor: dedicated, learned, funny, supportive, humane, and whip-smart. At every stage, Ben has made this a better book, and at every stage, he has been a joy to work with. Brit Hvide dealt with our various requests, questions, and stumbles with a professionalism that was even more impressive than her patience. Our copyeditor, Phil Bashe, was commendably conscientious and frighteningly well informed (or at least a wizard at using Google). We are thankful for him and the whole production and marketing team, including Amar Deol, Marie Florio, Alison Forner, Cary Goldstein, Allison Har-Zvi, Beth Maglione, Anne Tate Pearce, Ciara Robinson, Ellen Sasahara, Jackie Seow, and Dana Trocker.

Having worked on this book for four years on opposite coasts, we have learned that the major steps forward tend to come in frequent and lengthy face-to-face conversations. These conversations are fueled by large quantities of caffeine. We are truly grateful for the plethora of excellent coffee shops to be found in Berkeley, Boston, Chicago, Denver, New Haven, New York, Seattle, and Washington, DC. Probably not surprisingly, it was in the last location that the charming woman at the neighboring table felt compelled to jump in with an extremely well-informed critique of the DC Court of Appeals' decision on proxy access. Thanks to her, too.

All that travel hints at just the smallest part of what we owe our two families. Jacob thanks his parents, Margaret and Thom, who gave him a childhood full of love and learning, and his own children, Ava and Owen, who asked whether Dad was "*still* working on that book" enough to make clear they wanted him to finish up and spend more time with them (better late than never). In raising Ava and Owen, his mother-in-law, Anneke, has been there since their early years; without her, this book would not have been possible and family life would have been much less rich. To Oona, a partner in scholarship as well as marriage and parenthood, no words are adequate, but these from Pablo Neruda are at least a start: "To feel the love of people whom we love is a fire that feeds our life."

Sadly, Paul's parents did not live to see this book's completion, but their ideas, commitments, and life experiences helped to shape it. Those experiences include the life-altering opportunities that came from Stan Pierson's eligibility for the GI Bill. Paul thanks Sidra and Seth, who have been way more supportive of and interested in this project than any dad has the right to expect. Without Tracey Goldberg's magical mix of support, patience, ingenuity, and respect for all that this project required, none of this would have happened. Nor would it have felt worth the effort.

Can't build it alone indeed.

NOTES

Introduction: Prosperity Lost

1. In *Our Declaration* (New York: Liveright, 2014), the political theorist Danielle Allen argues convincingly that the twin affirmations in the Declaration's opening—of rights and representative government—should be seen as interlinked, and indeed that the period commonly separating them in reprints of the Declaration may well be a transcription error.

2. Jonathan Elliot, *The Debates in the Several State Conventions of the Adoption of the Federal Constitution* (Philadelphia: J.B. Lippincott Company, 1907), Volume III, online at www.constitution.org/rc/rat_va_13.htm.

3. Garry Wills, *James Madison* (New York: Times Books, 2002), p. 27.

4. Our own thinking on this subject is informed strongly by the excellent discussions in Garry Wills, *A Necessary Evil: A History of American Distrust of Government* (New York: Simon & Schuster, 1999), and Paul Starr, *Freedom's Power: The True Force of Liberalism* (New York: Perseus, 2007).

5. James Madison, *Journal of the Constitutional Convention* (Chicago: Robert O. Law, 1893), p. 354.

6. Mariana Mazzucato, *The Entrepreneurial State: Debunking Public vs. Private Sector Myths* (London: Anthem Press, 2013).

7. Adam Smith, *An Inquiry into the Nature and Causes of the Wealth of Nations*, ed. Charles J. Bullock (Edinburgh, Scot.: Stevenson, 1843).

8. Charles E. Lindblom, *Politics and Markets* (New York: Basic Books, 1977).

9. Smith, *The Wealth of Nations*, Bk. I, Ch. 10; Bk. V, Ch. 2.

10. Ibid., Bk. IV, Ch. 2; Bk. I, Ch. 10. We are indebted to Deborah Boucoyannis for illuminating this neglected side of Smith's thinking. See her "The Equalizing Hand: Why Adam Smith Thought the Market Should Produce Wealth Without Steep Inequality," *Perspectives on Politics* 11, no. 4 (2013): pp. 1051–70.

11. Holman W. Jenkins, "A Better Way to Bring 'Elites' into Line," *Wall Street Journal*, September 4, 2015, www.wsj.com/articles/a-better-way-to-bring-elites-into-line-1441406810.

12. Angus Maddison, "Historical Statistics of the World Economy: 1–2008 AD" (University of Groningen Growth and Development Centre, 2010).

13. Oskar Burger, Annette Baudisch, and James W. Vaupel, "Human Mortality Improvement in Evolutionary Context," *Proceedings of the National Academy of the Sciences of the United States of America* 109, no. 44 (2012): pp. 18210–14.

14. J. David Hacker, "Decennial Life Tables for the White Population of the United

States, 1790–1900," *Historical Methods: A Journal of Quantitative and Interdisciplinary History* 43, no. 2 (2010): pp. 45–79, doi:10.1080/01615441003720449.

15. Thomas Piketty, *Capital in the Twenty-First Century*, trans. Arthur Goldhammer (Cambridge, MA: Belknap Press, 2014), p. 87.

16. Angus Deaton, *The Great Escape: Health, Wealth, and the Origins of Inequality* (Princeton, NJ: Princeton University Press, 2015), p. 93.

17. J. William Fulbright, "The War and Its Effects: The Military-Industrial-Academic Complex" in *Super-State: Readings in the Military-Industrial Complex*, ed. Herbert I. Schiller and Joseph D. Phillips (Urbana: University of Illinois Press, 1970), pp. 171–78; Gar Alperovitz and Lev Daly, *Unjust Deserts: How the Rich Are Taking Our Common Inheritance* (New York: New Press, 2009).

18. Burton W. Folsom, *The Myth of the Robber Barons: A New Look at the Rise of Big Business in America* (Herndon, VA: Young America's Foundation, 1987).

19. David Greenberg, "Hating Woodrow Wilson: The New and Confused Attacks on Progressivism," *Slate*, October 22, 2010, www.slate.com/id/2202431; Steven Teles, "How the Progressives Became the Tea Party's Bête Noir" in *The Progressives' Century: Democratic Reform and Constitutional Government in the United States*, ed. Stephen Skowronek, Stephen Engel, and Bruce Ackerman (New Haven, CT: Yale University Press, forthcoming).

20. Jonah Goldberg, *Liberal Fascism: The Secret History of the American Left from Mussolini to the Politics of Meaning* (New York: Doubleday, 2007), p. 80.

21. Paula Span, "How Did Woodrow Wilson Become America's Most Hated President?" *American History*, January 2014.

22. Ibid.

23. Richard H. K. Vietor, "Government Regulation of Business," in *Cambridge Economic History of the United States*, ed. S. L. Engerman and R. E. Gallman (New York: Cambridge University Press, 2000), pp. 969–1012.

24. Span, "How Did Woodrow Wilson Become America's Most Hated President?"

25. William E. Kovacic and Marc Winerman, "The Federal Trade Commission as an Independent Agency: Autonomy, Legitimacy, and Effectiveness," *Iowa Law Review* 100 (2015): p. 2087.

26. Woodrow Wilson, *Constitutional Government in the United States* (New York: Columbia University Press, 1908), p. 169.

27. George Will, "Not a State-Broken People," *Real Clear Politics*, July 26, 2010, www.realclearpolitics.com/articles/2010/07/26/not_a_state-broken_people_106463.html.

28. Ibid.

29. Wills, *James Madison*, pp. 27–29.

30. Ibid.; David Brian Robertson, *The Original Compromise: What the Constitution's Framers Were Really Thinking* (New York: Oxford University Press, 2013).

31. Wills, *James Madison*, pp. 29–30.

32. James Madison, "The Federalist No. 58," *The Federalist Papers* (Mineola, NY: Dover Publications, 2014), p. 288.

33. Alexis de Tocqueville, *Democracy in America*, trans. Harvey C. Mansfield and Delba Winthrop (Chicago: University of Chicago Press, 2000).

34. Jerome Karabel, "'American Exceptionalism' and the Battle for the Presidency," *Huffington Post*, December 22, 2011, www.huffingtonpost.com/jerome-karabel/american-exceptionalism-obama-gingrich_b_1161800.html; "Ameri-

can exceptionalism," Google Books Ngram Viewer, https://books.google.com
/ngrams/graph?content=%22American+exceptionalism%22&year_start=
1800&year_end=2000&corpus=15&smoothing=3&share=&direct_url=
t1%3B%2C%22%20American%20exceptionalism%20%22%3B%2Cc0.

35. Ronald Reagan, "Remarks Accepting the Presidential Nomination at the Republican National Convention in Dallas, Texas," August 23, 2014, www.reagan
.utexas.edu/archives/speeches/1984/82384f.htm; Franklin D. Roosevelt, "Third
Inaugural Address," in *My Fellow Citizens: The Inaugural Addresses of the Presidents of the United States*, ed. Arthur Schlesinger and Fred L. Israel (New York:
Infobase, 2007), p. 296.

36. Jerome Karabel and Daniel Laurison, "Outlier Nation? American Exceptionalism and the Quality of Life in the United States" (working paper, Institute
for Research on Labor and Employment, University of California at Berkeley,
2011).

37. These performance indicators are discussed in detail in chapter 1.

38. Piketty, *Capital*, p. 484.

39. Rick Perlstein, "What Mitt Romney Learned from His Dad," *Rolling Stone*, January 17, 2012, www.rollingstone.com/politics/news/what-mitt-romney-learned
-from-his-dad-20120117.

40. Jacob S. Hacker and Paul Pierson, "Romney Is the Right Man for America: George
Romney, That Is," *Washington Post*, February 10, 2012, www.washingtonpost
.com/opinions/romney-is-the-right-man-for-america-george-romney-that-is
/2012/02/07/gIQAdGwo4Q_story.html.

41. Michael Kranish and Scott Helman, *The Real Romney* (New York: HarperCollins,
2012).

42. T. George Harris, *Romney's Way: A Man and an Idea* (Englewood Cliffs, NJ:
Prentice-Hall, 1998). See also Chris Bachelder, "Crashing the Party: The Ill-
Fated 1968 Presidential Campaign of Governor George Romney," *Michigan Historical Review*, Fall 2007.

43. Perlstein, "What Mitt Romney Learned from His Dad."

44. Nelson Lichtenstein, *Walter Reuther: The Most Dangerous Man in Detroit* (Chicago: University of Illinois Press, 1995), p. 230.

45. Newell G. Bringhurst and Craig L. Foster, *The Mormon Quest for the Presidency*
(Independence, MO: John Whitmer, 2008), p. 61.

46. Tom Loftus, *The Art of Legislative Politics* (Washington, DC: Congressional
Quarterly Press, 1994), p. 130.

47. Dean J. Kotlowski, *Nixon's Civil Rights: Politics, Principle, and Policy* (Cambridge, MA: Harvard University Press, 2009), pp. 54–69.

48. Geoffrey Kabaservice, *Rule and Ruin: The Downfall of Moderation and the Destruction of the Republican Party, from Eisenhower to the Tea Party* (New York:
Oxford University Press, 2012), pp. 116, 130.

49. Ibid., p. 116.

50. Kranish and Helman, *The Real Romney*, pp. 329–30.

51. Greta R. Krippner, *Capitalizing on Crisis: The Political Origins of the Rise of Finance* (Cambridge, MA: Harvard University Press, 2011), p. 2.

52. Ralph Gomory and Richard Sylla, "The American Corporation," *Daedalus* 142,
no. 2 (2013): pp. 102–18.

53. Krippner, *Capitalizing on Crisis*, pp. 7–10.

54. Gomory and Sylla, "The American Corporation," p. 106.
55. Ibid., p. 108.
56. Mark S. Mizruchi, *The Fracturing of the American Corporate Elite* (Cambridge, MA: Harvard University Press, 2013), p. 42.
57. Lee Edwards, *Goldwater: The Man Who Made a Revolution* (Washington, DC: Regnery, 1995).

PART I: THE RISE OF THE MIXED ECONOMY

ONE: Coming Up Short

1. John Komlos, "On the Biological Standard of Living of Eighteenth-Century Americans: Taller, Richer, Healthier," *Research in Economic History* 20 (2001): pp. 223–48.
2. David McCullough, *John Adams* (New York: Simon & Schuster, 2002), p. 72.
3. Lyn Ragsdale, *Vital Statistics on the Presidency: Washington to Clinton* (Washington, DC: CQ Press, 1996).
4. Komlos, "Taller, Richer, Healthier"; Dora L. Costa and Richard H. Steckel, "Long-Term Trends in Health, Welfare, and Economic Growth in the United States" in *Health and Welfare During Industrialization*, ed. Richard H. Steckel and Roderick Floud (Chicago: University of Chicago Press, 1996), pp. 47–89, 50–51.
5. William R. Polk, *The Birth of America: From Before Columbus to the Revolution* (New York: HarperCollins, 2006), p. 149.
6. Alexis de Tocqueville, *Democracy in America*, trans. Harvey C. Mansfield and Delba Winthrop (Chicago: University of Chicago Press, 2000).
7. J. Hector St. John Crevecoeur, "Letter III: What Is an American," in Letters from an American Farmer (1782) via the University of Virginia, http://xroads.virginia.edu/~hyper/CREV/letter03.html.
8. Maddison, "Historical Statistics of the World Economy"; Peter H. Lindert and Jeffrey G. Williamson, "American Incomes 1774–1860" (working paper, National Bureau of Economic Research, Cambridge, MA, 2012).
9. Costa and Steckel, "Long-Term Trends."
10. Timothy J. Hatton and Bernice E. Bray, "Long Run Trends in the Heights of European Men, 19th–20th Centuries," *Economics & Human Biology* 8 (2010): pp. 405–13.
11. Komlos, "Taller, Richer, Healthier"; John Komlos and Benjamin E. Lauderdale, "Underperformance in Affluence: The Remarkable Relative Decline in U.S. Heights in the Second Half of the 20th Century," *Social Science Quarterly* 88 (2007): pp. 283–305.
12. See Hatton and Bray, "Long Run Trends" for European data, and Costa and Steckel, "Long-Term Trends" for American data.
13. Anne Case and Christina Paxson, "Stature and Status: Height, Ability and Labor Market Outcomes," *Journal of Political Economy* 116 (2008): pp. 499–532; John Komlos and Marieluise Baur, "From the Tallest to (One of) the Fattest: The Enigmatic Fate of the American Population in the 20th Century," *Economics & Human Biology* 2 (2004): pp. 57–74.
14. Hatton and Bray, "Long Run Trends," pp. 5–7.
15. Komlos and Lauderdale, "Underperformance in Affluence."

16. *Society at a Glance 2009: OECD Social Indicators* (Paris: Organization for Economic Cooperation and Development, 2009).

17. Komlos and Baur, "From the Tallest to (One of) the Fattest"; Burkhard Bilger, "The Height Gap," *New Yorker*, April 5, 2014.

18. *Society at a Glance 2009*, p. 108.

19. Komlos and Baur, "From the Tallest to (One of) the Fattest," pp. 63–64.

20. Costa and Steckel, "Long-Term Trends," pp. 51–53; Richard Steckel, "Heights and Health in the United States: 1710–1950," in *Stature, Living Standards, and Economic Development*, ed. John Komlos (Chicago: University of Chicago Press, 1994), pp. 153–70.

21. Marco Sunder, "The Height Gap in 19th-Century America: Net-Nutritional Advantage of the Elite Increased at the Onset of Modern Economic Growth," *Economics & Human Biology* 11 (2013): pp. 245–58.

22. Hatton and Bray, "Long Run Trends," p. 4.

23. *Society at a Glance 2009*.

24. Komlos and Baur, "From the Tallest to (One of) the Fattest."

25. *National Accounts of OECD Countries* (Paris: Organization for Economic Cooperation and Development, 2015).

26. Arthur Max, "Dutch Reach New Heights," *USA Today*, September 16, 2006.

27. Nermeen Shaikh, "Interview with Amartya Sen: A More Human Theory of Development," AsiaSociety.org, December 6, 2004.

28. Mariana Mazzucato, *The Entrepreneurial State: Debunking Public vs. Private Sector Myths* (London: Anthem Press, 2013).

29. Fred Block and Matthew R. Keller, *State of Innovation: The US Government's Role in Technology Development* (New York: Paradigm, 2011).

30. William D. Nordhaus, "The Health of Nations: The Contribution of Improved Health to Living Standards," in *Measuring the Gains from Medical Research: An Economic Approach*, ed. Kevin M. Murphy and Robert H. Topel (Chicago: University of Chicago Press, 2003).

31. Walter Isaacson, *Steve Jobs* (New York: Simon & Schuster, 2015), p. 123.

32. Alex Berenson, "Pinning Down the Money Value of a Person's Life," *New York Times*, June 11, 2007.

33. Christopher J. L. Murray, Steven H. Woolf, and Laudan Aron, *U.S. Health in International Perspective: Shorter Lives, Poorer Health* (Washington, DC: National Academy of Sciences, 2013).

34. Ibid.

35. Christopher J. L. Murray et al., "The State of US Health, 1990–2010: Burden of Diseases, Injuries, and Risk Factors," *Journal of the American Medical Association* 310 (2013): pp. 591–606.

36. Murray, Woolf, and Aron, *Shorter Lives, Poorer Health*.

37. "Annual Estimates of the Resident Population for Selected Age Groups by Sex for the United States, States, Counties, and Puerto Rico Commonwealth and Municipios: April 1, 2010 to July 1, 2014," US Census Bureau, accessed October 1, 2015, http://factfinder.census.gov/faces/tableservices/jsf/pages/product-view.xhtml?src=bkmk.

38. Anne Case and Angus Deaton, "Rising Morbidity and Mortality in Midlife among White Non-Hispanic Americans in the 21st Century," *Proceedings of the National Academy of Sciences* 112, no. 49 (2015): pp. 15078–83.

39. Murray, Woolf, and Aron, *Shorter Lives, Poorer Health*, pp. 40–41; Stephen C. Schoenbaum et al., "Mortality Amenable to Health Care in the United States: The Roles of Demographics and Health Systems Performance," *Journal of Public Health Poli*cy 32 (2011): pp. 407–29.
40. Murray, Woolf, and Aron, *Shorter Lives, Poorer Health*.
41. Ibid.
42. Murray, Woolf, and Aron, *Shorter Lives, Poorer Health*, pp. 44–45.
43. Ibid., pp. 66–68.
44. Calculated from "OECD Health Statistics" (Paris: Organization for Economic Cooperation and Development, 2015) using the same seventeen rich nations in Murray, Woolf, and Aron, *Shorter Lives, Poorer Health*.
45. "OECD Health Statistics."
46. Murray, Woolf, and Aron, *Shorter Lives, Poorer Health*.
47. Ellen Nolte and Martin McKee, "Variations in Amenable Mortality—Trends in 16 High-Income Nations," *Health Policy* 103 (2011): pp. 47–52.
48. Claudia Goldin and Lawrence Katz, *The Race Between Education and Technology* (Cambridge, MA: Harvard University Press, 2010); Patricia J. Gumport, Mari Iannozzi, Susan Shaman, and Robert Zemsky, *The United States Country Report: Trends in Higher Education from Massification to Post-Massification* (Stanford, CA: National Center for Postsecondary Improvement, 1997).
49. Richard J. Murnane, "U.S. High School Graduation Rates: Patterns and Explanations," *Journal of Economic Literature* 51 (2013): pp. 370–422.
50. "Education at a Glance 2014: OECD Indicators" (Paris: Organization for Economic Cooperation and Development, 2014).
51. James J. Heckman and Paul A. LaFontaine, "The American High School Graduation Rate: Trends and Levels," *Review of Economic Statistics* 92 (2010): pp. 244–62.
52. "Labour Market Outcomes of Vocational Education in Europe: Evidence from the European Union Labour Force Survey" (Luxembourg: European Centre for the Development of Vocational Training, 2013)
53. Jeremy Travis and Bruce Western, *The Growth of Incarceration in the United States: Exploring Causes and Consequences* (Washington, DC: National Academies Press, 2014); Roy Walmsley, *World Prison Population List*, 10th ed. (London: International Centre for Prison Studies, 2014).
54. Heckman and LaFontaine, "American High School Graduation Rate."
55. Murnane, "U.S. High School Graduation Rates."
56. "Education at a Glance 2014."
57. "OECD Skills Outlook 2013" (Paris: Organization for Economic Cooperation and Development, 2014).
58. Joy Resmovits, "International Tests Show East Asian Students Outperform World as U.S. Holds Steady," *Huffington Post*, December 11, 2012.
59. "Skills Outlook 2013."
60. Sean F. Reardon, "The Widening Academic Achievement Gap Between the Rich and the Poor: New Evidence and Possible Explanations," in *Whither Opportunity? Rising Inequality and the Uncertain Life Chances of Low-Income Children*, ed. Richard J. Murnane and Greg J. Duncan (New York: Russell Sage Foundation Press, 2011); Eduardo Porter, "In Public Education, Edge Still Goes to Rich," *New York Times*, November 5, 2013.
61. Porter, "Edge Still Goes to Rich."

62. Albert Wat, *Dollars and Sense: A Review of Economic Analyses of Pre-K* (Washington, DC: Pre-K Now, May 2007).

63. "Education at a Glance 2012: OECD Indicators" (Paris: Organization for Economic Cooperation and Development, 2012).

64. "Main Economic Indicators 2015" (Paris: Organization for Economic Cooperation and Development, 2015).

65. Carmen DeNavas-Walt and Bernadette D. Proctor, *Income and Poverty in the United States: 2013* (Washington, DC: US Census Bureau, 2014).

66. Ibid.

67. Lane Kenworthy, *When Does Economic Growth Benefit People on Low to Middle Incomes—and Why?* (London: Resolution Foundation Commission on Living Standards, November 2011).

68. Francine D. Blau and Lawrence M. Kahn, "Female Labor Supply: Why Is the US Falling Behind?" *American Economic Review* 103 (2013): pp. 251–56.

69. Robert J. Gordon, "Two Centuries of Economic Growth: Europe Chasing the American Frontier" (Northwestern University and NBER Paper Prepared for Economic History Workshop, Northwestern University, October 17, 2002).

70. Ibid.

71. Anthony B. Atkinson, "The Distribution of Earnings in OECD Countries," *International Labour Review* 146 (2007); Anthony B. Atkinson, Thomas Piketty, and Emmanuel Saez, "Top Incomes in the Long Run of History," *Journal of Economic Literature* 49 (2011): pp. 3–71.

72. Anthony Shorrocks, Jim Davies, and Rodrigo Lluberas, *Global Wealth Report 2014* (Zurich: Credit Suisse Research Institute, 2014), https://publications.credit-suisse.com/tasks/render/file/?fileID=60931FDE-A2D2-F568-B041B58C5EA591A4.

73. Tami Luhby, "America's Middle Class: Poorer Than You Think," *CNN Money*, June 6, 2011.

74. Fabrice Martin and Marco Mira d'Ercole, "Household Wealth Inequality across OECD Countries: New OECD Evidence," *OECD Statistics Brief*, June 2015, No. 21.

75. Werner Sombart, *Why Is There No Socialism in the United States?* (New York: International Arts & Sciences Press, 1976).

76. Joseph P. Ferrie, "The End of American Exceptionalism? Mobility in the U.S. Since 1850" (working paper, National Bureau of Economic Research, Cambridge, MA, 2005).

77. Miles Corak, Lori Curtis, and Shelley Phipps, "Economic Mobility, Family Background, and the Well-Being of Children in the United States and Canada" (discussion paper, Institute for the Study of Labor, Bonn, Ger., 2010).

78. Peter Adamson, *Child Well-Being in Rich Countries: A Comparative Overview* (Florence, It.: UNICEF Office of Research, 2013).

79. Sara Rosenbaum and Robert Blum, "How Healthy Are Our Children?" *Future of Children* 25, no. 1 (2015): pp. 11–34.

80. William H. Press, "What's So Special About Science (And How Much Should We Spend on It?)" *Science* 342 (2013): pp. 817–22.

81. Robert D. Atkinson and Stephen J. Ezell, *Innovation Economics* (New Haven, CT: Yale University Press, 2012), p. 2.

82. *National Patterns of R&D Resources: 2011–12 Data Update* (Arlington, VA: Na-

tional Science Foundation, National Center for Science and Engineering Statistics, 2013), www.nsf.gov/statistics/nsf14304.

83. Justin Hicks and Robert D. Atkinson, *Eroding Our Foundation: Sequestration, R&D, Innovation, and U.S. Economic Growth* (report by the Information Technology and Innovation Foundation, 2012).

84. Richard R. Nelson and Paul M. Romer, "Science, Economic Growth, and Public Policy," in *Technology, R&D, and the Economy,* ed. Bruce L. R. Smith and Claude E. Barfield (Washington, DC: Brookings Institution and American Enterprise Institute), pp. 49–74.

85. *Science and Engineering Indicators 2012* (Arlington, VA: National Science Foundation, 2012), chap. 4, www.nsf.gov/statistics/seind12/pdf/seind12.pdf; Robert D. Atkinson, Stephen Ezell, and Luke A. Stewart, *The Global Innovation Policy Index* (Washington, DC: Information Technology and Innovation Foundation and the Kauffman Foundation, March 2012), www2.itif.org/2012-global-innovation-policy-index.pdf?_ga=1.64198505.795725122.1447676955.

86. Hicks and Atkinson, *Eroding Our Foundation.*

87. *Antibiotic Resistance Threats in the United States, 2013* (Atlanta: Centers for Disease Control and Prevention, 2013), www.cdc.gov/drugresistance/pdf/ar-threats-2013-508.pdf.

88. Jason Millman, "It's Going to Take a Lot More Ice Buckets to Fill the NIH Funding Gap," *Wonkblog* (blog), *Washington Post*, August 21, 2014, www.washingtonpost.com/news/wonkblog/wp/2014/08/21/its-going-to-take-a-lot-more-ice-buckets-to-fill-the-nih-funding-gap.

89. Keith Humphreys, "Eating the Seed Corn in the Health Research World," *Washington Monthly*, December 5, 2013, www.washingtonmonthly.com/ten-miles-square/2013/12/eating_the_seed_corn_in_the_he048061.php.

90. Robin Harding, Richard McGregor, and Gabriel Muller, "US Public Investment Falls to Lowest Level Since War," *Financial Times*, November 3, 2013, www.ft.com/intl/cms/s/0/f0e71a16-4487-11e3-a751-00144feabdc0.html#slide0.

91. Don Lee, "Shoddy U.S. Roads and Bridges Take a Toll on the Economy," *Los Angeles Times*, August 14, 2014, www.latimes.com/nation/la-na-roads-economy-20140815-story.html; Ed Lee and Annise Parker, "America's Urban Water Crisis," *Politico*, September 9, 2014, www.politico.com/magazine/story/2014/09/aging-water-infrastructure-110774.html?wpisrc=nl-wonkbk&wpmm=1#.VBB4cihy9UQ.

92. Josh Bivens, "Public Investment: The Next 'New Thing' for Powering Economic Growth" (briefing paper, Economic Policy Institute, Washington, DC, 2012).

93. M. Ishaq Nadiri and Theofanis P. Mamuneas, *Contribution of Highway Capital to Industry and National Productivity Growth* (report prepared by Apogee Research for the Federal Highway Administration Office of Police Development, September 1996), http://ntl.bts.gov/lib/5000/5800/5807/growth.pdf.

94. Xavier Sala-I-Martín et al., *The Global Competitiveness Index 2014–2015: Accelerating a Robust Recovery to Create Productive Jobs and Support Inclusive Growth* (Switzerland: World Economic Forum, 2015).

95. *2013 Report Card for America's Infrastructure* (report by the American Society of Civil Engineers, 2013).

96. "America's Transport Infrastructure: Life in the Slow Lane," *Economist*, April 28, 2011.

97. Stephen Blank, Graham Parsons, and Juan Carlos Villa, "Freight Transportation Infrastructure Policies in Canada, Mexico & the US: An Overview and Analysis" (working paper, North American Transportation Competitiveness Research Council, 2008).

98. Sabrina Eaton, "Rep. Ryan Says China and India Outspend U.S. on Infrastructure," *PolitiFact*, August 9, 2011.

99. "Changsha - Guangzhou on Chinese High-Speed Train Beijing - Guangzhou (part 5)," YouTube video, www.youtube.com/watch?v=Nvjk-4Ft5_0; "Changsa Railway Station," China Highlights, www.chinahighlights.com/china-trains/changsha-railway-station.htm.

100. Lindsay H. Jones, "Beyoncé Did Not Cause Superdome's Super Bowl Blackout," *USA Today*, February 4, 2013, www.usatoday.com/story/sports/nfl/2013/02/04/super-bowl-superdome-blackout-beyonce/1890419.

101. Frank T. Princiotta, *Global Climate Change: The Technology Challenge* (New York: Springer, 2011), p. 323.

102. Joseph E. Aldy, "A Preliminary Review of the American Recovery and Reinvestment Act's Clean Energy Package," *Review of Environmental Economics and Policy* (2011).

103. Richard S. J. Tol, "The Marginal Damage Costs of Carbon Dioxide Emissions: An Assessment of the Uncertainties," *Energy Policy* 33 (2005): pp. 2064–74.

104. *2015 World Development Indicators* (Washington, DC: World Bank, 2015), http://data.worldbank.org/sites/default/files/wdi-2015-frontmatter.pdf.

105. Angel Hsu et al., *2014 Environmental Performance Index: Full Report and Analysis* (New Haven, CT: Yale Center for Environmental Law & Policy, 2014).

106. *Obesity Update 2014* (Paris: OECD Directorate for Employment, Labour and Social Affairs, Organization for Economic Cooperation and Development, June 2014), www.oecd.org/els/health-systems/Obesity-Update-2014.pdf.

107. Ruopeng An, "Health Care Expenses in Relation to Obesity and Smoking Among U.S. Adults by Gender, Race/Ethnicity, and Age Group: 1998–2011," *Public Health* 129 (2015): pp. 29–36.

108. Donald F. Behan and Samuel H. Cox, *Obesity and Its Relation to Mortality and Morbidity Costs* (Schaumburg, IL: Society of Actuaries, December 2010).

109. Neville Owen, "Sedentary Behavior: Emerging Evidence for a New Health Risk," *Mayo Clinic Proceedings* 85 (2010): pp. 1138–41; "Profiling Food Consumption in America," in *Agriculture Fact Book 2001–2002* (Washington, DC: US Department of Agriculture, 2003), pp. 13–22.

110. See "Weight Management," in *California Nutrition and Physical Activity Guidelines for Adolescents* (report by the California Department of Public Health, 2013), www.cdph.ca.gov/programs/NutiritionandPhysicalActivity/Documents/MO-NUPA-Guidelines.pdf; Lisa Young, "The Battle Against Big Soda Continues," *Huffington Post*, June 26, 2012; Cheryl D. Fyar, Qiuping Gu, and Cynthia L. Ogden, *Anthropometric Reference Data for Children and Adults: United States, 2007–2010*, CDC Vital and Health Statistics 252, no. 11 (October 2012).

111. Christopher Ingraham, "The Average American Woman Now Weighs as Much as the Average 1960s Man," *Washington Post Wonkblog*, June 12, 2015, www.washingtonpost.com/news/wonk/wp/2015/06/12/look-at-how-much-weight-weve-gained-since-the-1960s.

112. Henry R. Luce, "The American Century," first published in *Life*, February 17, 1941, accessible at www.informationclearinghouse.info/article6139.htm.

TWO: The Great Divide

1. Herrman L. Blumgart, "Caring for the Patient," *New England Journal of Medicine* 270 (1964): pp. 449–56.
2. Kevin G. Kinsella, "Changes in Life Expectancy 1900–1990," *American Journal of Clinical Nutrition* (1992): pp. 1196S–1202S.
3. CDC, *Health, United States, 2014* (Hyattsville, MD: National Center for Health Statistics, 2015), p. 85.
4. Kinsella, "Changes in Life Expectancy."
5. Angus Deaton, *The Great Escape: Health, Wealth, and the Origins of Inequality* (Princeton, NJ: Princeton University Press, 2015).
6. Kinsella, "Changes in Life Expectancy"; Karen N. Eggleston and Victor R. Fuchs, "The New Demographic Transition: Most Gains in Life Expectancy Now Realized Late in Life," *Journal of Economic Perspectives* 26 (2012): pp. 137–56.
7. Olli Kangas, "One Hundred Years of Money, Welfare and Death: Mortality, Economic Growth and the Development of the Welfare State in 17 OECD Countries 1900–2000," *International Journal of Social Welfare* 19 (2010): pp. S42–S59.
8. David Cutler and Grant Miller, "The Role of Public Health Improvements in Health Advances: The 20th Century United States" (working paper, National Bureau of Economic Research, Cambridge, MA, 2004).
9. Oskar Burger, Annette Baudisch, and James W. Vaupel, "Human Mortality Improvement in Evolutionary Context," *Proceedings of the National Academy of Sciences of the United States of America* 109, no. 44 (2012): pp. 18210–14.
10. Ibid.
11. Ibid.
12. Richard A. Easterlin, "The Worldwide Standard of Living Since 1800," *Journal of Economic Perspectives* 14, no. 1 (2000): pp. 7–26.
13. CDC, "Achievements in Public Health, 1900–1999: Healthier Mothers and Babies," *Morbidity and Mortality Weekly Report* 48, no. 38 (1999): pp. 849–58.
14. Ibid.
15. Rose Goff, "Factors in the Drop in United States Infant Mortality: 1900–1940," (Carnegie Mellon University Research Showcase 5, 2010).
16. Doug Wead, *All the Presidents' Children: Triumph and Tragedy in the Lives of America's First Families* (New York: Atria Books, 2003), pp. 347–48.
17. CDC, "Healthier Mothers and Babies."
18. David Cutler has done more than any other health economist to chart and explain changing patterns of longevity in the twentieth century. The first part of this chapter (on health gains) would not have been possible without his pioneering work. David M. Cutler and Ellen Meara, "Changes in the Age Distribution of Mortality over the 20th Century" (working paper, National Bureau of Economic Research, Cambridge, MA, 2001).
19. Ibid.
20. William D. Nordhaus, "The Health of Nations: The Contribution of Improved Health to Living Standards" in *Measuring Gains from Medical Research: An Eco-*

nomic Approach, ed. Kevin M. Murphy and Robert H. Topel (Chicago: University of Chicago Press, 2003).

21. Cutler and Meara, "Changes in Age Distribution of Mortality," pp. 7–8.

22. Ibid., p. 11; Kwang-Sun Lee, "Infant Mortality Decline in the Late 19th and Early 20th Centuries: The Role of Market Milk," *Perspectives in Biology and Medicine* 50, no. 4 (1987): pp. 585–602.

23. Ibid., pp. 587–88.

24. David Cutler, Angus Deaton, and Adriana Lleras-Muney, "The Determinants of Mortality" (working paper, National Bureau of Economic Research, Cambridge, MA, 2006), pp. 31–32.

25. Lee, "Market Milk," pp. 589–90.

26. Cutler and Miller, "Role of Public Health Improvements in Health Advances," pp. 1–22.

27. Ibid., p. 3.

28. Ibid., p. 19.

29. Cutler and Meara, "Changes in Age Distribution of Mortality."

30. Dora L. Costa and Richard H. Steckel, "Long-Term Trends in Health, Welfare, and Economic Growth in the United States" in *Health and Welfare During Industralization*, ed. Richard H. Steckel and Roderick Floud (Chicago: University of Chicago Press, 1996).

31. Simon Szreter, "Economic Growth, Disruption, Deprivation, Disease, and Death: On the Importance of the Politics of Public Health for Development," *Population and Development Review* 23, No. 4 (1997): pp. 693–728.

32. Richard A. Easterlin, "How Beneficent Is the Market? A Look at the Modern History of Mortality," *European Review of Economic History* 3, no. 3 (1999): pp. 257–94.

33. Michael R. Haines, "The Urban Mortality Transition in the United States," (historical working paper, National Bureau of Economic Research, Cambridge, MA, 2001).

34. Cutler, Deaton, and Lleras-Muney, "Determinants of Mortality," p. 32.

35. Easterlin, "How Beneficent Is the Market?"

36. Alexandra Minna Stern and Howard Merkel, "The History of Vaccines and Immunization: Familiar Patterns, New Challenges," *Health Affairs* 24, no. 3 (2005): pp. 611–21, 612–14.

37. Byrd S. Leavell, "Thomas Jefferson and Smallpox Vaccination," *Transactions of the American Clinical and Climatological Association* 88 (1977): pp. 119–27.

38. Easterlin, "How Beneficent Is the Market?" pp. 271–72.

39. Stern and Merkel, "History of Vaccines and Immunization," pp. 614–16.

40. Roy M. Anderson and Robert M. May, "Modern Vaccines: Immunisation and Herd Immunity," *Lancet* 335 (1990): pp. 641–45.

41. Walter A. Orenstein and Alan R. Hinman, "The Immunization System in the United States and the Role of School Immunization Laws," *Vaccine* 17 (1999): pp. S19–S24.

42. Phillip Musgrove, "Public and Private Roles in Health," in *Health Economics in Development* (Washington, DC: World Bank, 2004): pp. 35–76, 45.

43. Cutler, Deaton, and Lleras-Muney, "Determinants of Mortality," pp. 97–120.

44. Roswell Quinn, "Rethinking Antibiotic Research and Development: World War II and the Penicillin Collaborative," *American Journal of Public Health* (2013): pp. 426–34.

45. Ibid.

46. Kristin Jarrell, "Regulatory History: Elixir Sulfanilamide," *Journal of GXP Compliance* 16, no. 3 (2012): pp. 12–14.
47. Quinn, "Rethinking Antibiotic Research and Development," pp. 427–28.
48. Ibid., p. 430.
49. Ibid., p. 432.
50. Alan M. Garber and Jonathan Skinner, "Is American Health Care Uniquely Inefficient?" *Journal of Economic Perspectives* 22, no. 4 (2008): pp. 27–50.
51. Eggleston and Fuchs, "New Demographic Transition," p. 138.
52. Cutler and Meara, "Age Distribution of Mortality over the 20th Century," pp. 17–18.
53. Jacob S. Hacker, *The Divided Welfare State: The Battle over Public and Private Social Benefits in the United States* (New York: Cambridge University Press, 2002).
54. Robert Fogel, "Economic Growth, Population Theory, and Physiology: The Bearing of Long-Term Processes on the Making of Economic Policy," *American Economic Association* 84, no. 3 (1994): pp. 369–95.
55. Peter L. Singer, "Federally Supported Innovations" (report by the Information Technology and Innovation Foundation, 2014).
56. Gar Alperovitz and Lew Daly, *Unjust Deserts: How the Rich Are Taking Our Common Inheritance* (New York: New Press, 2009).
57. NIH, *The Benefits of Medical Research and the Role of the NIH* (Washington, DC: National Institutes of Health, 2000), p. 27.
58. Alperovitz and Daly, *Unjust Deserts*.
59. Cutler and Meara, "Age Distribution of Mortality over the 20th Century," pp. 20–21.
60. Daniel Sullivan and Till von Wachter, "Job Displacement and Mortality: An Analysis Using Administrative Data," *Quarterly Journal of Economics* (2009): pp. 1265–306.
61. Jonathan Cylus, M. Maria Glymour, and Mauricio Avendano, "Do Generous Unemployment Benefit Programs Reduce Suicide Rates? A State Fixed-Effect Analysis Covering 1968–2008," *American Journal of Epidemiology* 180, no. 1 (2014): 45–52.
62. Kangas, "One Hundred Years of Money, Welfare and Death," p. S56.
63. There is also suggestive evidence that larger welfare states are associated with higher levels of self-reported well-being (aka "happiness"). Dylan Matthews, "Do Bigger Governments Lead to Happier People?" *Wonkblog* (blog), *Washington Post*, December 23, 2013, www.washingtonpost.com/blogs/wonkblog/wp/2013/12/23/do-bigger-governments-lead-to-happier-people.
64. Szreter, "Economic Growth, Disruption, Deprivation, Disease, and Death," pp. 693–728.
65. Angus Maddison, "Historical Statistics of the World Economy: 1–2008 AD" (University of Groningen Growth and Development Centre, 2010).
66. Robert J. Gordon, "Is U.S. Economic Growth Over? Faltering Innovation Confronts the Six Headwinds" (working paper, National Bureau of Economic Research, Cambridge, MA, 2012), pp. 7–8.
67. Julian Alston, Jennifer James, Matthew Anderson, and Philip Pardey, *Persistence Pays: U.S. Agricultural Productivity Growth and the Benefits from Public R&D Spending* (New York: Springer, 2010).
68. Gordon, "Is U.S. Economic Growth Over?," pp. 8–10.
69. Maddison, "Historical Statistics of the World Economy."

70. Ibid.

71. Robert Shackleton, "Total Factor Productivity Growth in Historical Perspective" (working paper, US Congressional Budget Office, Washington, DC, 2013).

72. Robert M. Solow, "Growth Theory and After," *American Economic Review* 78, no. 3 (1988): pp. 307–17.

73. Ibid., p. 309.

74. Robert M. Solow, "Technical Change and the Aggregate Production Function," *Review of Economics and Statistics* 39, no. 3 (1957): pp. 312–20.

75. Despite a powerful explication by Alperovitz and Daly. This section is indebted to their lucid arguments about the implications of the Solow residual for our understanding of national wealth.

76. William J. Baumol, *The Free-Market Innovation Machine: Analyzing the Growth Miracle of Capitalism* (Princeton, NJ: Princeton University Press, 2002), p. 134.

77. Robert E. Hall and Charles I. Jones, "Why Do Some Countries Produce So Much More Output Per Worker Than Others?" *Quarterly Journal of Economics* 114, no. 1 (1999): pp. 83–116.

78. Mark A. Lemley, "The Myth of the Sole Inventor" (Stanford public law working paper, 2011).

79. Christopher A. Cotropia and Mark A. Lemley, "Copying in Patent Law," *North Carolina Law Review* 87 (2009).

80. Simon Kuznets, "Economic Growth and Income Inequality," *American Economic Review* 45, no. 1 (1955): pp. 1–28.

81. Joel Mokyr, *The Lever of Riches: Technological Creativity and Economic Progress* (New York: Oxford University Press, 1990), p. 3.

82. "Simon Kuznets—Autobiography," Nobelprize.org, February 12, 2013, www.nobel prize.org/nobel_prizes/economic-sciences/laureates/1971/kuznets-bio.html.

83. Solomon Fabricant, "Toward a Firmer Basis of Economic Policy: The Founding of the National Bureau of Economic Research," in *Toward a Firmer Basis of Economic Policy*, ed. Solomon Fabricant (Cambridge, MA: National Bureau of Economic Research, 1961), pp. 1–16.

84. Carol S. Carson, "The History of the United States National Income Accounts: The Development of an Analytical Tool," *Review of Income and Wealth* 21, no. 2 (1975): pp. 153–81.

85. Ibid., p. 160.

86. Steven Landefeld, "GDP: One of the Great Inventions of the 20th Century," *Bureau of Economic Analysis Survey of Current Business* (2000): pp. 7–14.

87. Carson, "The History of the United States National Income Accounts," pp. 156–57.

88. Simon Kuznets, "Modern Economic Growth: Findings and Reflections," *American Economic Association* 63, no. 3 (1973): pp. 247–58.

89. Kuznets, "Economic Growth and Income Inequality," p. 31.

90. Daron Acemoglu and James Robinson, *Why Nations Fail: The Origins of Power, Prosperity, and Poverty* (New York: Crown, 2012).

91. Ibid., pp. 402–3.

92. Ibid., pp. 43–44.

93. Ibid., p. 42.

94. Ibid., pp. 75–76.

95. Vito Tanzi and Ludger Schuknecht, *Public Spending in the 20th Century: A Global Perspective* (New York: Cambridge University Press, 2000), p. 6.

96. Max Weber, "Politics as a Vocation," in *Max Weber: Selections in Translation*, ed. W. G. Runciman, trans. Eric Matthews (New York: Cambridge University Press, 2011), pp. 212–25.

97. See data on "Expense (% of GDP)" in World Bank, 2015 *World Development Indicators* (Washington, DC: World Bank, 2015).

98. Daron Acemoglu and James A. Robinson, "The Political Economy of the Kuznets Curve," *Review of Development Economics* 6, no. 2 (2002): pp. 183–203.

99. Charles I. Jones, "U.S. Economic Growth in a World of Ideas," *American Economic Review* 92, no. 1 (2002): pp. 220–39.

100. Ibid., p. 226.

101. James Flynn, "The Mean IQ of Americans: Massive Gains 1932 to 1978," *Psychological Bulletin* 99 (1984): pp. 29–51.

102. Clancy Blair, David Gamson, Steven Thorne, and David Baker, "Rising Mean IQ: Cognitive Demand of Mathematics Education for Young Children, Population Exposure to Formal Schooling, and the Neurobiology of the Prefrontal Cortex," *Intelligence* 33, no. 1 (2005): pp. 93–106.

103. Jones, "U.S. Economic Growth in a World of Ideas," p. 228.

104. Goldin and Katz, *The Race Between Education and Technology*.

105. John R. Lott, Jr. "Why Is Education Publicly Provided? A Critical Survey," *Cato Journal* 7, no. 2 (1987): pp. 475–501.

106. Milton Friedman, "The Role of Government in Education," in *Economics and the Public Interest*, ed. Robert A. Solo (New Brunswick, NJ: Rutgers University Press, 1955).

107. Eric A. Hanushek and Ludger Woessmann, "How Much Do Educational Outcomes Matter in OECD Countries?" *Economic Policy* (2011): pp. 427–91.

108. Harvey Brooks, "National Science Policy and Technological Innovation," in *The Positive Sum Strategy: Harnessing Technology for Economic Growth*, ed. Ralph Landau and Nathan Rosenberg (Washington, DC: National Academies Press, 1986).

109. Stephen W. MacMahon, Jeffrey A. Cutler, Curt D. Furberg, and Gerald H. Payne, "The Effects of Drug Treatment for Hypertension on Morbidity and Mortality from Cardiovascular Disease: A Review of Randomized Controlled Trials," *Progress in Cardiovascular Diseases* 29, no. 3 (1986): pp. 99–118.

110. Cutler, Deaton, and Lleras-Muney, "Determinants of Mortality," p. 104.

111. Brooks, "National Science Policy and Technological Innovation," p. 121.

112. Ibid., p. 119.

113. David Bollier, *Public Assets, Private Profits: Reclaiming the American Commons in an Age of Market Enclosure* (Washington, DC: New America Foundation, 2001), p. 49.

114. Alperovitz and Daly, *Unjust Deserts*, p. 76.

115. National Science Board, *Science and Engineering Indicators 2012*, chap. 5, p. 8.

116. Bollier, *Public Assets, Private Profits*, p. 50.

117. Brooks, "National Science Policy and Technological Innovation," pp. 121–23.

118. Ibid., pp. 123–24.

119. Hall and Jones, "Why Do Some Countries Produce So Much More Output Per Worker Than Others?" p. 114.

120. Albert Fishlow, "Transportation in the 19th and Early 20th Centuries," in *The Cambridge Economic History of the United States*, vol. 2, *The Long Nineteenth Century*, ed. Stanley L. Engerman and Robert E. Gallman (New York: Cambridge

University Press, 2000), p. 601. The Nobel laureate Robert Fogel tried to produce a calculation of the economic effect of the railroads, however, and sparked a continuing controversy within economics about just how important they were. Robert Fogel, "Notes on the Social Saving Controversy," *Journal of Economic History* 39, no. 1 (1979): pp. 1–54.

121. "Improving Transportation," The U.S. Army Corps of Engineers: A Brief History," www.usace.army.mil/About/History/BriefHistoryoftheCorps/Improving Transportation.aspx.

122. Ibid.

123. Gordon, "Is U.S. Economic Growth Over?" pp. 8–9.

124. Alperovitz and Daly, *Unjust Deserts*.

125. E. S. Lincoln, *A Chronological History of Electrical Development* (New York: National Electrical Manufacturers Association, 1946).

126. Richard R. Nelson and Gavin Wright, "The Rise and Fall of American Technological Leadership: The Postwar Era in Historical Perspective," *Journal of Economic Literature* 30, no. 4 (1992): pp. 1931–62.

127. Richard F. Weingroff, "The Man Who Changed America, Part 1," Public Roads 66.5 (2003).

128. Alperovitz and Daly, *Unjust Deserts*, p. 19.

THREE: The Trouble with Markets

1. In the lingo of economists, these goods are "nonexcludable."

2. Quoted in Joseph E. Stiglitz, "Knowledge as a Global Public Good," in *Global Public Goods: International Cooperation in the 21st Century*, ed. Inge Kaul, Isabelle Grunberg, and Marc Stern (New York: United Nations Development Programme, 1999), p. 308.

3. Adam Smith, *An Inquiry into the Nature and Causes of the Wealth of Nations*, ed. Charles J. Bullock (Edinburgh, Scot.: Stevenson, 1843) Bk. I, Ch. 2.

4. The careful reader will note that positive externality arguments morph into public goods arguments as the private benefits decline relative to the public benefits. The market won't produce pure public goods at all. Most products yielding positive externalities can sustain private markets (for example, purely private education markets), but these markets will generally be much smaller than we should want them to be.

5. David Firestone, "Romney in Ohio: Want College? Can't Afford It? Too Bad," *Taking Note Blog* (blog), *New York Times*, March 5, 2012, takingnoteblog.nytimes.com/2012/03/05/Romney-in-ohio-want-college-cant-afford-it-too-bad.

6. There are other big problems too. One, which we discuss later in this chapter, is myopia: Prospective students are likely to systematically underestimate their personal gains from education. Moreover, without government intervention, there will be formidable difficulties in constructing loan markets for those with very limited assets who wish to invest in the development of their own human capital.

7. Michael Greenstone et al., "Lower Pollution, Longer Lives: Life Expectancy Gains If India Reduced Particulate Matter Pollution," *Economic and Political Weekly* 1, no. 8, (2015): pp. 41–46.

8. *State of the Air 2014* (report by the American Lung Association, 2014), www.stateoftheair.org/2014/assets/ALA-SOTA-2014-Full.pdf.

9. The following is from EPA, *"The Benefits and Costs of the Clean Air Act from 1990 to 2020* (Final Report of the Environmental Protection Agency, April 2011).

10. All figures from Daniel Bell, *The Coming of Post-Industrial Society: A Venture in Social Forecasting* (New York: Basic Books, 1973), p. 171.

11. Census data reported by the EPA, accessed October 1, 2014, at http://cfpub .epa.gov/eroe/index.cfm?fuseaction=detail.viewInd&lv=list.listByAlpha&r= 239789&subtop=225.

12. Although beyond a certain point (which we have long since reached), it turns out that part of the solution to this problem is even greater density—since sprawl is particularly damaging to the environment.

13. For an excellent introduction to the recent debate about lead and crime, see Kevin Drum, "America's Real Criminal Element: Lead," *Mother Jones*, January/ February 2013.

14. Jonathan Levy, Jonathan Buonocore, and Katherine von Stackelberg, "The Public Health Costs of Traffic Congestion: A Health Risk Assessment," *Environmental Health* 9, no. 65 (2010).

15. For a broad overview of the data, see Shlomo Angel, *Planet of Cities* (Cambridge, MA: Lincoln Institute of Land Policy, 2012), chap. 6.

16. Enrico Moretti, *The New Geography of Jobs* (New York: Houghton Mifflin, 2012); Edward Glaeser, *Triumph of the City* (New York: Penguin Press, 2011).

17. Henry Adams, *The Education of Henry Adams: An Autobiography* (Boston and New York: Houghton Mifflin, 1918), pp. 494–95.

18. MG Sieler, "Eric Schmidt: Every 2 Days We Create as Much Information as We Did up to 2003," *Tech Crunch*, http://techcrunch.com/2010/08/04/schmidt-data.

19. Derek de Solla Price, *Science Since Babylon* (New Haven, CT: Yale University Press, 1961). For a nice discussion, see Bell, *Coming of Post-Industrial Society*, pp. 177–87.

20. Dennis Overbye, "Chasing the Higgs," *New York Times*, March 4, 2013.

21. Alexis C. Madrigal, "Reading the Privacy Policies You Encounter in a Year Would Take 76 Workdays," *Atlantic*, March 1, 2012, www.theatlantic.com /technology/archive/2012/03/reading-the-privacy-policies-you-encounter-in -a-year-would-take-76-work-days/253851.

22. *AT&T Mobility LLC v. Concepcion*, 563 U.S. 321, 2011; Melissa Bell, "Know What You're Signing Before Clicking 'I Accept,'" *Washington Post*, August 12, 2011.

23. Daniel Kahneman, *Thinking, Fast and Slow* (New York: Farrar, Straus and Giroux, 2011). See also Richard H. Thaler and Cass R. Sunstein, *Nudge: Improving Decisions About Health, Wealth, and Happiness* (New Haven, CT: Yale University Press, 2008).

24. Kahneman, *Thinking, Fast and Slow.*

25. In one famous study, participants were asked to draw a number randomly before being asked to estimate the solution to a problem. Those who drew higher numbers in the random drawing gave much higher estimates of the answer to the problem, even though the two tasks clearly had nothing to do with each other.

26. Brigitte C. Madrian and Dennis F. Shea, "The Power of Suggestion: Inertia in 401(k) Participation and Savings Behavior," *Quarterly Journal of Economics* 116, no. 4 (2001): pp. 1149–87.

27. Thaler and Sunstein, *Nudge*, p. 75.

28. It is worth noting that many conservatives are quick to attack such behavior when they think it leads to public overconsumption ("entitlements," "takers"), but they are resolutely silent when it leads to private overconsumption.

29. Kahneman, *Thinking, Fast and Slow*, pp. 138–39.
30. Ola Svenson, "Are We All Less Risky and More Skillful Than Our Fellow Drivers?" *Acta Psychologica* 47 (1981): pp. 143–48; K. Patricia Cross, "Not Can, but Will College Teaching Be Improved?" *New Directions for Higher Education* (1977): pp. 1–15.
31. Stan Luger, *Corporate Power, American Democracy, and the Automobile Industry* (Cambridge: Cambridge University Press, 2000), p. 61. This discussion relies on Luger's account, pp. 54–75.
32. National Highway Traffic Safety Administration (NHTSA), *An Analysis of the Significant Decline in Motor Vehicle Traffic Fatalities in 2008* (Washington, DC: NHTSA, June 2010), p. 27.
33. Though here, as in so many areas, the relative performance of the United States has declined over time. Most rich countries have made much greater progress on traffic safety in the last generation. Transportation Research Board of the National Academies, *Achieving Traffic Safety Goals in the United States: Lessons from Other Nations* (Special Report, 2011).
34. NHTSA, *Lives Saved Calculations for Seatbelts and Frontal Airbags* (Department of Transportation, Report, December 2009).
35. "Childhood Obesity Facts," Centers for Disease Control and Prevention, August 2015, www.cdc.gov/healthyyouth/obesity/facts.htm.
36. George A. Akerlof and Robert J. Shiller, *Phishing for Phools: The Economics of Manipulation and Deception* (Princeton, NJ: Princeton University Press, 2015).
37. Jennifer Erickson and David Madland, "Retirement Labels and Retirement Receipts Could Save American Investors Billions Each Year," Center for American Progress, July, 1, 2015, www.americanprogress.org/issues/economy/news/2015/07/01/115509/retirement-labels-and-retirement-receipts-could-save-american-investors-billions-each-year/
38. Thaler and Sunstein, *Nudge*, p. 144.
39. Akerlof and Shiller, *Phishing for Phools*, p. 150.
40. Paul Starr, "Liberalism After Socialism," *American Prospect*, Fall 1991, http://prospect.org/article/liberalism-after-socialism.
41. Alicia H. Munnell, Wenliang Houand, and Anthony Webb, "NRRI Update Shows Half Still Falling Short" (brief by the Center for Retirement and Research, December 2014).
42. Milton Friedman, "A Monetary and Fiscal Framework for Economic Stability," *American Economic Review* 3 (1948): pp. 245–64.
43. Quoted in John Cassidy, *How Markets Fail: The Logic of Economic Calamities* (New York: Farrar, Straus and Giroux, 2009), p. 11.
44. Smith, *Wealth of Nations*, Bk. I, Ch. 10.
45. Boucoyannis, "The Equalizing Hand."
46. Quoted in Luigi Zingales, *A Capitalism for the People: Recapturing the Lost Genius of American Prosperity* (New York: Basic Books, 2012), p. 38.
47. Quoted in Steve Fraser, *Wall Street: A Cultural History* (London: Faber and Faber, 2005), p. 158.
48. Joseph Stiglitz, *The Price of Inequality: How Today's Divided Society Endangers Our Future* (New York: Norton, 2012).
49. Daniel Carpenter and David A. Moss, "Introduction," in *Preventing Regulatory Capture: Special Interest Influence and How to Limit It*, ed. Carpenter and Moss (Cambridge: Cambridge University Press, 2013), pp. 1–22.

50. EPA, "Coal Ash Basics," Environmental Protection Agency, accessed October 1, 2015, www2.epa.gov/coalash/coal-ash-basics.
51. EPA, "Electricity Sector Emissions," Environmental Protection Agency, accessed October 1, 2015, www3.epa.gov/climatechange/ghgemissions/sources /electricity.html; Jennifer Duggan and Craig Segall, "Closing the Floodgates: How the Coal Industry Is Poisoning Our Water and How We Can Stop It" (report by the Environmental Integrity Project and the Sierra Club, 2013), p. 1.
52. Nicholas Z. Muller, Robert Mendelsohn, and William Nordhaus, "Environmental Accounting for Pollution in the United States Economy," *American Economic Review* 101 (August 2011): pp. 1649–75. To be clear, the implication of Nordhaus's analysis is not that coal should not be produced at all, but that it should be far more expensive (which would lower but not eliminate demand) than it is.
53. John Kenneth Galbraith, *American Capitalism: The Concept of Countervailing Power* (Houghton, 1952).
54. Zingales, *Capitalism for the People*.
55. Ibid., p. 221.
56. Luigi Zingales, "Does Finance Benefit Society?" January 2015, http://faculty .chicagobooth.edu/luigizingales/papers/research/finance.pdf.

FOUR: How America Got Rich

1. *Time*, April, 3, 1944, pp. 1, 52–57. The cover is accessible at http://content.time .com/time/covers/0,16641,19440403,00.html.
2. G. Pascal Zachary, *Endless Frontier: Vannevar Bush, Engineer of the American Century* (New York: Free Press, 1997), p. 183.
3. Ibid., p. 52.
4. Ibid., pp. 250–59.
5. Ibid. p. 369.
6. Vannevar Bush, *Science: The Endless Frontier: A Report to the President by Vannevar Bush, Director of the Office of Scientific Research and Development, July 1945* (Washington, DC: US Government Printing Office, 1945).
7. Zachary, *Endless Frontier*, p. 260.
8. J. William Fulbright, "The War and Its Effects: The Military-Industrial-Academic Complex" in *Super-State: Readings in the Military-Industrial Complex*, ed. Herbert I. Schiller and Joseph D. Phillips (Urbana: Univerisity og Illinois Press, 1970) pp. 171–77.
9. James Ledbetter, "Guest Post: James Ledbetter on 50 Years of the 'Military-Industrial Complex,'" *Schott's Vocab* (blog), *New York Times*, January 25, 2011, http://schott.blogs.nytimes.com/2011/01/25/guest-post-james-ledbetter -on-50-years-of-the-military-industrial-complex/?_r=0. Henry Giroux claims (without direct evidence) that Eisenhower initially used the phrase "military-industrial-academic." Henry Giroux, *University in Chains: Confronting the Military-Industrial-Academic Complex (The Radical Imagination)* (London: Routledge, 2007).
10. Zachary, *Endless Frontier*, p. 241.
11. Ibid., p. 218.
12. Arthur H. Frazier, *United States Standards of Weights and Measures: Their Creation and Creators* (Washington, DC: Smithsonian Institution Press, 1978).

13. Gordon G. Lee, "The Morrill Act and Education," *British Journal of Educational Studies* 12, no. 1 (1963): pp. 19–40.

14. Ibid., pp. 28–29; Mark R. Nemec, "The Morrill Act of 1862 and Coordination Shaping the American University and the American State," in *Ivory Towers and Nationalist Minds* (Ann Arbor: University of Michigan Press, 2006), p. 64.

15. Claudia Goldin and Lawrence Katz, *The Race Between Education and Technology* (Cambridge, MA: Harvard University Press, 2010), pp. 257–58.

16. Zachary, *Endless Frontier*, p. 183.

17. Ibid., p. 115.

18. Bush, *Science*.

19. Zachary, *Endless Frontier*, p. 369.

20. David Mayhew, "The Long 1950s as a Policy Era," in *The Politics of Major Policy Reform in Postwar America*, ed. Jeffrey A. Jenkins and Sidney M. Milkis (Cambridge: Cambridge University Press, 2014), pp. 4–11.

21. Jennifer Delton, "Rethinking Post-World War II Anticommunism," *Journal of the Historical Society* 10, no. 1 (2010): pp. 1–41.

22. Goldin and Katz, *The Race Between Education and Technology*, p. 4.

23. Robert Gordon, "Is U.S. Economic Growth Over? Faltering Innovation Confronts the Six Headwinds," (working paper, National Bureau of Economic Research, Cambridge, MA 2012) p. 1; Robert Shackleton, "Total Factor Productivity Growth in Historical Perspective," (working paper, US Congressional Budget Office, Washington, DC, 2013).

24. Nelson W. Polsby, *Political Innovation in America: The Politics of Policy Initiation* (New Haven, CT: Yale University Press, 1985); William A. Blanpied, "Science and Technology in Times of Transition: the 1940s and 1990s," in *Science & Engineering Indicators 2000* (Washington, DC: National Science Foundation, 2000), pp. 1–4.

25. Richard F. Weingroff, "Federal-Aid Highway Act of 1956: Creating the Interstate System," *Public Roads* 60, no. 1 (1996).

26. Arthur A. Goldsmith, "Economic Rights and Government in Developing Countries: Cross-National Evidence on Growth and Development," *Studies in Comparative International Development* 32, no. 2 (1997): pp. 29–44.

27. Joseph E. Stiglitz, "Some Lessons from the East Asian Miracle," *World Bank Research Observer* 11, no. 2 (1996): pp. 151–176.

28. Andrew Sheng and Xiao Geng, "The Night-Watchman State's Last Shift," Project Syndicate, May 22, 2013, www.project-syndicate.org/commentary/reframing-the-state-market-relationship-by-andrew-sheng-and-geng-xiao.

29. Milton Friedman, *Bright Promises, Dismal Performance—An Economist's Protest* (San Diego: Harcourt Brace Jovanovich, 1983), p. 61.

30. "US Real Per Capita GDP from 1870–2001," *Social Democracy for the 21st Century: A Post Keynesian Perspective* (blog), September 24, 2012 http://socialdemocracy21stcentury.blogspot.com/2012/09/US-real-per-capita-gdp-from-18702001.html; N. S. Balke and R. J. Gordon, "The Estimation of Prewar Gross National Product: Methodology and New Evidence," *Journal of Political Economy* 97, no. 1 (1989): pp. 38–92; Angus Maddison, *The World Economy: Historical Statistics* (Paris: Organization of Economic Cooperation and Development, 2003).

31. Dora L. Costa and Richard H. Steckel, "Long-Term Trends in Health, Welfare, and Economic Growth in the United States" in *Health and Welfare During In-*

dustralization, ed. Richard H. Steckel and Roderick Floud (Chicago: University of Chicago Press, 1996), pp. 47–90.

32. Richard A. Epstein, *The Classical Liberal Constitution* (Cambridge, MA: Harvard University Press, 2014); Folsom, *Myth of the Robber Barons*; Larry Schweikart and Lynne Pierson Doti, *American Entrepreneur: The Fascinating Stories of the People Who Defined Business in the United States* (New York: AMACOM, 2009); Max M. Edling, *A Revolution in Favor of Government: Origins of the U.S. Constitution and the Making of the American State* (New York: Oxford University Press, 2003), pp. 9–11.

33. Edling, *Revolution in Favor of Government*.

34. Ibid., 132; David Brian Robertson, *The Constitution and America's Destiny* (Cambridge: Cambridge University Press, 2005), p. 52.

35. Robertson, *Constitution and America's Destiny*, pp. 86–87.

36. David Brian Robertson, *The Original Compromise: What the Constitution's Framers Were Really Thinking* (New York: Oxford University Press, 2013), pp. 4–5.

37. Ibid., pp. 225–29.

38. Henry Adams, *History of the United States During the Second Administration of James Madison*, vol. 3 (New York: Charles Scribner's Sons, 1921), p. 195.

39. Erik Reinert, *How Rich Countries Got Rich and Why Poor Countries Stay Poor* (London: Constable, 2007), p. 23.

40. George Washington, "Washington's Farewell Address 1796," the Avalon Project, Yale Law School, http://avalon.law.yale.edu/18th_century/washing.asp.

41. Brian Balogh, *A Government Out of Sight: The Mystery of National Authority in Nineteenth-Century America* (New York: Cambridge University Press, 2009).

42. "That government is best which governs least. (Quotation)" the Jefferson Monticello, accessed October 1, 2015, https://www.monticello.org/site/jefferson/government-best-which-governs-least-quotation.

43. Edling, *Revolution in Favor of Government*, pp. 216–18.

44. Balogh, *A Government Out of Sight*, p. 117.

45. Ibid., pp. 122–130.

46. Robert J. Allison, "The Communications Revolution," *Reviews in American History* 24, no. 4 (1996): pp. 596–600.

47. Balogh, *A Government Out of Sight*, pp. 167–80; "Historical Statistics of the United States: Colonial Times to 1970, Part 2" (Washington, DC: US Census Bureau, 1975); "Milestones: 1801–1929," US Department of State, accessed October 1, 2015, https://history.state.gov/milestones/1801-1829/louisiana-purchase.

48. Though Jefferson was in Paris when the public-schools section was added to his initial draft. John M. Merriam, "The Legislative History of the Ordinance of 1787," Proceedings of the American Antiquarian Society (April 1888), 314.

49. Thomas K. McCraw, *The Founders and Finance: How Hamilton, Gallatin, and Other Immigrants Forged a New Economy* (Cambridge, MA: Belknap Press, 2012), p. 248.

50. Richard White, *Railroaded: The Transcontinentals and the Making of Modern America* (New York: W. W. Norton, 2011), p. 24.

51. McCraw, *Founders and Finance*, p. 248.

52. Guy S. Callender, "The Early Transportation and Banking Enterprises of the States in Relation to the Growth of Corporations," *Quarterly Journal of Economics* 27 (1902).

53. Ibid., p. 6.

54. Goldin and Katz, *The Race Between Education and Technology*, p. 132.

55. Ibid., p. 134.

56. Ibid., p. 162.

57. Maury Klein, "The Robber Barons' Bum Rap," *City Journal* (Winter 1995): www .city-journal.org/html/5_1_a2.html. Also, Folsom, *Myth of the Robber Barons*.

58. Christopher Levenick, "Seven Myths about the Great Philanthropists," *Philan-thropy*, Winter 2011, www.philanthropyroundtable.org/topic/excellence_in _philanthropy/seven_myths_about_the_great_philanthropists.

59. J. Bradford DeLong, "Robber Barons" (working paper, National Bureau of Eco-nomic Research, Cambridge, MA, 1997), p. 1.

60. Albro Martin, "Railroads and the Equity Receivership: An Essay on Institu-tional Change," *Journal of Economic History* 34, no. 3 (1974): pp. 685–709.

61. Allen D. Boyer, "Activist Shareholders, Corporate Directors, and Institutional Investment: Some Lessons from the Robber Barons," *Washington and Lee Law Review* 50, no. 3 (1993): pp. 977–1042, 1007–9.

62. Edward L. Glaeser and Andrei Shleifer, "The Rise of the Regulatory State," *Journal of Economic Literature* 41, no. 2 (2003): pp. 401–25.

63. Martin, "Railroads and the Equity Receivership," p. 685.

64. R. Christopher Whalen, *Inflated: How Money and Debt Built the American Dream* (New York: Wiley, 2010), pp. 46–49.

65. Charles W. Calomiris, *U.S. Bank Deregulation in Historical Perspective* (New York: Cambridge University Press, 2006), pp. 141–46.

66. "US Business Cycle Expansions and Contractions," National Bureau of Eco-nomic Research, accessed October 1, 2015, www.nber.org/cycles.html; Victor Zarnowitz, *Business Cycles: Theory, History, Indicators, and Forecasting* (Chi-cago: University of Chicago Press, 1992), pp. 221, 226.

67. Burton W. Folsom, *The Myth of the Robber Barons: A New Look at the Rise of Big Business in America* (Herndon, VA: Young America's Foundation, 1987).

68. Matthew Josephson, *The Robber Barons: The Great American Capitalists, 1861–1901* (San Diego: Harcourt, 1934), p. 354.

69. Thomas Piketty, *Capital in the Twenty-First Century*, trans. Arthur Goldhammer (Cambridge, MA: Belknap Press, 2014), pp. 347–50.

70. Thomas Jefferson, "Jefferson to Madison: Fontainebleau Oct 28, 1785" in *The Republic of Letters: The Correspondence Between Thomas Jefferson and James Madison*, ed. James Morton Smith (New York: Norton, 1985), p. 390.

71. John Adams, "John Adams to James Sullivan: 26 May 1776" in *The Founders' Constitution*, accessed October 1, 2015, via University of Chicago Press, http:// press-pubs.uchicago.edu/founders/documents/v1ch13s10.html; John Adams, *A Defence of the Constitutions of Government of the United States*, Volume 1 (Phil-adelphia: Budd and Bartram, 1797), p. 182.

72. Noah Webster, "Examination by Noah Webster" in *Pamphlets on the Constitu-tion of the United States: Published During Its Discussion by the People, 1787–1788*, ed. Paul Leicester Ford (Brooklyn: 1888), p. 59.

73. Ralph L. Nelson, *Merger Movements in American Industry 1895–1956* (Washing-ton, DC: National Bureau of Economic Research, 1959), pp. 100–3.

74. Alfred D. Chandler, "The Information Age in Historical Perspective," in *A Na-tion Transformed by Information: How Information Has Shaped the United States*

from Colonial Times to the Present, ed. Alfred D. Chandler and James W. Cortada (New York: Oxford University Press, 2000), pp. 10–13.

75. Richard R. John, "Recasting the Information Infrastructure for the Industrial Age," in *A Nation Transformed by Information: How Information Has Shaped the United States from Colonial Times to the Present*, ed. Alfred D. Chandler and James W. Cortada (New York: Oxford University Press, 2000).
76. Ibid., p. 75.
77. White, *Railroaded*, p. 234.
78. Ibid., pp. 22–23.
79. Ibid., p. 512.
80. John Fabian Witt, *The Accidental Republic: Crippled Workingmen, Destitute Widows, and the Remaking of American Law* (Cambridge, MA: Harvard University Press, 2006).
81. White, *Railroaded*, pp. 463–65.
82. Ibid., p. 254.
83. Theodore Roosevelt, "Theodore Roosevelt Defines His New Nationalism Platform, Osawatomie, Kansas, August 31, 1910," in *Live from the Campaign Trail: The Greatest Presidential Campaign Speeches of the Twentieth Century and How They Shaped Modern America*, ed. Michael A. Cohen (New York: Walker, 2008), p. 47.
84. Glaeser and Shleifer, "The Rise of the Regulatory State," pp. 407–8.
85. Richard H. K. Vietor, "Government Regulation of Business," in *Cambridge Economic History of the United States*, ed. S. L. Engerman and R. E. Gallman (New York: Cambridge University Press, 2000), pp. 969–1012.
86. Melvin I. Urofsky, *Louis D. Brandeis: A Life* (New York: Schocken, 2012); Brian Balogh, *A Government Out of Sight*, pp. 330–31.
87. Balogh, *A Government Out of Sight*, pp. 15–16.
88. *Louis K. Liggett Co. v. Lee*, U.S. 301 (1933).
89. Michael D. Reagan, "The Political Structure of the Federal Reserve System," *American Political Science Review* 55, no. 1 (1961): pp. 64–76, 66.
90. Robert Kuttner, *Debtors' Prison: The Politics of Austerity Versus Possibility* (New York: Random House, 2013), pp. 17–18.
91. "FDR: From Budget Balancer to Keynesian," FDR Library and Museum, accessed October 1, 2015, www.fdrlibrary.marist.edu/aboutfdr/budget.html; Douglas Irwin, "What Caused the Recession of 1937–38?," Center for Economic and Policy Research, November 6, 2015, www.voxeu.org/article/what-caused-recession-1937-38-new-lesson-today-s-policymakers.
92. Robert Shackleton, "Total Factor Productivity Growth in Historical Perspective," (working paper, US Congressional Budget Office, Washington, DC, 2013), p. 5.
93. Federal Works Agency, *Final Report on the WPA Program, 1935–1943* (Washington, DC: US Government Printing Office, 1946), pp. 134–36.
94. Carol Ballentine, "Taste of Raspberries, Taste of Death: The 1937 Elixir Sulfanilamide Incident," *FDA Consumer Magazine*, June 1981, www.fda.gov/aboutfda/whatwedo/history/productregulation/sulfanilamidedisaster/default.htm.
95. Frank Levy and Peter Temin, "Inequality and Institutions in 20th Century America" (working paper, National Bureau of Economic Research, Cambridge, MA, 2007).
96. Carolyn Jones, "Mass-Based Income Taxation: Creating a Taxpaying Culture, 1940–1952," in *Funding the Modern American State, 1941–1995: The Rise and*

Fall of the Era of Easy Finance, ed. W. Elliot Brownlee (Cambridge: Cambridge University Press, 1996): pp. 107–47.

97. Theodore R. Marmor, Jerry L. Mashaw, and Philip L. Harvey, *America's Misunderstood Welfare State: Persistent Myths, Enduring Realities* (New York: Basic, 1992), p. 31.

98. Michele Landis Dauber, *The Sympathetic State: Disaster Relief and the Origins of the American Welfare State* (Chicago: University of Chicago Press, 2012); Theda Skocpol, *Protecting Soldiers and Mothers: The Political Origins of Social Policy in United States* (Cambridge, MA: Belknap Press, 1995); Balogh, *A Government Out of Sight*, p. 3.

99. Balogh, *A Government Out of Sight*, p. 363; Jacob S. Hacker and Paul Pierson, "Business Power and Social Policy: Employers and the Formation of the American Welfare State," *Politics and Society* 30, no. 2 (2002): pp. 277–325.

100. Edwin Amenta, *Bold Relief* (Princeton, NJ: Princeton University Press, 2000); Daniel T. Rodgers, *Atlantic Crossings: Social Politics in a Progressive Age* (Cambridge, MA: Belknap Press, 2000).

101. Friedrich August Hayek, *The Road to Serfdom* (New York: Routledge, 1944).

102. Roy Lubove, *The Struggle for Social Security* (Cambridge, MA: Harvard University Press, 1968), p. 175.

103. Cass Sunstein, *The Second Bill of Rights: FDR's Unfinished Revolution and Why We Need It More Than Ever* (New York: Basic Books, 2006), p. 12.

104. Carl E. Horn and Herbert A. Schaffner, *Work in America: An Encyclopedia of History, Policy, and Society* (New York: ABC-CLIO, 2003), p. 471.

105. Philip Dray, *There Is Power in a Union* (New York: Anchor, 2010); Frances Perkins, *The Roosevelt I Knew* (New York, Penguin Classics, 2011), p. 220.

106. Leo Wolman, "Union Membership in Great Britain and the United States" (working paper, National Bureau of Economic Research, Cambridge, MA, 1973), p. 2; Jake Rosenfeld, *What Unions No Longer Do* (Cambridge, MA: Harvard University Press, 2014).

107. Gerald Mayer, *Union Membership Trends in the United States* (Washington, DC: Congressional Research Service, 2004), p. 11.

108. Rosenfeld, *What Unions No Longer Do*, p. 4.

109. Ibid., pp. 183–95.

110. Ibid., p. 2.

111. Vannevar Bush, *Pieces of the Action* (New York: Morrow, 1970), p. 4.

112. James T. Sparrow, *Warfare State: World War II Americans and the Age of Big Government* (New York: Oxford University Press, 2011), p. 263.

113. John Bound and Sarah Turner, "Going to War and Going to College: Did World War II and the G.I. Bill Increase Educational Attainment for Returning Veterans?" *Journal of Labor Economics* 20, no. 4 (2002): pp. 784–815.

114. Economic Policy Institute (EPI), *State of Working America*, 12th ed. (Washington, DC: EPI, 2012), p. 59.

115. Dominick Pratico, *Eisenhower and Social Security: The Origins of the Disability Program* (Lincoln, NE: iUniverse, 2001).

116. Rexford Santerre and Stephen Neun, *Health Economics: Theory, Insights, and Industry Studies* (South-Western College, 2009), p. 345.

117. Pratico, *Eisenhower and Social Security*.

118. Frank Fitzpatrick, *And the Walls Came Tumbling Down: The Basketball Game*

That Changed American Sports (Lincoln: University of Nebraska Press, 2000), pp. 113–14.

119. Ibid., p. 33.

120. Frank Fitzpatrick, "Texas Western's 1966 Title Left Lasting Legacy," *ESPN Classic*, November 19, 2003, https://espn.go.com/classic/s/013101_texas_western _fitzpatrick.html.

121. Fitzpatrick, *Walls Came Tumbling Down*, p. 26.

122. Ibid., p. 121.

123. Sandra Day O'Connor, *The Majesty of the Law: Reflections of a Supreme Court Justice* (New York: Random House, 2007), p. 136.

124. Putting aside the creation of Medicaid, the major programs of the War on Poverty were the Food Stamps Act of 1964, the Economic Opportunity Act of 1964 (Job Corps; Volunteers in Service to America, or VISTA; the federal work-study program; creation of the Office of Economic Opportunity), and the Elementary and Secondary Education Act of 1965. Only food stamps counts as direct income support.

125. David Brooks, *Bobos in Paradise: The New Upper Class and How They Got There* (New York: Simon & Schuster, 2000), pp. 25–26.

126. Ibid.

127. Nicholas Lemann, *The Big Test: The Secret History of the American Meritocracy* (New York: Farrar, Straus and Giroux: 1999), p. 121.

128. Ibid.

129. Camille L. Ryan and Julie Siebens, *Educational Attainment in the United States: 2009* (Washington, DC: US Census Bureau, 2012), p. 3.

130. Walter W. McMahon, *Higher Learning, Greater Good: The Private and Social Benefits of Higher Education* (Baltimore: Johns Hopkins University Press, 2009), pp. 301–2.

131. Pell Institute, *Reflections on Pell: Championing Social Justice Through 40 Years of Educational Opportunity* (Washington, DC: Pell Institute, 2003), p. 53.

132   Ibid., p. 45.

133. Franklin D. Roosevelt, "Message to the Conference on Economic Conditions of the South," July 4, 1938, *The American Presidency Project*, ed. Gerhard Peters and John T. Woolley, www.presidency.ucsb.edu/ws/?pid=15670.

134. National Emergency Council, *Report on Economic Conditions of the South* (Washington, DC: US Government Printing Office, 1938), p. 29.

135. FRED, "State and Regional Personal Income Per Capita" (Federal Reserve Economic Data, Economic Research Division, Federal Reserve Bank of St. Louis, updated February 2, 2015), accessible at http://research.stlouisfed.org/fred2.

136. Gunnar Myrdal, *An American Dilemma: The Negro Problem and Modern Democracy* (New Brunswick, NJ: Transaction, 1944), p. 951.

137. Timothy Besley, Torsten Persson, and Daniel Sturm, "Political Competition and Economic Performance: Theory and Evidence from the United States" (discussion paper, Department of Economics, University of Munich, Ger., 2006), pp. 17–19.

138. FRED, "State and Regional Personal Income Per Capita."

139. Jac C. Heckelman, "Income Convergence Among U.S. States: Cross-Sectional and Time Series Evidence," *Canadian Journal of Economics* 46, no. 3 (2013): pp. 1085–109.

140. Gavin Wright, "The New Deal and the Modernization of the South," *Federal History* (2010): pp. 58–73.

141. Ibid., pp. 66–67.

142. John S. Kiernan, "2015's States Most & Least Dependent on the Federal Gov-

ernment," *WalletHub*, https://wallethub.com/edu/states-most-least-dependent
-on-the-federal-government/2700/#main-findings.

143. Glaeser and Shleifer, "Rise of the Regulatory State," pp. 993–95.
144. Ibid., pp. 990–91.
145. Price V. Fishback, "Social Welfare Expenditures in the U.S and the Nordic Countries 1900–2003" (working paper, National Bureau of Economic Research, Cambridge, MA, 2010), pp. 17–18.
146. US Department of Health and Human Services, *The Health Consequences of Smoking: 50 Years of Progress. A Report of the Surgeon General* (Atlanta: US Department of Health and Human Services, Centers for Disease Control and Prevention, National Center for Chronic Disease Prevention and Health Promotion, Office on Smoking and Health, 2014).
147. Ibid., p. 801.
148. Ibid., pp. 701–5.
149. Ibid., p. 7.
150. CDC, "Smoking & Tobacco Use: Fast Facts," Centers for Disease Control and Prevention, accessed October, 1, 2015, www.cdc.gov/tobacco/data_statistics/fact _sheets/fast_facts.
151. *The Health Consequences of Smoking*, p. 18.
152. Theodore R. Holford et al., "Tobacco Control and the Reduction in Smoking-Related Premature Deaths in the United States, 1964–2012," *Journal of the American Medical Association* 311, no. 2 (2013): pp. 164–71.
153. *The Health Consequences of Smoking*, p. 33.
154. Ibid., p. 34.
155. Benjamin Woolley, *Virtual Worlds: A Journey in Hype and Hyperreality* (New York: Science, 1993).
156. H. Peter Alesso and Craig F. Smith, *Connections: Patterns of Discovery* (Hoboken, NJ: Wiley, 2008), pp. 56–59.
157. John Markoff, "Computer Visionary Who Invented the Mouse," *New York Times*, July 3, 2013, www.nytimes.com/2013/07/04/technology/douglas-c-engelbart -inventor-of-the-computer-mouse-dies-at-88.html?_r=0.

FIVE: "An Established and Useful Reality"

1. "The Carpenter and Raskob Letters," *New York Times*, December 21, 1934, quoted in Jared A. Goldstein, "The American Liberty League and the Rise of Constitutional Nationalism," *Temple Law Review* 86 (2014): pp. 287–330.
2. Ibid.
3. Quoted in William E. Leuchtenburg, *Franklin D. Roosevelt and the New Deal, 1932–1940* (New York: Harper & Row, 1963), pp. 183–84.
4. Quoted in Kim Phillips-Fein, *Invisible Hands: The Making of the Conservative Movement from the New Deal to Reagan* (New York: W. W. Norton, 2009), p. 31.
5. Robert M. Collins, *The Business Response to Keynes, 1929–1964* (New York: Columbia University Press, 1981), p. 91.
6. Ibid.
7. Ibid., p. 93.
8. Ibid., pp. 121–22.
9. David Vogel, "Why Businessmen Distrust Their State: The Political Conscious-

ness of American Corporate Executives," *British Journal of Political Science* 8, no. 1 (1978): pp. 45–78.

10. Quoted in John B. Judis, *The Paradox of American Democracy: Elites, Special Interests, and the Betrayal of Public Trust* (New York: Routledge, 2000), p. 55.

11. Collins, *Business Response*, p. 48.

12. Ibid., p. 38.

13. Ibid., pp. 54–55.

14. Ibid., p. 78.

15. James T. Sparrow, *Warfare State: World War II Americans and the Age of Big Government* (New York: Oxford University Press, 2011), p. 122.

16. Quoted in Collins, *The Business Response to Keynes*, p. 12.

17. Sparrow, *Warfare State*, p. 127.

18. Ibid., pp. 5, 10.

19. Ibid. p. 152.

20. Ibid. pp. 146–47.

21. Robert M. Collins, *More: The Politics of Economic Growth in Postwar America* (New York: Oxford University Press), 2000, p. 42.

22. Arthur Herman, *Freedom's Forge: How American Business Produced Victory in World War II* (New York: Random House, 2012), p. 248.

23. Quoted in Mark S. Mizruchi, *The Fracturing of the American Corporate Elite* (Cambridge, MA: Harvard University Press, 2013), p. 42.

24. Kim McQuaid, *Uneasy Partners: Big Business and American Politics, 1945–1990* (Baltimore: Johns Hopkins University Press, 1994), p. 15.

25. Our discussion of the CED draws heavily on the excellent accounts in Collins, *Business Response to Keynes*; Judis, *Paradox of American Democracy*; and Mizruchi, *American Corporate Elite*.

26. Collins, *Business Response*, p. 62.

27. Ibid., p. 57.

28. Quoted in Judis, *Paradox of American Democracy*, p. 67.

29. Collins, *Business Response*, p. 57.

30. Ibid., p. 206.

31. Ibid., p. 147.

32. James Weinstein, *The Corporate Ideal in the Liberal State, 1900–1918* (Boston: Beacon Press, 1968). See also Mizruchi, *American Corporate Elite*, chap. 1.

33. Marion Bayard Folsom, "Social Security Administration Project" (Columbia University Oral History Collections, 1976), pp. 57–58.

34. Geoffrey Kabaservice, *Rule and Ruin: The Downfall of Moderation and the Destruction of the Republican Party, from Eisenhower to the Tea Party* (New York: Oxford University Press, 2012).

35. Ibid., p. 202.

36. Ibid., p. 20.

37. Samuel Lubell, *The Future of American Politics*, quoted in Sidney Blumenthal, *The Strange Death of Republican America: Chronicles of a Collapsing Party* (New York: Union Square Press, 2008), p. 13.

38. Alf Landon speech in Milwaukee, September 1936, quoted in Ed Berkowitz and Larry DeWitt, "Social Security from the New Deal to the Great Society: Expanding the Public Domain," in *Conservatism and American Political Development*, ed. Brian Glenn and Steven Teles (New York: Oxford University Press, 2009), p. 69.

39. Ira Katznelson, *Fear Itself: The New Deal and the Origins of Our Time* (New York: W. W. Norton, 2013).

40. Dwight D. Eisenhower, "Personal and confidential to Edgar Newton Eisenhower, November 8, 1954," in *The Papers of Dwight David Eisenhower*, ed. L. Galaambos and D. van Ee, doc. 1147, (Baltimore, MD: The Johns Hopkins University Press, 1996); World Wide Web facsimile by the Dwight D. Eisenhower Memorial Commission of the print edition, http://www.eisenhowermemorial .org/presidential-papers/first-term/documents/1147.cfm.

41. "President's News Conference of April 17, 1957," in Dwight D. Eisenhower, *Public Papers of the Presidents of the United States* (Washington: Office of the Federal Register, 1958), p. 284; Hal Boyle, "Milton Eisenhower in the Political Spotlight and on Political Spot," *Spokane Daily Chronicle*, October 28, 1955.

42. See for example Aaron Friedberg, *In the Shadow of the Garrison State: America's Anti-Statism and Its Cold War Grand Strategy* (Princeton, NJ: Princeton University Press, 2000).

43. Dwight D. Eisenhower, "1952 Speech to the American Federation of Labor," quoted in David M. Kotz, *The Rise and Fall of Neoliberal Capitalism* (Cambridge, MA: Harvard University Press, 2015), pp. 26–27.

44. "Annual Message Transmitting the Economic Report to Congress," January 28, 1954. Quoted in Godfrey Hodgson, *America in Our Time: From World War II to Nixon—What Happened and Why* (New York: Vintage, 1995), p. 100.

45. David Mayhew, "The Long 1950s as a Policy Era," in *The Politics of Major Policy Reform in Postwar America*, ed. Jeffrey A. Jenkins and Sidney M. Milkis (Cambridge: Cambridge University Press, 2014), p. 29, emphasis added.

46. This thesis is explored in Collins, *More*, as well as Mayhew, "Long 1950s."

47. Phillips-Fein, *Invisible Hands*, p. 141.

48. Judis, *Paradox of American Democracy*, p. 82.

49. Recording of Conversation between LBJ and Humphrey, March 2, 1965, quoted in David Brockman, "The 'Problem of Preferences': Medicare and Business Support for the Welfare State," *Studies in American Political Development* 26, no. 2 (2012).

50. Ibid.; Folsom, Oral History Collections, p. 147.

51. Collins, *More*, p. 104.

52. Allen J. Matusow, *Nixon's Economy: Booms, Busts, Dollars, and Votes* (Lawrence: University Press of Kansas), 1998, p. 3.

53. Leonard Silk, "Nixon's Program—'I Am Now a Keynesian,'" *New York Times*, January 10, 1971.

54. Richard Nixon, "Statement About Labor Day, 1969," the American Presidency Project, www.presidency.ucsb.edu/ws/?pid=2211.

55. Mizruchi, *American Corporate Elite*, pp. 153–76.

56. Barack Obama, "Obama's Remarks to the Business Roundtable," *Washington Wire* (blog), *Wall Street Journal*, March 12, 2009, http://blogs.wsj.com/washwire /2009/03/12/obamas-remarks-to-the-business-roundtable.

57. Benjamin C. Waterhouse, *Lobbying America: The Politics of Business from Nixon to NAFTA* (Princeton, NJ: Princeton University Press, 2013), pp. 257–60.

58. Ibid., p. 13.

59. Greta R. Krippner, *Capitalizing on Crisis: The Political Origins of the Rise of Finance* (Cambridge, MA: Harvard University Press, 2011), pp. 7–10.

60. Jonathan A. Knee, *The Accidental Investment Banker: Inside the Decade That Transformed Wall Street* (New York, Random House, 2007), p. xxiii.

61. Obama, "Remarks to the Business Roundtable."

62. Barack Obama, "The House Upon a Rock" (remarks on April, 14, 2009), accessible at www.whitehouse.gov/blog/2009/04/14/ldquothe-house-upon-a-rockrdquo.

63. Caren Bohan, "White House to Business: Can't We Be Friends?" *Reuters*, November 3, 2010.

64. Ibid.

65. Eamon Javers, "Inside Obama's Bank CEOs Meeting," *Politico*, April 4, 2009, www.politico.com/story/2009/04/inside-obamas-bank-ceos-meeting-020871.

66. Noreen Nielsen, "Big Polluters' Big Ad Spending in the 2012 Elections," Center for American Progress, November 7, 2012, www.americanprogressaction.org/issues/green/news/2012/11/07/44116/big-polluters-big-ad-spending-in-the-2012-elections.

67. Jonathan Alter, "Schwarzman: 'It's a War' Between Obama, Wall St." *Newsweek*, August 15, 2010, www.newsweek.com/schwarzman-its-war-between-obama-wall-st-71317?piano_t=1.

68. Dinesh D'Souza, "How Obama Thinks," *Forbes*, September 9, 2010, www.forbes.com/forbes/2010/0927/politics-socialism-capitalism-private-enterprises-obama-business-problem.html.

69. Michael Grunwald, *The New New Deal: The Hidden Story of Change in the Obama Era* (New York: Simon & Schuster, 2013), pp. 140–43.

70. Ibid., pp. 142–43.

71. Ibid., p. 19.

72. Ibid., pp. 180–205.

73. Ibid., p. 149.

74. David Lightman, "Tidal Wave of Outside Money Swamping 2010 Elections," *McClatchyDC*, October 4, 2010, www.mcclatchydc.com/news/politics-government/article24595864.html.

75. Grunwald, *New New Deal*, p. 399.

76. Mizruchi, *American Corporate Elite*, pp. 53–55.

77. Elizabeth Williamson, "Obama Slams 'Fat Cat' Bankers," *Wall Street Journal*, December 14, 2009, www.wsj.com/articles/SB126073152465089651; Rebecca Christie, "Obama's Tax Pitch: The Income Gap That Millionaires Should Fill," *BloombergBusiness*, October 6, 2010, www.bloomberg.com/news/articles/2010-10-06/obama-pre-election-tax-battle-shift-pits-millionaires-against-middle-class.

78. Arthur C. Brooks, "America's New Culture War: Free Enterprise vs. Government Control," *Washington Post*, May 23, 2010, www.washingtonpost.com/wp-dyn/content/article/2010/05/21/AR2010052101854.html.

PART II: THE CRISIS OF THE MIXED ECONOMY

SIX: American Amnesia

1. Bob Woodward, *The Agenda: Inside the Clinton White House* (New York: Simon & Schuster Paperbacks, 2005), p. 161.

2. Dwight D. Eisenhower, "To Edgar Newton Eisenhower, November 8, 1954," in

The Papers of Dwight David Eisenhower: The Presidency: The Middle Way, vol. 14, ed. Daun Van Ee (Baltimore: Johns Hopkins Press, 1996), p. 1386.

3. Woodward, *The Agenda*.

4. Dwight D. Eisenhower, "Address to Congress on the State of the Union: February 2, 1953," in *State of the Union: Presidential Rhetoric from Woodrow Wilson to George W. Bush*, ed. Deborah Kalb, Gerhard D. Peters, and John Turner Woolley (Washington, DC: CQ Press, 2007), pp. 452–65.

5. William J. Clinton, "Address Before a Joint Session of Congress on Administration Goals: February 17, 1993," in *State of the Union*, pp. 966–76.

6. Paul Samuelson, *Economics: The Original 1948 Edition* (York, PA: Maple Press, 1997), p. 39.

7. Shobhana Chandra, "Paul Samuelson, Nobel-Winning Economist, Dies at 94," *BloombergBusiness*, December 13, 2009, www.bloomberg.com/bw/stories/2009 -12-13/paul-samuelson-nobel-winning-economist-dies-at-94businessweek -business-news-stock-market-and-financial-advice.

8. Samuelson, *Economics*.

9. William F. Buckley, *God and Man at Yale: The Superstitions of "Academic Freedom"* (Washington, DC: Regnery, 1986), p. 71.

10. Mark Skousen, "The Perseverance of Paul Samuelson's Economics," *Journal of Economic Perspectives* 11, no. 2 (1997): pp. 137–52.

11. Milton Friedman, interview by John Hawkins, *Right Wing News*, February 25, 2012, http://rightwingnews.com/interviews/an-interview-with-milton-friedman-2.

12. Barry Goldwater, *The Conscience of a Conservative* (Shepherdsville, KY: Victor, 1960), p. 15.

13. Daniel T. Rodgers, *Age of Fracture* (Cambridge, MA: Belknap Press, 2011), p. 47.

14. Ibid., p. 27.

15. Ronald Reagan, "Reagan's First Inaugural: 'Government is not the solution to our problem; government is the problem.'" Heritage Foundation, January 20, 1981, www.heritage.org/initiatives/first-principles/primary-sources/reagans-first -inaugural-government-is-not-the-solution-to-our-problem-government-is -the-problem.

16. David L. George, *The Rhetoric of the Right: Language Change and the Spread of the Market* (New York: Routledge, 2013), p. 44.

17. Geoffrey Nunberg, *Talking Right: How Conservatives Turned Liberalism into a Tax-Raising, Latte-Drinking, Sushi-Eating, Volvo-Driving, New York Times-Reading, Body-Piercing, Hollywood-Loving, Left-Wing Freak Show* (New York: PublicAffairs, 2007), p. 127.

18. George, *The Rhetoric of the Right*, p. 37.

19. Ibid., pp. 116–17.

20. Ibid., p. 94.

21. John Gerring, *Party Ideologies in America, 1828–1996* (New York: Cambridge University Press, 1998), p. 234.

22. We are grateful to B. Dan Wood for providing us with this data. For more on presidential discourse about the economy, see B. Dan Wood, *The Politics of Economic Leadership: The Causes and Consequences of Presidential Rhetoric* (Princeton, NJ: Princeton University Press, 2007).

23. Jacob Jensen, Ethan Kaplan, Suresh Naidu, and Laurence Wilse-Samson, "The

Dynamics of Political Language" (conference draft, Brookings Institution, Washington, DC, September 13, 2012).

24. Angus Burgin, *The Great Persuasion: Reinventing Free Markets Since the Depression* (Cambridge, MA: Harvard University Press, 2015).

25. John Maynard Keynes, *The General Theory of Employment, Interest and Money* (New York: Lulu Press, 2013), pp. 383–84.

26. Upton Sinclair, *I, Candidate for Governor: And How I Got Licked* (Berkeley, CA: University of California Press, 1994), p. 109

27. Paul Krugman, *Peddling Prosperity: Economic Sense and Nonsense in the Age of Diminished Expectations* (New York: W. W. Norton, 1995), pp. 40–47.

28. Benjamin C. Waterhouse, *Lobbying America: The Politics of Business from Nixon to NAFTA* (Princeton, NJ: Princeton University Press, 2013), p. 137.

29. I. M. Destler, *American Trade Politics* (Washington, DC: Institute for International Economics, 2005), pp. 53–57.

30. Ibid., pp. 41–43.

31. Justin McCarthy, "Americans Name Government as No. 1 U.S. Problem," *Gallup*, March 12, 2015, www.gallup.com/poll/181946/americans-name-government-no -problem.aspx.

32. John Logan Palmer, *The Reagan Experiment: An Examination of Economic and Social Policies Under the Reagan Administration* (Washington, DC: Urban Institute, 1982), p. 109.

33. Waterhouse, *Lobbying America*, p. 202. Carter was particularly hurt because of the tendency for voters to evaluate presidential performance based on economic conditions the year prior to the election—which in Carter's case were abysmal, even though overall income growth during his tenure was relatively healthy. See Andrew Healy and Gabriel S. Lenz, "Substituting the End for the Whole: Why Voters Respond Primarily to the Election-Year Economy," *American Journal of Political Science* 58, no. 1 (2014): pp. 31–47.

34. Peter G. Peterson, *The Education of an American Dreamer: How a Son of Greek Immigrants Learned His Way from a Nebraska Diner to Washington, Wall Street, and Beyond* (New York: Twelve, 2009), p. 169.

35. Ibid., p. 62.

36. Ibid., pp. 216–29.

37. Ken Auletta, *Greed and Glory on Wall Street: The Fall of the House of Lehman* (New York: Warner, 1986).

38. David Carey and John E. Morris, *King of Capital: The Remarkable Rise, Fall, and Rise Again of Steve Schwarzman and Blackstone* (New York: Crown Business, 2012).

39. Greta R. Krippner, *Capitalizing on Crisis: The Political Origins of the Rise of Finance* (Cambridge, MA: Harvard University Press, 2011).

40. Ibid., pp. 81–82.

41. Simon Johnson and James Kwak, *13 Bankers: The Wall Street Takeover and the Next Financial Meltdown* (New York: Pantheon Books, 2010), p. 71.

42. Adolf A. Berle and Gardiner C. Means, *The Modern Corporation and Private Property* (New Brunswick, NJ: Transaction Publishers, 1991).

43. Marina Von Neumann Whitman, *New World, New Rules: The Changing Role of the American Corporation* (Cambridge, MA: Harvard Business School Press, 1999), p. 9.

44. Jeff Madrick, *Age of Greed: The Triumph of Finance and the Decline of America, 1970 to the Present* (New York: Vintage Books, 2012), pp. 83–84.

45. Roberta Romano, "A Guide to Takeovers: Theory, Evidence and Regulation," *Yale Journal on Regulation* 9, no. 119 (1992).

46. David P. Gregory, "The NLRB and the Politics of Labor Law," *Boston College Law Review* 27, no. 37 (1985): pp. 39–52.

47. Paul Roberts, *The Impulse Society: America in the Age of Instant Gratification* (New York: Bloomsbury, 2012), p. 153.

48. Peter F. Drucker, *The New Society: The Anatomy of Industrial Order* (New Brunswick, NJ: Transaction Publishers, 2011), p. 103.

49. Whitman, *New World, New Rules*, p. 96.

50. Eileen Applebaum and Rosemary Batt, *Private Equity at Work: When Wall Street Manages Main Street* (New York: Russell Sage Foundation, 2014), p. 15.

51. Auletta, *Greed and Glory*, p. 8.

52. Ann Crittenden, "Reaping the Big Profits from a Fat Cat," *New York Times*, August 7, 1983, www.nytimes.com/1983/08/07/business/reaping-the-big-profits-from-a-fat-cat.html?pagewanted=all.

53. Lizzy Ratner, "Olin Foundation, Right-Wing Tank, Snuffing Itself," *New York Observer*, May 9, 2005, http://observer.com/2005/05/olin-foundation-rightwing-tank-snuffing-itself.

54. Carl O'Donnell, "What Does It Take to Make the Forbes 400? Increasingly More and More," *Forbes*, October 3, 2014, www.forbes.com/sites/carlodonnell/2014/10/03/what-does-it-take-to-make-the-forbes-400-increasingly-more-and-more.

55. United Press International, "'Money Is Power'—Judge's Ruling," August 24, 1983, www.upi.com/Archives/1983/08/24/Money-is-power-judges-ruling/8171430545600.

56. Kerry A. Dolan and Luisa Kroll, "Inside the 2014 Forbes 400: Facts and Figures About America's Wealthiest," *Forbes*, September 29, 2014, www.forbes.com/sites/kerryadolan/2014/09/29/inside-the-2014-forbes-40facts-and-figures-about-americas-wealthiest.

57. Liyan Chen, "Tracking a Decade of America's Richest in Six Charts," *Forbes*, October 2, 2014, www.forbes.com/sites/liyanchen/2014/10/02/tracking-a-decade-of-americas-richest-in-six-charts.

58. Stephen N. Kaplan and Joshua Rauh, "It's the Market: The Broad-Based Rise in the Return to Top Talent," *Journal of Economic Perspectives* 27, no. 3 (2013): pp. 35–56.

59. Ken Auletta, "The Fall of Lehman Brothers: The Men, Money, the Merger," *New York Times*, February 24, 1985, www.nytimes.com/1985/02/24/magazine/the-fall-of-lehman-brothers-the-men-the-money-the-merger.html?pagewanted=all.

60. Joel Bel Bruno, "Blackstone CEO Collected $400M in '06," *USA Today*, June 6, 2011, http://usatoday30.usatoday.com/money/economy/2007-06-11-3445583551_x.htm.

61. Carey and Morris, *King of Capital*, pp. 294–95.

62. Ibid., p. 263.

63. Ibid., pp. 1–3.

64. "The Top 25 Moneymakers: The New Tycoons," *Institutional Investor's Alpha*, April 24, 2007, www.institutionalinvestorsalpha.com/Article/1329029/Search/The-Top-25-Moneymakers-The-New-Tycoons.html.

65. Landon Thomas Jr., "Stephen Schwarzman of Blackstone Feels the Agony of

Victory," *New York Times*, September 4, 2015, www.nytimes.com/2015/09/06 /business/dealbook/stephen-schwarzman-of-blackstone-feels-the-agony-of -victory.html?_r=0.

66. Emmanuel Saez, "Striking It Richer: The Evolution of Top Incomes in the United States (Update with 2007 Estimates)" (update to paper in *Pathways* magazine, August 2009). This analysis, based on data compiled jointly by Saez and Thomas Piketty, is accessible at http://elsa.berkeley.edu/~saez/TabFig2007. xls.

67. Jon Bakija, Adam Cole, and Bradley T. Heim, "Jobs and Income Growth of Top Earners and the Causes of Changing Income Inequality: Evidence from U.S. Tax Return Data" (working paper, April 2012).

68. Drucker, *New Society*, p. 41.

69. Jennifer Burns, *Goddess of the Market: Ayn Rand and the American Right* (New York: Oxford University Press, 2009), p. 173.

70. Cary Schneider and Sue Horton, "Ayn Rand's 'Atlas Shrugged': What the Critics Had to Say in 1957," *Los Angeles Times*, http://articles.latimes.com/2012/aug/26 /opinion/la-oe-schneider-atlas-shrugged-reviews-20120826.

71. Rob Clarfield, "Who Is John Galt?" *Forbes*, February 15, 2012, www.forbes .com/sites/robclarfeld/2012/02/15/who-is-john-galt.

72. Greg Sargent, "Is Mitt Romney the Candidate of the 'One Percent'?" *The Plum Line* (blog), *Washington Post*, November 28, 2011, www.washingtonpost.com /blogs/plum-line/post/is-mitt-romney-the-candidate-of-the-one-percent/2011 /11/28/gIQAHLBZ5N_blog.html.

73. Jeff Elder, "VC Perkins: Ignore Protesters Against Silicon Valley's Rich," *Wall Street Journal*, February 14, 2014, http://blogs.wsj.com/digits/2014/02/14/vc -perkins-ignore-protesters-against-silicon-valleys-rich.

74. Chrystia Freeland, "Super-Rich Irony," *New Yorker*, October 8, 2012, www .newyorker.com/magazine/2012/10/08/super-rich-irony.

75. Kevin Rose, "Pursuing Self-Interest in Harmony with the Laws of the Universe and Contributing to Evolution Is Universally Rewarded," *New York*, April 10, 2011, http://nymag.com/nymag/features/ray-dalio-2011-4.

76. Barry Eichengreen, *Hall of Mirrors: The Great Depression, The Great Recession, and the Uses-and-Misuses-of History* (New York: Oxford University Press, 2014), pp. 69–70.

77. Thomas Philippon and Ariell Reshef, "Wages and Human Capital in the U.S. Finance Industry: 1909–2006," *Quarterly Journal of Economics* 127 (2012): pp. 1551–1609.

78. But the most significant subsidies are implicit guarantees that governments will aid significant financial institutions rather than risk the consequences of their failures. These guarantees were made explicit during the crisis. In 2008 about $2.2 trillion in emergency aid was pumped into the financial system, with $900 billion provided by the Treasury and $1.3 trillion by the Federal Reserve. Since then, the Fed has been lending to banks at rock-bottom rates, enabling them to earn a relatively safe returns on that money and build back their decimated balance sheets. See Anant Admati and Martin Hellwig, *The Bankers' New Clothes: What's Wrong with Banking and What to Do about It* (Princeton, NJ: Princeton University Press, 2014), pp. 129–31.

79. Susan Holmberg and Michael Umbrecht, "Understanding the CEO Pay Debate:

A Primer on America's Ongoing C-Suite Conversation" (white paper, Roosevelt Institute, New York, 2014).

80. Freedland, "Super-Rich Irony"; Rob Wile, "Here's the Angry 'Class Warfare' Letter That Hedge Fund Manager Leon Cooperman Sent to Obama," *Business Insider*, October 4, 2012, www.businessinsider.com/here-is-the-full-text-of-leon-coopermans-letter-to-president-obama-2012-10#ixzz31u8CswFX.

81. Charles Riley, "Tom Perkins' Big Idea: The Rich Should Get More Votes," *CNN Money*, February 2, 2014, http://money.cnn.com/2014/02/14/investing/tom-perkins-vote.

82. Peter Thiel, "The Education of a Libertarian," *Cato Unbound*, April 13, 2009, www.cato-unbound.org/2009/04/13/peter-thiel/education-libertarian.

83. Patri Friedman, "Beyond Folk Activism," *Cato Unbound*, April 6, 2009, www.cato-unbound.org/2009/04/06/patri-friedman/beyond-folk-activism.

84. Kevin Roose, "The Government Shutdown Has Revealed Silicon Valley's Dysfunction Fetish," *New York*, October 16, 2013, http://nymag.com/daily/intelligencer/2013/10/silicon-valleys-dysfunction-fetish.html.

85. Peterson, *Education*, p. 305.

86. "Pete Peterson Giving Away a Fortune to Keep the American Dream Alive," *U.S. News*, October 15, 2010, www.usnews.com/opinion/articles/2010/10/15/pete-peterson-giving-away-a-fortune-to-keep-the-american-dream-alive.

87. "No More Free Lunch for the Middle Class," *New York Times*, January 17, 1982, www.nytimes.com/1982/01/17/magazine/no-more-free-lunch-for-the-middle-class.html?pagewanted=all.

88. Peterson, *Education*, p. 340.

89. Peter G. Peterson, *Will America Grow Up Before It Grows Old? How the Coming Social Security Crisis Threatens You, Your Family, and Your Country* (New York: Random House, 1996), p. 48.

90. Peter G. Peterson, *Running on Empty: How the Democratic and Republican Parties Are Bankrupting Our Future and What Americans Can Do About It* (New York: Farrar, Straus and Giroux, 2005), pp. 122–23.

91. Peter G. Peterson and Neil Howe, *On Borrowed Time: How the Growth in Entitlement Spending Threatens America's Future* (New Brunswick, NJ: Transaction Publishers, 2009), p. 32.

92. Jackie Calmes, "Rubinomics Recalculated," *New York Times*, November 23, 2008, www.nytimes.com/2008/11/24/us/politics/24rubin.html.

93. Ken Brown and David Enrich, "Rubin, Under Fire, Defends His Role at Citi," *Wall Street Journal*, November 29, 2008, www.wsj.com/articles/SB122791795940965645.

94. Lawrence Summers, Interview, *PBS*, April 24, 2001, www.pbs.org/wgbh/commandingheights/shared/minitext/int_lawrencesummers.html.

95. Clea Benson, "Summers After Government Saw Wealth Surge to $7 Million," *Bloomberg*, August 8, 2013, http://www.bloomberg.com/news/articles/2013-08-02/summers-after-government-saw-wealth-surge-to-17-million.

96. Ari Berman, "How the Austerity Class Rules Washington," *Nation*, November 7, 2011, www.thenation.com/article/how-austerity-class-rules-washington.

97. Lawrence Jacobs and Benjamin Page, "Deficits, Social Security, and the American Public," *Huffington Post*, May 25, 2011, www.huffingtonpost.com/lawrence-jacobs/deficits-social-security_b_630215.html.

98. Derek Thompson, "Has the Media Totally Forgotten About the Unemployed?" *Atlantic*, May 17, 2011, www.theatlantic.com/business/archive/2011/05/has-the-media-totally-forgotten-about-the-unemployed/239048.

99. Josh Bivens and Heidi Shierholz, "Three Years into Recovery, Just How Much Has State and Local Austerity Hurt Job Growth?," *Economic Policy Institute*, July 6, 2012, www.epi.org/blog/years-recovery-state-local-austerity-hurt.

100. "Paul Ryan, Deficit Hawk or Dove?" *Economist*, *Free Exchange* (blog) January 7, 2011, www.economist.com/blogs/freeexchange/2011/01/paul_ryan_and_american_fiscal_policy.

101. Dan Eggen, "Many Deficit Commission Staffers Paid by Outside Groups," *Washington Post*, November 10, 2012, www.washingtonpost.com/wp-dyn/content/article/2010/11/10/AR2010111006850.html.

102. David Grant, "Fix the Debt: CEOs Launch Drive for 'Grand Bargain.' Is Washington Listening?" *Christian Science Monitor*, October 25, 2012, www.csmonitor.com/USA/Politics/2012/1025/Fix-the-Debt-CEOs-launch-drive-for-grand-bargain.-Is-Washington-listening.

103. Matthew G. Miller, "Billionaire Greene Goes Long on U.S. While Bemoaning Jobs Crisis," *BloombergBusiness*, January 21, 2015, www.bloomberg.com/news/articles/2015-01-21/billionaire-greene-goes-long-on-u-s-while-bemoaning-jobs-crisis.

104. Ernest Hemingway, *The Snows of Kilimanjaro and Other Stories* (New York: Simon & Schuster, 1955), p. 23. This was Hemingway's retelling. The actual quote was, "Let me tell you about the very rich. They are very different from you and me." Ralph Keyes, *The Quote Verifier* (New York: St. Martins, 2006), pp. 179–180.

105. Benjamin I. Page, Larry M. Bartels, and Jason Seawright, "Democracy and the Policy Preferences of Wealthy Americans," *Perspectives on Politics* 11, no. 1 (March 2013): pp. 51–73.

106. Martin Gilens and Benjamin I. Page, "Testing Theories of American Politics: Elites, Interest Groups, and Average Citizens," *Perspectives on Politics* (2014): 564–81.

107. Chrystia Freeland, *Plutocrats: The Rise of the New Global Super-Rich and the Fall of Everyone Else* (New York: Penguin Books, 2012), p. 79.

108. Leslie McCall, *The Undeserving Rich: American Beliefs about Inequality, Opportunity, and Redistribution* (New York: Cambridge University Press, 2013), p. 148.

109. James A. Stimson, *Tides of Consent: How Public Opinion Shapes American Politics* (New York: Cambridge University Press, 2004).

110. Marc J. Hetherington, *Why Trust Matters: Declining Political Trust and the Demise of American Liberalism* (Princeton, NJ: Princeton University Press, 2006), p. 45.

111. "Trust in Government," *Gallup*, 2015, www.gallup.com/poll/5392/trust-government.aspx.

112. Lane Kenworthy, Sondra Barringer, Daniel Duerr, and Garrett Andrew Schneider, "The Democrats and Working Class Whites," June 10, 2007, https://lanekenworthy.files.wordpress.com/2014/07/2007thedemocratsandworkingclasswhites.pdf.

113. This analysis is based on American National Election Series data, which can be found at www.electionstudies.org/studypages/download/datacenter_all_NoData.php.

114. Christopher Ellis and James A. Stimson, *Ideology in America* (New York: Cambridge University Press, 2012), p. 85.

SEVEN: We're Not in Camelot Anymore

1. Benjamin C. Waterhouse, *Lobbying America: The Politics of Business from Nixon to NAFTA* (Princeton, NJ: Princeton University Press, 2013), p. 77.

2. Lee Drutman, *The Business of America Is Lobbying: How Corporations Became Politicized and Politics Became More Corporate* (New York: Oxford University Press, 2015), pp. 36–38.

3. Mark S. Mizruchi, *The Fracturing of the American Corporate Elite* (Cambridge, MA: Harvard University Press, 2013), pp. 155–56.

4. Waterhouse, *Lobbying America*, p. 235.

5. Mizruchi, *American Corporate Elite*.

6. Waterhouse, *Lobbying America*, p. 87.

7. Quoted in Leonard Silk and David Vogel, *Ethics and Profits: The Crisis of Confidence in American Business* (New York: Simon & Schuster, 1976), p. 65.

8. Waterhouse, *Lobbying America*, pp. 130–32.

9. Ibid., p. 235.

10. Mizruchi, *American Corporate Elite*.

11. Waterhouse, *Lobbying America*, p. 233.

12. Jeffrey H. Birnbaum, "Former Powerhouse, Back at the Table," *Washington Post*, July 12, 2004, www.washingtonpost.com/wp-dyn/articles/A42902-2004Jul11.html.

13. Mizruchi, *American Corporate Elite*, pp. 64–67.

14. Alison Leigh Cowan, "Executives Are Fuming over Data on Their Pay," *New York Times*, August 25, 1992, p. D1.

15. Mary Williams Walsh with Claudia H. Deutsch, "Is True Reform Possible?" *New York Times*, July 14, 2002, p. C1.

16. Arthur Levitt, *Take On the Street: What Wall Street and Corporate America Don't Want You to Know* (New York: Pantheon, 2002), pp. 112–18.

17. Joseph E. Stiglitz, *The Roaring Nineties: A New History of the World's Most Prosperous Decade* (New York: W. W. Norton, 2011), p. 117.

18. Waterhouse, *Lobbying America*, p. 64.

19. On the leadership's effort to consolidate its position as power brokers, see Jacob S. Hacker and Paul Pierson, "The Republican Machine," chap 5., in *Off Center: The Republican Revolution and the Erosion of American Democracy* (New Haven, CT: Yale University Press, 2005),

20. Helene Cooper, "GOP, Stung by Large Donations to Democrats, Takes Tougher Stand Against Corporate America," *Wall Street Journal*, January 9, 1997, p. A14.

21. Mizruchi, *American Corporate Elite*, p. 255.

22. Peter H. Stone, "GOP Jousts with Business Roundtable," *National Journal*, January 11, 1997, p. 75.

23. Birnbaum, "Back at the Table."

24. Peter H. Stone, "Business Strikes Back," *National Journal*, October 25, 1997, p. 2130.

25. Ibid.

26. Data on lobbying expenditures is from the Center for Responsive Politics website, www.opensecrets.org/lobby/clientsum.php?id=D000032202&year=2015.

27. Louis Jacobson, "Lobbying: The Roundtable's Turnaround," *National Journal*, June 28, 2003; Birnbaum, "Back at the Table."

28. Birnbaum, "Back at the Table."

29. Chris Frates, "Engler to Head Business Roundtable," *Politico*, December 21, 2010, http://www.politico.com/story/2010/12/engler-to-head-business-round table-046671.

30. Paul Starr, *Remedy and Reaction: The Peculiar American Struggle over Health Care Reform* (New Haven, CT: Yale University Press, 2011), p. 220.

31. Lori Montgomery, "Business Leaders Say Obama's Economic Policies Stifle Growth," *Washington Post*, June 23, 2010.

32. Jia Lynn Yang, "CEOs from Far and Wide Band Against Financial Bill Provision," *Washington Post*, May 14, 2010, p. A11.

33. On the many ways that executives can use their leverage over boards to influence their compensation, see Lucian Bebchuk and Jesse Fried, *Pay Without Performance: The Unfulfilled Promise of Executive Compensation* (Cambridge, MA: Harvard University Press, 2004).

34. For a more extended discussion of *Business Roundtable v. SEC*, see Haley Sweetland Edwards, "He Who Makes the Rules," *Washington Monthly*, March/April 2013.

35. David D. Kirkpatrick, "New Judge Sees Slavery in Liberalism," *New York Times*, June 9, 2005, www.nytimes.com/2005/06/09/politics/new-judge-sees-slavery-in -liberalism.html.

36. *Business Roundtable v. SEC* (DC Circuit Court of Appeals 2011), accessible at www.cadc.uscourts.gov/internet/opinions.nsf/89BE4D084BA5EBDA852578D 5004FBBBE/$file/10-1305-1320103.pdf.

37. Bo Becker, Daniel Bergstresser, and Guhan Subramanian, "Does Shareholder Proxy Access Improve Firm Value? Evidence from the Business Roundtable Challenge," *Journal of Law and Economics* 56, no. 1 (2013).

38. "An Interview with the President," *Democracy in America* (blog) *Economist*, August 2, 2014, www.economist.com/blogs/democracyinamerica/2014/08/barack -obama-talks-economist.

39. "About," Business Roundtable, accessed October 1, 2015, http://businessround table.org/about.

40. A copy of the Powell memo is available online at the Washington and Lee School of Law, http://law2.wlu.edu/deptimages/Powell%20Archives/PowellMemoran dumTypescript.pdf.

41. Waterhouse, *Lobbying America*, p. 59.

42. Kim Phillips-Fein, *Invisible Hands: The Making of the Conservative Movement from the New Deal to Reagan* (New York: W. W. Norton, 2009), p. 200.

43. Waterhouse, *Lobbying America*, p. 63.

44. Ibid., p. 58.

45. Ibid., p. 214.

46. Ibid., pp. 218–20.

47. Greg Johnson, "Business Groups' Feel Recession Pinch: Chambers of Commerce, Others Are Hurting as Businesses Trim Memberships to Cut Costs," *Los Angeles Times*, October 8, 1991, http://articles.latimes.com/1991-10-08/business/fi-136 _1_membership-levels.

48. Kirk Victor, "Deal Us In," *National Journal*, April 3, 1993, pp. 805–9.

49. Richard L. Berke, "Clinton Finds a Friendlier Chamber of Commerce," *New York Times*, April 14, 1993.

50. John Judis, "Abandoned Surgery: Business and the Failure of Health Reform," *American Prospect*, December 19, 2001.

51. Jack Nelson, "Conservatives Strain GOP, Chamber of Commerce Ties," *Los Angeles Times*, April 9, 1993.

52. Berke, "Clinton Finds Friendlier Chamber of Commerce."

53. Nelson, "Conservatives Strain Ties."

54. On the rise of the NFIB, see McGee Young, *Developing Interests: Organizational Change and the Politics of Advocacy* (Lawrence: University Press of Kansas, 2010), pp. 76–82.

55. Victor, "Deal Us In."

56. Judis, "Abandoned Surgery."

57. Nelson, "Conservatives Strain Ties."

58. Alyssa Katz, *The Influence Machine: The U.S. Chamber of Commerce and the Corporate Capture of American Life* (New York: Penguin Random House, 2015), p. 62.

59. Robert D. Hershey, "President of the U.S. Chamber Will Resign After 21 Years," *New York Times*, February 25, 1997.

60. Melinda Henneberger, "Master Persuader Will Run the Leading Business Lobby," *New York Times*, June 24, 1997.

61. Phillips-Fein, *Invisible Hands*, p. 200.

62. David R. Mayhew, *Divided We Govern: Party Control, Lawmaking and Investigations, 1946–2002* (New Haven, CT: Yale University Press, 2005), p. 75.

63. Heather Cox Richardson, *To Make Men Free: A History of the Republican Party* (New York: Basic Books, 2014), pp. 317–18.

64. "Chamber of Commerce, 2015," Center for Responsive Politics, accessed October 1, 2015, www.opensecrets.org/outsidespending/recips.php?cmte=US+Chamber+of+Commerce&cycle=2014.

65. Anne Palmer, "Super PACs Rival Chamber," *Politico*, March 23, 2012, www.politico.com/story/2012/03/chambers-new-competition-super-pacs-074382.

66. Sheryl Gay Stolberg, "Pugnacious Builder of the Business Lobby," *New York Times*, June 1, 2013.

67. See chap. 3 in Kenneth P. Vogel, *Big Money* (New York: Public Affairs, 2014).

68. Alyssa Katz, "Why the Chamber of Commerce Isn't Looking Out for Small Businesses," *Inc.*, July 20, 2015, www.inc.com/alyssa-katz/why-the-chamber-of-commerce-isnt-looking-out-for-small-business.html.

69. James Verini, "Show Him the Money," *Washington Monthly*, July 10, 2010.

70. "Changing of the Business Guard," *Nation's Business* 85, no. 8 (1997): pp. 62–63.

71. Jeffrey H. Birnbaum, "A Quiet Revolution in Business Lobbying," *Washington Post*, February 5, 2005.

72. Ibid., p. A1.

73. Jim VandeHei, "Major Business Lobby Wins Back Its Clout by Dispensing Favors," *Wall Street Journal*, September 11, 2001, p. A1.

74. Eric Lipton, Mike McIntire, and Don Van Natta Jr., "Top Corporations Aid U.S. Chamber of Commerce Campaign," *New York Times*, October 21, 2010.

75. Carol D. Leonnig, "Corporate Donors Fuel Chamber of Commerce's Political Power," *Washington Post*, October 18, 2012.

76. Lipton, McIntire, and Van Natta, "Corporations Aid Chamber."

77. All lobbying figures in this paragraph are from the Center for Responsive Politics website, www.opensecrets.org.

78. David Steinbach, "Billion Dollar Baby: U.S. Chamber Is First to Hit Lobbying Milestone," Center for Responsive Politics, July 23, 2013, www.opensecrets.org/news/2013/07/billion-dollar-baby-us-chamber-is-first-to-hit-lobbying-milestone.

79. Sean Sullivan, "The Chamber of Commerce Just Endorsed a Democrat," *Washington Post*, September 3, 2014. The Chamber endorsed thirty-eight Democrats in 2008, twenty-one in 2010, and five in 2012.

80. "The Institute for Legal Reform: The U.S. Chamber's Corporate Conduit" (report by US Chamber Watch, October 2011).

81. T. R. Goldman, "A Legal Strike Force at the U.S. Chamber of Commerce Picks Key Supreme Court Cases for Amicus Intervention," *California Lawyer*, July 2014, www.callawyer.com/clstory.cfm?eid=935765&wteid=935765_Inside_the_Chamber.

82. US Chamber Watch, "The Institute for Legal Reform: The U.S. Chamber's Corporate Conduit," October 2011.

83. US Chamber Watch, "Corporate Conduit."

84. Goldman, "Legal Strike Force."

85. Ibid.

86. *AT&T Mobility LLC v. Concepcion*, 131 S. Ct. 1740 2011; Jessica Silver-Greenberg and Robert Gebeloff, "Arbitration Everywhere, Stacking the Decks of Justice," *New York Times*, October 31, 2015.

87. Goldman, "Legal Strike Force."

88. Quoted in James Verini, "Show Him the Money," *Washington Monthly*, July 10, 2010.

89. Jim VandeHei, "Major Business Lobby Wins Back Its Clout by Dispensing Favors," *Wall Street Journal*, September 11, 2001, p. A1.

90. Drew Armstrong, "Insurers Gave U.S. Chamber $86 Million Used to Oppose Obama's Health Law," *BloombergBusiness*, November 17, 2010.

91. Verini, "Show Him the Money."

92. VandeHei, "Business Lobby Dispensing Favors"; Lipton, McIntire, and Van Natta, "Top Corporations Aid Chamber."

93. Christ Frates, "AHIP Gave More Than $100 Million to Chamber's Efforts to Derail Health Care Reform," *National Journal* Blog, June 13, 2012, www.healthcare-now.org/blog/ahip-gave-more-than-100-million-to-chambers-efforts-to-derail-health-care-reform.

94. Armstrong, "Insurers Gave Chamber $86 Million."

95. "Chamber of Commerce of the United States of America—Contact Us," US Chamber of Commerce, accessed July 28, 2014, www.uschamber.com/about-us/chamber-commerce-united-states-america-contact-us. Emphasis added.

96. Armstrong, "Insurers Gave Chamber $86 Million."

97. For detailed documentation of this point, see Mark Smith, *American Business and Political Power* (Chicago: University of Chicago Press, 2000), pp. 40–54.

98. William J. Lanouette, "Chamber's Ponderous Decision-Making Leaves It Sitting on the Sidelines," *National Journal*, July 24, 1982, p. 1299. Emphasis added.

99. Danny Hakim, "Big Tobacco's Staunch Friend in Washington: U.S. Chamber of Commerce," *New York Times*, October 9, 2015.

100. Ibid.

101. Robert D. Hershey Jr., "Chamber of Commerce Is Budgeting," *New York Times*, October 1, 1983.

102. The description of the Vail event is drawn from Daniel Schulman, *Sons of Wichita: How the Koch Brothers Became America's Most Powerful and Private Dynasty* (New York: Grand Central, 2014), pp. 304–7.

103. Adam Bonica, Nolan McCarty, Keith T. Poole, and Howard Rosenthal, "Why Hasn't Democracy Slowed Rising Inequality?" *Journal of Economic Perspectives* Vol. 27, no. 3 (2013): pp. 103–24.

104. Andrew Goldman, "The Billionaire's Party," *New York Magazine*, July 25, 2010.

105. Isaac Martin, *Rich People's Movements: Grassroots Campaigns to Untax the 1%* (New York: Oxford University Press, 2013).

106. Phillips-Fein, *Invisible Hands*, p. 3.

107. Lee Fang, *The Machine: A Field Guide to the Resurgent Right* (New York: New Press, 2013), pp. 107–8.

108. Brian Doherty, *Radicals for Capitalism: A Freewheeling History of the Modern American Libertarian Movement* (New York: Public Affairs, 2007), p. 407.

109. Schulman, *Sons of Wichita*, p. 42.

110. William T. Miller, "The Birch Society," *Time*, May 12, 1961, p. 124.

111. Schulman, *Sons of Wichita*, p. 55.

112. Quoted in Schulman, *Sons of Wichita*, pp. 98, 102.

113. Gregg Easterbrook, "Ideas Move Nations: How Conservative Think Tanks Have Helped Changed the Terms of Political Debate," *The Atlantic*, January 2006, www.theatlantic.com/past/politics/poliblog/eastidea.htm.

114. Charles Koch speech in Dallas, 1974. A link to a copy of the speech is in Nicholas Confessore, "Quixotic '80 Campaign Gave Birth to Kochs' Powerful Network," *New York Times*, May 17, 2014.

115. Doherty, *Radicals for Capitalism*, p. 16.

116. Schulman, *Sons of Wichita*, p. 263.

117. John Maynard Keynes, *General Theory of Employment, Interest and Money* (New York: Lulu Press, 2013), pp. 383–384.

118. Doherty, *Radicals for Capitalism*, p. 410.

119. Quoted in Doherty, *Radicals for Capitalism*, p. 99.

120. Robert Paarlberg, *The United States of Excess: Gluttony and the Dark Side of American Exceptionalism* (New York: Oxford University Press, 2015), pp. 73–75.

121. Jane Mayer, "The Kochs v. Cato: Winners and Losers," *New Yorker*, June 27, 2012. See also Mayer, "Covert Operations," *New Yorker*, August 30, 2010.

122. The last figure is from Vogel, *Big Money*, p. 6.

123. Matea Gold, "Koch-Backed Political Network, Built to Shield Donors, Raised $400 Million in 2012 Elections," *Washington Post*, January 5, 2014; Matea Gold, "An Expanding Koch Network Aims to Spend $300 Million to Shape Senate Fight and 2016," *Washington Post*, June 18, 2014.

124. Gold, "Koch-Backed Network Raised $400 Million."

125. Vogel, *Big Money*, p. 125.

126. Matea Gold, "An Expanding Koch Network Aims to Spend $300 Million to Shape Senate Fight and 2016," *Washington Post*, June 18, 2014.

127. Mike Allen and Jim VandeHei, "The Koch Brothers' Secret Bank," *Politico*, September 11, 2013.

128. Matea Gold, "Koch-Backed Network, Built to Shield Donors, Raised $400 Million in 2012 Elections," *Washington Post*, January 5, 2014.

129. Ibid.

130. Schulman, *Sons of Wichita*, p. 295.

131. Vogel, *Big Money*, p. 7.

132. Vogel, *Big Money*, pp. 3, 14; Schulman, *Sons of Wichita*, p. 292; Matea Gold, "A Rare Look Inside the Koch Brothers Political Empire," *Washington Post*, February 5, 2014.

133. Ibid.

134. Hayley Peterson, "Internal Memo: Romney Courting Kochs, Tea Party," *Washington Examiner*, November 2, 2011, www.washingtonexaminer.com/internal-memo-romney-courting-kochs-tea-party/article/940551.

135. Theda Skocpol and Vanessa Williamson, *The Tea Party and the Remaking of American Conservatism* (New York: Oxford University Press, 2011), pp. 102–4.

136. Ashley Parker, " 'Koch Primary' Tests Hopefuls in the G.O.P." *New York Times*, January 20, 2015, www.nytimes.com/2015/01/21/us/koch-seminar-is-early-proving-ground-for-gop-hopefuls.html.

137. Ibid.

EIGHT: This Is Not Your Father's Party

1. David Karol, "Defining Dissidence Down," *The Monkey Cage* (blog), May 9, 2012, http://themonkeycage.org/2012/05/defining-dissidence-down.

2. Nate Silver, "A Risky Rationale Behind Romney's Choice of Ryan," *FiveThirtyEight* (blog), *New York Times*, August 11, 2012, http://fivethirtyeight.blogs.nytimes.com/2012/08/11/a-risky-rationale-behind-romneys-choice-of-ryan.

3. "HOUSE_SORT11 Rank Ordering," Voteview, accessed October 15, 2015, http://voteview.org/HOUSE_SORT112.HTM; Aaron Blake, "Bachmann: Obamacare 'Literally Kills' People," *Washington Post*, March 21, 2013, www.washingtonpost.com/news/post-politics/wp/2013/03/21/bachmann-obamacare-literally-kills-people/; Ed Kilgore, "Springtime for Bachmann," *New Republic*, March 17, 2011, www.newrepublic.com/article/the-permanent-campaign/85365/michele-bachmann-2012-gop-presidential-nominee.

4. All figures are based on DW-Nominate Scores developed by Keith Poole and Howard Rosenthal. Rankings available at http://voteview.com/dwnl.htm.

5. Jacob S. Hacker and Paul Pierson, "Confronting Asymmetric Polarization," in *Solutions to Political Polarization in America*, ed. Nathaniel Persily (New York: Cambridge University Press, 2015), pp. 59–72.

6. Jeffrey A. Segal and Albert D. Cover, "Ideological Values and the Votes of U.S. Supreme Court Justices," *American Political Science Review* 83, no. 2 (1989): pp. 557–65; Alex Greer, "Ranking the Most Conservative Modern Supreme Court Justices," InsideGov, June 30, 2015, http://supreme-court-justices.insidegov.com/stories/5048/most-conservative-modern-supreme-court-justice.

7. Michael Cooper, "Conservatives Sowed Idea of Health Care Mandate, Only to Spurn It Later," *New York Times*, February 14, 2012, www.nytimes.com/2012/02/15/health/policy/health-care-mandate-was-first-backed-by-conservatives.html?_r=0.

8. Henry J. Aaron, "How Not to Reform Medicare," *New England Journal of Medicine* 364 (2011): pp. 1588–89; Timothy Stolzfus Jost, "Consensus and Conflict in Health System Reform—The Republican Budget Plan and the ACA," *New England Journal of Medicine* 364 (2011); Edwin Park, Kathy Ruff-

ing, and Paul N. Van de Water, *Proposed Cap on Federal Spending Would Force Deep Cuts in Medicare, Medicaid, and Social Security* (Washington, DC: Center on Budget Policy and Priorities, 2011), http://www.cbpp.org/research/proposed-cap-on-federal-spending-would-force-deep-cuts-in-medicare-medicaid-and-social.

9. Sidney Plotkin and William E. Scheuerman, *Private Interest, Public Spending: Balanced-Budget Conservatism and the Fiscal Crisis* (Boston: South End Press, 1994), pp. 13–21.

10. For details, see Hacker and Pierson, *Winner Take All Politics*, pp. 212–18.

11. Pew Research Center for the People and the Press, "Tax System Seen as Unfair, In Need of Overhaul: Wealthy Not Paying Fair Share Top Complaint," Pew Research Center, December 20, 2011, www.people-press.org/2011/12/20/tax-system-seen-as-unfair-in-need-of-overhaul.

12. Austin Nichols and Jesse Rothstein, "The Earned Income Tax Credit" (working paper, Institute for Research on Labor and Employment, University of California at Berkeley, 2015).

13. Leonard E. Burman, "Tax Evasion, IRS Priorities, and the EITC" (statement of Leonard E. Burman before the United States House of Representatives Committee on the Budget; On Waste, Fraud, and Abuse in Federal Mandatory Programs, 2003).

14. Steve Benen, "Ten-to-One Isn't Good Enough for the GOP," *Political Animal* (blog), *Washington Monthly*, August 12, 2011, www.washingtonmonthly.com/political-animal/2011_08/tentoone_isnt_good_enough_for031484.php#.

15. "The Non-Taxpaying Class," *Wall Street Journal*, November 20, 2002, www.wsj.com/articles/SB1037748678534174748.

16. David Korn, "Secret Video: Romney Tells Millionaire Donors What He *Really* Thinks of Obama Voters," *Mother Jones* Blog, September 17, 2012, www.motherjones.com/politics/2012/09/secret-video-romney-private-fundraiser.

17. Greg Sargent, "Joni Ernst's Hog-Castrating Ideology, Revealed!" *The Plum Line* (blog), *Washington Post*, October 16, 2014, www.washingtonpost.com/blogs/plum-line/wp/2014/10/16/joni-ernsts-hog-castrating-ideology-revealed.

18. Timothy Noah, "Medicare and Brimstone," *New Republic*, August 24, 2012. Following the 2012 election, Ryan repudiated the "maker/taker" distinction. Paul Ryan, "A Better Way Up from Poverty," *Wall Street Journal*, August 15, 2014.

19. An audio of Ryan's 2005 remarks to the Atlas Society is available at http://atlassociety.org/commentary/commentary-blog/4971-paul-ryan-and-ayn-rands-ideas-in-the-hot-seat-again.

20. Alec MacGillis, "Eric Cantor's Wall Street Job Isn't Paying Him What He's Really Worth," *New Republic*, September 2, 2014, www.newrepublic.com/article/119298/eric-cantors-new-wall-street-job-underpaying-him.

21. Jake Tapper, "Did Obama Say, 'If You've Got a Business, You Didn't Build That'?" *Politics*(blog), ABCNews.com, July 12, 2012, http://abcnews.go.com/blogs/politics/2012/07/did-obama-say-if-youve-got-a-business-you-didnt-build-that.

22. Thomas E. Mann and Norman J. Ornstein, *It's Even Worse Than It Looks: How the American Constitutional System Collided with the New Politics of Extremism* (New York: Basic Books, 2012).

23. Mark Tushnet, "Constitutional Hardball," *John Marshall Law Review* 37, no. 2 (2004).

24. To avoid getting bogged down in side arguments, it excludes two very signifi-

cant episodes that we would be inclined to include: the Supreme Court's decision in *Bush v. Gore*, and the willingness of four GOP appointees to strike down
the entirety of the Affordable Care Act—the signature statutory result of the
Democrats' sweeping electoral victory in 2008 (and a bill that essentially no
prominent figures regarded as raising major constitutional issues during the
long and intense debate over passage).

25. Mann and Ornstein, *It's Even Worse Than It Looks*, p. xiv. Mann and Ornstein
credit the term "insurgent outlier" to Yale political scientist Stephen Skowronek.

26. Sean Theriault, *The Gingrich Senators: The Roots of Partisan Warfare in Congress*
(New York: Oxford University Press, 2013).

27. Adrian Wooldridge and John Micklethwait, *The Right Nation: Conservative
Power in America* (New York: Penguin Books, 2004).

28. Douglas J. Amy, *Government Is Good: An Unapologetic Defense of a Vital Institution* (Indianapolis: Dog Ear, 2011), pp. 185–87.

29. Matt Grossmann and David A. Hopkins, "Ideological Republicans and Group
Interest Democrats: The Asymmetry of American Party Politics," *Perspectives
on Politics*, March, 2015, pp. 119–39.

30. Gary Jacobson, "The Electoral Origins of Polarized Politics: Evidence from the
2010 Cooperative Congressional Election Study," *American Behavioral Scientist*
(2012): p. 14.

31. Nicolas A.Valentino and David O. Sears, "Old Times There Are Not Forgotten:
Race and Partisan Realignment in the Contemporary South," *American Journal
of Political Science* 49, no. 3 (2005): pp. 672–88; Ilyana Kuziemko and Ebonya
Washington, "Why Did the Democrats Lose the South? Using New Data to Re-
solve an Old Debate," (unpublished manuscript, Princeton University, 2015);
M. V. Hood, Quentin Kidd, and Irwin L. Morris, *The Rational Southerner: Black
Mobilization, Republican Growth and the Partisan Transformation of the Ameri-
can South* (New York: Oxford University Press, 2012).

32. For documentation of the role of such dog-whistle dynamics in the develop-
ment of the modern GOP, see the detailed discussions in Ian Haney Lopez,
*Dog Whistle Politics: How Coded Racial Appeals Have Reinvented Racism and
Wrecked the Middle Class* (New York: Oxford University Press, 2014), and Doug
McAdam and Karina Kloos, *Racial Politics and Social Movements in Postwar
America* (New York: Oxford University Press, 2014).

33. Valentino and Sears, "Old Times There Are Not Forgotten."

34. Michael Tesler, "The Spillover of Racialization into Health Care: How President
Obama Polarized Public Opinion by Racial Attitudes and Race," *American Journal of Political Science* 56, no. 3 (2012): pp. 690–704.

35. Daniel J. Hopkins, "The Diversity Discount: When Increasing Ethnic and Racial
Diversity Prevents Tax Increases," *Journal of Politics* 71, no. 1 (2009): pp. 160–77;
Jessica Troustine, "One for You, Two for Me: Support for Public Goods Investment
in Diverse Communities" (working paper, University of California, Merced, 2013).

36. Jean M. Twenge, Nathan T. Carter, and W. Keith Campbell, "Time Period, Gen-
erational, and Age Differences in Tolerance for Controversial Beliefs and Life-
styles in the United States, 1972–2012," *Journal of Social Forces* 94, no. 1 (2015).

37. Amy Mitchell, Jeffrey Gottfried, Jocelyn Kiley, and Katerina Eva Matsa, "Political Polarization and Media Habits," Pew Research Center, October 21, 2014,
www.journalism.org/2014/10/21/political-polarization-media-habits.

38. Jill Lepore, "Bad News: The Reputation of Roger Ailes," *New Yorker*, January 20, 2014.

39. Jonathan Martin and Keach Hagey, "Republican Primary: Complicated, Contractual," *Politico*, September 27, 2010.

40. David Schoetz, "Frum: Now We Work for Fox," *ABC News Nightline*, March 23, 2010, http://blogs.abcnews.com/nightlinedailyline/2010/03/david-frum-on-gop-now-we-work-for-fox.html.

41. Jeffrey M. Berry and Sarah Sobieraj, *The Outrage Industry: Political Opinion Media and the New Incivility* (New York: Oxford University Press, 2014), p. 129.

42. Jackie Calmes, " 'They Don't Give a Damn About Governing': Conservative Media's Influence on the Republican Party" (Shorenstein Center on Media, Politics and Public Policy Discussion Paper Series, Harvard University, July 2015), appendix C.

43. Gregory Martin and Ali Yurukoglu, "Bias in Cable News: Real Effects and Polarization" (working paper, National Bureau of Economic Research, Cambridge, MA, December 2014).

44. Kevin Arceneaux, Martin Johnson, Rene Lindstadt, and Ryan J. Vander Wielen, "The Influence of News Media on Political Elites: Investigating Strategic Responsiveness in Congress," *American Journal of Political Science* (2015).

45. Jonathan M. Ladd, *Why Americans Hate the Media and How It Matters* (Princeton, NJ: Princeton University Press, 2012), pp. 122–25.

46. Theda Skocpol and Vanessa Williamson, *The Tea Party and the Remaking of American Conservatism* (New York: Oxford University Press, 2011), p. 132.

47. Calmes, "They Don't Give a Damn," p. 9.

48. Lee Drutman, "The Political 1% of the 1% in 2012," Sunlight Foundation, June 24, 2013, http://sunlightfoundation.com/blog/2013/06/24/1pct_of_the_1pct.

49. Adam Bonica and Howard Rosenthal, "The Wealth Elasticity of Political Contributions by the Forbes 400" (working paper, September 26, 2015). Available at SSRN: http://ssrn.com/abstract-2668780.

50. Michael Beckel and Russ Choma, "Super PACs, Nonprofits Favored Romney Over Obama: Citizens United Decision Helped Romney Neutralize Obama's Fundraising Advantage," Center for Responsive Politics, October 30, 2012, www.opensecrets.org/news/2012/10/super-pacs-nonprofits.

51. Kenneth P. Vogel and Mackenzie Weinger, "The Tea Party Radio Network," *Politico*, April 17, 2014, www.politico.com/story/2014/04/tea-party-radio-network-105774.

52. Turnout, in fact, is a key explanation for Republicans' big statehouse edge: governors are overwhelmingly elected in nonpresidential election years, when turnout is much lower. Only nine states hold gubernatorial elections alongside the presidential race. Anthony Fowler, "Regular Voters, Marginal Voters and the Electoral Effects of Turnout," *Political Science Research and Methods* 3, no. 2 (2015): 205–19.

53. Neil Shah, "Smallville, USA, Fades Further," *Wall Street Journal*, March 27, 2014.

54. Jonathan Chait, "Who Needs to Win to Win?" *New York*, February 3, 2013.

55. Megan Garber, "The State of Wyoming Has Two Escalators: And They're Totally Fine with That," *Atlantic*, July 17, 2013.

56. Ben Highton, "How the Senate Is Biased Toward Republicans," *The Monkey Cage* (blog), *Washington Post*, January 31, 2014.

57. Calculated from data on Senate elections available at www.fec.gov/pubrec

/electionresults.shtml and Senate seat shares available at www.senate.gov /history/partydiv.htm.

58. Chait, "Who Needs to Win to Win?"

59. Gary Jacobson, "Eroding the Electoral Foundations of Political Polarization," in *Solutions to Political Polarization in America*, ed. Nathan Persily (New York: Cambridge University Press, 2015), p. 85.

60. Alan I. Abramowitz, "Beyond Confrontation and Gridlock: Making Democracy Work for the American People," in *Solutions to Partisan Polarization*, ed. Persily, p. 201. On the absence of swing voters in swing districts, see Jonathan Rodden, "Geography and Gridlock in the United States," in *Solutions to Partisan Polarization*, ed. Persily, pp. 104–20.

61. Paul Waldman, "Still Waiting for That GOP Fever to Break," *American Prospect*, February 11, 2013, http://prospect.org/article/still-waiting-gop-fever-break.

62. Christopher H. Achen and Larry M. Bartels, "Blind Retrospection: Why Shark Attacks Are Bad for Democracy" (working paper, Center for the Study of Democratic Institutions, Vanderbilt University, Nashville, TN, 2013).

63. Alex Seitz-Wald, "How Newt Gingrich Crippled Congress," *Nation*, January 30, 2012, www.thenation.com/article/how-newt-gingrich-crippled-congress.

64. Sheryl Gay Stolberg, "Gingrich Stuck to Caustic Path in Ethics Battles," *New York Times*, January 26, 2012.

65. Ibid.

66. "Language: A Key Mechanism of Control" (GOPAC memo, 1994). The text is available at "Words Gingrich Governed By," *New York Times*, January 27, 2012, www.nytimes.com/interactive/2012/01/27/us/politics/27gingrich-text.html.

67. Quoted in Dan Balz and Ronald Brownstein, *Storming the Gates: Protest Politics and the Republican Revival* (Boston: Little, Brown, 1996), p. 121.

68. Ibid.

69. Ibid., p. 140.

70. Ibid., p. 135.

71. "Congress and the Public," *Gallup* Historical Trends, 2015, www.gallup.com /poll/1600/congress-public.aspx.

72. Data via Voteview, accessed October 1, 2015, https://voteviewblog.wordpress .com/author/voteviewblog/page/2. Note: this updated post indicates Obama is now the second most moderate, slightly to the left of LBJ.

73. Joshua Green, "Strict Obstructionist," *Atlantic*, January/February 2011.

74. For a compilation of polling on the subject, see PollingReport.com, www.polling report.com/congress.htm.

75. Alec MacGillis, *The Cynic: The Political Education of Mitch McConnell* (New York: Simon & Schuster, 2014), p. 85.

76. Ibid., pp. 105–6.

77. Juraj Medzihorsky, Levente Littvay, and Erin K. Jenne, "Has the Tea Party Era Radicalized the Republican Party? Evidence from Text Analysis of the 2008 and 2012 Republican Primary Debates," *PS: Political Science & Politics* 47, no. 4 (2014): pp. 806–12.

78. Jennifer Rubin, "10 Signs the Tea Party Is in Decline," *Right Turn* (blog), *Washington Post*, March 10, 2014, www.washingtonpost.com/blogs/right-turn/wp /2014/03/10/10-signs-the-tea-party-is-in-decline.

79. Tom Hamburger, "The Biggest Winner in Primaries: U.S. Chamber of Com-

merce," *Washington Post*, May 21, 2014, www.washingtonpost.com/news/post
-politics/wp/2014/05/21/the-biggest-winner-in-primaries-u-s-chamber-of
-commerce.

80. Quoted in Peter Hamby, "Company Men: The U.S. Chamber Flexes Its New
Political Muscle," CNN.com, 2014, www.cnn.com/interactive/2014/politics
/hamby-midterms-chamber-tea-party.

81. Jada F. Smith, "Chamber to Split with Tea Party in Primaries, *The Caucus* (blog),
New York Times, January 8, 2014, http://thecaucus.blogs.nytimes.com/2014/01
/08/chamber-to-split-with-tea-party-in-g-o-p-primaries/?_r=0. Emphasis added.

82. Neil King Jr. and Patrick O'Connor, "GOP, Business Recast Message," *Wall
Street Journal*, December 25, 2013.

83. Sean Sullivan, "The Chamber of Commerce Just Endorsed a Democrat," *Washington Post*, September 3, 2014.

84. Rebekah Wilce, "Spending for ALEC Member Tillis Breaks All Records in NC
Senate Race," PR Watch, Center for Media and Democracy, October 21, 2014,
www.prwatch.org/news/2014/10/12633/spending-alec-member-tillis-breaks
-all-records-nc-senate-race; Edward Martin, "Business's Man: House Speaker
Thom Tillis Is North Carolina's Most Focused Free-Market Legislative Leader
in a Long Time—Maybe Ever," *Business North Carolina*, April 2012, www.busi
nessnc.com/articles/2012-04/business-s-man-category.

85. Iowa Public Television, "Ernst Calls for Abolishing IRS, Dept. of Education,
and EPA," April 24, 2014, www.iptv.org/iowapress/story.cfm/story/11721
/ip_20140424_4131_ernst_cutting_spending; Ed Kilgore, "Third Strike for
Joni Ernst," *Political Animal* (blog), *Washington Post*, October 6, 2014, www
.washingtonmonthly.com/political-animal-a/2014_10/third_strike_for_joni
_ernst052356.php#.

86. Molly Ball, "The Making of a Conservative Superstar," *Atlantic*, September 17,
2014.

87. Mann and Ornstein, *It's Even Worse Than It Looks*.

88. Kasia Anderson, "Barney Frank, Ever the Politician, Predicts Hillary Clinton Is
'Gonna Win' in 2016," *Truthdig*, November 4, 2015, www.truthdig.com/report/
item/barney_frank_on_clinton_sanders_gop_20151104.

89. John Brinkley, "Ex Im Bank Survives Tea Party Attack, Girds for the Next One,"
Forbes, September 23, 2014, http://onforb.es/1rtLJuu.

90. Brett LoGiurato, "The Tea Party Is on the Verge of Its Biggest-Ever Victory in
Washington," *Business Insider*, June 24, 2014, www.businessinsider.com/ex
-im-bank-victory-tea-party-2014-6.

91. Zachary A. Goldfarb and Holy Yeager, "Long-Building Conservative Anger at
Export-Import Bank Reaches Boiling Point," *Washington Post*, June 28, 2014,
www.washingtonpost.com/business/economy/long-building-conservative
-anger-at-export-import-bank-reaches-boiling-point/2014/06/27/cce4a87a
-fe01-11e3-b1f4-8e77c632c07b_story.html.

92. Glenn Kessler, "Tom Cotton's Invented Version of Farm Bill History," *Washington Post*, September 23, 2014, www.washingtonpost.com/news/fact-checker
/wp/2014/09/23/tom-cottons-invented-version-of-farm-bill-history.

NINE: The Modern Robber Barons

1. Quoted in Eli F. Heckscher, *Mercantilism*, vol. 1 (New York: Routledge, 2013), p. 36.
2. Matthew Josephson, *The Robber Barons* (Boston: Mariner Books, 1934), p. vii.
3. Theo Francis and Ryan Knutson, "Wave of Megadeals Tests Antitrust Limits in the U.S.," *Wall Street Journal*, October 19, 2015, www.wsj.com/articles/wave-of -megadeals-tests-antitrust-limits-in U-S-1445213306.
4. "Health Care Spending in the United States & Selected OECD Countries," Kaiser Family Foundation, April 12, 2011, http://kff.org/health-costs/issue-brief /snapshots-health-care-spending-in-the-united-states-selected-oecd-countries.
5. *The 2015 Long-Term Budget Outlook* (Washington, DC: US Congressional Budget Office, June 2015), www.cbo.gov/sites/default/files/114th-congress-2015-2016 /reports/50250-LongTermBudgetOutlook-4.pdf.
6. Jamelle Bouie, "GOP Aims to Cut $40 Billion Out of Food Stamps to Foil Illusory 'Cheaters,'" *Daily Beast*, September 5, 2013, www.thedailybeast.com/articles /2013/09/05/gop-aims-to-cut-40-billion-out-of-food-stamps-to-foil-illusory -cheaters.html.
7. "2013 Comparative Price Report Variation in Medical and Hospital Prices by Country" (report by the International Federation of Health Plans, 2013), pp. 17–18.
8. Zack Cooper, Stuart Craig, Martin Gaynor, and John Van Reener, "Why Is Health Care Spending on the Privately Insured in Grand Junction, Colorado, So High? Prices, Competition, and Health Care Spending" (working paper, National Bureau of Economic Research, Cambridge, MA, 2015).
9. Drew Altman, "High Health-Care Prices: More Talk Than Action," *Wall Street Journal*, January 12, 2015.
10. Edward D. Kleinbard, *We Are Better Than This: How Government Should Spend Our Money* (New York: Oxford University Press, 2014), p. 320.
11. Elizabeth Warren, David Himmelstein, Deborah Thorne, and Steffie Woolhander, "Medical Bankruptcy in the United States, 2007: Results of a National Study," *American Journal of Medicine* 20, no. 10 (2009): pp. 1–6.
12. *Health Care Costs: A Primer—Key Information on Health Care Costs and Their Impact*, (Menlo Park, CA: Henry J. Kaiser Family Foundation, May 2012), http://kff.org/report-section/health-care-costs-a-primer-2012-report.
13. www.cms.gov/Research-statistics-data-and-systems/Statistics-Trends-and -Reports/NationalHealthExpendData/Downloads/tables.pdf, Table 21.
14. "The Facts on Medicare Spending and Financing," Henry J. Kaiser Family Foundation, July 24, 2015, http://kff.org/medicare/fact-sheet/medicare-spending -and-financing-fact-sheet.
15. Louis Jacobson, "John Boehner Says U.S. Health Care System Is Best in World," *Politifact*, July 5, 2012, www.politifact.com/truth-o-meter/statements/2012/jul /05/john-boehner/john-boehner-says-us-health-care-system-best-world.
16. Leah A. Burke and Andrew R. Ryan, "The Complex Relationship Between Cost and Quality in US Health Care," *AMA Journal of Ethics* 16, no. 2 (2014): pp. 124–30.
17. Margaret E. Guerin-Calvert and Guillermo Israilevich, *Assessment of Cost Trends and Price Differences for U.S. Hospitals* (report by the American Hospital Association, March 2011), p. 4; Kelly J. Devers, Linda R. Brewster, and Lawrence P. Casalino, "Changes in Hospital Competitive Strategy: A New Medical Arms Race?" *Health Services Research* 38 (2003): pp. 447–69.

18. *Health at a Glance 2011: OECD Indicators* (Paris: Organization for Economic Co-operation and Development, 2011), pp. 108–11.

19. Ellen Nolte and C. Martin McKee, "Measuring the Health of Nations: Updating an Earlier Analysis," *Health Affairs* 27, no. 1 (2008): pp. 58–71.

20. Elisabeth Rosenthal, "In Need of a New Hip, but Priced Out of the U.S.," *New York Times*, August 3, 2013, www.nytimes.com/2013/08/04/health/for-medical-tour ists-simple-math.html?pagewanted=all&_r=0; Christopher Ingraham, "You Just Finished Your Tax Return. What's the Chance You'll Get Audited," *Washington Post*, April 15, 2014, https://www.washingtonpost.com/news/wonk/wp/2014/04/15 /you-just-finished-your-tax-return-whats-the-chance-youll-get-audited/.

21. Elisabeth Rosenthal, " 'Paying Till It Hurts': Why American Health Care Is So Pricey," Interview by Terry Gross, *WUNC 91.5*, August 7, 2013, http://wunc .org/post/paying-till-it-hurts-why-american-health-care-so-pricey#stream/0.

22. Steven Brill, "Bitter Pill: Why Medical Bills Are Killing Us," *Time*, April 4, 2013, http://time.com/198/bitter-pill-why-medical-bills-are-killing-us.

23. Michelle M. Mello, Amitabh Chandra, Atul A. Gawande, and David M. Studdert, "National Costs of the Medical Liability System," *Health Affairs* 29, no. 9 (2010): 1569–77.

24. Lisa Schencker, "Medical Liability Premiums Flat as California Battles over Caps," *Modern Healthcare*, October 30, 2014, www.modernhealthcare.com /article/20141030/MAGAZINE/310309965.

25. Victor R. Fuchs, "Why Do Other Rich Nations Spend So Much Less on Health-care?" *Atlantic*, July 23, 2014, www.theatlantic.com/business/print/2014/07 /why-do-other-rich-nations-spend-so-much-less-on-healthcare/374576.

26. Ranked Sectors, Center for Responsive Politics, accessed October 15, 2015, www.opensecrets.org/lobby/top.php?indexType=c&showYear=a.

27. Bruce Bartlett, "Medicare Part D: Republican Budget-Busting," *Economix* (blog), *New York Times*, November 19, 2013, http://economix.blogs.nytimes .com/2013/11/19/medicare-part-d-republican-budget-busting/?_r=0.

28. David D. Kirkpatrick and Duff Wilson, "One Grand Deal Too Many Costs Lobbyist His Job," *New York Times*, February 12, 2010, www.nytimes.com/2010 /02/13/health/policy/13pharm.html; Wendell Porter, "Why Health Care Costs So Much: Both Parties Suck at Teat of Medical-Industrial Complex," *Huffington Post*, August 25, 2014, www.huffingtonpost.com/wendell-potter/why-health -care-costs-so_b_5708501.html.

29. Thomas Edsall, "The Trouble with That Revolving Door," *New York Times*, December 18, 2011, http://campaignstops.blogs.nytimes.com/2011/12/18/the-trouble-with -that-revolving-door/; Lichtenstein, et al., "Judged Frequency of Lethal Events," *Journal of Experimental Psychology: Human Learning and Memory* 4:6 (1978): 555.

30. Elliot Gerson, "To Make America Great Again, We Need to Leave the Country," *Atlantic*, July 10, 2012, www.theatlantic.com/national/archive/2012/07 /to-make-america-great-again-we-need-to-leave-the-country/259653/2.

31. Maxwell Palmer and Benjamin Schneer, "How and Why Retired Politicians Get Lucrative Appointments on Corporate Boards," *The Monkey Cage* (blog), *Washington Post*, February 1, 2015, www.washingtonpost.com/blogs/monkey-cage /wp/2015/02/01/how-and-why-retired-politicians-get-lucrative-appointments -on-corporate-boards.

32. Dan Eggen and Kimberly Kindy, "Former Lawmakers and Congressional Staffers Hired to Lobby on Health Care," *Washington Post*, July 6, 2009,

www.washingtonpost.com/wp-dyn/content/article/2009/07/05/AR200907
0502770.html?sid=ST2009070502858.

33. Ida Hellander, David U. Himmelstein, and Steffie Woolhandler, "Medicare Over-payments to Private Plans, 1985–2012: Shifting Seniors to Private Plans Has Already Cost Medicare US$282.6 Billion," *International Journal of Health Services* 43, no. 2 (2013): pp. 305–19.

34. J. Bradford DeLong, "The Greater Depression," Project Syndicate, August 28, 2014, www.project-syndicate.org/commentary/j--bradford-delong-argues-that-it-is-time-to-call-what-is-happening-in-europe-and-the-us-by-its-true-name.

35. Luigi Zingales, "Can Wonks Save Finance from Itself?" *BloombergView*, January 11, 2015, www.bloombergview.com/articles/2015-01-11/academics-can-help-save-finance-from-itself.

36. Stephen C. Cecchetti and Enisse Kharroubi, "Reassessing the Impact of Finance on Growth" (working paper, Bank for International Settlements, Basel, Switzerland, July 2012).

37. Stephen C. Cecchetti and Enisse Kharroubi, "Why Does Financial Sector Growth Crowd Out Real Economic Growth?" (working paper, Bank for International Settlements, Basel, Switzerland, February 2015).

38. William Lazonick, "Profits Without Prosperity," *Harvard Business Review*, September 2014, https://hbr.org/2014/09/profits-without-prosperity.

39. Catherine Rampell, "Out of Harvard, and into Finance," *Economix* (blog), *New York Times*, December 21, 2011, http://economix.blogs.nytimes.com/2011/12/21/out-of-harvard-and-into-finance.

40. Elliot Gerson, "Losing Rhodes Scholars to Wall Street's Siren Call," *Washington Post*, November 21, 2009, www.washingtonpost.com/wp-dyn/content/article/2009/11/20/AR2009112003374.html.

41. Thomas Philippon, "Finance vs. Wal-Mart: Why Are Financial Services so Expensive?" in *Rethinking the Financial Crisis*, ed. Alan Blinder, Andrew W. Lo, and Robert M. Solow (New York: Russell Sage Foundation, 2012): pp. 235–46.

42. For all data on campaign finance and spending of FIRE industry, see "Finance, Insurance & Real Estate Sector Profile, 2014," Center for Responsive Politics, accessed October 1, 2015, www.opensecrets.org/lobby/indus.php?id=F&year=2014.

43. Simon Johnson and James Kwak, *13 Bankers: The Wall Street Takeover and the Next Financial Meltdown* (New York: Pantheon Books, 2010), p. 5.

44. Clea Benson, "Summers After Government Saw Wealth Surge to $7 Million," *Bloomberg*, August 8, 2013, www.bloomberg.com/news/articles/2013-08-02/summers-after-government-saw-wealth-surge-to-17-million.

45. Robert Reich, "Greenspan, Summers, and Why the Economy Is Out of Whack," May 25, 2011, *Huffington Post*, www.huffingtonpost.com/robert-reich/greenspan-summers-and-why_b_524874.html.

46. William D. Cohan, "Rethinking Robert Rubin," BloombergBusiness, September 30, 2012, www.bloomberg.com/bw/articles/2012-09-19/rethinking-robert-rubin#p1.

47. Johnson and Kwak, *13 Bankers*, pp. 185–86.

48. Alan Blinder, *After the Music Stopped: The Financial Crisis, the Response, and the Work Ahead* (New York: Penguin Press, 2014), p. 75.

49. Peter Boone and Simon Johnson, "Shooting Banks," *New Republic*, February 24, 2010, www.newrepublic.com/article/politics/shooting-banks.

50. Johnson and Kwak, *13 Bankers*, p. 205; for evidence of the continuing existence

of such subsidies after the crisis, see IMF, Global Financial Stability Report Moving from Liquidity-to Growth-Driven Markets (Washington, DC: International Monetary Fund, 2014), pp. 101–32.

51. Richard A. Posner, *A Failure of Capitalism: The Crisis of '08 and the Descent into Depression* (Cambridge, MA: Harvard University Press, 2009), p. xii.

52. Greta R. Krippner, "The Financialization of the American Economy," *Socio-Economic Review* 3 (2005): pp. 173–208, 185.

53. Benjamin C. Waterhouse, *Lobbying America: The Politics of Business from Nixon to NAFTA* (Princeton, NJ: Princeton University Press, 2013), p. 237.

54. "David Hirschmann, President and CEO," US Chamber of Commerce, accessed October 1, 2015, www.theglobalipcenter.com/david-hirschmann.

55. Marianne Bertrand and Sendhil Mullainathan, "Are CEOs Rewarded for Luck? The Ones Without Principals Are," *Quarterly Journal of Economics* 116, no. 3 (2001): pp. 901–32.

56. Lucian A. Bebchuk, Martijn Cremers, and Urs Peyer, "The CEO Pay Slice," (discussion paper, John M. Olin Center for Law, Economics, and Business at Harvard Law School, Cambridge, MA, 2010).

57. Sally Bakewell, "Carbon-Intensive Investors Risk $6 Trillion 'Bubble,' Study Says," *BloombergBusiness*, April 18, 2013; Michael Greenstone, "If We Dig Out All Our Fossil Fuels, Here's How Hot We Can Expect It to Get," *New York Times*, April 8, 2015.

58. Steve Connor and Michael McCarthy, "World On Course for Catastrophic 6° Rise, Reveal Scientists," *Independent* (UK), October 22, 2011, www.independent .co.uk/environment/climate-change/world-on-course-for-catastrophic-6deg -rise-reveal-scientists-1822396.html.

59. Nicholas Stern, "Stern Review: The Economics of Climate Change" (report to the Prime Minister and Chancellor of Exchequer of the United Kingdom, October 30, 2006).

60. "Counting the Cost of Energy Subsidies," *IMF Survey Magazine*, July 17, 2015, www.imf.org/external/pubs/ft/survey/so/2015/NEW070215A.htm.

61. "Restoring the Quality of Our Environment" (Report of the Environmental Pollution Panel, President's Science Advisory Panel, the White House November 1965).

62. "Special Message to Congress on Conservation and Restoration of Beauty," February 8, 1965, www.lbjlib.utexas.edu/johnson/archives.hom/speeches.hom/650208.asp.

63. Lisa Lerer, "Is Cap and Trade Dems' Next 'BTU'?" *Politico*, July 13, 2009, www .politico.com/story/2009/07/is-cap-and-trade-dems-next-btu-024843.

64. Dan Roberts, "White House Insists Tough New Carbon Restrictions Are Legal Under Clean Air Act," *Guardian* (Manchester), August 3, 2015, www.theguardian .com/environment/2015/aug/02/obama-white-house-emissions-cuts-clean-air-act.

65. These figures are from the Center for Responsive Politics, Opensecrets.org, accessed June 1, 2015.

66. House Oversight Committee, "Political Interference with Climate Change Science Under the Bush Administration" (report by the Oversight and Government Reform Committee of the House of Representatives, United States Congress, December 10, 2007).

67. David Biello, "Editing Scientists: Science and Policy at the White House," *Scientific American*, October 22, 2009, www.scientificamerican.com/article/white -house-editing-scientists.

68. Quoted in Eric Pooley, *The Climate War: True Believers, Power Brokers, and the Fight to Save the Earth* (New York: HarperCollins, 2010), p. 50.
69. Naomi Oreskes and Eric M. Conway, *Merchants of Doubt: How a Handful of Scientists Obscured the Truth on Issues from Tobacco Smoke to Global Warming* (New York: Bloomsbury, 2010).
70. Richard Lazarus, "Super Wicked Problems and Climate Change: Constraining the Present to Liberate the Future," *Cornell Law Review* 94, no. 1153 (2009): pp. 1153–234.
71. Pooley, *Climate War*, pp. 40–41.
72. Robert J. Brulle, "Institutionalizing Delay: Foundation Funding and the Creation of U.S. Climate Change Counter-Movement Organizations," *Climatic Change* 122 (2014): 681–94.
73. Riley E. Dunlap and Peter J. Jacques, "Climate Change Denial Books and Conservative Think Tanks: Exploring the Connection," *American Behavioral Scientist* 57, no. 6 (2013): pp. 699–731.
74. Brulle, "Institutionalizing Delay."
75. Aaron M. McCright and Riley E. Dunlap, "The Politicization of Climate Change and Polarization in the American Public's Views of Global Warming, 2001–2010," *Sociological Quarterly* 52 (2011): 155–94.
76. See the excellent analysis in Theda Skocpol, "Naming the Problem: What It Will Take to Counter Extremism and Engage Americans in the Fight Against Global Warming," prepared for the Symposium on the Politics of America's Fight Against Global Warming, Harvard University, January 2013, www.scholarsstrategynetwork.org/sites/default/files/skocpol_captrade_report_january_2013_0.pdf.
77. Pooley, *Climate War*, p. 139.
78. Ibid., p. 170.
79. Thomas J. Donohue, "Managing a Changing Climate: Challenges & Opportunities for the Buckeye State" (remarks in Columbus, Ohio, May 2, 2008).
80. Andrew Clark, "US Firms Quit Chamber of Commerce over Climate Change Position," *Guardian* (Manchester), September 29, 2009; Terry Tamminen, *Cracking the Carbon Code: The Key to Sustainable Profits in the New Economy* (New York: Palgrave Macmillan, 2011), p. 100.
81. Frederick Mayer, "Stories of Climate Change: Competing Narratives, the Media, and U.S. Public Opinion 2001–2010" (discussion paper, Shorenstein Center on the Press, Politics, and Public Policy, Harvard University, Cambridge, MA, February 2012).
82. McCright and Dunlap, "The Politicization of Climate Change."
83. Ronald Brownstein, "GOP Gives Climate Science a Cold Shoulder," *National Journal*, October 9, 2010.
84. "Totals by Sector," Center for Responsive Politics, accessed October 1, 2014, www.opensecrets.org/overview/sectors.php.
85. "Top Industries/Interest Groups," Center for Responsive Politics, accessed October 1, 2014, www.opensecrets.org/overview/industries.php.
86. Brody Mullins and Neil King Jr., "GOP Chases Wall Street Donors," *Wall Street Journal*, February 4, 2010, www.wsj.com/articles/SB10001424052748703575004575043612216461790.
87. Ronald D. Orol, "If Senate OKs Bank Bill, Expect a Year of Debate: Boehner," *MarketWatch*, March 17, 2010, http://www.marketwatch.com/story/a-year-more-of-bank-reform-debate-likely-boehner-2010-03-17.

88. Edward Wyatt and Eric Lichtblau, "A Finance Overhaul Fight Draws a Swarm of Lobbyists," *New York Times*, April 19, 2010, www.nytimes.com/2010/04/20 /business/20derivatives.html.

89. James Verini, "Show Him the Money," *Washington Monthly*, July 10, 2010.

90. Peter Dreier, "Lessons from the Health-Care Wars," *American Prospect*, March 27, 2010, http://prospect.org/article/lessons-health-care-wars-0.

91. Pooley, *The Climate War*, p. 393.

92. Ryan Grim, "Dick Durbin: 'Banks Frankly Own the Place,'" *Huffington Post*, May 25, 2011, www.huffingtonpost.com/2009/04/29/dick-durbin-banks -frankly_n_193010.html.

93. Steven Brill, Interview by Norah O'Donnell, *CBS News*, January 5, 2015, www .youtube.com/watch?v=sfnwgo3ErQY.

94. Alex Wayne and Drew Armstrong, "Tauzin's $11.6 Million Made Him Highest Paid Health-Law Lobbyist," *Bloomberg News*, November 29, 2011, www.bloom berg.com/news/articles/2011-11-29/tauzin-$-11-6-million-made-him-highest -paid-health-law-lobbyist.

95. CBO, "Add a "Public Plan" to the Health Insurance Exchanges," Options for Reducing the Deficit: 2014 to 2023, November 13, 2013, www.cbo.gov/budget -options/2013/44890.

96. Mike Konczal, "2013 Year Was a Bad Year for Wall St. Lobbyists," *New Republic*, December 29, 2013, www.newrepublic.com/article/116064/2013-financial -reform-went-way-better-anyone-expected.

97. "Dodd-Frank Progress Report," Davis Polk, accessed October 1, 2015, www .davispolk.com/Dodd-Frank-Rulemaking-Progress-Report.

98. Ben Protess, "Wall Street Seeks to Tuck Dodd-Frank Changes in Budget Bill," *New York Times*, December 9, 2014, http://dealbook.nytimes.com/2014/12/09 /wall-street-seeks-to-tuck-dodd-frank-changes-in-budget-bill.

99. Morris M. Kleiner, *Stages of Occupational Regulation: Analysis of Case Studies* (Kalamazoo, MI: Upjohn Institute, 2013), p. 8.

100. Steve Teles, "The Scourge of Upward Redistribution," *National Affairs*, Fall 2015, www.nationalaffairs.com/publications/detail/the-scourge-of-upward-redis tribution.

101. Tom Geoghegan, "Why Is Broadband More Expensive in the US?," *BBC News*, October 28, 2013, www.bbc.com/news/magazine-24528383; Micah Singleton, "Here's How Terrible U.S. Broadband Service Really Is," *Daily Dot*, September 5, 2014, www.dailydot.com/politics/us-broadband-speed-cost-infographic.

102. Duff Wilson and Janet Roberts, "Special Report: How Washington Went Soft on Childhood Obesity," *Reuters*, April 27, 2012, www.reuters.com/article/2012/04 /27/us-usa-foodlobby-idUSBRE83Q0ED20120427.

103. Suzanne Mettler, *Degrees of Inequality: How the Politics of Higher Education Sabotaged the American Dream* (New York: Basic Books, 2014), p. 34.

104. *For Profit Higher Education: The Failure to Safeguard the Federal Investment and Ensure Student Success* (report by the Senate Committee on Health, Education, Labor, and Pensions, 2012).

105. David Deming, Claudia Goldin, and Lawrence Katz, "For-Profit Colleges," *Future of Children* 23, no. 1 (2013): pp. 137–63; "Fact Sheet," For Profit U, accessed October 1, 2015, http://forprofitu.org/fact-sheet.

106. Mettler, *Degrees of Inequality*, p. 95.

TEN: A Crisis of Authority

1 Thomas P. Slaughter, *The Whiskey Rebellion: Frontier Epilogue to the American Revolution* (New York: Oxford University Press, 1988), p. 12.

2. David Brian Robertson, *The Original Compromise: What the Constitution's Framers Were Really Thinking* (New York: Oxford University Press, 2013), p. 192.

3. Alexander Hamilton, "The Federalist No. 50," in Alexander Hamilton, James Madison, and John Jay, *The Federalist Papers* (Mineola, NY: Dover Publications, 2014), p. 138.

4. Slaughter, *Whiskey Rebellion*, p. 5.

5. Rachel Bade, "Republicans Seek to Cripple IRS," *Politico*, December 11, 2014, www.politico.com/story/2014/12/republicans-irs-regulations-113484.

6. Nina E. Olson, "National Taxpayer Advocate Annual Report to Congress 2014" (report to Congress, Internal Revenue Service, 2015).

7. Chuck Marr, Joel Friedman, and Brandon Debot, "IRS Funding Cuts Continue to Compromise Taxpayer Service and Weaken Enforcement," Center on Budget and Policy Priorities, www.cbpp.org/research/federal-tax/irs-funding-cuts -continue-to-compromise-taxpayer-service-and-weaken-enforcement?fa= view&id=4156.

8. GAO, "Tax Gap: IRS Could Significantly Increase Revenues by Better Targeting Enforcement Resources" (report to Congressional Requesters by the United States Government Accountability Office, December 2012).

9. "IRS Releases New Tax Gap Estimates; Compliance Rates Remain Statistically Unchanged From Previous Study," Internal Revenue Service, January 6, 2012, www.irs.gov/uac/IRS-Releases-New-Tax-Gap-Estimates;-Compliance-Rates -Remain-Statistically-Unchanged-From-Previous-Study.

10. Richard Rubin, "IRS Audits of High-Income U.S. Households Drop to 6-Year Low," *BloombergBusiness*, February 24, 2015, www.bloomberg.com/news /articles/2015-02-24/irs-audits-of-high-income-households-hit-lowest-level -since-2009.

11. Ron Johnson, "Interview by Laurie Rice," Atlas Society, January 16, 2013, http://atlassociety.org/commentary/commentary-blog/5155-video-interview -sen-ron-johnson-and-atlas-shrugged-.

12. The Atlas Society, "Video Interview: Sen. Ron Johnson and *Atlas Shrugged*," January 16, 2013, http://atlassociety.org/commentary/commentary-blog/5155-video-interview -sen-ron-johnson-and-atlas-shrugged-.

13. Morgan Little, "Maine Governor Says IRS Not as Bad as Gestapo—Yet," *Los Angeles Times*, July 12, 2012, http://articles.latimes.com/2012/jul/12/news/la-pn -maine-governor-says-irs-not-as-bad-as-gestapo-yet-20120712.

14. Hadas Gold, "S.C. GOP on IRS: 'Obama's Gestapo,'" *Politico*, July 31, 2013, www.politico.com/story/2013/07/south-carolina-republicans-irs-094964.

15. Noah Rothman, "All the President's Apologists," *Commentary*, June 1, 2014, www.commentarymagazine.com/articles/all-the-presidents-apologists.

16. Brett LoGiurato, "Jon Stewart Destroys Obama over the IRS Scandal," *Business Insider*, May 14, 2013, www.businessinsider.com/jon-stewart-obama-irs -scandal-benghazi-daily-show-may-13-2013-5.

17. To be sure, the hassles may have discouraged groups from applying or pursuing their applications. But the only group caught up in the review that actually lost

its tax-exempt status was the Maine chapter of the progressive group Emerge America, which the IRS determined to be a partisan entity. Denials and revocations of this sort, it turns out, are exceedingly rare—and, with the pressure on the IRS, becoming more so. In 2013, tax-exempt status was denied to fewer than one quarter of one percent of applications for "social welfare" 501(c)4 status (down from nearly 4 percent in the early 1980s, Julia Patel, "Hobbled IRS Can't Stem 'Dark Money' Flow," Center for Public Integrity, July 15, 2015; Josh Hicks, "Senate Panel Hits Auditor but Clears IRS of Bias in Targeting Scandal," *Washington Post*, September 5, 2014, www.washingtonpost.com/news/federal -eye/wp/2014/09/05/senate-panel-clears-irs-of-bias-in-targeting-scandal-but-hits-auditor.

18. David Cay Johnston, *Perfectly Legal: The Covert Campaign to Rig Our Tax System to Benefit the Super Rich—and Cheat Everybody Else* (New York: Penguin, 2005), p. 146.

19. Ibid., p. 157.

20. Tanina Rostain and Milton C. Regan Jr., "The IRS Under Siege," in *Confidence Games: Lawyers, Accountants, and The Tax Shelter Industry* (Cambridge, MA: MIT Press, 2014), p. 19.

21. Vanessa Williamson, "Paying Taxes: Understanding Americans' Tax Attitudes" (doctoral dissertation, Harvard University, Cambridge, MA, 2015).

22. Alexander Hamilton, "Alexander Hamilton on the Adoption of the Constitution," delivered June 24, 1788, www.nationalcenter.org/AlexanderHamilton.html.

23. George Will, "The Danger of a Government with Unlimited Power," *Washington Post*, June 3, 2010, www.washingtonpost.com/wp-yn/content/article/2010/06 /02/AR2010060203278.html.

24. Charles Murray, *By the People: Rebuilding Liberty Without Permission* (New York: Crown, 2015) pp. 133, 138; Charles Murray, "Rebuilding Liberty Without Permission," *Cato's Letter*, 13, no. 2 (Spring 2015): p. 3.

25. Garry Wills, *Necessary Evil: A History of American Distrust of Government* (New York: Simon & Schuster, 1999), pp. 77–78.

26. James Wilson, "Madison Debates: Jul 14," The Avalon Project, July 14, 1787, http://avalon.law.yale.edu/18th_century/debates_714.asp.

27. Zachary A. Goldfarb, "S&P Downgrades U.S. Credit Rating for First Time," *Washington Post*, August 6, 2011, www.washingtonpost.com/business/econ omy/sandp-considering-first-downgrade-of-us-credit-rating/2011/08/05 /gIQAqKeIxI_story.html.

28. Nancy LeTourneau, "An Insurgency by Any Other Name," *Washington Monthly*, May 27, 2015, www.washingtonmonthly.com/political-animal-a/2015_05/an _insurgency_by_any_other_nam055752.php.

29. Dan Amira, "Mitch McConnell Admits That Hostage-Taking Is Exactly What the GOP Did," *New York*, August 3, 2011, http://nymag.com/daily/intelligencer /2011/08/mitch_mcconnell_okay_fine_were.html.

30. "What's Happening with the Debt Ceiling Explained," *Mother Jones*, August 2, 2011, www.motherjones.com/mojo/2011/06/whats-happening-debt-ceiling -explained.

31. Dan Merica, "1995 and 2013: Three Differences Between Two Shutdowns," CNN .com, October 4, 2013, www.cnn.com/2013/10/01/politics/different-government -shutdowns.

32. Andrew Flowers, "Why We Still Can't Afford to Fix America's Broken Infra-

structure," *FiveThirtyEight*, June 3, 2014, http://fivethirtyeight.com/features
/why-we-still-cant-afford-to-fix-americas-broken-infrastructure.

33. College Board, "Inflation-Adjusted Maximum Pell Grant and Published Prices
at Public and Private Nonprofit Four-Year Institutions over Time," Trends in
Higher Education, accessed October 15, 2015, http://trends.collegeboard.org
/student-aid/figures-tables/inflation-adjusted-max-pell-grant-prices-public
-private-nonprofit-four-time.

34. Amanda Terkel, "112th Congress Set to Become Most Unproductive Since
1940s," *Huffington Post*, December 28, 2012, www.huffingtonpost.com/2012/12
/28/congress-unproductive_n_2371387.html.

35. Ezra Klein, "14 Reasons Why This Is the Worst Congress Ever," *Wonkblog* (blog),
Washington Post, July 13, 2012, www.washingtonpost.com/blogs/wonkblog
/wp/2012/07/13/13-reasons-why-this-is-the-worst-congress-ever.

36. Public Policy Polling, "Congress Losing Out to Zombies, Wall Street, and . . .
Hipsters," October 8, 2013, http://publicpolicy.com/2013/10/Congress-losing
-out-to-zombies-wall-street-and-hipsters.html.

37. "Non-Defense Discretionary Programs," Center on Budget and Policy Priorities,
April 30, 2014, www.cbpp.org/research/policy-basics-non-defense-discretion
ary-programs.

38. Peter R. Orszag, "Congress's Budget Game Gets Uglier," *BloombergView*, May 4,
2015, www.bloombergview.com/articles/2015-05-04/congress-s-cynicism-on
-the-budget-is-getting-worse.

39. Robert Greenstein, "Budget Deal, Though Imperfect, Represents Significant
Accomplishment and Merits Support," Center on Budget and Policy Priorities,
October 27, 2015, www.cbpp.org/press/statements/greenstein-budget-deal
-though-imperfect-represents-significant-accomplishment-and.

40. ASCE, 2013 Report Card for America's Infrastructure (report by the American
Society for Civil Engineers, 2013).

41. FHWA, "Deficient Bridges by State and Highway System 2014," Federal Highway Administration: Bridges & Structures, December 2014, www.fhwa.dot.gov
/bridge/nbi/no10/defbr14.cfm.

42. Rebecca Strauss, "Finally a Highway Bill, But Big Financing Problems Remain,"
Council on Foreign Relations, December 3, 2015, http://blogs.cfr.org/renewing
-america/2015/12/03/finally-a-highway-bill-but-big-financing-problems
-remain.

43. Kristen Doerer, "The Highway Trust Fund Keeps Bridges from Falling Down, but
Will Congress Reauthorize It?" *PBS News Hour*, October 27, 2015, www.pbs
.org/newshour/making-sense/highway-trust-fund-keeps-bridges-falling-will
-congress-pay-bill.

44. Derek Thompson, "A Map of the World's Most Dangerous Countries for Drivers," *Atlantic*, February 18, 2014, www.theatlantic.com/international/archive
/2014/02/a-map-of-the-worlds-most-dangerous-countries-for-drivers/283886.

45. Ron Nixon, "Human Cost Rises as Old Bridges, Dams and Roads Go Unre-
paired," *New York Times*, November 5, 2015.

46. Robert Putnam, "The Strange Disappearance of Civic America," *American Prospect*, December 19, 2001, http://prospect.org/article/strange-disappearance
-civic-america.

47. CSPI, "Keep America's Food Safe: The Case for Increased Funding at FDA," Cen-

ter for Science in the Public Interest, accessed October 1, 2015, www.cspinet
.org/foodsafety/fdafunding.html.

48. Ibid.

49. *Analytical Perspectives, Budget of the United States Government, Fiscal Year 2013* (Washington, DC: US Government Printing Office, 2013), p. 113.

50. Mike Alberti, "The Incredible Shrinking Federal Workforce," Remapping Debate, accessed October 1, 2015, www.remappingdebate.org/map-data-tool /incredible-shrinking-federal-workforce.

51. Brian Naylor, "GOP Targets Federal Workers' Salaries," *NPR*, November 11, 2010, www.npr.org/2010/11/11/131250179/gop-eyes-cutting-federal-bureaucracy -to-save-money.

52. Joe Spiering, "Lummis-Mulvaney Bill Cuts Federal Workforce by Attrition Introduced legislation expected to save billions, limit size of government," Congressman Cynthia Lummis, January 20, 2015, http://lummis.house.gov/news /documentsingle.aspx?DocumentID=398191.

53. John D. Donahue, *The Warping of Government Work* (Cambridge, MA: Harvard University Press, 2008); pp. 167–80.

54. Kendall Breitman, "Federal Worker Job Satisfaction Hits a Low," *Politico*, December 9, 2014, www.politico.com/story/2014/12/2014-federal-agency-rankings -job-satisfaction-low-113415.

55. Paul Chassy and Scott Amey, *Bad Business: Billions of Taxpayer Dollars Wasted on Hiring Contractors* (report by the Project on Government Oversight, September 13, 2011); David Cay Johnston, "The U.S Government Is Paying Through the Nose for Private Contractors," *Newsweek*, December 12, 2013, www.news week.com/us-government-paying-through-nose-private-contractors-224370.

56. John Dilulio, "Want Better, Smaller Government? Hire Another Million Federal Bureaucrats," *Washington Post*, August 29, 2014, www.washingtonpost.com /opinions/want-better-smaller-governmenthire-1-million-more-federal-bureau crats/2014/08/29/c0bc1480-2c72-11e4-994d-202962a9150c_story.html.

57. Timothy M. LaPira and Herschel F. Thomas, "Revolving Door Lobbyists and Interest Representation," *Interest Groups & Advocacy* 3 (2014): pp. 4–29.

58. Lee Drutman and Steven Teles, "Why Congress Relies on Lobbyists Instead of Thinking for Itself," *Atlantic*, March 10, 2015, www.theatlantic.com/politics/ar chive/2015/03/when-congress-cant-think-for-itself-it-turns-to-lobbyists/387295.

59. Jordi Blanes i Vidal, Mirko Draca, and Christian Fons-Rosen, "Revolving Door Lobbyists," *American Economic Review* 102, no. 7 (2012): pp. 3731–48.

60. Lee Drutman and Steven Teles, "A New Agenda for Political Reform," *Washington Monthly*, May 2015, www.washingtonmonthly.com/magazine/marchapril may_2015/features/a_new_agenda_for_political_ref054226.php?page=all.

61. Kevin Sack, Sheri Fink, Pam Belluck, and Adam Nossiter, "How Ebola Roared Back," *New York Times*, December 29, 2014, www.nytimes.com/2014/12/30 /health/how-ebola-roared-back.html.

62. Bob Cesca, "The Unforgivable Hysteria of the News Media's Ebola Coverage," *Daily Banter*, October 13, 2014, http://thedailybanter.com/2014/10/unforgivable -hysteria-american-news-medias-ebola-coverage.

63. Justin McCarthy, "Ebola Debuts on Americans' List of Top U.S. Problems," *Gallup*, October 21, 2014, www.gallup.com/poll/178742/ebola-debuts-americans -list-top-problems.aspx.

64. Harvard School of Public Health, "Poll: Most Believe Ebola Likely Spread by Multiple Routes, Including Sneezing, Coughing," news release, October 15, 2014, www.hsph.harvard.edu/news/press-releases/poll-finds-most-believe-ebola-spread-by-multiple-routes; Amy Norton, "Ebola Panic Starting to Fade, Poll Finds," *CBS News*, November 8, 2014, www.cbsnews.com/news/ebola-panic-starting-to-fade-poll-finds.

65. Justin McCarthy, "Americans Name Government No. 1 U.S. Problem," *Gallup*, March 12, 2015, www.gallup.com/poll/181946/americans-name-government-no-problem.aspx.

66. "The White House Correspondents' Dinner. Aired 10-11p ET," CNN.com, www.cnn.com/TRANSCRIPTS/1504/25/se.04.html.

67. Ron Fournier, "The Scariest Thing About Ebola: Americans' Lack of Trust in Institutions," *National Journal*, October 7, 2014.

68. Charles Krauthammer, "Election Day Looking Like a Referendum on Competence," *Washington Post*, October 30, 2014, www.washingtonpost.com/opinions/charles-krauthammer-election-day-looking-like-a-referendum-on-competence/2014/10/30/81bccc4c-6067-11e4-91f7-5d89b5e8c251_story.html.

69. Brian Stelter, "Rush Limbaugh Thinks 'They' Think We All Deserve Ebola," *CNN Money*, October 21, 2014, http://money.cnn.com/2014/10/21/media/stelter-response-to-rush-limbaugh.

70. Brian Tashman, "Michael Savage: Obama Wants to Bring Ebola Epidemic to America, Should Resign," *Right Wing Watch*, October 2, 2014, www.rightwingwatch.org/content/michael-savage-obama-wants-bring-ebola-epidemic-america-should-resign#sthash.GrtwhYNk.dpuf.

71. Alex Pappas, "Rand Paul: Obama Foolishly Letting 'Political Correctness' Influence Ebola Decisions," *Daily Caller*, October 1, 2014, http://dailycaller.com/2014/10/01/rand-paul-obama-foolishly-letting-political-correctness-influence-ebola-decisions/#ixzz3qMSmsxn5.

72. McCarthy, "Americans Name Government as No. 1 U.S. Problem."

73. "NIH Research Funding Trends," Federation of American Societies for Experimental Biology, accessed October 1, 2015, www.faseb.org/policy-and-government-affairs/data-compilations/nih-research-funding-trends.aspx.

74. Brett Norman, "Ebola Highlights CDC Fund Crunch," *Politico*, October 2, 2014, www.politico.com/story/2014/10/ebola-dcd-funding-111556.

75. "Fact Sheet: Impact of Sequestration on the National Institutes of Health," National Institutes of Health, June 3, 2013, www.nih.gov/news-events/news-releases/fact-sheet-impact-sequestration-national-institutes-health.

76. Max Nisen, "Bill Gates: Here's the Biggest Problem with Capitalism," *Business Insider*, March 14, 2014, www.businessinsider.com/bill-gates-problem-with-capitalism-2013-3.

77. Sam Stein, "Ebola Vaccine Would Likely Have Been Found by Now If Not for Budget Cuts: NIH Director," *Huffington Post*, October 12, 2014, www.huffingtonpost.com/2014/10/12/ebola-vaccine_n_5974148.html; Roger Runningen and Kathleen Hunter, "Ebola Cases Follow Cuts in Preparedness, Research Funding," *BloombergBusiness*, October 13, 2014, www.bloomberg.com/news/articles/2014-10-13/ebola-case-in-u-s-sparks-talks-on-more-respnose-funding?wpisrc=nl-wonkbk&wpmm=1.

78. Jonathan Cohn, "Why Public Silence Greets Government Success," *American*

Prospect, May 8, 2015, http://prospect.org/article/why-public-silence-greets
-government-success.

79. Gregory J. Wawro, "Testimony Prepared for the Senate Committee on Rules and
    Administration" April 22, 2010.

80. "Senate Action on Cloture Motions," United States Senate, accessed October 1,
    2015, www.senate.gov/pagelayout/reference/cloture_motions/clotureCounts.htm.

81. Russell Wheeler, "Judicial Nominations and Confirmations: Fact and Fic-
    tion," Brookings Institution, December 30, 2013, www.brookings.edu/blogs
    /fixgov/posts/2013/12/30-staffing-federal-judiciary-2013-no-breakthrough
    -year.

82. Barry J. McMillion, "President Obama's First-Term U.S. Circuit and District
    Court Nominations: An Analysis and Comparison with Presidents Since Rea-
    gan" (report by the Congressional Research Service, May 2, 2013).

83. Ibid.

84. Dahlia Lithwick and Carl Tobias, "Vacant Stares: Why Don't Americans Worry
    About How an Understaffed Federal Bench Is Hazardous to Their Health?,"
    Slate, September 27, 2010, http://www.slate.com/articles/news_and_politics
    /jurisprudence/2010/09/vacant_stares.htmlw.

85. Al Kamen and Paul Kane, "Did 'Nuclear Option' Boost Obama's Judicial Ap-
    pointments?" *In the Loop* (blog), *Washington Post*, December 17, 2014, www
    .washingtonpost.com/blogs/in-the-loop/wp/2014/12/17/did-nuclear-option
    -boost-obamas-judicial-appointments.

86. Thomas E. Mann and Norman J. Ornstein, *It's Even Worse Than It Looks: How
    the American Constitutional System Collided with the New Politics of Extremism*
    (New York: Basic Books, 2012), p. 98.

87. Suzanna Andrews, "The Woman Who Knew Too Much," *Vanity Fair*, October
    31, 2011, www.vanityfair.com/news/2011/11/elizabeth-warren-201111.

88. Jim Puzzanghera, "GOP Stalls Confirmation of Consumer Agency Nominee,"
    Los Angeles Times, September 7, 2011, http://articles.latimes.com/2011/sep/07
    /business/la-fi-consumer-bureau-cordray-20110907.

89. Julian Hattem, "Obama Dealt Second Court Defeat over NLRB Recess Ap-
    pointments," *The Hill*, May 16, 2013, http://thehill.com/regulation/labor
    /300273-court-rules-against-nlrb-recess-appointment.

90. Melanie Trottman, "High Hurdles for Labor Board Nominees," *Washington
    Wire* (blog), *Wall Street Journal*, May 16, 2013, http://blogs.wsj.com/washwire
    /2013/05/16/high-hurdles-for-labor-board-nominees.

91. Christopher Rowland, "Deadlock by Design Hobbles Election Agency," *Boston
    Globe*, July 7, 2013, www.bostonglobe.com/news/nation/2013/07/06/america
    -campaign-finance-watchdog-rendered-nearly-toothless-its-own-appointed
    -commissioners/44zZoJwnzEHyzxTByNL2QP/story.html?s_campaign=sm_tw.

92. Cynthia L. Bauerly and Ellen L. Weintraub, "Statement of Reasons in MUR
    5937" (report of the Federal Election Commission, 2009).

93. Eric Lichtblau, "F.E.C. Can't Curb 2016 Election Abuse, Commission Chief
    Says," *New York Times*, May 2, 2015, www.nytimes.com/2015/05/03/us
    /politics/fec-cant-curb-2016-election-abuse-commission-chief-says.html?_r=0.

94. Theodoric Meyer, "Under Obama, More Appointments Go Unfilled," *Pro-
    Publica*, February 27, 2013, http://www.propublica.org/article/under-obama
    -more-appointments-go-unfilled.

95. White House, "President Obama Announces More Key Administration Posts," news release, November 19, 2014, www.whitehouse.gov/the-press-office/2014/11/19/president-obama-announces-more-key-administration-posts; Anne Joseph O'Connell, *Waiting for Leadership: President Obama's Record in Staffing Key Agency Positions and How to Improve the Appointments Process* (report by the Center for American Progress, April 2010).
96. Jennifer Steinhauer, "Senate Confirms Loretta Lynch as Attorney General After Long Delay," *New York Times*, April 23, 2015, www.nytimes.com/2015/04/24/us/politics/loretta-lynch-attorney-general-vote.html.
97. Mann and Ornstein, *It's Even Worse Than It Looks*, p. 95.
98. Dan Froomkin, "How the Mainstream Press Bungled the Single Biggest Story of the 2012 Campaign," *Huffington Post*, December 7, 2012, www.huffingtonpost.com/dan-froomkin/republican-lies-2012-election_b_2258586.html. The quotes that follow are from this source.

Conclusion: The Positive-Sum Society

1. McKinsey Global Institute, "The Power of Parity," September 2015, www.mckinsey.com/insights/growth/how_advancing_womens_equality_can_add_12_trillion_to_global_growth; McKinsey & Company, "The Economic Impact of the Achievement Gap in America's Schools," April 2009, http://mckinseyonsociety.com/downloads/reports/Education/achievement_gap_report.pdf.
2. James Madison, "The Federalist No. 10," in Alexander Hamilton, James Madison, and John Jay, *The Federalist Papers* (Mineola, NY: Dover Publications, 2014).
3. James Madison, "The Federalist No. 51," in Hamilton, Madison, and Jay, *The Federalist Papers* (Mineola, NY: Dover Publications, 2014).
4. Adam Winkler, "Is the Filibuster Unconstitutional?" *New Republic*, March 7, 2013, www.newrepublic.com/article/112606/filibuster-unconstitutional.
5. Tom McCarthy, "Senate Approves Change to Filibuster Rule After Repeated Republican Blocks," *Guardian* (Manchester), November 21, 2013, www.theguardian.com/world/2013/nov/21/harry-reid-senate-rules-republican-filibusters-nominations.
6. Francis Fukuyama, *Political Order and Political Decay: From the Industrial Revolution to the Globalization of Democracy* (New York: Farrar, Straus and Giroux, 2014).
7. Ida A. Brudnick, Congressional Salaries and Allowances in Brief (Washington, DC: Congressional Research Service, 2014).
8. Anthony Madonna and Ian Ostrander, "If Congress Keeps Cutting Its Staff, Who Is Writing Your Laws? You Won't Like the Answer," *The Monkey Cage* (blog), *Washington Post*, August 20, 2015, www.washingtonpost.com/blogs/monkey-cage/wp/2015/08/20/if-congress-keeps-cutting-its-staff-who-is-writing-your-laws-you-wont-like-the-answer.
9. Tom Berstein and Max Stier, "Good Government Starts with Good People" (report by the Partnership for Public Service, 2011).
10. Drutman and Teles, "New Agenda for Political Reform."
11. Daniel D'Addario and Charlotte Alter, "Watch John Legend and Common's Stirring Acceptance Speeches at the Oscars," *Time*, February 22, 2015, http://time.com/3717055/oscars-2015-best-original-song-john-legend-common-selma.

12. "Issues Related to State Voter Identification Laws," US General Accounting Office, October 8, 2014, www.gao.gov/products/GAO-14-634.

13. Justin Levitt, *The Truth About Voter Fraud* (New York: Brennan Center for Justice, 2007).

14. Keith G. Bentele and Erin E. O'Brien, "Jim Crow 2.0? Why States Consider and Adopt Restrictive Voter Access Policies," *Perspectives on Politics* 11, no. 4 (2013): pp. 1088–116.

15. Sean McElwee, "Why the Voting Gap Matters," Demos, October 23, 2014, www.demos.org/publication/why-voting-gap-matters.

16. Jan E. Leighley and Jonathan Nagler, *Who Votes Now?* (Princeton, NJ: Princeton University Press, 2013).

17. Sean McElwee, "Why Voting Matters: Large Disparities in Turnout Benefit the Donor Class," Demos, September 16, 2015, www.demos.org/publication/why-voting-matters-large-disparities-turnout-benefit-donor-class.

18. Charles Stewart III, "Waiting to Vote in 2012," *Journal of Law and Politics* 28, no. 4 (2013): pp. 439–63.

19. Mark Schmitt, "Political Opportunity: A New Foundation for Political Reform," Brennan Center for Justice, February 5, 2015, www.brennancenter.org/publication/political-opportunity-new-framework-democratic-reform.

20. Bruce Ackerman and Ian Ayres, *Voting with Dollars: A New Paradigm for Campaign Finance* (New Haven, CT: Yale University Press, 2002).

21. Paul Blumenthal, "President Obama's SOPA Stance Could Cost Campaign Money, Says Hollywood Lobbyist Chris Dodd," *Huffington Post*, January 19, 2012.

22. Dave Lee, "Sopa and Pipa Protests Not Over, Says Wikipedia," *BBC News*, March 8, 2012.

23. Stan Schroeder, "SOPA Explodes on Twitter, Generates 2.4 Million Tweets," Mashable, January 19, 2012, http://mashable.com/2012/01/19/sopa-tweets/#Ol12mxvACGqm.

24. Cecilia Kang, "SOPA Critics Send Petition to Congress, Warn Against Bill," *Washington Post*, December 16, 2011, www.washingtonpost.com/business/economy/sopa-critics-send-petition-to-congress-warn-against-bill/2011/12/15/gIQAhLzfwO_story.html.

25. Richard B. Freeman, "Spurts of Union Growth: Defining Moments and Social Processes," in *The Defining Moment: The Great Depression and the American Economy in the Twentieth Century,* ed. Michael Bordo, Claudia Goldin, and Eugene White (Chicago: University of Chicago Press, 1998), pp. 265–95.

26. Josh Eidelson, "Alt-Labor," *American Prospect*, January 29, 2013, http://prospect.org/article/alt-labor; Rose Hackmanin, "Alt-Labor: A New Union Movement or the Same Old Song?," *Guardian* (Manchester), October 20, 2015, www.theguardian.com/money/2014/may/01/low-wage-new-union-walmart-fast-food.

27. Nicholas Confessore, "Tale of a Lost Cellphone, and Untold Static," *New York Times*, June 21, 2006.

28. Clay Shirky, *Here Comes Everybody: The Power of Organizing Without Organizations* (New York: Penguin Press, 2008).

29. Patrick Emmenegger, "The Long Arm of Justice: U.S. Structural Power and International Banking," *Business and Politics* 17, no. 3 (2015): pp. 473–93.

30. Enrico Moretti, *The New Geography of Jobs* (New York: Houghton Mifflin, 2012).

31. Jac C. Heckelman, "Income Convergence Among U.S. States: Cross-Sectional and Time Series Evidence," *Canadian Journal of Economics* 46, no. 3 (2013): p. 1094.

32. FRED, "State and Regional Personal Income Per Capita."

33. Bettina H. Aten, Eric B. Figueroa, and Troy M. Martin, *Regional Price Parities for States and Metropolitan Areas, 2006–2010, Survey of Current Business* (Washington, DC: Bureau of Economic Analysis, 2012), pp. 229–42, 235.

34. Jens Manuel Krogstad and Michael Keegan, "15 States with the Highest Share of Immigrants in Their Population," Pew Research Center, May 14, 2014, www.pewresearch.org/fact-tank/2014/05/14/15-states-with-the-highest-share-of-immigrants-in-their-population/

35. Sarah Burd-Sharps, Kristen Lewis, Eduardo Borges Martins, *The Measure of America: American Human Development Report, 2008–2009* (New York: Columbia University Press, 2008), p. 163; Philip Longman, "Oops! The Texas Miracle that Isn't," *Washington Monthly*, March/April/May 2014; Renee Loth, "What's the Matter with Texas," *Boston Globe*, August 20, 2011.

36. Peter Georgescu, "Capitalists Arise: We Need to Deal with Income Inequality," *New York Times*, August 7, 2015.

37. Ed Pilkington and Suzanne Goldenberg, "ALEC Facing Funding Crisis from Donor Exodus in Wake of Trayvon Martin Row," *Guardian* (Manchester), December 3, 2013.

38. Brian Fung, "Google: We're Parting with the Climate Change Skeptics at ALEC," *Washington Post*, September 22, 2014.

39. Quoted in Benjamin Page, Jason Seawright, and Mathew Lacombe, "Stealth Politics by U.S. Billionaires" (Paper Presented at the Annual Meeting of the American Political Science Association, September 2015).

40. Kenneth S. Baer, *Reinventing Democrats: The Politics of Liberalism from Reagan to Clinton* (Lawrence: University Press of Kansas, 2000).

41. Milan Kundera, *The Book of Laughter and Forgetting* (New York: Perennial Classics, 1999).

42. *Role of Government Survey* (report by *Washington Post*, Kaiser Family Foundation, and Harvard University, 2010).

43. Michael Tomasky, "Democrats Are Petrified of Defending Government—But They Need to Start," *Daily Beast*, December 4, 2014, www.thedailybeast.com/articles/2014/12/04/democrats-are-petrified-of-defending-government-but-they-need-to-start.html.

44. Suzanne Mettler, *The Submerged State: How Invisible Government Policies Undermine American Democracy* (Chicago: University of Chicago Press, 2011).

45. Peter Schuck, *Why Government Fails So Often: And How It Can Do Better* (Princeton, NJ: Princeton University Press, 2014).

46. Bianca DiJulio, Jamie Firth, and Mollyann Brodie, "Kaiser Family Foundation April 2015 Tracking Poll," Henry J. Kaiser Family Foundation, April 21, 2015, http://kff.org/health-costs/poll-finding/kaiser-health-tracking-poll-april-2015.

47. Bianca DiJulio, Jamie Firth, and Mollyann Brodie, "ACA Advertising in 2014–Insurance and Political Ads," Henry J. Kaiser Family Foundation, October 30, 2014, http://kff.org/report-section/aca-advertising-in-2014-key-findings.

48. Robert Kagan, *Adversarial Legalism: The American Way of Law* (Cambridge, MA: Harvard University Press, 2001).

INDEX

American Truckers Associations, 218, 221
America's Cup (1992), 228
Amtrak, 41, 319
Amway, 228
Anderson, Robert, 143
Anschutz, Phil, 235–36
anthrax, 52
antibiotics, 40, 51, 52–54
anti-Semitism, 115
Apple, 3, 4, 29, 85
Archey, William, 215, 216, 218
Armey, Dick, 216, 233–34, 241
Army Corps of Engineers, US, 67
ARPANET, 66, 130
Articles of Confederation, 2, 11–12, 105, 304, 313
"As We May Think" (Bush), 129
asymmetric information, 80, 84–87, 275
Atkinson, Bill, 29
Atlanta, Ga., 274
Atlantic Monthly, 129
Atlas Shrugged (Rand), 184–85, 307
Atlas Society, 246, 307
atomic energy, 101
attorney generals, state, 223
ATT v. Concepcion, 225
Atwater, H. Brewster, Jr., 206
audits, 306–7, 310
austerity, 192, 317
auto industry, 83, 93, 127, 145
Automobile Manufacturers Association, 133
automobiles, 57, 68–69, 76
  accidents and, 319
  safety of, 83–84, 127
average net wealth, 36
Axis powers, 230

Bachmann, Michelle, 241
Baier, Bret, 244
Bain Capital, 16
Ball, George, 175
Balogh, Brian, 107
bank failures, 116, 187
banking secrecy, 354
bank panics, 10, 111
bankruptcies, medical, 275
banks, 85, 93, 286, 297, 299, 300
Barbour, Haley, 236
Bartels, Larry, 194, 259
Bartlett, Bruce, 278–79
Baucus, Max, 279

Baumol, William, 59
Beck, Glenn, 10, 114, 236, 253, 255, 326
behavioral economics, 81
Bell, Alexander Graham, 112
Bell & Howell, 174, 175
Bell Labs, 100
Bennett, Bob, 264
Benton, William, 141, 142, 143
Berkeley, Calif., 302
Berle, Adolf A., Jr., 177
Berry, Jeff, 253
Beyoncé, 41
binding arbitration, 225
bipartisanship, 219
blackouts, 41–42
Blackstone, 157, 175–76, 181, 182–83, 184
Blinder, Alan, 285
Bloomberg, Michael, 182
Bloomberg News, 306
Boehner, John, 209, 216, 217–18, 241, 260, 264, 267, 268, 276, 297, 298, 316
Boeing, 210, 268, 333
Bohr, Niels, 38
Bolivia, 57
bonds, 138
Book of Laughter and Forgetting, The (Kundera), 361
Boston police strike (1919), 119
Boston Tea Party, 304
Bowles, Erskine, 193
Boxer, Barbara, 206
Bradford, Ralph, 133
Brandeis, Louis, 115
breast milk, 49
Bridge of Spies (film), 361–62
bridges, 318
Bridgewater Associates, 186
Brill, Steven, 277, 299
broadband access, 301–2
Brookings Institution, 247
Brooks, David, 123
Brooks, Harvey, 65, 66
Brown, Janice Rogers, 212
Brown, Scott, 327, 333
Browner, Carol, 218
Brownstein, Ronald, 295
Brulle, Robert, 293
Btu tax, 290
Buckley, William F., Jr., 168
budget deficits, 194
Buffett, Warren, 91, 196, 284, 358
Bulgaria, 301